E5

D0533021

Route of the Hussar Brigade, 1808-9
   "   "   "   "   1813-14
Hussar Brigade action, 1808-9
   "   "   "   "   1813-14

From
CORUNNA
To
WATERLOO

WITH THE HUSSARS
1808 *to* 1815

by

JOHN MOLLO

Pen & Sword
MILITARY

First published in Great Britain in 1997
Republished by
PEN AND SWORD MILITARY
an imprint of
Pen and Sword Books Ltd
47 Church Street, Barnsley
South Yorkshire S70 2AS

ISBN 978 1 78346 239 1

Printed and bound in England by
CPI Group (UK) Ltd, Croydon, CR0 4YY

Pen & Sword Books Ltd incorporates the imprints of
Pen & Sword Books Ltd incorporates the imprints of Pen & Sword Archaeology, Atlas,
Aviation, Battleground, Discovery, Family History, History, Maritime, Military, Naval,
Politics, Railways, Select, Social History, Transport, True Crime, and
Claymore Press, Frontline Books, Leo Cooper, Praetorian Press,
Remember When, Seaforth Publishing and Wharncliffe.

For a complete list of Pen and Sword titles please contact
Pen and Sword Books Limited
47 Church Street, Barnsley, South Yorkshire, S70 2AS, England
E-mail: enquiries@pen-and-sword.co.uk
Website: www.pen-and-sword.co.uk

IN MEMORY OF C.C.P.L. (R. 1892)
Author, artist and Carthusian

'I think the Prince [Regent Colonel of the 10th Hussars] will be highly
delighted that his "Dolls" were the only ones kept engaged on that day,
[at Morales] and came off so brilliantly. . .'
(JSAR Vol 44 p.101)

Contents

Maps

Acknowledgements

This account of the beginnings of the Hussar regiments of the British army originated in research carried out in the early sixties for the planned sixth volume of the late C.C.P. Lawson's *History of the Uniforms of the British Army*, and it is to him that I have dedicated it, in commemoration of nearly twenty years of friendship and collaboration. The bulk of the work was completed in the early 1970s, and consequently many of the people and institutions from whom I then received so much help are no longer with us. From the first I have had ready and comprehensive answers to my numerous questions from the Marquess of Anglesey and Mr S.P.G. Ward and general encouragement from Michael Barthorp and my brother, Boris, who read the original draft and made many useful suggestions for its improvement. The Army Museums Ogibly Trust, under its successive secretaries, has been a treasure house of information, particularly of a pictorial nature, as have the libraries of the Royal United Services Institution, the British Museum and the War Office, now Ministry of Defence. The late Mrs John Nicholas Brown allowed unrestricted access to her incomparable collection of military drawings and prints, a tradition which has, since her death, been carried on by its present curator, Peter Harrington.

Many people responded generously to my requests to examine family papers and diaries. In the early days Mr. Robert Mackworth-Young, the Royal Librarian, and Miss Jennifer Sharwood, Curator of Prints and Drawings, Royal Collection, patiently answered my numerous queries. The Duchess of Beaufort allowed me to examine the Badminton papers with the assistance of Mr. S. Bywater. Lt.-Colonel C.T. Mitford-Slade and the Somerset Record Office made notable efforts to find the missing diary of Sir John Slade and Mr F.R. Hodge and Major J.S. Sutherland allowed me to make transcripts of the invaluable Hodge papers lodged in the Queen's Own Hussars Museum. Major Simon Murray of the 15th/19th Hussars allowed me to examine the Adjutant's diaries, now in their regimental museum in Newcastle-on-Tyne. The Hon. J. Wyndham, Miss D. Beatrice Harris and Miss Gordon Williams gave me much information on the Wyndham family and took time and trouble to guide me to the West Sussex Record Office. The University College of North Wales provided copies of the Hughes diary and the Department of Manuscripts, Nottingham University, copies of the letters of Captain Mellish. More recently

I am indebted to Colonel Robin Merton for permission to examine the archives of the 10th Hussars and through the years the London Library and its helpful staff have been of great assistance.

Last, but not least, my thanks go to my wife, Louise, who has lived with this project for much of our married life and who has patiently tramped across many apparently featureless stretches of foreign soil in the firm belief that they meant something special to me, and finally to our son, Thomas, a baby when I started writing this book and who, now that it is finished, is himself a serving officer.

Hungerford, 1997

CHAPTER ONE
The Colonel of Dragoons

At half-past five on the morning of Monday, 25 February, 1793, Sir Gilbert Elliot was up and about to see the three battalions of the Foot Guards march off from Horse Guards en route for Greenwich, and thence to Holland. The 2,000 men drawn up on parade, 'all young and all fine', were, he wrote, 'animated by a spirit natural on the occasion, not to mention spirits of a different sort, of which they had had more than one could wish. Many of them were too drunk to walk straight'. As the grenadier companies moved off the men burst into 'God Save The King!', which moved the Monarch 'a good deal'. He was riding a white charger and looked like an equestrian statue. The thirty-one-year-old Prince of Wales was also present, wearing his 'new Light Horse uniform', which was 'very handsome and theatrical', but displayed 'an amount of bulk', which certainly amused Sir Gilbert and his companion, and 'probably all beholders'.[1]

The crisis which had led to the departure of the Foot Guards had been brought to a head by the French invasion of the Austrian Netherlands. On 21 January, 1793, Louis XVI had been sent to the guillotine and the following month the French Republic, already at war with Austria and Prussia, declared war on Britain. Austria was unwilling to commit the bulk of her army to the defence of the Low Countries, so a coalition of Austrian, British, Hanoverian and Prussian troops was hastily assembled for the purpose. The available British troops, consisting of two infantry brigades and twenty squadrons of cavalry, were rushed to Holland, under the command of the King's second son, the Duke of York.

In order to account for the presence of the Prince of Wales, in full uniform, that cold February morning, and his subsequent involvement in the affairs of the British Army, it is necessary to go back thirteen years, to the time of his coming of age. Prince George and his next younger brother, Prince Frederick, later to become Duke of York, with only a year and four days separating them, were very close and had been educated together from an early age. Their first tutor, the Earl of Holdernesse, gave them a rigorous grounding in the Classics, but was afterwards driven to comment that, while the Royal brothers could be taught Latin and Greek with ease, 'they could never be taught to understand

1

the value of money'. Both Princes inherited the strong military traditions of the House of Brunswick, which were, at first, encouraged. At the age of five Prince George was felt to be too timid, so he was given a battery of twenty-one one-pounder brass guns, complete with travelling carriages, on his birthday, in order to correct this tendency. Later, however, the King began to discourage the military sciences in his eldest son, while fostering them in Prince Frederick. The latter was taken by his father to numerous reviews and was placed in the charge of General Smith, an engineer, under whose guidance he studied all the best foreign military writers. In the process the gardens of Kew House were transformed into the terrain of the Seven Years War, where the battles of Frederick's 'great' namesake were refought over again. Clearly much of this rubbed off onto his elder brother.

When they reached the ages of eighteen and seventeen respectively their joint education came to an end. Prince Frederick, appointed colonel by brevet, left to complete his military education in Hanover, in November, 1780. There the Duke of Brunswick, considered to be one of the first soldiers of the age, was to be his mentor. The Prince of Wales was grudgingly allowed an establishment of his own, and on his birthday the King gave a far from flattering summary of his son's attainments, while one of his tutors, Bishop Hurd, held an even more pessimistic view of his pupil's prospects: 'He will be either the most polished gentleman or the most accomplished blackguard in Europe; perhaps both.'

The Prince of Wales, separated for the first time from his beloved brother, was subjected to numerous irksome restrictions, which, however, he skilfully managed to evade. Before long, encouraged by his dissolute uncles, the Dukes of Cumberland and Gloucester, he was well on the way to becoming the leader of London society at one of its most brilliant periods. The reclusive habits of his parents had made them unpopular with the upper classes, but their son and heir was welcomed by the fashionable world with open arms.

In 1783 the Peace of Versailles brought the American war to an end and before long anglomane French nobles began once again to appear in London society. They were extremely worldly and were to have considerable influence on the susceptible Prince of Wales. Three in particular became his close companions and were largely responsible for some of his less attractive characteristics. The most highly-born was Louis-Phillipe-Joseph, Duc de Chartres, who after the death of his father in 1785, became Duc d'Orléans, a prince who should have been one of the most powerful supporters of the French throne, but who became one of its inveterate enemies. His political opposition to his cousin, Louis XVI, was inspired by little more than a strong desire for popularity. His real interest was pleasure; he went up in balloons, dabbled in magic with Count Cagliostro, kept numerous racehorses and gave frequent dinners, or rather orgies, at the Château de Mousseaux, for his rowdy friends and the prettiest 'disreputables' in Paris; he won vast sums gambling in London, where

2

few had a good word for him. 'With the huge Orléans property', Carlyle wrote of him:

> With the Duke of Penthiévre for father-in-law, he will one day be the richest man in France. Meanwhile his hair is falling out, his blood is quite spoiled – by early transcendentalism of debauchery. Carbuncles stud his face, dark studs in a ground of burnished copper.

Disappointed in a naval career, he turned to the army, requesting, and obtaining, in 1778, the specially created post of Colonel-General of Hussars, and in 1783 a regiment of the same name was raised, of which he was made Colonel. It was in the blue and red Hussar uniform of *Mestre de Camp Commandant of the Régiment Colonel-Général* that Sir Joshua Reynolds painted him in 1785. The result, a handsome full-length, which flatteringly concealed the carbuncles, was, for a time at least, given pride of place in Carlton House, the Prince of Wales's London residence. In 1789, having taken a prominent part in the revolution in France, 'Vile Egalité' retired to England, where his treatment of Louis XVI put him in bad odour with the Prince. He returned to France in July, 1790, and three years later was one of the deputies who voted for the execution of the King. Early in 1793 the French General Doumouriez, and the young Duc de Chartres, Orléans' son, deserted from the French 'Army of the North' and, as a reprisal, all remaining members of the Bourbon family were arrested. On 4 November, 1793, the Duc d'Orléans was tried, sentenced and executed in Paris, all within two hours.

The second intimate of the Prince, the Duc de Lauzun, was a soldier of note, well-known and liked in London, having been a constant visitor for fifteen years. He had stayed on after the signing of the Franco-American treaty in 1777 and had been kindly treated by the King, who invited him to ride with him in the lanes around Richmond, while they discussed the worsening political situation. Nevertheless, it was not long before Lauzun was himself in America at the head of the Legion which bore his name; and at the siege of Yorktown, which effectively ended Britain's efforts to defeat the rebels, he came up against the celebrated Banastre Tarleton and his 'British Legion'. Tarleton had expressed a wish to 'shake hands with the great Duke', and before long an occasion presented itself. Lauzun led his Hussars against Tarleton's Dragoons, broke them, and drove them into the trenches at Gloucester. Tarleton himself was badly wounded, and many of his men taken prisoner. As Duc de Biron, a title which he inherited in 1788, Lauzun became a leading member of the egalitarian movement and, like Orléans, took a prominent part in the early stages of the French Revolution.

The third of this trio, the Marquis de Conflans, was tall, handsome and skilled in all forms of physical exercise. A man of intelligence and wit, he was excessively profligate; but though everyone spoke ill of him, they were delighted to see him. He was colonel of the Hussar regiment which bore his name and the story was told of him that, at a mess dinner, seeing a veteran officer empty a glass, holding nearly a pint of wine, in a single swallow, not to be outdone, he removed one of his boots, filled it and drank it off to the officer's health. The Comte de Lautrec had a wolf cub which followed at his heels like a dog, so M de Conflans at once procured a dancing bear, dressed it in a Hussar jacket, and stood it solemnly behind his chair with a plate in its paws. Conflans, who, perhaps fortunately, died before the Revolution broke out, lived as much in London as he did in Paris, and was generally regarded as the keeper of the Prince of Wales's conscience in matters of profligacy, being blamed, not without reason, for instilling the worst morality in his pupil. The Prince was deeply impressed by these three French notables, all of whom had, at one time or another, served as Hussar officers, and it was in their company that he first became aware of that particular branch of the cavalry and developed a taste for the outlandish clothing and riotous entertainments of a Hussar mess.

The title of 'Hussar', which so stirred the imagination of the Prince of Wales, was originally given to certain wild tribes of Hungarian horsemen who existed on plunder. There are various theories as to its exact provenance, one being that it is a corruption of the Magyr *husz ara*, meaning 'the price of twenty', referring to the custom of taking one member of every twentieth household for military service; and another that it comes from *husz ar*, meaning 'twenty acres', a feudal holding which required military service of its tenant. The original Hussars were descended from the same Tartar stock as Cossacks, whom they resembled closely in dress and tactics. Mounted on hardy ponies, clothed in fur and skins, and armed with spears and scimitars, they were a formidable foe. As the frontiers of Christendom were extended, so these wild tribesmen were formed into village settlememts, tamed, and recruited to serve as a local militia. The first regular body of Hussars was formed by Matthias Corvinus, King of Hungary, about 1485, and Louis II had some of them in his army at Mohacs, where he lost his life in 1526. During the Thirty Years War (1618–48) their services were much in demand by both sides, and it is from this period that the earliest descriptions of Hussar dress date. It was, we are told, quite different from that of other troops

They have a kind of doublet which scarce reaches to the waist; the sleeves are very tight, and are turned back with a button. They have large breeches, or pantaloons, like long hose. They have boots up to the knee, without knee-guards, the feet of which are rounded, with small iron heels. The shirts of the men are very short, and are seldom changed, for which reason many of them are made of blue cotton. Their cloaks are scarcely longer than their doublets, and they wear them to one side until it rains. Their caps are long and they edge them with fur; the greater part have shaven heads, and they leave only a small tuft on the right side.

Their officers were equally magnificent with caps decorated with fine *aigrettes*

4

and strips of silver to mark the number of combats in which they had taken part.

After the defeat of the Turks at the gates of Vienna in 1683 Louis XIV persuaded the Hungarian nobles to take up arms against Austria, and towards 1692 the first Hussars took service with France. The defeat of the French at Blenheim in 1704 led to Austria taking reprisals against the Hungarian nobles, many of whom were stripped of their possessions and exiled. Some, like Count Ladislaw de Bércheny, fled to France and offered their swords to Louis XIV, but, with Austrian territory closed to them, Hungarian recruits could only be obtained from provinces under Turkish control. Some time before 1720 Count Bércheny in search of recruits, journeyed into Wallachia, armed with a letter to the French Ambassador at the Sublime Porte. His mission was successful and he returned with the first batch of one hundred officers and men, with which to begin forming his regiment. During the wars of the Polish Succession (1733–35) and the Austrian Succession (1741–48) the Bércheny Hussars established a formidable reputation, and their Colonel eventually became Inspector-General of Hussars and a Marshal of France.

Hussars were not easy to handle and, being so often on advanced detached duties, were 'much accustomed' to deserting and selling their horses. It was said that the Hungarians forgave a Hussar the crime of desertion provided he returned from the enemy lines with a better horse. If they got their men and horses back their captains tended to turn a blind eye to desertion, but when taken 'sword in hand' there was no escape from draconian punishment, a fact which detracted somewhat from the valour of the French Hussars, as they were almost entirely deserters from enemy armies. Gradually Hungarians became so few that they were usually kept together in one squadron in each regiment. The Hussar regiment raised in 1743 by the Baron de Beausobre consisted entirely of Germans, recruited in Alsace and Lorraine. Gradually the net was spread wider to include people living along the banks of the Rhine as far as Coblenz.

By 1760 any Frenchman, provided his usual tongue was German, was permitted to serve in the hitherto exclusively foreign regiments, and in 1773 German was adopted as the normal language of command in French Hussar regiments. Hussars were first taken into the Prussian service in 1721 and by 1745 there were eight regiments. General Warnery, who had first-hand experience of their conduct during the Seven Years War, was not over-impressed by the martial qualities of the native-born Hungarian. At first, he wrote, 'none were admitted but Hungarians, deserters, or others, but afterwards Germans were received, and in course of time, Poles, experience having proved, that it was not necessary to be born in Hungary to become a good Hussar.'

Hussars first appeared in the British Isles during the 1745 uprising in the service of both Prince Charles Edward Stewart, and the Duke of Cumberland. The latter had a mounted bodyguard, recruited from the German States and Austria, known as the "Duke of Cumberland's Hussars". Dressed in green jackets with fur caps and pelisses in proper Hussar style, sixteen of them saw action at Culloden. After the Seven Years War, although there were no true

Hussars in the British Army, their reputation was well-known in military circles. Smith's *Military Dictionary* of 1779 devoted much space to a highly coloured recital of their feats. As they were irregular troops their tactics were 'extremely active'. Before an attack they laid themselves 'so flat on the necks of their horses' it was 'hardly possible to discover their force'. Once within pistol shot:

> . . . they raise themselves with such surprising quickness, and begin the fight with such vivacity on every side, that unless an enemy is accustomed to their method of engaging, it is very difficult for troops to preserve their order.

In retreat they were no less spectacular. Their horses had 'so much fire' and they were such excellent horsemen that no other cavalry could come up with them. They leaped ditches and swam across rivers with 'surprising facility'; they never camped, so were not encumbered 'with any kind of camp equipage, saving a kettle and a hatchet to every six men'. At that time Smith concluded, 'the Emperor Queen of Hungary' and the King of Prussia exceeded 'every country in this description of troops'.

Much of this was romantic nonsense, as events in the American Revolution were to prove. Of the 400 Hussars of the Duc de Lauzun's 'Foreign Volunteers' one squadron was entirely Hungarian, while the others contained a frightening mix of Poles and Irish, but in their various engagements with the several regiments of British and Loyalist Light Dragoons, including the British Legion, the honours appear to have been fairly evenly divided. General Warnery, summing up the qualities of Hussars, had to admit grudgingly that:

> It is in the Hussars that the best officers of cavalry are formed, for this plain reason, that they are most frequently in presence of, and engaged with the enemy, often on detachments, charged with the execution of difficult and delicate enterprizes, affording them frequent opportunities of exercising their capacities, and which obliges them to form their resolutions on the spot, and determine, without hesitation; the most important of all military qualifications . . .

On the other hand he was sure that ordinary Light Dragoons, when properly trained, could render the same service. What was the purpose in making the natives of a country masquerade in a 'foreign dress' that was more expensive and, at the same time, the most inconvenient that can be imagined?

* * *

From the moment the two royal brothers had been separated in 1780 they had kept up a regular correspondence. Frederick bowed to his elder brother's superior taste in matters of dress and much of their correspondence dealt with sartorial matters, both civilian and military. Frederick wanted a 'Vandyke' dress for a masquerade and asked George to order one for him,[2] but when, on 23 March, 1782, he was gazetted Colonel of the 2nd Troop of Horse Grenadier Guards, the latter was asked to turn his attention from the intricacies of 'lyloch silk . . . with pale buff puffs and knots' to the more solid qualities of superfine scarlet and gold lace. The King, with his habitual parsimony, had only ordered the full dress, but George took it upon himself to order the 'frock' uniform as well. In November, 1782, Frederick was made a major general, and no doubt deputed his brother to provide him with all the necessary details of the required uniform[3].

After leaving London in the early summer of 1783 the Prince's undesirable French friends had moved on to Berlin, where the aged Frederick the Great was holding his annual manoeuvres, and Prince Frederick, getting wind of this, persuaded his mentor the Duke of Brunswick to let him attend. He was immediately taken up by the wizened old warrior, who insisted on his young namesake accompanying him to all the reviews and field-days. Frederick was in his seventh heaven and faithfully reported everything he saw to his father. Writing on 6 June, he gave a memorable eye-witness account of the old Frederick the Great:

> He is short and small but wonderfully strong made, not very well upon his legs, but on horseback, Your Majesty would be astonished to see him . . . I cannot say His Majesty's wardrobe is the best I ever saw; he always wears the uniform of the Army, as it is called, which is a blue coat, with red cape and cuffs and a large shoulder knot. His coat is always buttoned quite down to the bottom, a very bad old uniform sword, a pair of black velvet breeches very greasy and dirty, and [a] pair of boots, which, never being blacked, are become quite red. However, with all this he has exceedingly the air of a gentleman and something exceedingly commanding in his look.

Prince Frederick and his military mentor, Colonel Grenville, visited Potsdam, Berlin and Magdeburg. Berlin society, he told the Prince of Wales, was 'very agreeable', except, apparently, for our old friends the French nobles, whom he described as 'a parcel of Frenchman, just freshly imported'. After Berlin Prince Frederick and Colonel Grenville moved on to Vienna where they saw the Austrian Army which they thought 'indeed very, very far behind the Prussians'.

Two years later Prince Frederick, now Duke of York, a lieutenant general and Colonel of the Coldstream Guards, visited his Prussian namesake for the second and last time. He and Lord Cornwallis, of Yorktown fame, were present at the last dinner given by Frederick the Great on the evening that he suffered his fatal stroke. Once again the Duke sent his father a detailed description of the reviews he had just attended in Silesia, which had been spectacular in the extreme, one of the highlights being twenty-nine battalions of infantry marching in one line, 'which was never attempted before' and he supposed never would be again, the distance from one flank to the other being 7,640 paces, or over three and a half miles. As for the cavalry:

> One day the king chose, without any previous notice, that the five and thirty squadrons of Cuirassiers and Dragoons should charge in one line *en muraille* and the forty squadrons of Hussars in the second line. Never was there seen so fine a sight; there was not a single horse out of his place until the word, Halt, was given, when, as the Commander was at the head of the right squadron, it was impossible for the squadron on the left to hear it in time enough, so that they advanced about twenty paces too far forward.

The Potsdam manoeuvres were fine but the King's illness and the terrible weather 'took away considerably from their lustre'. The manner in which Frederick had been treated by the King and the Prince of Prussia was more flattering than he could possibly express. 'But enough of military matters', he concluded, 'lest you should accuse me of being Prussian mad.'

*   *   *

After his first bout of enthusiasm, when the Duke of York first went to Hanover and the French nobles came to London, the Prince of Wales seemed to have abandoned his interest in military pursuits. But in 1787, after an absence of nearly six and a half years, Frederick returned home, leaving behind his younger brothers, Ernest and Adolphus, who were studying at Göttingen, and Edward, who was serving as a colonel in the Hanoverian Foot Guards. After their long separation the two older brothers spent most of their time together. By the end of December Grenville was writing that he and his charge were being 'thoroughly initiated into all the extravagances and debaucheries of this most *virtuous* metropolis'. The return of the Duke of York, however, had served to rekindle the spark of military ardour in the Prince's breast and in the spring of 1788 the first reference to the connection between the latter and the 10th Light Dragoons occurs. The Prince had apparently been in the habit of frequenting the mess of the regiment and, on his attending a field-day with the Duke of York, it had been suggested to him by the Colonel that it would make him and the whole regiment happy, if, 'as they bore the name of the Prince of Wales's Regiment, he would do them the honor of appearing at their head' before the King; but the latter quashed the idea out of hand, in a manner that hurt the Prince 'a good deal'.

The regiment with which the Prince's name was to become so inextricably connected was one of several Dragoon regiments raised in 1715, at the time of the troubles in Scotland. In 1755, in common with the three regiments of Dragoon Guards and four other regiments of Dragoons, it was augmented by a seventh, or 'Light' Troop. This first feeble attempt to keep up with the development of light cavalry on the Continent was very half-hearted and, on the return of the regiment from the Seven Years War, the Light Troop was disbanded. In 1759, however, the first entire regiment of Light Dragoons, the 15th, was raised, to be followed during the next few years by several more. The excellent performance of the 16th and 17th Light Dragoons during the American War led to the conversion of six more Dragoon regiments in 1783, including the 10th. On 27 September, 1783, the regiment was 'honoured' with the title of the '10th or Prince of Wales's Own Regiment of Light Dragoons'. At the same time it was permitted to wear the Prince of Wales's badge of the three ostrich feathers and the motto *'Ich Dien'*. On 18 May, 1784, its uniform was changed from red to blue, faced with pale yellow. At the same time a new style of uniform was introduced, consisting of a blue sleeveless 'upper jacket', or 'shell', which reached to just below the hips, worn over a sleeved 'under jacket'. Both garments were frogged and looped on the breast, with silver or white braid, and were vaguely hussar-like in character. The headdress was changed to the cumbersome 'Tarleton' helmet, much beloved by the King. This consisted of a peaked leather skull, bound round with a leopard-skin turban, with a large silver Prince of Wales's feathers fastened on the left side and surmounted, from front to rear, by a black fur crest.

In 1785 the 10th were stationed at Hounslow Barracks providing the royal escorts between Weymouth, Windsor and London, a duty which the Dragoons had taken over from the Household Cavalry at the beginning of George III's reign; it was probably during the course of these royal journeyings that the Prince of Wales first came into contact with the regiment that was to become so much his own.

* * *

In the summer of 1791 the Duke of York was back again in Berlin, hoping to volunteer for service with the Prussian Army. In the event he had to content himself with attending reviews and paying court to the Princess Frederica of Prussia, whom he married the same year. The Prince of Wales took this opportunity of presenting his brother with a comprehensive shopping list, which revealed his revived interest in uniforms, and in Hussars in particular. Among other items he wanted 'the compleat uniforms, accoutrements, saddle, bridle &c., of one of Zieten's[4] Hussars . . . as well as one of the Officers compleat uniforms, cloathing, sword, cap, saddle, bridle, chabrack, pistols, in short, everything compleat'. He apologized for giving his brother so much trouble, but as he knew, he had 'long intended to have these over, as one day or other they may give us some little ideas for our own troops'.

The Prince's unofficial connection with the 10th became more open in 1792. Throughout the summer there were reports of field-days, sumptuous dinners for the officers and a buzz of activity at a large camp on Bagshot Heath. Relations between the Prince of Wales and his father, which had reached an all-time low during the King's recent illness and the subsequent 'Regency

Crisis', seemed to have improved considerably, for when the latter visited the camp on 23 July he was accompanied, not only by the Duke of York, but also by the Prince. They watched the assembled regiments perform various evolutions which were carried out 'with great skill and activity', and afterwards the Prince 'gave a dinner, at which many persons of fashion, from the neighbourhood and from the camp, were present'. The following day there was a grand field-day, in which the Prince took an active part. Shortly after half past eight, *The Times* reported:

> ... the action began by the grand guard of cavalry being drove in after a good deal of skirmishing; a heavy cannonade commenced from the field pieces posted on the flanks of the three redoubts, and in half an hour's time the fire became general through the whole line for above twenty minutes, when the two regiments of cavalry [the 10th and 11th Light Dragoons] on the left headed by the PRINCE OF WALES, charged the hollow-way about half a mile in front, which had a truly grand effect.

The whole spectacle, the report continued, was 'uncommonly fine', and when part of the heath caught fire, to the alarm of the onlookers, it added much 'to the grandness of the occasion'. On the 26th the Prince dined with 'his' regiment, having first taken the precaution of sending two hogsheads of claret to the officers, to which, according to *The Times* 'they seemed to have done justice'. On 9 August there was another review prior to the departure of the regiments to their 'respective quarters', and soon after they marched off, leaving their tents standing to be 'picked up by Mr TROTTER', the enterprising army contractor who had supplied them all.[5]

The following year steps were taken to regularize the Prince's position, and to give him some permanent rank in the army. At the King's suggestion he was given 'a Letter of Service to act with the 10th Dragoons, till an opportunity should arise of the present Colonel exchanging to some other Regiment'. The actual letter, which was dated 26 January, read as follows:

> The King having been graciously pleased to appoint your Royal Highness Colonel Commandant of the 10th (or the Prince of Wales's Own) Regiment of (Light) Dragoons, I have the honor to acquaint your Royal Highness therewith, and to signify to you his Majesty's pleasure that you do obey such orders as you shall receive from his Majesty, the Commander-in-Chief, or other your superior officer.

The Prince's commission in the rank of colonel, when it was announced in the *London Gazette* in the following June, was back-dated to 19 November, 1782, by which strategem the Prince became the 'first Colonel at the head of a Regiment' in the Army. The King was later to claim that he had only given his son this commission 'on the solemn assurance . . . that no higher rank was meant hereafter to be claimed from it', and that the application arose only from the Prince's desire 'of being employed in forming' the 10th and 'in going with it to camp', which he could not do without some military rank. For the moment, however, the Prince was well enough pleased and thanked his father with his usual extravagance. He begged to be permitted to assure the King that 'in whatever situation in life' he might deign to place him, there was no one existing 'who, both in heart and mind' could be 'more truly, or more sincerely devoted & attached' to his sacred person than himself. It was, no doubt, in this glow of gratitude and loyalty, that he donned his 'Light Horse' uniform and turned out into the cold to see the Foot Guards off to Holland.

*   *   *

The fist year of war turned out to be disappointing and the royal brothers serving abroad had little to report. 1794, however, was to prove more eventful. In January Prince Ernest was transferred from the command of the 9th Hanoverian Light Dragoons to that of the 2nd Hanoverian Dragoons. He was not very pleased at the change; he had served five years in the Light Dragoons and he was 'damn'd to enter into the heavy cavalry', for no man could hate 'cuirassier service' more than he did. The campaigning season, however, began with three brilliant cavalry actions. On 24 April two squadrons of the 15th Light Dragoons and two of Austrian Hussars attacked the French cavalry in and around the village of Villers-en-Cauchie, near Cambrai, utterly routing them and inflicting the loss of 1,200 men killed and three pieces of cannon. The Emperor of Austria, who was in the area, was only just saved from being taken prisoner and, as a result, silver medals and the Knighthood of the Order of Maria Theresa were given to the officers concerned.[6]

Two days later General Otto, at the head of Mansell's brigade of heavy cavalry, caught the left flank of the General Chappuis's French army 'in the air', near the village of Beaumont and, in a surprise attack, rolled up his entire force. Chappuis himself was captured, while his army streamed back into Cambrai in disorder. By this stroke alone the Duke of York defeated 30,000 Frenchmen in thirty minutes. He told the Prince of Wales that:

Nothing could have exceeded the courage and spirit of the British cavalry on the 24th and 26th of last month. The [15th] Light Dragoons are really the astonishment of everybody, and all the foreigners allow they had no idea of such a corps. Every day, however, proves more and more the necessity of our having some Hussars or at least some troops mounted upon lighter horses and more fit for the outpost duties than our Light Dragoons, who are really too good to be flund [sic] away on every occasion.

On 10th May the French resumed the offensive and 30,000 men under Pichegru met the British between Tournai and Lille. Once again the Duke of

York spotted a flank 'in the air', this time the right, which he promptly attacked with a strong force of cavalry. On this occasion the French formed square and managed to avoid total destruction, but were pushed back towards their centre, which was then attacked by the British infantry near the village of Willems. Eventually the French line broke, pursued by the British cavalry, leaving thirteen guns and over 400 prisoners in British hands. The next day the French counter-attacked and drove back the Austrians. Among the casualties was Prince Ernest. 'Early have I got wounded,' he told the Prince in English, which, after his long stay in Germany, seemed to be getting somewhat rusty. He had suffered

> a strong contusion on my left arm occasion'd by the wind of a twelf [sic] pound shot; my arm is quite dead except the elbow & fingers. When the pitcher goes daily to the well at last it breaks, so is my arm with me, for three days running I have been in a fire. I had the command of a battalion and two squadrons to strengthen the outposts. They had forgot me, and by God, *j'étais prez d'être entouré*. However Goodwill and the determin [sic] bravery of my lads saved me.

After this brilliant beginning the coalition suffered a series of reverses, largely through lack of co-operation by the Austrian forces, which was soon followed by their withdrawal from Flanders. The British, outnumbered, had no course open to them but a gradual retreat, which began early in July and continued through the bitterly cold winter of 1794–5. The supply services, medical arrangements, and discipline all broke down and the army was eventually embarked at Bremen and shipped back to England. The coalition had proved a disastrous failure. Austria and Prussia were far more interested in the partition of Poland than in the conquest of France, and the subsidies provided by England were used for the former rather than the latter purpose. The result was that by 1795 Belgium had been annexed by France and Holland had been converted into the puppet Batavian Republic, Prussia had been bribed into making peace, and Bonaparte, after the Italian campaign of 1796, which led to the humiliation of Austria by the treaty of Campo Formio, had emerged as a military genius of the first order.

In spite of the heavy responsibilities of extricating the British army from an extremely awkward situation, the Duke of York managed to find time to write to the Prince on his birthday. The latter, it seems, was still hankering after items of Hussar uniform for his collection:

> Prince William informed me that you wished to have the cloathing and accoutrements of the Corps of Uhlans raised by Monsieur de Wiedenbrock. Wiedenbrock has nothing more to do with them and they have been changed from Uhlans to Hussars. I will take care to send you over a compleat cloathing and accoutrements of them as they are at present. There are three other Corps of Hussars raising of which if you

please I will send you over the cloathing; [they are] The Prince de Roban's, the Duke de Choiseul's, and Hompesch's.

The Duke must have deputed Prince Ernest to collect these items, for in November the latter informed the Prince that he was getting 'all the cloathing of the new corps' and would send them over as soon as possible.

The Duke of York returned to England in December, 1794, having given up the command of the British and Hanoverian contingent to General Walmoden, and in February, 1795, was made field marshal and successor to Lord Amherst as Commander-in-Chief; Prince Ernest was not allowed home until 1796.

* * *

The 10th Light Dragoons were not destined to see service in the Duke of York's campaign and remained peacefully in quarters in the south of England. A fortnight or so after watching the departure of the Foot Guards Sir Gilbert Elliot reported that the Prince was becoming 'impatient of his present inglorious life' and wished to 'have his share of the glory that is going'. He was quite happy to serve under the Duke of York, but did not relish remaining at home 'merely as a parade officer or an idle spectator of the great events in Europe', which Sir Gilbert felt was 'creditable to him, and it would be a way to recover charactor and favour with the country'.

In the summer of 1793 a large military camp was assembled at Waterdown, in Kent, and, when it eventually broke up, the 10th and some of the Militia regiments were permitted to go into camp near Brighton. The Prince, delighted at the prospect of having his own regiment stationed near his beloved pavilion, set about making elaborate preparations for its reception. By 5 August the ground for the encampment, 'a delightful spot by the sea-side' to the west of the town, towards Shoreham, was already marked out and the wells partly dug. The Prince, *The Times* reported, intended to 'dine at the mess every day and be in actual service in all respects'. A large temporary building was being erected to serve as the mess-house and a marquee, one of the most elegant ever made in Britain, was set up near the ruins of the old church in Hove. It contained several rooms, including a 'spacious kitchen', with 'all sorts of conveniences attached'. The chairs in the 'State Room' alone were said to have cost £1,000, and the rest of the furniture was to be of 'corresponding elegance'.

When the regiment finally reached Brighton that morning it was met by the Prince in person and led to the camp ground. The Prince's 'tent' was put up and that night he slept in it. A week later, the Prince's birthday was celebrated in style, with the ringing of bells and the firing of salutes. He gave a 'very superb entertainment' to the officers of his regiment in the marquee and in the evening there was a ball at the Castle Hotel, which was 'numerously attended'. The next day the Militia arrived on the outskirts of Brighton from Waterdown and were 'formed in battalions, in which order they moved, keeping good wheeling distance'. Crowds of people came out to meet them and conspicuous among the spectators was the Prince 'in the honourable garb of his regiment, looking both the Soldier and the Prince'.

Early in September a gale blew down much of the camp, including the Prince's marquee. The Prince himself was unhurt as, 'except on the night when he is Colonel of the Camp, his residence is in the Pavilion', but the inclement weather and the destruction of his marquee must have blunted the edge of his military ardour, for on the 12th of the month he was back in London. The camping season was, in any case, almost over and on the 18th *The Times* reported that 'a total suspension of everything active has taken place'. In the event the regiment left at the end of October and moved into quarters at Chichester; by the 22nd *The Times* revealed that 'universal torpor' pervaded the camp. The Prince's first wartime summer 'in the field' ended with something of a let-down when he was informed that, as Prince of Wales, 'he could not with propriety go through the different ranks of General Officers, but must remain a Colonel or [as King in due course] Command the Army'. In short he was not to look for promotion to general officer rank but 'remain the first Colonel at the head of a Regiment'. The Prince replied that he would much rather remain as 'Colonel Commandant' of the 10th 'until either this or some other' regiment became 'perfectly' his own.

In June of the following year the 10th returned to Brighton, setting up their tents at Goldstone Bottom, and the Prince spent all that summer 'manoeuvring his regiment'. Early in August it was reviewed on the downs and the men were complimented on their 'soldier-like appearance and the exact manner in which they went through their military evolutions'. On 30 August there was a 'sham-fight' during which the Prince led his regiment into action, making several charges 'upon the supposed enemy with great judgement and effort'. All the 'beauty and fashion' of the neighbourhood was present at these military spectacles, and even Mrs Fitzherbert turned out on horseback dressed 'in the Prince's uniform'.[7] In October the 10th struck their tents and moved to Croydon and then went on 'King's Duty' at Windsor, Hounslow and Hampton Court.

In the months that followed, the Prince was chiefly concerned with his forth-coming marriage to his cousin the Princess Caroline of Brunswick. In the interval of waiting for his bride, however, he managed to find time to revive the question of his promotion. On studying the *Gazette* of 28 February, 1795, he was infuriated to discover that his nineteen-year-old cousin Prince William of Gloucester, whose commission dated from 1794, had been promoted to major general and had now become his immediate superior. He wrote to the Secretary of State for War, Henry Dundas, on 1 March complaining 'as a much injured man in my capacity as a soldier for my Sovereign'. Dundas's reply was prevaricative in the extreme; the Prince's having received the command of a regiment 'without it's being a step to higher promotion in the Army' was entirely the fault of himself and Pitt importuning the King; the King would feel that 'the heir apparent of the British Empire ought to rest the glory of his life upon pursuits very different from those that could result from any military occupation or military attainment'; the Prince might gratify the wishes and expectations of the people more 'by studying to cultivate and improve the blessings of peace rather than by addressing himself to the manoeuvres of military discipline'. As a final twist he reminded the Prince that Parliament was about to go into the matter of his debts.[8]

On receiving this missive the Prince wrote to the King direct, saying that if he had known of the condition he would have dropped the request rather than have submitted to 'so humiliating a limitation'. The 'boon' he asked of the King was 'the rank of General, or Lt-General' so dated as to give him seniority in such degree as the King might 'deem expedient'. Here the matter rested for the moment, both the King and his eldest son being involved in matters of dynastic importance, namely the latter's impending marriage. Three days after the wedding, however, the Prince received the King's reply which was no less deflating than that from Dundas. He had purposely avoided replying, he wrote, until the arrival of Princess Caroline should engage the Prince's attention and 'divert it from objects certainly not so pleasing to the nation'. He was sorry the Prince had 'again applied' but could not depart from what he has 'uniformly thought right'.

In spite of these setbacks the Prince clearly enjoyed himself with the 10th and was popular with the younger officers. Jack Slade, who joined the regiment in 1780, recalled the hard drinking that took place in the mess. Once, when one of them asked for a song, the Prince enquired affably which one he would have. 'The one your Royal Highness sang last night', came the reply. 'Oh,' said the Prince, 'that is a two bottle song, let us have some more wine first'. The glasses in the mess were made without stems, so that they could only be set down when empty, and when the pace got too hot Slade used quietly to empty his under the table.[9] The members of the mess were a surprisingly mixed group. On the one hand there were those of the 'highest rank and fashion', like Lords Petersham, Edward Somerset, and the brothers Charles and Robert Manners, while on the other several were of considerably less exalted rank like George Leigh, who spent most of his life on the racecourse, George Quentin, the Hanoverian horsemaster and son of a Göttingen merchant, Charles Palmer, the son of the wealthy Bath brewer and spermaceti merchant, and last, but by no means least, the celebrated dandy, George Bryan Brummell, son of a successful Government fuctionary.

Brummell, who entered the regiment in June, 1794, had his first encounter with Royalty when, as a boy at Eton, he had been presented to the Prince of Wales on the terrace at Windsor Castle. Sixteen years old and 'adorned in the rich uniform of the Tenth, which his slight but handsome figure was well calculated to show off', Cornet Brummell at once found himself 'in the highest society in the country'. His military career, however, was less distinguished. He was present at the Prince's wedding and accompanied his royal Colonel to Windsor for the honeymoon, as a kind of *Chevalier d'honneur*. In all he spent so much time in attendance on the Prince that the 'gallant Tenth did not benefit much from his services', and when he did condescend to parade with them the results were usually spectacular.

The celebrated story of how he could only recognize his troop, when on parade, by means of an old soldier with a 'bottle nose', is typical of Brummell's military prowess. Slade had a similar, if less well-known, story. On this occasion a loose charger was seen galloping down the ranks as the regiment stood formed up. 'Whose horse is that?', bawled the sorely-tried Colonel. Mr Brummell's, Sir!' 'Send him here!'. 'What have you to say?' demanded the Colonel, with many expletives. 'The fact is, Colonel,' drawled Brummell in his best dandiacal manner, 'that my horse is a very fine animal and wanted to show off his paces, so I let him go,' a reply which merely added fuel to the fire. After little more than three years of such antics, Brummell left the 10th, on hearing, it is said, that the regiment was ordered to Manchester. He could not possibly go 'on foreign service' and be so far away from London.[10]

* * *

When, for whatever reason, a vacancy occurred the Prince took considerable trouble to fill the place with a suitable candidate. During the first few years of his command he secured for the regiment such catches as Lord Robert Manners, younger brother of the Duke of Rutland, and Frederick Ponsonby, Lord Bessborough's son. In the latter case the Prince was not above trying what might be called a 'hard sell' by making a direct approach to Lord Bessborough. Having heard 'by chance', he began, that Lord Bessborough intended his son for the Army, he was letting him know that the 'most advantageous opportunity offers itself at this moment for the young man' in the 10th. 'By various exchanges that have lately taken place in my regiment,' he continued, 'several cornetcies are become vacant', and if the 'young man' bought one of these, which the Prince pointed out was 'but £650', he would in a matter of weeks 'probably become either a Lieutenant or next for purchase for a Lieutenancy, an advantage which is not to be imagined to any person who means to make the Army their profession'. 'I need not I trust add,' he continued,

> that in coming into my regiment, every attention will be shewn to your son, but that it is also no detriment to know, that he is coming into a regiment, supposed to be one of the first in the service, and of which the Corps of Officers is entirely composed of men of Fashion and Gentlemen, and the most regular and orderly Corps of young men that exists.

One wonders whether Jack Slade would have recognized his riotous fellow subalterns from this description, and it was perhaps just as well that Lady Bessborough did not see the Prince's letter to the Duke of York, dated 15 September, in which he enclosed a medical certificate for Captain Fuller, one of the senior members of that 'regular and orderly Corps'. He was 'laid up', the Prince explained, 'with a very serious venereal attack, nothing fresh but an old business which has hitherto only been patched up, but which [Dr.] Keate assures him now with perseverance he will make him completely rid of.' All in all Slade had a somewhat jaundiced view of the Prince's character: 'Of kind words and fair promises I always found the Prince of Wales liberal to excess, but, as to his promises, he never kept them.'

In peacetime the 'purchase' system was the only path to promotion, while in wartime vacancies caused by death in action could be filled up by the next senior officer in succession without purchase. When a vacancy occurred the senior officer in the next lower rank had the moral right to be offered 'his step' at the regulation price, but many ploys were practised in order to obtain a higher price. Commission brokers were employed, auctioning resorted to, and a poor officer might see three or four of his juniors buy their way over his head. If there was a block in his promotion prospects an officer with money to spare might exchange, or buy his way, into a regiment with better prospects by paying over the odds, while officers ordered abroad against their will could often exchange with those willing to go for a cash payment. When the Duke of York became Commander-in-Chief in February, 1795, he started to tackle the whole problem of the 'scandalous abuses that have, of late, crept into the mode of officering the Army'. In March, 1795, he ordered a circular letter to be sent to the colonels of regiments asking for an immediate return of the numbers of captains under twelve years of age and lieutenant colonels under the age of eighteen. Eventually he put an end to a system whereby someone like the unnamed youth, cited by Oman, 'who had the advantage of being wealthy, a peer, and possessed of great family influence in Parliament' could work his way up from Lieutenant to Lieutenant-Colonel in a single year. By 1811 a system had been introduced whereby a minimum service in each rank was required before promotion was allowed and no officer under orders for foreign service could exchange, except in the case of ill-health. The cost of commissions in the Dragoons and Dragoon Guards varied from £735 for a Cornetcy to £4,982 for a Lieutenant-Colonelcy, the big jump being between a Lieutenancy (£997.10s), and a Captaincy (£2,782.10s).[11]

With the exception of the short spell of duty in Manchester, which had driven Beau Brummell from the regiment, the 10th spent the rest of the first part of the war in various parts of southern England. Much of the time was spent on the south coast, where one of their duties was to help in the prevention and apprehension of the numerous smugglers. The soldiers, in particular, detested 'Coast Duty', and often worked hand in glove with the inhabitants, to the extent of helping with the unloading when their officers' backs were turned. As a result incentives were offered in the shape of rewards for 'seizures'. These, like naval prize money, were distributed in proportions, which varied from the single share of privates, drummers and trumpeters, to the 150 shares which fell to the Colonel.

One of the hazards of being stationed on the coast was illustrated when a recruiting sergeant of the 10th was found guilty of embezzling 'money the property of one of his comrades'. For this crime he was sentenced to 400 lashes and to be drummed out of the regiment. The first part of the sentence was, however, remitted, but the latter part was carried into execution the next day in the face of the 'whole line'. The ensuing ceremony lasted for more than an hour, the culprit being 'exhibited with a halter about his neck'. Meanwhile the Royal Navy, in the person of one Sealey, a member of the press gang, was lurking in the crowd, ready to snap him up at the end of the ceremony. The soldiers were 'no sooner appraised' of this than with cries of 'No pressing!' . . . 'No pressing!' . . . 'By G— we will have no pressing!' they surrounded the unfortunate Sealey and pushed him over the cliff, 'where he was followed and pelted with pebbles till his face was almost covered with blood'. He would probably have been killed if a Quartermaster of the 10th had not rushed to his aid. The disgraced recruiting sergeant did not, however, escape so easily, but was 'afterwards secured, and by a file of men escorted on board the tender at Shoreham' to embark on a naval career.[12]

In July, 1798, the 10th moved to Canterbury, where the Prince took up residence at Charlton Court and busied himself with regimental matters. The horses were one cause of worry. They were at least eighty short, what with the 'cast horses' that had died 'from the hurry of our march from Dorchester', and from the glanders, which seemed to be 'rather spreading'. He was still riled that he was 'to a certain degree' under the command of Prince William. He complained bitterly to his mother about the 'dull stupid boy' being a major-general 'attended by two Aides de Camp' on account of his 'high birth & consequence', while his own 'birth, rank, consequence, education, age & time of life', was 'all to go for nothing'. 1799 began with rumours that the 10th might go on foreign service, but summer came without any orders being received and in August the King reviewed the regiment on Winkfield Plain. The King was pleased with the state of the regiment. 'He spoke most kindly,' Princess Elisabeth informed her brother, '& said out & out they road [sic] the best of any.' Expecting every moment to be sent to Holland, the regiment moved to Barham Down, six miles from Canterbury, where the Prince reviewed it on the 30th, apparently quite reconciled at not being allowed to accompany it on active service.

A year later, when the regiment was again at Windsor, Hounslow and Hampton Court for another spell of Escort Duty, it was very nearly sent on active service once more, but yet again it came to nothing. In fact the 10th Light Dragoons were to miss any involvement in the whole of the first part of the war, because during August and November, 1800, the first attempts were made to negotiate a peace with France through an intermediary, a Mr Otto, the Agent for French Prisoners. These early negotiations failed, but Mr Otto remained in England, and on 21 March, 1801, they were re-opened. This time they were more successful and on 30th September a reply accepting the British proposals was received from Bonaparte and at seven o'clock on the evening of 1 October Lord Hawkesbury and Mr Otto signed the 'Preliminaries of Peace' in Downing Street. The news being a complete surprise, London was unprepared for celebration and, as the *Morning Post* reported, 'The illumination, so far from being general, was principally confined to a few streets'. The Royal Mail coaches, hastily placarded with PEACE WITH FRANCE in bold capitals, and with the drivers wearing a sprig of laurel in their hats, spread the news to the provinces.

*   *   *

The outbreak of war in 1793 caught the British Army unprepared, as was usually the case. The cavalry were in a particularly bad state of neglect; regiments were widely dispersed and employed for most of the time in what was little more than police work. The officers, especially the subalterns, were badly paid and had little incentive to perform their duties with anything approaching professional enthusiasm. Nevertheless, some of the regiments which took part in the campaign in the Low Countries had managed to distinguish themselves in action. On taking up his office as Commander-in-Chief, the Duke of York embarked on a wide programme of reforms. He began by circulating Dundas's drill book to commanding officers, with the object of standardizing the exercise and movements of regiments. While the infantry continued to puzzle out the intricacies of Dundas's *Rules and Regulations,* 'Old Pivot', as he was irreverently called, addressed himself to the problems of cavalry drill. The new cavalry manual, which introduced the practice of executing movements 'by threes', was made compulsory in 1795. Finally, in 1796, the *Rules and Regulations for the Sword Exercise of the Cavalry,* drawn up by the celebrated fencing-master Henry Angelo and illustrated with figures of the 10th and 16th Light Dragoons, was published and two years later a uniform code of trumpet signals was introduced.

In March, 1796, the Duke set up a Board of General Officers to enquire into the clothing, saddlery and equipment of the cavalry, which produced its findings the following May. As far as the clothing was concerned, it recommended that a short-waisted jacket should replace the former combination of sleeved waistcoat and sleeveless 'shell', or outer waistcoat. A new pattern of saddlery was introduced and the old-fashioned 'housings', which only partly covered the horse's withers, were done away with. The suggestion that the light cavalry should be issued with a bayonet was not accepted and their arms and equipment remained unchanged.

The Board also pointed out that the breed of black horses, which provided the cavalry with its mounts, was now 'either extinct or completely transformed', being only suitable for draught work. Fortunately, two developments which took place during the reign of George III helped to solve this particular problem. The first was the phenomenal increase in the popularity of fast fox-hunting, which led to the development of a new type of horse, with a large proportion of thoroughbred blood, able to carry a weight of up to sixteen stone over all sorts of fences at almost racing speed. As far as the military were concerned, the native English 'hunter' soon showed that, provided he was reasonably well fed, he compared favourably with all types of Continental remount, and in the approach march, followed by a charge, was soon to prove himself unequalled.[13]

The second development was that of the Mail Coach service, the brainchild of John Palmer, the father of Charles Palmer of the 10th Light Dragoons. When it was introduced in 1784 his plan of carrying the mails in specially designed lightly sprung mail coaches, in the charge of an armed guard, instead of unarmed, unpunctual and badly-organized 'post boys', was an immediate success. The speeds required to operate the new mail service efficiently led to the introduction of the 'coach-horse', capable of trotting steadily on the new hard roads for long distances at speeds of up to eight miles an hour without excessive fatigue. The heavy draught animal was no longer in demand and the 'blood' horse established its superiority on the road, as it had on the hunting field. The Board reported that this type of horse was fitted to take the place of the blacks in the ranks of the cavalry. Thus, by the end of the 18th century, there were two types of horse available, both of which were ideal for military use: the light, medium, or heavy 'hunter', which was suitable for the cavalry, and the 'coach-horse', which enabled the formation of an efficient horse artillery arm.

The last recommendation of the Board was that a veterinary surgeon, a saddler and an armourer should be attached to every regiment of cavalry. Prior to the establishment of the Royal Veterinary College in 1791, by the Frenchman Charles Vidal de St Bel, English veterinary surgeons had, according to one historian, 'followed principles which were hardly free from the taint of witchcraft and sorcery'. The welfare of cavalry horses was the responsibility of regimental farriers, and the Board's recommendation was that they should be sent to the college for training, but this proved impracticable. In April, 1796, therefore, a veterinary officer was attached to each regiment at an annual salary of £95, or, alternatively, half that sum was provided to support a student at the college. In the following September veterinary surgeons were given the King's Commission and pay of seven shillings a day. By 1802 all cavalry regiments had fully trained veterinary surgeons, saddlers and armourer-sergeants, and there was considerable hope of improved efficiency in these departments.

In spite of these reforms, there was still a basic weakness in the training of the cavalry. Little was required of them beyond the immaculate performance of the various squadron and regimental movements, in line and column, and such important matters as outpost duty and reconnaissance were virtually ignored. The so-called '(Light) Dragoons' were in fact used in the field as heavy cavalry, for the attack or 'charge', and the need for 'proper' light cavalry, or 'hussars', had already been the subject of much discussion between the Prince of Wales, the Duke of York and Prince Ernest. It was partly with this in mind, and partly from his love of military finery, that the first was so avidly collecting examples of hussar clothing and equipment from the Continent. A lone voice, that of General Money, who had served with the French Army, complained that in England, the most strongly enclosed country in the world, not a single cavalryman was properly armed or trained for dismounted work. Quoting the success of the French *Chasseurs à Cheval* in the recent Italian campaign, he pleaded for the introduction of similar regiments in the British Army. Until 'this new system of horse-chasseurs be adopted in Austria and Prussia,' he wrote, 'whom we copy in most things, nothing will be done,' on account of what he called 'jack-boot predudice'.[14]

CHAPTER TWO
Ipswich Swells

On 27 March, 1802, the Treaty of Amiens was finally signed and the Government, little knowing how short would be the respite, hastened to reduce the size of the Army. The '*Parish* Corps', the myriad bodies of Fencible Cavalry and Volunteer Infantry, could be disbanded without causing too much distress, but the cuts in the regular Army were more serious.[1] By July the Prince of Wales could write to Lord Paget, Colonel of the 7th Light Dragoons, that it was 'quite melancholy to see our poor wretched skeleton regiments'. He had inspected the 11th Light Dragoons and had not been impressed; their men were 'small and punchy', presumably in the equestrian sense of short-legged and thickset, 'which I do not think meets your ideas any more than it does mine'. He was not specific as to what these ideas were, but subsequent events suggest that he and Paget were already discussing the possibility of turning their respective regiments into Hussars.

On the outbreak of war the only Hussar regiments in British pay were foreign, composed of French *émigrés* or German deserters from the French army.[2] The one approximation to a hussar regiment in the British Army proper was the 25th Light Dragoons, who, during the campaign in the Low Countries, called themselves 'Gwynn's Hussars'. Sergeant Landsheit of the *émigré* Hompesch Hussar thought they were far from achieving the panache of the genuine article. When his regiment returned from the West Indies in 1796 they were offered the chance to re-enlist in the British Army. In their red shakos, richly ornamented blue jackets and scarlet sabretaches, 'suspended by slings of such length as to keep it dangling at our heels', they considered themselves 'prodigious dandies' and they were not at all impressed by the party of the 25th who came to seek recruits. They were, Landsheit recalled,

> dressed in dirty grey jackets, leather helmet caps fearfully heel-balled, white leather breeches, and shoes and long black gaiters. They wore white feathers thrust into the sides of the helmets, and sabretaches tucked up so as to descend no lower than the hips. On the whole we had never seen such spectacles; and hence, though the non-commissioned officers exerted themselves with laudable pertinacity in the cause, not one man could they get from us.

In short they were dowdy, old-fashioned and totally without style, criticisms which the Prince of Wales, Prince Ernest and Lord Paget, Colonel of the 7th Light Dragoons, felt could, with justification, be applied to the British light cavalry in general.

After the Prince and the Duke of York had inspected the Hompesch Hussars at Southampton, 'Not content to feast us . . . upon roasted sheep and hogsheads of ale', Landsheit wrote, the Prince announced that he had adopted them as his own regiment, 'and taking away our old buttons, gave us new – richly plated and stamped with the ostrich feathers and motto of the principality'. Unfortunately the Prince's partiality failed to save the regiment from being disbanded in 1798. The following year Landsheit, and a hundred or so survivors from the Hompesch Hussars, joined another *émigré* regiment, the York Hussars, then stationed on the Isle of Wight, where it was being brought up to strength from recruits collected from the prison-hulks, 'and the wrecks of almost all the foreign regiments in English service'. In February, 1800, they moved to Weymouth, still in a miserable state, 'half naked, without arms, without horses, and totally ignorant of their duty'. In May, however, a new colonel, Robert Long, who was later to command the 15th Light Dragoons, arrived and lost no time in 'introducing English drill, English habits, English distinctions and English punishments'. To the 'old soldiers', mainly Germans, who knew their duty thoroughly, his proceedings were 'vexatious in the extreme'. In their old regiment the horses were always in the peak of condition, each man running to the stables, feeding and cleaning his horse, as soon as the trumpet sounded 'Stables'. Under the new régime the men were paraded by troops with sponges suspended from their buttons, curry-combs in their hands and 'brushes so disposed that the orderly-officer might see them'; then, after a lengthy inspection, they were marched to the stables by squads. The rest of the day was taken up with foot and horse parades, and carbine, sword and pistol drill; 'in a word, one continued series of drills and parades from break of day till it was time to lie down again'.

What was even more distressing to the German Hussars was the introduction of the cat-o'-nine-tails in place of the traditional *bastinado*[3]. Men began to desert, 'and the more they deserted, the faster flew the lash, till there were comparatively few among the privates to whom it had not been applied'. The culmination occurred when six men stole a boat from the harbour and attempted to sail to France, but landed by mistake in Guernsey and were recaptured. Two of them were sentenced to be shot, and the remainder flogged, before being sent to a 'condemned corps'.[4] But, in spite of the horrors of lash and firing parties, life in the York Hussars had its lighter moments.When the Royal Family came to Weymouth the King frequently inspected them. One particular morning he stopped in front of a private and asked him where he came from. 'Oh!' he exclaimed when told, 'a Saxon, a Saxon, – a fine nation, a fine nation, very good soldiers, very good soldiers'. In a similar fashion he spoke to a Swede and a Hanoverian. The next man was tall, with a dark oval face, piercing black eyes, hair like a raven's wing and an enormous pair of moustaches. The King gazed at him for some time and then asked,

> What countryman are you?. 'A Hungarian', replied Forksh, whose name being rendered into English signifies a wolf. 'All excellent soldiers the Hungarians,' cries the King, 'all excellent soldiers,' and then, as if attracted by the peculiar curl of the man's moustachios, he put forth his hand and began gently to twist one of them. It is impossible to say what motive could have actuated Forksh, for he never gave a satisfactory account of it; but the king had hardly seized his moustache, when he made a sort of snap like a dog at the royal hand, which was instantly withdrawn.

The whole parade burst out laughing, including the Prince of Wales, who, as he passed by, slipped a guinea into the hand of the impassive Forksh. From that day the York Hussars became 'mighty favourites with the King', but it did not save them when, in June, 1802, they were transported back to the Isle of Wight and were offered the choice of re-enlisting in a British regiment or of taking ship for Germany. Over two-thirds of a total strength of 331 elected to return home.

With the disbandment of the foreign Hussar regiments, the British Army was left without any of what the Prince of Wales, the Duke of York, Prince Ernest and others considered proper light cavalry, and the time now seemed ripe to put their plans into action. Perhaps the King's attachment to the York Hussars had softened his objections, for in early 1803 the two royal Colonels were permitted to dress one troop of their respective regiments as a Hussar Troop.[5] When the 10th Light Dragoons moved to Brighton in April, 1803, the Prince flung himself heart and soul into supervising the change, sending Captain Quentin over to see Colonel Long, who was still on the Isle of Wight with the remnants of the York Hussars, in order to obtain non-commissioned officers and privates for the new troop. Long recommended Landsheit as a suitable recruiting sergeant and the latter was left with the task of hanging on to any likely recruits, with orders 'to keep them in good humour' until Quentin returned to approve them. This turned out to be an expensive business. By the time Quentin returned, Landsheit had been forced to advance a pound, out of his own pocket, to each of his twelve recruits. This time Quentin brought the Regimental Sergeant-Major of the 10th with him,

> a Belgian, by name du Pré, and as thorough a coxcomb as I have ever chanced to see in his station. Covered in silver lace and gorgeously apparelled, he would scarcely stoop to notice so humble a personage as myself; and as to the recruits with them, he would hold no intercourse further than was requisite in parading them for inspection.

On this second visit Quentin was querulous and suspicious, and when

Landsheit asked for his money back he was told sharply that he might seek repayment where he could, but from Quentin he should never receive it. When it was pointed out to Quentin that the men were not yet attested and could withdraw whenever they wished, he 'lowered his tone' and promised to pay the money back that evening. Landsheit, concluding that it would not be to his advantage to join the 10th, booked himself a passage to Weymouth for the following morning. At nine o'clock he waited on Captain Quentin, who handing him his twelve pounds 'without scruple', told Landsheit that he 'would not suit him' and that he would therefore 'dispence' with his services. 'I am very glad, Captain Quentin', Landsheit replied, 'for to be plain with you, it was my intention to take the very step in which you have anticipated me. Neither you nor your sergeant-major will do for me, so I wish you good morning.' Thus the worthy Sergeant departed from the scene, to re-enlist, eventually, in the 20th Light Dragoons.

If Captain Quentin would not do for Sergeant Landsheit, he was indispensable to the Prince of Wales. A tall, dry, somewhat humourless Hanoverian, George Quentin was already thirty-three when he joined the 10th Light Dragoons as a Cornet in 1794. Acknowledged to have been 'the most compleat horseman in Europe', he was soon appointed riding-master to the 10th, much to the satisfaction of the Prince, 'with whom he was a great favourite'. Half a century later Lord William Lennox recalled that Quentin 'was the first to introduce the foreign cavalry seat' into England, and that he was particularly knowledgeable on the subject of hussars. He 'knew how the pelisse should be slung, and the proper cut of the hessian boot.' Under his auspices the men were 'well set up, so much that the new system captivated the heart of the heir to the throne'.[6]

The alterations with which the 10th were busying themselves consisted in changing the old bearskin-crested 'Tarleton' helmet for the tall cylindrical 'Mirliton', or 'Flugel-cap', and providing the men with fur-trimmed pelisses, knotted 'barrel' sashes and Hungarian high-mounting saddles. These last, common in central Europe, were of eastern origin, having been introduced by the Mongol horsemen who flooded into Hungary in the 13th Century. The basic construction consisted of two wooden sideboards glued and pegged to high wooden front and rear arches, between which a rawhide seat was suspended and attached to the sideboards by leather thonging. A separate padded seat, or 'pilch', hooked over the front and rear arches, and the whole was placed on the horse's back on top of a folded blanket. The suspended seat was intended to take the weight of the rider and his baggage off the horse, although a badly made Hungarian saddle, or one with twisted or warped sideboards could cause the dreaded sore back, the bane of the cavalrymans's life. Finally, the Prince bought forty of Mr Ezekiel Baker's new rifled carbines, similar to those already in use in the 'Experimental Rifle Corps', then training at Shorncliffe under Sir John Moore.[7] The 10th Light Dragoons were thus the first British cavalry regiment to be armed with rifles.

*　*　*　*

In March, 1803, sterner matters were about to engage the attentions of the British Army. To the numerous Britons taking advantage of the peace to visit Paris the First Consul had been polite, if a little distant, but the Government at home was not so sure about the friendliness of his intentions.[8] While many of the opposition were abroad sightseeing, a Bill was brought in establishing the Militia at 72,000 men, 49,000 of whom were to be embodied at once for twenty-one days' training, and in May a second Bill enabled certain corps of Yeomanry and Volunteers to remain in being. The fears with regard to Bonaparte's intentions were soon justified as he continued his relentless annexation of the continent, swallowing up Italy, Switzerland and Holland, and handing over the lands beyond the Rhine to a parcel of German princelings. British protests were made in vain. In February, 1803, the French Government demanded the evacuation of Malta, in accordance with an article in the Treaty of Amiens, which provided for the return of the island to the Knights of St John of Jerusalem. In reply the British Ambassador, Lord Whitworth, drew the attention of the French to their aggrandizements carried out subsequently to the signing of the Treaty. After a series of unsuccessful negotiations the situation gradually deteriorated until, at a stormy meeting held on 13 March, Bonaparte charged the British with trying to drag France into hostilities. Finally, on 12th May, Lord Whitworth requested his passport and the two countries were once again at war.

For the next two years, while Britain stood alone, Bonaparte's plans were centred on the invasion of England. A camp was formed at Boulogne, in which the huge 'Army of the Coasts of the Ocean' was assembled to await the signal of the newly-proclaimed Emperor of the French. A vast arsenal was established at Antwerp, and all along the coast, from the Texel to Brest, fleets of barges and transports were gradually collected together. In the face of these threatening gestures the British once again looked to their defences. The Navy and Army were strengthened, the Militia embodied and 30,000 volunteers enrolled to arm and drill in preparation for the expected invasion.

Not since the days of the Armada had Britain been pervaded with such patriotism and warlike spirit, and the royal princes were much in evidence. The imperturbable figure of the Duke of York was to be seen posting from one part of the country to another, now reviewing the troops on Rushmere Heath near Ipswich, now at Thanet inspecting the 15th Light Dragoons, or at Shorncliffe with Sir John Moore and the Light Brigade. Prince Ernest, now Duke of Cumberland, was in command of the Western District and the Duke of Cambridge the 'Home' District, while that 'dull stupid boy', Prince William of Gloucester, commanded the North-Western.

The Prince of Wales arrived at Brighton on 8 July, 1803, where once again a large camp was being established on the high ground behind the town. However, his main activities during this particular visit seem to have been giving dinner parties at the 'Red House', where he was staying while the Pavilion underwent considerable 'alterations and improvements', and arguing with his father on the vexed subject of promotion. At a time when the whole nation was in arms it irked the heir-apparent that he was still only a Colonel of Dragoons, but the King was adamant 'that no further mention should be made to him upon the subject'. When the Prince persevered, the King's reply was, as expected, short and to the point. 'Should the implacable enemy', he wrote, 'so far succeed as to land, you will have an opportunity of showing your zeal at the head of your Regiment.' The Prince decided to appeal to his brother, the Commander-in-Chief, but the latter was in a difficult position. He was bound to obey the King's wishes, but he was fond of his brother and there was always the possibility that, with the King in his present state of ill-health, the Prince of Wales might himself be King before long. He refused to get involved and eventually the Prince abandoned his importunings, but for some time after there was a noticeable cooling in the relations between the two brothers.

In October the Prince, back in residence at the Pavilion and anxious to know how quickly his regiment could turn out 'ready to face the enemy', button-holed Colonel Leigh after a concert one evening. The gallant colonel, ever ready to oblige his royal master, leaped on to his horse and rode to the barracks where he:

> commanded a black trumpeter on duty, to sound to arms. The man, in obedience to the mandate, raised the trumpet to his lips; but the surprise of the moment so greatly overpowered him, that he wanted breath to put it into execution. An English trumpeter, who overheard the order, as he lay in bed, in an instant arose, dashed open the window of his room, and without waiting for further advice, put his bugle in his mouth, gave the proper signal, and the troops, in every part, were, in an instant, in motion.

Aroused from their beds, the men turned out, accoutred and mounted, in time to have reached Brighton, a mile and a half away, in fifteen minutes. They were accompanied by the 'flying artillery', whose Captain, a 'handsome and agree-able Irishman', by the name of Bloomfield, was accustomed to accompany the Prince on the 'cello and had probably only just finished taking part in the concert.[9] Shortly after this, relations with the King worsened, the latter's displeasure taking the form of separating the Prince from his regiment, which was 'removed from Brighton to Guildford'. The Prince was furious, blamed the Duke of York for what he considered a deliberate insult and talked loudly of 'attending to the duty of his Regiment' by taking up residence in Guildford, but in the end Brighton proved too much of an attraction.

A more likely reason for the Prince staying away was the 'unpleasant-ness' among the officers of the 10th, which exploded into a full-blown row at Guildford. It seems to have been a resurgence of the ill-feeling caused when the Prince promoted Slade out of the regiment to clear the way for Leigh. The Prince's partiality for Leigh seems to have stemmed from the latter's reputation on the turf, which was, to say the least, shady, and his wide experience of equestrian matters, which was clearly of value to his patron, as he appears in the Prince's correspondence whenever there is anything to do with the buying and selling of horses. It appears that Leigh fell out with one of the two majors, Henry Seymour, and the officers then took sides for and against their commanding officer, Leigh's party going so far as to accuse the Paymaster, one Manby, of offering 'civilities' (or financial inducements) to officers who would 'give up the party of Colonel Leigh'. The Prince in turn accused Manby of being the 'chief cause' of the trouble. The dispute rumbled on throughout 1804, with the Paymaster unsuccessfully demanding some sort of enquiry that would put him right in the Prince's opinion and in the 'opinion of the World & the Regt', Major Seymour complaining about Colonel Leigh to the Prince and the Danish Baron Eben, another of the Prince's cronies, challenging Manby to a duel. Eventually the Duke of York stepped in and removed Manby from the regiment, at the same time recommending him for an appointment in the Commissariat on the grounds that, while he was very much involved in the 'great disputes', all the officers 'were a great deal to blame' and nothing that had come to his knowledge had 'impeached the integrity of Mr Manby'. As a result of this affair, which was, in some ways, a foretaste of what was to happen in 1814, Major Seymour left the regiment. Colonel Leigh and Baron Eben spent most of their time at Brighton in attendance on the Prince, the former as Equerry and the latter as stage manager for the celebrated 'Phantasmagoria', and other entertainments given at the Pavilion, while the general day-to-day running of the regiment was left entirely in the hands of Captain, now Major, Quentin.[10]

*　*　*

With the destruction of the French and Spanish fleets off Cape Trafalgar in October, 1805, and the abandoning of Napoleon's plans for the invasion of England, there was a general relaxation of the defence measures along the English coast. In consequence the 10th were moved to Romford, where during the next eighteen months the regiment was converted into hussars; at the same time the King also agreed to three other Light Dragoon regiments, the 7th, 15th and 18th, being converted.[11] At the very moment, however, when the cherished ambitions of the hussar faction were about to be crowned with success, the Prince of Wales seems to have lost interest in the whole thing. The 'degrading treatment' he had received at the hands of the King, the coolness between himself and the Duke of York, the removal of the invasion threat, and with it the possibility of promotion and glory, and perhaps the sheer inconvenience of having to drag himself away from the delights of Brighton to visit his squabbling officers in such an outlandish spot as Romford, seem to have turned his mind towards more peaceful pursuits.

The torch of progress now passed to the Duke of Cumberland, whose regiment, the 15th Light Dragoons, moved to the Weymouth area in July, 1805, and thence to the village of Radipole, where a brigade consisting of the 1st

Light Dragoons of the newly-formed King's German Legion and the 15th Light Dragoons, under the command of General Slade, was encamped.[12] The whole force in the area, amounting to some 11,000 men, was under the command of the Duke of Cumberland, and during that summer he kept them hard at work with many 'instructive field-days'. When the camp finally broke up at the end of September the 15th Light Dragoons moved into Radipole Barracks.

Barrack life was a relatively new experience for the British soldier, for until 1792 there were very few permanent barracks in the British Isles. Ever since the formation of a standing army Parliament had been reluctant to keep soldiers separate from civil life, and in peacetime many had been allowed to follow their trades, while the cavalry horses were turned out to grass. It was William III who introduced the system of quartering troops in 'victualling houses', a system which the increase in military activity, brought about by the war with France in 1703, aggravated the already discontented inn-keepers, but it was not until 1792, when William Pitt established the office of Barrackmaster-General, that the great boom in barrack building began. With the increase in manufacturing industries and agitation among the workers, there was a need to station small bodies of troops in towns to act as police. It was this want of a police force, rather than the prospect of war, which led Pitt to take action to improve the situation. In spite of the scandalous corruption and malpractice which was rife in the Barrackmaster-General's office, within a few years over 200 barracks had been built, holding 146,000 infantry and 17,000 cavalry.

The forty-eight new cavalry barracks were very small, only two of them being intended to hold more than six troops. Their sites were chosen for a variety of reasons. The frequent visits of the Royal Family to Weymouth, for instance, and the need to station a cavalry escort in the neighbourhood, led to the construction of the long low stable blocks, with their paling fences and cottage gardens, along the Radipole road.[13] On the east coast the constant need for cavalry to help suppress smuggling led to the building of the barracks on the road leading out of Ipswich towards Rushmere Heath, and its consequent choice as one of the centres where troops were trained for overseas service. Much can be learned about life in barracks from Colonel Long's manuscript orders, which contain detailed instructions for keeping the barrack rooms clean, very necessary to judge by what were evidently common practices:

> The men are strictly forbidden to throw filth or dust of any kind against the walls or ceilings ... or to spit about the floor. No water, ashes, bones, potatoe parings, or other dust to be on any account thrown in the coal boxes, or in the streets in front of the barrack room doors – every kind of filth is to be collected in coal buckets and taken to the ash or dung pit. ...

A certain rough justice was invoked to deal with sanitary problems:

The children are not to be permitted to commit nuisances about the buildings, or streets, and when a Dragoon is detected in doing so, he must be made to remove every similar nuisance which may occur until he can discover another so offending, who will of course take this duty until a third is detected and so on.

The men's rations of a pound of meat and bread a day, supplemented by other foodstuffs bought at their own expense, were cooked by a Room Orderly appointed daily. The dinners were to be 'dressed' in the kitchens and eaten in the barrack rooms 'at one and the same time, when the trumpet sounded'. The Officer of the Day, and occasionally other troop officers, visited the rooms at meal-times, the former, in the case of the 7th Hussars at Ipswich, having 'previously inspected the Kitchens, and ascertained the quality and quantity of the different messes'.

The King and Queen, as they had done in the days of the York Hussars, often passed through the camp and Major General Baron von Linsingen and his German Dragoons soon 'became an object of His Majesty's notice'. Although speaking hardly a word of English, the light cavalry, in particular, were found, when manoeuvring with the 15th, 'to be no less efficient' and 'gained the approbation of the inspecting Generals'. As the 1st and 2nd Light Dragoons of the Legion seem from the first to have been dressed as hussars, their efficiency must have been an important factor in overcoming the King's last lingering objections to this class of cavalry.

The Duke of Cumberland, the tallest and most elegant of the Royal brothers, was given a somewhat sinister appearance by the wound to his left eye, which many people thought accorded well with his perceived character. In 1801 he obtained the Colonelcy of the 15th Light Dragoons and from the start took a deep interest in regimental affairs, although there was considerable disquiet over the way in which he exercised his command. He was accused of introducing 'picketting', a traditional military punishment on the continent, by which the victim was suspended by his wrists, with one bare foot resting on a wooden stake.[14] Public reaction to the rumours of its use was heightened by interest in the current proceedings against Colonel Thomas Picton, who was accused of sanctioning the use of picketting, while Governor of Trinidad, to extract information from a young girl, Luise Calderon, 'the interesting subject of the people of England's philanthropy', but in fact the known accomplice of robbers.[15] Another complaint against the Duke of Cumberland was that he preferred German to English officers, on the grounds, it was said, that the former were more 'servile': it was even 'whisper'd that to several of his own officers he has gone so far as to hold up his cane'. The truth of the matter would seem to be that, having seen active service commanding a regiment of Hanoverian light dragoons, he was well aware of what could be achieved by German discipline, but his attempts to instil 'foreign' methods into an English regiment did not accord with the somewhat lax attitude of both the officers and the men.[16] Anxious, in view of the forthcoming changes, for a commanding officer with some experience of Hussars, he soon obtained the services of Colonel Long, who, as former commander of the York Hussars, came with a strong recommendation from the King.

* * *

In January, 1806, a new recruit called Tale, entered the ranks of the 15th Light Dragoons. He was later the author of a small volume entitled *Jottings from my Sabretache* and wrote under the pen-name of 'Chelsea Pensioner'. He picks up, more or less, where Sergeant Landsheit left off.[17] Long's detailed instructions for recruiting parties, originally compiled for the York Hussars, and clearly still in use in the 15th Light Dragoons, placed considerable limitations on whom they could and could not enlist, the latter including anyone who had served in the Marines or in the Sea Service 'in any capacity', indentured apprentices, and anyone who had served in another regiment 'without attentive examination of his discharge', these sometimes being altered 'to cover disgrace and a disreputable discharge'. Yeomanry and Volunteers were fair game 'if any can be procured'. On the physical side they were not to take anyone who was not

> perfectly straight and well made, none to be taken that are in-kneed, bow-legged, subject to fits, that have ruptures, running sores on any part of their bodies, scald heads, blear eyes, defect in speech, or hearing, whatsoever , nor . . . any one that have recd. Corporal punishment, nor under any pretence attest a recruit without previous examination of a surgeon . . .

Generally, no man was to be taken without first enquiring into his former conduct, character, and occupation, nor any 'Vagrants, Stragglers, or Beggars of any description', and recruiting-parties were enjoined to try and procure men 'born and bred in the Country and neighbourhood', preferably those who have been 'bred up as Labourers, and to the Plough'. 'Fine growing lads from 16 years of age' could be engaged provided they were at least 5 feet 6 inches tall, men from sixteen to twenty-four provided they were 5 feet 7 inches tall, and men from twenty-four to twenty-eight provided they were 5 feet 7½ inches tall. New recruits had first to be attested before a civil magistrate, and a receipt taken for the sums of money respectively received and 'agreed upon', before the papers were forwarded to the recruit's Commanding Officer. In all the 'bounty' which, offered by the recruiting-sergeant, as an inducement to the recruit, the reward given to the bring-in of the recruit, and other incidental expenses, set Colonel Long back by the sum of £13. 14s 1d. for each new enlistment.

The experiences of young Tale show how the recruiting parties of the 15th Light Dragoons managed to stretch Colonel Long's orders. Apprenticed to a 'chronometer maker of some eminence', he was strolling through Westminster when he saw a huge recruiting poster, emblazoned with the figure of a light dragoon 'mounted on a dashing steed and brandishing a sabre'. He was at once accosted by a splendid-looking 'blade of a light horseman *in full fig*', who, without beating about the bush excited the youth's fancy with 'a glowing account of the glories, the delights, the privileges, and what not of a soldier's life', and it was not long before he had taken the King's shilling, which was rapidly removed from him thanks to the products of 'Mr Whitbread – great in politics, and in malt'.[18]

The new recruit was below the regulation height, so it was agreed that he should pretend to be younger than he really was. Next he was led off to nearby St James's Palace, to be vetted by the Colonel, whose 'noble and commanding frame', dressed in blue, with the broad blue ribbon of the Garter across his chest, greatly impressed him. Within seconds he was standing shoeless before the Royal Duke to be measured. After 'a minute and searching optical examination' he was pronounced to be a 'Good-looking lad, . . . very good-looking; but short – too short'. Fortunately the 'good and excellent old Lieutenant', who had accompanied him to the interview, stepped into the breach and overruled the objections of the Duke by setting forth his 'youth, healthy appearance, and certainty of growth'.

Eventually, after the gruelling experience of a medical examination and a long journey, our hero found himself at Radipole barracks. But his problems were not yet over, for the Adjutant, Lieutenant Charles Jones, 'a fierce-looking, red-whiskered officer, of rather small stature', soon discovered he was a runaway apprentice, and ordered him into arrest. After a few days of 'durance in the black hole', he was led before Colonel Long, who, realizing he was resolved to stay in the regiment, 'in a kind and persuasive manner contrasted, in strong and glowing colours, the glories of a soldier's life with the more ignoble pursuit of fiddling away at, and filing watch-wheels'. The next few weeks were spent in the guardroom, while enquiries were made into his case. In the meantime he was employed by the Commanding Officer in copying out the voluminous instructions the latter was composing for the regiment. Eventually he managed to persuade his relations that he really did wish to become a soldier and was freed from his indentures. He now set about learning his duties in good earnest, and, being able to write and 'perform little offices for the non-commissioned officers', was spared many of the 'vexatious employments . . . such as fatigue-parties, double horses, &c'. He 'eschewed the quill' and stuck to the sword, and in the twelve months that the regiment remained at Radipole became a 'full-blown hussar and mounted guard'.

The aspiring Hussar greatly admired his Commanding Officer, and no one, he thought, could have laboured more to reform the morals and discipline of the regiment. Apart from his untiring zeal, the Colonel possessed 'a thorough knowledge for perfecting the hussar in every branch, from his entrance into the barrack-room to his completion and fitness for the field'. In order to achieve this reformation flogging was 'unhappily a frequent necessity', but more, he thought, 'in accordance with the usage of the day, than from a penchant on the part of Colonel Long for the odious infliction'. There were many bad characters in the regiment who had been accepted owing to the need to fill up the regiment in wartime. Also the custom of making officers furnish a certain number of men in order to gain a step in promotion resulted in 'strong infusions, not only from the off-scourings of society', but also of 'liberated gaol-birds'.

Through Long's efforts a high moral tone was inculcated and bullying and swearing were put down. In conducting drills 'noise and force of lungs' gave way to gentler methods 'calculated to draw out the capabilities of the recruit, without souring his temper'. When their basic training was completed the regiment was treated to a few 'field-days' and 'sham-fights', the former of which, being 'generally dashed through with life and spirit . . . were looked for rather with pleasure than otherwise'.

* * *

During 1806 and the first half of 1807 the conversion of the 7th, 10th, 15th and 18th Light Dragoons to Hussars went on apace. The Duke of Cumberland and Lord Paget supervised the operation closely, helped by Baron von Linsingen and his King's German Legion Hussars. The Prince of Wales seemed, for the reasons already mentioned, to have lost interest in the whole business. In the early flush of his enthusiasm his position as a leader of fashion had naturally led him to rebel against what he considered to be the old-fashioned dress and customs favoured by the King. Hussar dress – outlandish, outrageous and foreign – was an ideal vehicle for the expression of his opposition to his royal father. Led by him, the 'hussar craze' became the military manifestation of the same desire for 'exclusivity' that pervaded the upper realms of London society at the beginning of the nineteenth century, and was responsible for the rise of the 'Dandy'; in fact, the two were inextricably bound up, as many of the leading dandies had, at one time or another, been hussar officers. Three of the four regiments were commanded by royal princes and an extremely wealthy peer, Lord Paget, all of whom considered themselves leaders of the fashionable world. It followed that they chose to officer their regiments with members of the exclusive set of which Brummell, Lord Petersham and the two Lords Manners, all of whom had at one time or another served in the 10th, were founder members, and it is not surprising that they wished to bring to their military activities some of the 'fineness' which they were at such pains to cultivate in their civilian lives. For a regiment to be 'fine' it had to be clothed in the finest uniforms, be mounted on the best horses and be armed with the best weapons that money could buy. But this was not enough – to be really fine one had to be different from the common herd. Hussars were smart not only because of their exclusive and exotic dress, but because they were new and experimental. The interest in 'Light Troops', which had declined after the American war, had been rekindled and was being carefully fostered, in the case of the infantry, by Sir John Moore at Shorncliffe.

The cavalry, however, had lagged behind, until the advent of the hussar, but now, alongside the Hungarian flummery, there was a genuine desire to create a new elite light cavalry in place of the dowdy and run-of-the-mill light dragoons.

The changes in the dress and equipment of the light dragoons, made in 1796, had already tended to make them look like continental Hussars, without taking the final plunge into what was thought of by many as 'Germanization'. They had been given the stirrup-hilted curved sabres known as 'Hungarian broadswords', and short blue jackets braided across the front like the hussar's dolman. A lack of pockets in this, it was said, led to the adoption of the hussar's small bag hanging from his sword-belt, known as a sabretache. Finally contact with foreign hussars during the recent campaign on the Continent had resulted in the adoption of the mirliton in place of the old 'Tarleton' helmet, and in the affectation of the officers wearing non-regulation fur-lined pelisses, heavily trimmed with black braid.

Thus, although on the face of it the change to 'Hussar Clothing and Equipment' involved little more than substituting fur caps for the helmets and providing the men with pelisses, barrel sashes, Hungarian 'high-mounting' saddles, special pistols and carbines, the whole operation took some eighteen months to complete. The 7th were ready first, in September, 1806, and the 10th and 15th were more or less complete by the middle of 1807. Almost immediately, in the summer of 1807, the three regiments were assembled at Ipswich, under the command of Lord Paget, who, now a major general, had been in the neighbourhood for several years, training up his own and the other cavalry regiments that had passed through from time to time.

* * *

The 15th Hussars marched out of Radipole Barracks early in July, 1807, a move hailed with delight by the men, especially the 'Johnny Raws' whose:

> ears had been tickled by the old files into delightful anticipations of the pleasures consequent upon a long march; not only as regards change of scene and circumstances, but as partaking of the more solid advantages of placing one's self three times a day under the landlord's mahogany, and gratifying at each and every spread, the inner man.

The reality, of course, did not quite live up to the anticipation. At the time innkeepers were bound to provide non-commissioned officers and men on the march with 'Full Diet and Small Beer', but the niggardly payment which they received for these meals – about sixteen pence per day – produced the opposite of a warm welcome. Some of the larger inns, especially those on the line of march leading to points of embarkation, sometimes had to cater for several hundred men, and many publicans were forced to close down to avoid ruin.[19]

The 15th broke their journey at Hounslow to enable the Duke of Cumberland to spend some time with his regiment. On 20 July they were reviewed by the Duke of Cambridge, then commanding the Home District. As this was the first time one of the new hussar regiments had appeared in public there was a great deal of interest, and the *Morning Post* reported the proceedings in detail. The regiment was formed on Hounslow Heath, about a mile and a half from the barracks, 'in their new clothing . . . superb to a degree not before seen in this country'. The Duke of Cumberland wore regimental uniform and Lord Paget, who was among the spectators, was in 'one of the most splendid uniform hussar dresses we have ever seen out of a drawing room'. The only thing that spoiled the brilliancy of the occasion was the cloud of black dust rising from the peaty ground, which rendered 'many of the manoeuvres invisible' and took much of the shine out of the new uniforms.

By the end of July the Hussar Brigade was fully assembled, with the 7th and 10th at Ipswich and the 15th at nearby Woodbridge. The daily routine was similar in each regiment. In the mornings the squadrons paraded separately in 'watering', 'field-day', or 'marching' order. One morning was spent in the riding school and one in an inspection of the horses by the Veterinary Surgeon. In the afternoons one or other squadron drilled under the adjutant and its respective officers, while on Saturday afternoons there was an inspection of the barrack rooms and 'Necessaries'. On Sundays, after Divine Service, 'at half past nine o'clock' the surgeon inspected the men by Troops.

The training programme devised by Lord Paget and his staff was far more comprehensive than has been previously supposed and seems to have been far more like a cavalry version of Shorncliffe. According to the newly-appointed Corporal Tale,[20] the three-strong regiments, and a troop of 'flying artillery', were frequently out on windmill-studded Rushmere Heath, good open cavalry country:

> The rapidity of movement, sounds from so many voices in command, the clangour of trumpets and roars from cannon . . . produced upon me at first a bewildering sensation; but these displays were, I should say, exciting to the mind of the young soldier. The only drawback of these stirring scenes was felt on our return to barracks, and the clearing ourselves of the black dust of Rushmere, clouds of which enveloped us in every movement. On all occasions we were covered with dust or with mud.

In the case of the 15th, Colonel Long adopted the then extremely unusual method of making selections from the best foreign military writers on the duties of light cavalry and hussars in the field and on service. These were then copied by the non-commissioned officers into their notebooks, the regiment split up into small groups, each under an officer or NCO, and the 'varied nature of service and operations called into play in a campaign were practised'. On the following day each Squad Leader submitted a written report to the

Adjutant, 'particularizing the duties performed by his detachment, accompanied by any other observations he might deem proper, such as describing the aspect and features of the country traversed'.

The main ritual of the dragoon's day, and the one which made his life so much more burdensome than that of the infantryman, was morning, noon and evening 'Stables', when the men, wearing their stable caps, jackets, 'trowsers' and buckled shoes instead of boots proceeded to the stables to muck out and groom their mounts. Apart from having to look after his horse, the dragoon had a mass of other articles, including his saddlery and 'horse appointments' to keep clean and in good repair, and he himself was expected to turn out in 'high style'. NCOs were given a list of points to look out for. The caps were to fit well, with the feather and cap-lines clean and white. The dragoon's ears, eyes and hands were to be 'clean washed', and his hair 'well tyed combed and platted'. This 'abominable system' meant that the dragoon had to find a comrade to act as valet before he could emerge from his barrack room, and before every parade 'tie for tie' and 'plat for plat' echoed from one end of the room to the other. Fortunately a General Order of 20 July, 1808, dispensed with queues, or pigtails, much to the fury of purists like the Prince of Wales and the Duke of Cumberland.[21]

Proceeding downwards from the dragoon's leather stock to his gloves and spurs, sword and carbine, the orders specified how every item was to fit well and be free from 'any stain' or hint of rust. This minute inspection, however, only covered the man – there was still his horse and all the equipment carried in Marching Order. The task of keeping all this up to scratch might be 'at first vexing and unpalatable from the tediousness and length of the examination', but its importance in cavalry training was given much emphasis. It was vital that the 'multiplicity of trappings and strappings' with which the horse was burdened were 'so nicely adjusted as to remove all chances of injury or torture in making a long march'.

When not supervising stables or parading with their troops, the officers had plenty of spare time, but life for an officer of hussars was far from cheap. In 1806 a Board of Officers was assembled to enquire into the 'expence attending the equipment of a Subaltern officer' on first joining the 15th Hussars, and the annual income necessary to enable him 'to support himself in that situation as an Officer and Gentleman'. After adding up the cost of two horses and their appointments, camp equipage, dress, arms, accoutrements and 'sundries', the total came to £458. But this was not the whole story, for the Board's report concluded by pointing out that no allowance had been made for pocket money; that, to live in comfort, a private servant was 'almost absoloutely necessary'; that no allowance had been made for changes in the patterns of uniforms and appointments; nor had the initial cost of the officer's commission, about £725 for a cornetcy in the dragoons, been taken into account. Thus, although the Board gave no definite figure, it appeared that a cornet of hussars needed at least £1,000 to launch himself, and between £400 and £500 a year to keep himself in the manner expected of him. That the Prince of Wales generally allowed those officers 'under his protection' an annual allowance of only £200 meant that they were kept on a very tight rein indeed.[22]

Frugality, however, was not high on the list of priorities of the officers of the Hussar Brigade. At the top end of the scale, Lord Paget rented the house of a Captain Studd, who told the diarist Farington in March, 1805, that he paid 500 guineas a year for the use of it. Paget kept about thirty servants and in 1804 his bill for 'coals and small beer only' had come to £500, but, fortunately for the local tradesmen, he paid his bills with great regularity. He had also, by this time of his life, acquired a considerable reputation for dandyism and set a very high standard of turn-out in his regiment and in the Hussar Brigade in general. He was much aped by his officers, and Ball Hughes, a wealthy young officer of the 7th, later to figure prominently in dandy circles as 'The Golden Ball', modelled himself, where coats, hats and boots were concerned, entirely on his Colonel, to such an extent, Captain Gronow recalled, that 'everything that his noble commander said or did was law to him'.

The events of the summer and autumn of 1807 occupied many columns of the *Ipswich Journal*. On 18 July the 10th Hussars marched into the King's Barracks and quarters in Ipswich, from 'Rumford', and on 1 August the 15th Hussars passed through the town on their way to Woodbridge. In the middle of September the Duke of Cumberland came to visit his regiment and on the 21st Lord Paget gave 'a most sumptuous entertainment' at Gooding's coffee house in his honour. All the staff of the garrison and the officers of the Hussar Brigade were invited, and they sat down to dinner, about a hundred in number, 'all dressed in the most elegant regimentals'. On 1 October the Duke returned the compliment with a similar affair at the same premises, when the bands of the 7th Hussars and the West Kent Militia, 'with the drums and fifes of the Derby . . . performed in a capital style several pieces of martial music'.

Transformed from a sleepy country town into a military version of Bath, Ipswich was definitely the place to be that summer. The town was full of 'well-known swells', who, when there were no reviews or field-days to disturb their pleasures, spent their time in as carefree manner as possible, racing and driving being the two main pastimes. Of those addicted to the former the most celebrated was the eccentric Captain Henry Mellish of the 10th, 'son to the late victualling contractor', who inherited a huge fortune when he was twenty-one. His extravagant behaviour became so notorious that the Prince of Wales is said to have been forced to give him permanent leave, lest his 'naughty ways should ruin half his brother officers'. In October, 1806, Farington reported that Mellish was owed £30,000 in gambling debts, half of it by the Duke of Sussex. The princely grandeur of his various establishments was legendary, with as many as forty racehorses in training, two of which won the St Leger in successive years, a drove of carriage-horses, hunters in Leicestershire, chargers at Brighton and horseflesh of all descriptions in London and Newmarket. Tall and thin with a very pale complexion, black hair, extraordinarily brilliant eyes and the long drooping moustache affected by hussar officers, he was said to have been 'as much the glass of ultra-fashion as Brummell himself'. When, in May, 1808, Mellish applied to go to Portugal as Aide-de-Camp to General Ferguson, the Prince insisted that he transfer to another regiment, and he left the 10th Hussars.

George Elers, an infantry officer on recruiting service, spent much of his time with the officers of the 10th, who numbered at least three peers of the realm, several Honourables, and 'Robarts the banker's son'. There was also 'a nice handsome little man of the name of Captain Derby [Darby]', who, it was 'whispered', was the son of the Prince of Wales and Lady Lade.

The Prince continued to take an interest in the affairs of his regiment, if from a distance, and at the time there appear to have been two or three of the younger officers who were recipients of his patronage. The first of these was a Frenchman – Antoine Geneviéve Heraclius Agénor, Comte de Grammont, the eldest son of the Duc de Guiche. Born at Versailles on 17th June, 1789, he was only four weeks old when his parents, somewhat unaccountably, left him in the charge of Queen Marie-Antoinette. When the mob broke into Versailles on 6 October he was carried to safety by one of the palace guards and reunited with his parents, with whom he went into exile. At the age of nine and a half he was given a sub-lieutenant's commission by Paul I of Russia, who used this tactful method of supporting the impoverished families who accompanied the Prince of Condé into exile. In 1800 he came to Edinburgh with his mother, and in 1802, as Comte de Grammont, was commissioned into the Swiss Regiment de Roll, then in British service. After two years at school he was gazetted into the *Chasseurs Brittaniques,* another *émigré* regiment, and in 1805, through the influence of the Duchess of Devonshire, was transferred to the 10th Light Dragoons. 'Leigh will settle with Greenwood [the Regimental Agent] about Grammont's pay', the Prince wrote airily to the Duchess, 'but he must join immediately'. Unfortunately, as has already been noted, the Prince's customary allowance of £200 per year was hardly sufficient for the 'style of high life' in the 10th, and if not paid promptly, as in young de Grammont's case, the recipient could find himself in considerable distress.

Another recipient of the Prince's patronage, Augustus George FitzClarence, the eldest son of the Duke of Clarence and the actress Mrs Jordan, was appointed to a cornetcy in the 10th in February, 1807, when he was only thirteen. He was at the Military College at Great Marlow, which the Duke of York had set up in 1802, and where the students, after entering at the age of thirteen, spent four years before taking up their commissions in the Army.[23]

After at first having a dull time in Ipswich, George Elers was eventually invited to dine in the mess of the 10th by his friend Harding and no longer 'moped about the town' by himself. He played billiards with his new friends during the day and cards, chiefly whist, at night. After a few weeks he had made considerable progress in Ipswich society, which enjoyed the use of a club possessing a reading room, coffee room and billiard table, all of which were open to officers for a moderate subscription. It was 'attended constantly by all the respectable part of the town, as well as of the country', and there were monthly subscription balls which were well attended by the military.

Some officers took to more energetic sports. In September, 1807, Wedderburn Webster, of the 10th, rode from Ipswich to London for a wager of 1,000 guineas. He was to complete the seventy-mile journey in five hours, but did it in four hours fifty minutes. Driving was another popular pastime and the 'Whip Club', formed in 1808, changed its name to the more celebrated 'Four in Hand Club' in the following year. The artist Robert Dighton, and his son Robert Junior, worked frequently at Ipswich, making watercolour portraits of the officers, their men, horses, and dogs. One of the latter's drawings, entitled 'well known Swells at Ipswich' and dated 1807, shows a four-in-hand being driven by a noisy group of hussar officers, dressed in the drab covert coats and red waistcoats worn by professional coachmen.

As befitted the true hussar, pipes were all the rage, and after Lord Paget declared that his brigade 'could not be quite perfect' without the traditional silver-mounted *meerschaums*, Mr Hudson, the London tobacconist, was summoned to Ipswich with his wares and succeeded in selling 'upwards of 500 pipes to the officers of the Brigade'. There were practical reasons for this fad, as the French light cavalryman Colonel de Brack recalled, some years later. It soothed the soldier, he wrote, occupied his spare time and thoughts, and kept him in bivouac close to his horse. While doing so, no one would attempt to steal his horse's food or the provisions from his wallets; he could spot any repairs needed to his saddlery; he could watch his comrade's horse while he went for water, forage or rations; and finally he had always to hand steel and tinder with which to light the bivouac fire.

1808 saw the brigade in the same quarters. A set of watercolours, commissioned from Robert Dighton Junior by the Duke of Cumberland, shows the officers and men of the Hussar Brigade as they appeared then: the 7th – 'The Lilywhites' – in blue jackets with white facings and lace, and brown fur busbies, with red cloth bags hanging over to one side; the 10th with pale yellow facings, white lace and red busby bags; and the 15th, with red facings, white lace, and black busbies with red bags, glower out of these paintings, their faces adorned with the black Mongol moustaches which were ordered to be worn in 1807. To the rest of the Army their appearance was outlandish and the general officer sent to inspect the 7th Hussars in 1808 did not fail to remark on the large caps which, in his opinion, disfigured both officers and men and reduced 'the effect and appearance of their height instead of adding to it'.

In the early summer of 1808 the brigade broke up. The 10th left Ipswich on 16 and 17 June, reaching Brighton on 10 August, two days before the Prince of Wales's birthday, when he reviewed all the troops in the district. It was a beautiful day and 'a very fine sight'. The Prince looked in better health and spirits than when last seen in public and 'with the splendour of his uniform afforded a pleasing gaze to upwards of twenty thousand spectators'. The advocates of the introduction of hussars into the British Army had finally won the day. The regiments concerned had been successfully, and spectacularly, converted into the finest light cavalry that could be imagined and after a year of intense training were in fighting trim. On 29 July, 1807, Lord Paget had written to his brother Arthur in Vienna, that he was:

> slaving away in Sun & Dust preparing for a Review instead of a Battle, either of which Events produce as many cricks as any other could name. I dont know if my Hussars would fight well, but they certainly look well, which is all we are likely to want of them . . .

When the call finally came in the summer of 1808 the Hussar brigade had been widely scattered. For Corporal Tale and the 15th Hussars at Romford:

> the war-blast was sounded in the form of an order for the immediate preparation of eight troops for service. Now all became recipients of new feelings, new life, new causes for excitement; and an uninterrupted scene of bustle and stir followed . . .; grinding swords, chopping, changing, and transferring men and cattle – in short, selecting the *élite* of both men and *materiel* of the regiment, in order to cope more effectively with our Gallic Neighbour on Spanish soil.

*   *   *

The chain of events which led to this warlike preparation started in 1807 when a French army invaded Portugal and forced the Royal family to flee to the Brazils. More French troops were massed in Spain, ostensibly to support Marshal Junot in Portugal, but their true purpose was revealed when Napoleon enticed Charles IV of Spain and his son Ferdinand across the border to Bayonne, and there 'persuaded' them to abdicate in favour of his brother Joseph. On 2 May, 1808, a rising in Madrid was the signal for riots and insurrections throughout the country. Later in the month emissaries from the provincial *Juntas* of northern Spain came to England in search of aid, although the two countries were nominally still at war. For once the British Government acted promptly. Peace was hurriedly signed and British agents, supplied with money and arms, were rushed to the provinces of Asturias and Galicia. In addition, a force of some 9,000 men, under the command of Sir Arthur Wellesley, which had originally been intended for a madcap descent on the Spanish colonies in America, was diverted to Portugal. Landing his force at the mouth of the Mondego River, Wellesley quickly inflicted two defeats on the French, the first at Rolica on 17 August, and the second four days later at Vimiero. The arrival of two senior generals, however, prevented him from exploiting his successes to the full and, on 31 August, the notorious Convention of Cintra was signed, under the terms of which Junot's army was repatriated in British ships, taking with it not only its baggage but also its plunder. The three generals who had signed the Convention, Sir Hew Dalrymple, Sir Harry Burrard and Sir Arthur Wellesley, were summoned back to explain their unpopular actions.

In the meantime a further 18,000 men had been despatched to Portugal under the command of Sir John Moore, and with them came Lord Paget, now a lieutenant general, in command, much to his disappointment, of an infantry division, but, finding that after the Convention of Cintra there were so many unemployed general officers kicking their heels around Lisbon, he decided to apply for leave. This was a fortunate decision, for the British Government, having successfully cleared Portugal of the French, now proposed to do as much for its new Spanish allies. 25,000 men of the Army of Portugal, now commanded by Sir John Moore, were to enter Spain to meet up with a further 12,000 men from England, under Sir David Baird, at Salamanca. The main body of Baird's force left Falmouth early in October and arrived off Corunna on the 13th where, as a foretaste of future Anglo-Spanish cooperation the Galician *Junta* refused permission for the troops to land until approval had been received from the central *Junta* at Aranjuez, a process which took two weeks to complete. The Spanish armies, of which so much was hoped, were numerous but badly led and equipped. Moreover both Moore and the Spaniards were woefully short of cavalry and, almost as an afterthought, the Hussar Brigade was added to Baird's force.[24] Lord Paget was given command of all the cavalry in the expeditionary force and returned to Spain with Baird, while command of the Hussar Brigade was given at the last moment to Jack Slade, who had recently been on the Staff in Ireland.

The 10th Hussars were to be commanded in the field by George Leigh, with Quentin and Palmer as the two majors, and the 7th Hussars by Hussey Vivian, but 'Bobby' Long was promoted out of the 15th Hussars, and his place taken by Colquhoun Grant. There seems to have been a breach between Long and his Colonel, and, both being obstinate men, the outcome was inevitable. Grant, who was Groom of the Bedchamber to Cumberland, was more of a courtier and less likely to argue with his Colonel. The fourteen-year-old George FitzClarence was fretting and fuming, longing to be away on service with his regiment, but his parents had misgivings. 'George is too young to go on service particularly with Light Cavalry', his father wrote to the Prince of Wales, 'and at the same time he cannot with propriety remain in your regiment and not go on service'. He questioned whether or not his son ought to exchange into a regiment not so likely to go abroad for some time. He had been taken away from Marlow in disgrace as 'his mind has been so bent on going on service that he has totally neglected his studies and made himself completely miserable'. A face-saving solution was found by attaching him to Slade's 'family' as an extra Aide-de-Camp, armed with the standard allowance of £200 a year from the Prince. In her last letter to him before he sailed his mother reminded him always to refer to his father as 'the Duke', or 'my Father', so as to 'prevent any little ridicule that might be excited by his calling him 'papa'.

41

CHAPTER THREE
In the Cause of Spain

The three regiments of Hussars converged on Portsmouth, marching in small groups, or 'Divisions', a day apart, so as not to overtax the facilities of the wayside alehouses.[1] As they arrived they were issued with camp equipment by the Ordnance Depot at Porchester Castle, consisting of wooden water barrels, or 'canteens', linen haversacks for rations, nose-bags and forage-cords, all of which increased the burden of the horses to twenty-one stone. Portsmouth harbour itself was as busy as ever, crowded with warships of 'every size and class', with 'Merchantmen, transports, victuallers, crowded round them, while to and fro boats were continually passing, as if all the maritime affairs of the whole world had been under discussion'. In the dockyard lay the 'crazy and unserviceable' transports in which the Hussars had to load themselves and their valuable 'cattle'. The transportation of horses by sea created a host of problems and comprehensive instructions on the subject were issued from Horse Guards. It was vital, for instance, that the horses should not be heated at the time of embarkation, and a long march on the last day was to be avoided. Each transport held from eighteen to twenty horses, placed in two rows in the hold, with their heads facing a wooden trough down the centre of the vessel. To prevent them lying down, their heads were secured to small upright posts, one between each horse, while their chests and haunches were padded with sheepskins to prevent them being skinned by the rolling of the ship. The dragoon was to wash the fetlocks and hooves of his horse at each stable hour, and was to be 'attentive to wash his Face, and particularly his Eyes and Nostrils, with a Sponge'. The greatest attention was to be paid to the ventilation of the hold, which was done by erecting 'Wind Sails', pieces of sacking hung from the deck into the main hatchway, 'the ends of which ought to be shifted to different parts of the hold'. In bad weather, when the hold was battened down 'great advantage' was to be found 'in washing the Manger with Vinegar and Water, and occasionally sponging the Nostrils of the Horse with the same'.

The 7th Hussars were the first to arrive, embarking on 2, 3, and 4 October, and Colonel Vivian was much relieved that he had got his regiment there without a single man appearing 'at any parade during the march the least in liquor'. The leading division had marched the last eighteen miles from Petersfield in pouring rain, and 'in that state', Captain Hodge recalled, 'wet, dirty, tired, our horses were embarked in the dockyard without being touched' – so much for General Orders. He and Major Kerrison boarded the same transport; but it was five in the evening before he had 'sufficiently finished' his duty to change out of his clothes, which had been wet through since seven in the morning – 'a pretty good taste of service' he thought. As they were loaded, the transports slipped down to St Helen's where they anchored. The officers remained on shore, and on the 5th, having received orders to go aboard their ships the next day, held a farewell dinner at the Fountain tavern.

For the next three days contrary winds prevented the convoy from sailing. On the 7th Hodge visited General Slade, who had just arrived on the *Egeira* Sloop-of-War, and found him and his staff 'most uncomfortably stowed five in a cabin'. The gale continued and that night both he and Kerrison were miserably seasick. The following day, as he was writing to his friend William Dacre Adams, it was still blowing a gale and the ship was pitching so much he could hardly write: 'I am dreadfully sick & obliged to hold my head while I write. Would that this voyage were over; I shall never like the name of St Helen's again.'

The next day, 9 October, the wind moderated and it was possible to go ashore or make ship visits. Captain Verner of the 7th Hussars arrived in Portsmouth to be confronted with the problem of getting his horses out to the transports at St.Helen's. Fortunately the sea was calm enough for him to put them aboard a float and he set off towards the regiment. The transports were some miles distant and, when they were eventually reached, the horses had to be slung aboard. It was a miracle that Verner's transport, a small Newcastle collier, 'a wretched sailor', and, as usual, grossly overcrowded, had room enough in the hold to take them aboard.[2]

On 14 October, the Royal Standard flying from the 'Platform at Portsmouth' announced the arrival of the Prince of Wales, and before long the brigadier was being rowed ashore to meet him at the dockyard, where part of the 10th Hussars were now embarking. The next day the Prince returned to the dockyard and addressed the men, 'expressing his conviction, that on the glorious service on which they were going, they would acquire honour to themselves and do him credit'. The men appeared 'sensibly affected' and gave him three cheers. The Prince was wearing the uniform of the 10th, and it was probably on this occasion that, apparently dissatisfied with Slade's appearance in a General's uniform presented him with his own sabre, jacket and pelisse.[3]

On the 16th the wind got up again and on the following day was blowing a gale which prevented the transports carrying the 10th from dropping down to St Helen's, until the 20th. At last, on the 22nd, the Commodore made the signal to weigh anchor and they 'stood out for Stokes Bay', the fleet, by Verner's reckoning, consisting of 'upwards of 70 sail of transports, besides Frigates and Gun Brigs'. They passed through the men-of-war at Spithead, which, 'with the whole of the Russian Fleet . . . exhibited a very fine sight', and reached Stokes Bay about four in the afternoon.[4]

The next day they were still there. At two in the afternoon the Duke of

Clarence came out to the *Sybille* Frigate, whose passengers included General Slade, George FitzClarence, Colonel Vivian and Major Paget, with the intention of going round the fleet. *Sybille* fired a salute and manned her yards, 'but rain coming on after HRH had visited one or two transports he returned to Portsmouth'. Berkeley Paget was thoroughly fed up with the Duke, who was 'continually jawing away and interrupting one'. He was mad and all the admirals, generals, and captains were 'heartily sick of him'.

That night turned out to be the most 'boisterous' so far and Hodge thought they were lucky to have been in the comparative shelter of Stokes Bay, for the next morning several of the ships at Spithead were found to have 'driven from their anchors', and one had gone ashore at Southsea Castle. From the 24th to the 27th the wind remained adverse and morale among the troops got lower and lower. 'Our situation', Hodge wrote, 'now is become on all accounts miserable and the delay not only unfortunate but dangerous'. The winter was coming on and the prospect of crossing the Bay of Biscay with 'a fleet of horse ships', was far from pleasant. They had not expected these delays and were poorly provided with the means of entertaining themselves. The few books that Hodge had brought with him he 'perused and reperused' and started teaching himself Spanish. They were also getting through their 'sea-stock' dangerously fast; Verner had already had to replenish his several times, and, as they were only provided with Spanish money, he had been forced to dip into his own reserves. On the 28th, however, there was a 'perfect calm', which the sailors said was the forerunner of a change of wind and, sure enough, that evening it swung round to the south-east.

That same day the leading division of the 15th Hussars marched into Portsmouth and started embarking under the busy-body eye of the Duke of Clarence. Thanks to the 'immense exertions of General Slade', he told the Prince of Wales, 'the 7th and 10th were thro' the Needles before dark, and would soon be clear of Old England'. There had been problems with the 15th, however, as when the time came to embark, neither Slade nor himself had been able to find a single officer with the men and horses, except for the Adjutant, Lieutenant Jones. 'To Slade and myself,' he boasted, 'does the King's service owe that regiment going abroad at all.' How different, he concluded, things were with the 7th and 10th.

At daybreak on Sunday 30 October, four weeks after the 7th Hussars had started embarking, the Commodore made the signal for sailing, 'a gun was fired, and the well-known Blue Peter hoisted'. At ten o'clock a second signal was made 'for all that were compleat with water to weigh and sail for Yarmouth Roads, there to wait for the 15th,' but according to Hodge it was not until the next afternoon that the fleet sailed with a fair wind. At half past four they were past the Needles, the freshening wind buffeting the transports as they left the shelter of the Solent. They would soon indeed be 'clear of Old England'.

As the fleet stood away from the coast and headed towards the Bay of Biscay the motion of Verner's transport grew more violent. The door of the cupboard in his cabin flew open, emptying its contents all over the place. At the same time the cord at the head of his cot broke, depositing him on the deck, where he hit his head on a locker. As though this were not enough a cask of beef broke free of its moorings and, rolling across the deck, blocked his cabin door. It was only the first of many mishaps. The next day the rolling of the ship was so bad that Hodge remained in his cot all morning, and even then, when he rose, it was at the 'expense of wh[a]t I had eaten before and the half of a basin of broth which I then swallowed'. At six he went back to bed 'and forced down a cup of tea and a small bit of dry toast'.

The thirty-five transports carrying the 15th Hussars finally left Stokes Bay on 2 November, 'under convoy of the *Endymion* Frigate'. As they slipped down the Solent a fine harvest moon threw up the details of either shore into sharp relief. Captain Gordon, on board the *Rodney*, 300 tons, struck by the strange light, dwelt on the 'melancholy idea of quitting friends and country, perhaps for ever,' but as the convoy met the first of the open sea his reveries came to an abrupt end and he was driven below by a violent attack of seasickness. That same afternoon the first fleet was well out into the Bay of Biscay. Hodge was feeling better and managed a little chicken, but Kerrison was still prostrate. The men, crammed below decks in appalling conditions, suffered dreadfully, but the horses were bearing up 'amazingly well'. Those who had never crossed the Bay, Verner wrote later,

> can form no conception of its grandeur. The storm was down but the swell continued, the waves were like mountains. The vessels were all within sight and some of them so close you could make yourself heard to those on board. The effect was very fine, at one moment alongside, the next wave raised it up and you could see underneath its keel. The water was so clear you could distinguish for several feet below the surface.

He and his friends dined on deck that day, while on board the *Sybille* Berkeley Paget passed the time pleasantly enough sitting on one of the frigate's quarterdeck guns, reading Shakespeare and *Gulliver's Travels* in the sunshine.

That night it blew violently and in the morning Verner's ship was floundering about without another sail in sight. The main part of the fleet, however, was 'all well and all together after the blowing weather but practically becalmed', and there was a 'sad falling off' in Hodge's estimate as to when they would reach Corunna. The next day the swell subsided, a breeze got up, and Verner's vessel, 'discovering' Cape Finisterre, had to 'go about and beat up against the wind', which they continued doing all that day and the following night, while the rest of the fleet scudded along in light but fair winds. Hodge was beginning to get worried about Roebeck's ship, which had not been sighted since they left the Needles. 'I hope he has met with no accident,' he wrote, 'but we none of us liked his ship before we started.'

On the 7th, while Hodge's ship was still beating about within five leagues of

Corunna, Verner's transport entered harbour. Most of the convoy was in and he was warmly welcomed by his Commanding Officer, who had given him up for lost. To Vivian's relief Hodge's transport came in the next day and the two somewhat queasy passengers dressed and went ashore, where the first sight that met their eyes was the resplendent figure of Lord Paget, prancing about on 'Elfi Bey'. They returned to dine on board, then hurried ashore again to attend the opera.

To most of the young bloods and 'Johnny Raws' of the Hussar Brigade Corunna was their first sight of a foreign land. It was situated on an irregular peninsula, the neck of which, separated from the mainland by a chain of bastions, was occupied by the town. This was 'regularly and neatly' built with a fine row of houses looking out over the harbour and commanding a magnificent view towards the coast of Ferrol. On the western side of this neck lay Orsan Bay, bounded to the north by a point on which stood the lofty lighthouse known as the 'Tower of Hercules'. On the eastern side was another bay, on the northern point of which stood the citadel. There was another fortress on St Diego's point to the south, and a third, that of St Antonio, on a rock in the entrance to the harbour, which 'yielded a good protection from marine attack'. But although strong, all the defences of Corunna were commanded 'nearly within musket-shot by the surrounding heights, in particular those of St Lucia'.[5]

On 6 November the *Amazon,* Captain Parker, anchored in Corunna, after a 'delightful' passage from Falmouth, with passengers of a less warlike kind on board. Lord and Lady Holland, accompanied by Lord John Russell, Mr Allen, Mr Chester, two maids, five 'men' and two carriages, had arrived on a voyage of pleasure, quite undeterred by the military activity taking place around them. Lady Holland thought her first view of the town and fortifications 'very pleasing', especially the rocky shore, and the great waves sweeping in from the Bay of Biscay.[6] When the first of the cavalry transports arrived the town and harbour were already full, so their passengers were confined to their ships until Baird's infantry had moved out, and Berkeley Paget, for one, suffered considerably from the ill-effects of those waves. 'An outer berth in Corunna harbour,' he wrote, 'is but a bad place. We had one when we anchored, for we could not get in further on account of the number of transports within, and I assure you we had not more sea in the Bay when we crossed it.'

The 7th Hussars started disembarking on the 9th and, according to Vivian, the scene was 'truly deplorable'. It rained in torrents. Because the harbour was too full for them to be able to 'haul up on the quays, the horses were slung into the water and most of them obliged to swim on shore.' According to Hodge, 'Such a scene of confusion, disorder, and mismanagement was never witnessed.' Most of the horses had to swim as much as a quarter of a mile, which was 'rather hard' for them, coming straight from 'the hot hold'. Once ashore, in spite of the fact that the regiment's Quartermasters had been sent ahead to prepare quarters, nothing was ready for the horses and they stood shivering in the streets for hours until they could be got into a large barn a mile out of town. The men were soaked through, and many of them had been separated from their baggage and had no dry clothes to put on. The inevitable result was that they drowned their sorrows in the all too easily available wine. 'So much for our first day,' wrote Hodge. He did not 'quarrel with the rough work . . . but with bad management. How easy it would have been for the disembarkation to have been deferred one day and a Quarter M[aste]r and two men per troop sent ashore to prepare. Then all would have been well, instead of a fine Regt. murdered.'

The next day the weather improved and the rest of the regiment disembarked, but 'being a fine day, the thing was not quite so bad'. Lady Holland walked out to the Tower of Hercules, a mile and three-quarters from the town. From here she could look down into the harbour filled with shipping. She could even make out the Hussars disembarking 'in small detachments from the transports'. Although 'not very well conducted for want of proper preparations,' she added, 'few horses perished.' Back in town she fell in with Major Howard of the 10th, and Lord Paget, who was 'uncommonly obliging and pleasing'. The Spaniards, struck by the latter's splendid appearance, had already christened him an *arrogante mozo y muy bizarro* – a haughty young man and very gallant. The *Corunna Diary,* reporting the disembarkation of the 10th Hussars, thought that it was 'impossible to conceive a finer corps of men and horses',[7] but some of the citizens thought that the fantastic dress of the hussars was neither warm in winter nor cool in summer, and utterly unsuitable for campaigning. The women were favourably impressed by the ruddy complexions, blue eyes and height of the British soldiers, but complained of a 'want of expression in their countenances, and delicacy in the shape of their limbs, especially about the knee'. They were, moreover, in general '*muy frios!*'

The British, for their part, had reservations about the Spanish, although the officers found them, on the whole, very hospitable. While some braved the discomforts of the best hotel, the *d'Ingleterra,* with its dirty waiters and table cloths, its *table d'hôte* – expensive at three shillings and fourpence – which consisted of meat, game, fish, and poultry, 'with a dessert and as much execrable *vino tinto*' as they cared to drink, others lived as guests of the inhabitants. On arriving at their new billets they were usually welcomed with a small cup of chocolate, a biscuit and a glass of water, handsomely served on 'large massive silver waiters'. Provisions were plentiful and good, especially poultry and fruit. The drawback was Spanish cooking, in particular the use of garlic, which generally proved too much for British stomachs. As hosts they were 'particularly attentive and kind', Lord Paget's insisting that he invite twenty of his friends to dinner. But when Berkeley Paget's landlady asked him to dine, 'a sorry meal' he made of it:

A touch of garlic I have no objection to, but my breath was taken away when one dish was put on the table, which was a sausage as large as a line-of-battle ship's main yard, cram full of garlic, a dish of macaroni poisoned with saffron, and a salad mixed with lamp-oil. I was obliged to eat out of compliment, and lie through thick and thin by saying I thought it delightful.

Major Griffith of the 15th Hussars felt that he cut a ridiculous figure, not speaking a word of Spanish, billeted with a merchant who had:

> two or three daughters besides a wife, and we all sleep . . . *in the same room,* for the recesses where the beds stand are open, and we dress and *undress* in each other's presence in the utmost sangfroid; . . . in the morning as soon as I am awake one of the handmaids presents herself with a large cup of Chocolate & dry toast which I am forced to eat in bed as I cannot make them understand that I would rather dress first; as soon as I *am* dressed and sat down . . . to write a letter, they all collect around me, cram me with apples, dry'd fruit &c. and pull and tumble all my things about in such away that I could with the greatest pleasure kick them downstairs.

Apart from the filth, upon which they were all agreed, opinions differed about the charms of Corunna itself. Hodge was amazed by it; 'The people, houses, vehicles, everything are so extraordinary that I can only describe it by saying that the pictures in *Gil Blas*' are an exact representation of all'. Colonel Vivian thought it a 'fine city and capable of improvement . . . and the *tout ensemble,* both for comfort and convenience, was very superior to anything we had been led to believe'. The streets were wide, the pavements excellent, and the shops well supplied, in spite of the blockade kept up by both the Royal Navy and the French. On 13 November the populace dressed up in their best clothes, the women, according to Hodge, in general 'in black and colored pelices trimmed with bugles with a veil which comes all over the head and reaches just below the shoulders'. The men, in spite of the fine weather, generally went about muffled in thick brown cloaks. One of the regular haunts was the playhouse, built in the ditch of the citadel, where Berkeley Paget was surprised to see Othello stab Desdemona in true Spanish style. 'The Spaniard imagines,' he supposed, 'that the stiletto is the only gentleman-like weapon, and disdains the bolster.' Like modern tourists, the visitors were most impressed with the dancing, which generally ended with the 'fandango or the bolero, danced by persons habited in the costume of Andalusia', whose admirably managed castanets added much to the spirit of the scene.

The rank and file, however, were not quite so impressed with Spanish hospitality. Sergeant Thomas, of the 7th Hussars, reported home to the Adjutant that:

> the accomodation for the men & horses here is very miserable, worse than the Regt. ever experienced before. The boasted civility of the Spaniards to the English is to be found only in the English papers. Their

conduct to us here quite the reverse; they grossly impose upon us in the price of every article we want. We have lost 12 horses since Embarkation, some were drowned in swimming them from the vessels to the shore.

The men, in spite of everything, were in high spirits, and the horses in good condition 'considering the long & rough journey & the scanty & bad provisions' they were now allowed. The regiment had been 'much harassed', but all were doing their duty with cheerfulness.[9]

After a tempestuous and disagreeable passage the 15th Hussars started disembarking on 13 November. They, too, had to lower their horses into the water and either tow or swim them ashore. The next morning the headquarters ship, which was overdue, arrived safely, and by 15 November the regiment was ashore, apart from one transport which was still missing. The entire brigade was now quartered in Corunna, or in the barracks at St Lucia, just outside the town, and everybody was busy with preparations for the march. That same day sightseeing and parties came to an end as the Hussar Brigade set off, amid rumours of the defeat of Blake's Spanish army. They were led by the 7th Hussars, in three divisions, a day apart, and followed by the 10th and the 15th. Sergeant Thomas wrote that they were going to march three or four hundred miles 'thro' a very barren country' and most of the horses were already in want of shoes. As there was no time to shoe the whole horse, the forefeet only were being attended to. Two Troops of the Royal Horse Artillery, B and C, were to accompany the Hussars, and a tenth division, commanded by Captain Gordon, of the 15th, was to act as a collecting party to gather up any stragglers. There was shortage of baggage mules and the bulk of the supplies had to be carried in bullock carts, hired by the day. They were of the crudest construction with solid wooden wheels on creaking ungreased axles. The Hussars themselves carried two or three days' provision of forage, which they had to collect themselves, and which was secured to their saddles by means of the forage cords.

The 'route' they were given, which was to be covered in twelve days, with two halting days to rest the horses, would take them as far as Astorga, some 180 miles along the *Caminho Réal*, which Gordon described as 'one of the finest public works in Europe'. Constructed, for the most part, half-way between the summit and the base of the various mountains through which it passed, it was carried, 'by gradual ascent, over some of the highest mountains in Galicia'. Augustus Schaumann, a Hanoverian serving as a Commissary with Sir John Moore's army, later described it as a 'noble piece of work, broad, frequently cut through the rock, and marked by milestones, after the manner of a great highway', stone pillars, set a league ('four English miles and about half a furlong') apart, showing the distance from Corunna.

The first stage of the journey took them to Betanzos, fourteen miles over a winding road through the gorse-covered hills of Galicia, which Vivian likened to Devon, but grander. The first division of the 7th was accompanied by Downman's B Troop of Horse Artillery; Hodge marched with the second, and

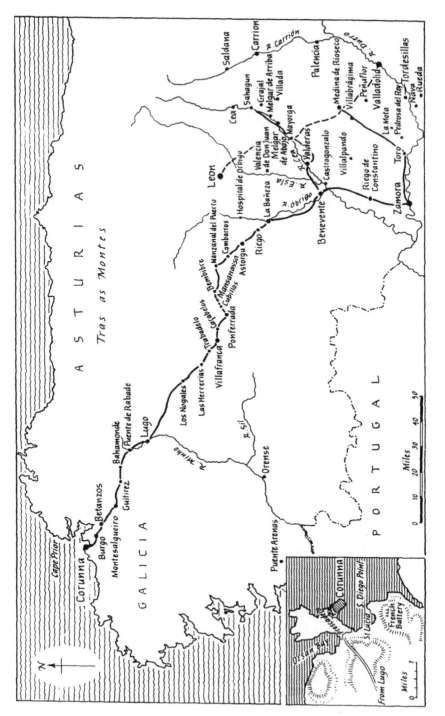

The unfavourable retreat 1808–9

Lord Paget, Colonel Vivian, Major Paget, the regimental band, Lord and Lady Holland and their retinue with the third. On the evening of the 16th Hodge and his men descended the hill into Betanzos. Situated on an arm of the sea, it was as 'small and . . . as miserable as a small Spanish town can be', Hodge noted in his diary, and moreover the commissariat was 'most shamefully managed here, as nothing was ready for men or horses'. The meat was 'stinking and the wine so infamous even the men would not take it'. How they were to do the next day he knew not.

On arrival in the town officers and men were allocated billets by the *Alcade*, or Mayor, to which they were directed by the troop quartermasters. The following day Major Paget, marching with the third division, was put up with a Spanish colonel's wife, who, after an excellent dinner, carried her guests off to a 'rout composed of half a dozen old tabbies'. Six days later Gordon, with the rear party, lodged with a poor *hildalgo* and his lady, who took him to a *tertulla*, or evening party, afterwards regaling him with 'hog's pudding and garlic à l'Espagnole'.

There were alternative halting places for the second stage of the march; Montesalgueiro, three leagues from Betanzos, or Guitirez, two leagues further on. Verner remembered the former as a 'wretched place . . . which the Colonel of the 10th Hussars christened Salt Hill although it had little claim to be compared with its namesake'.[10] Hodge stopped there as well on the 17th and was 'obliged to seize any sheds we could find for our horses, and very glad to get them'. He put fifty or so men and horses into the sheds, and the remaining 120 into a single house, where Vivian stayed the next night. It was a 'low house on a barren heath, 3 officers and 120 men all pigging it together in the straw'. When he considered the conditions he was surprised at the good turnout they made next morning. When, on the 21st, the leading division of the 15th Hussars arrived in the neighbourhood, Adjutant Jones was 'obliged to pitch tents for the accomodation of the men', as there was no room for them at the *venta*, or inn. It was an 'excessive cold night' and the wolves were so plentiful that they attacked the men as they slept. Three nights later Gordon, with the rear party, saw the carcasses of two 'wild dogs', shot by some of the men 'encamped on the moor'; they resembled wolves, but were smaller in size.

Two days of marching were enough to persuade Verner that they had 'made a great change for the worse', for not only were they having difficulty in getting rations and forage, but also 'great unwillingness' on the part of the locals to provide either. Occasionally they found themselves sharing the same quarters as the Spanish Muleteers, whose breakfasts came as a horrid shock to those brought up on the English variety:

An enormous quantity of garlic [was] cut into a pan, upon which was poured a quantity of oil; it was then placed upon the fire and when sufficiently warm bread thinly sliced was added. When all became well blended the contents were poured into an earthen dish and placed upon a table round which the muleteers sat each provided with a spoon, with which he helped himself from the dish. When the more substantial part was disposed of, the dish containing the oil was handed round, each taking a sup until all was finished . . .

Lord Paget and his party spent the night of the 18th in the inn at Guitirez, the best part of which he had gallantly secured for the Hollands. The next morning, before they left on a sightseeing tour of the cathedral town of Lugo, the Hollands watched Lord Paget muster his men and march off, 'proceeded by the band playing'. The next stage, to Bahamonde, a distance of two leagues, began to tell on the horses of the 7th, although the road was level and the pace slow. Two horses had been left at Betanzos, Hodge noted, and by the time the regiment met the enemy all would be very weak. It had been a bad policy, he thought, not to have let them recover themselves more at Corunna. On the 18th Lady Holland wrote in her journal that

The horses after 7 weeks confinement on a ship and then plunged into the sea to be swum ashore in a state of fever, have of course suffered severely, especially in their feet; besides the change of food from oats and hay to chopped straw and maize has affected their health. Seventeen were left at Betanzos. Three young men died, and on the road we saw several horses lying dead, and others who had fallen but could not rise . . .

The road to Bahamonde was 'highly picturesque', with bridges soaring dramatically over mountain torrents, but there was not a vestige of population or cultivation to be seen, 'the whole a barren heath or range of mountains covered with furze'. Opinions differed about Bahamonde itself. Hodge said it consisted of three miserable barns, while Gordon thought it a pleasant little village 'situated in an extensive and fertile plain watered by the Minho'. Hodge was certainly prejudiced as he and his men had marched all day through drenching rain and were soaked to the skin. When they arrived, the only place he could find to stable the horses was 'like a pigstie, with dirt up to their fetlocks'. Wrapped in his bearskin and blankets, he spent an uncomfortable night, plagued by fleas. The next morning his body looked as if he had leprosy, being completely covered in red spots, and his 'flannel dressing gown covered with the devourers'. Vivian suffered much the same the next night, sharing with Lord Paget and his staff, 'ten of us in one little room, and an antechamber full of lice, fleas, and all sorts of vermin'.

Another day's march brought the leading division to Lugo, four leagues from Bahamonde, situated on a plateau close to the source of the Minho. Vivian thought Lugo inferior, in most respects, to any English village, and in dirt surpassing anything he had ever beheld. On the 20th Lord Paget arrived with the last division of the 7th Hussars, and that same evening received an express from Sir David Baird, announcing that the French were in the vicinity of Astorga. He also received confirmation of Blake's defeat, and gave orders for the cavalry to push on to Astorga without halting. To speed up the march the baggage was to be reduced as much as possible, and as a result General Slade was 'reduced to two coats, two pairs of overalls, six shirts, six pairs of stockings, two pairs of boots, a knife, fork, and spoon' – and his bed.

The lack of co-operation from their supposed allies was now making the officers of the brigade very angry. 'The Spaniards may be an honourable generous fine nation', Hodge wrote in exasperation, 'but we have hitherto found nothing but knavery, incivility, falsehood and beastliness.' Gordon, on occasions, found it 'necessary to enforce obedience with threats and blows'. The *Alcade* was often little better than the lowest sort of peasant, while many were suspected of being 'well-affected' towards the enemy. Hodge went so far as to suggest that the contractors had been bribed by the enemy, 'for they fail in their agreements at the moment they are most needed'. His greatest difficulty was in getting carts to carry the men's tents, while Vivian was having trouble finding mules for the heavy cast-iron camp kettles, the basic cooking utensil, one of which served five men. The drivers of the carts, when they were finally coerced into action, were an 'obstinate ferocious set', who if hard pressed were liable to draw their knives, cut their oxen's throats and leave the baggage in the middle of the road.[11] On top of everything else the horses were now dropping fast. The 7th Hussars left thirty-one at Lugo, while those that kept going 'were far from being in a fit state for active service'.

Hodge and his men marched out of Lugo on the 21st. The next day the Hollands left for home and on the road back they passed General Slade, accompanied by 'young FitzClarence', grumbling furiously about the lack of assistance from the *Juntas*. Further on they met the 15th Hussars, who seemed in much better shape than the rest of the brigade. Their horses had, of course, been on board ship for a much shorter time, eleven days only, but apart from that, Tale put their superior condition down to Colonel Long's thorough training:

Of one thing I have personal knowledge as well as ocular proof; namely, that in the regimental returns rendered to the Brigade-Major, fewer casualties from sore backs were exhibited [by the 15th] than from any of the other regiments; . . . In addition to the ordinary burthen at home, clap a further weight of some three quarters of a hundred pounds in the shape of provender, provisions, ammunition, horseshoes, and nails &c., and the good or inefficient training of the cavalry soldier will soon be tested.

Travelling thus 'light', the Hussar Brigade pushed on to Astorga, over a difficult road which crossed two mountain ranges, and in worsening weather. At first the countryside was well-watered and cultivated, although the officers remarked on the lack of 'anything like a gentleman's country house', but gradually they entered wilder country. The march to Los Nogales, on the 22nd, was over winding mountain roads, with high cliffs on one side, and sheer drops of two or three hundred feet on the other, with a 'river rolling through a rocky bottom' far below them. The next day, between Los Nogales and Trabadelo, the men of the 7th Hussars changed their boots for shoes and led their horses up the three-and-a-half mile climb to the summit of the mountain. Here, on top of a nearby peak, 'to all appearance inaccessible', they saw the ruined ivy-clad walls of a large castle. It was the 'exact haunt of banditti', thought Hodge, reminded strongly of Mrs Radcliffe and her 'Gothick' novels.[12] Slade thought the road exceeded everything he had seen in Switzerland and made him quite tremble to look down. Another three miles or so and the head of the column entered Trabadelo, which was soon filled with lame horses. Vivian came up to the front of the first division to tell Hodge that the regiment was already reduced to a strength of 600, with more horses dropping all the time. The men, however, in spite of all their various hardships, including being without bread for three days, continued 'wonderfully healthy'.

The gradual descent to Villafranca, through chestnut woods and maize fields, was easier. The town lay in a small valley at the foot of the mountains commanding the passes into Galicia, and once there the country opened out into vineyards and cornfields. At Villafranca Cornet Phillips, of the 15th Hussars, was ordered to return to Lugo with the sick horses of the brigade, 170 in all, together with 160 men. He got them back safely, less four men and horses, whose fate his letters home fail to reveal. At Lugo he found Cornet Jenkins, with about 200 men and horses of the regiment, who had been captured by a French privateer, and 'Rifled of all their Armes & Appointments'. They had been released on parole that neither he nor his men would serve again during the 'present War'.[13]

Between Villafranca and Astorga there was another difficult pass, at Manzanal, four leagues short of Bembibre. It was on this stretch of road that Gordon passed large numbers of mules, laden with wine and led by well-armed muleteers dressed in 'a sort of cuirass of strong buff leather' and broad-brimmed hats. They reminded him strongly of the engravings in *Gil Blas*. The weather continued variable, hot, cold, wet and foggy by turns, but in spite of their appalling accommodation the men were, according to Vivian, bearing their privations without a murmur. When the first division of the 7th Hussars finally rode into Astorga on 26 November, after covering 160 miles in nine days, they had lost four men and left behind sixty horses.[14]

* * *

Two days later Sir John Moore, now at Salamanca, learned of the defeat of the Spanish armies of the centre and right at Tudela and decided on an imme-diate retreat to Portugal. Baird was ordered to retire on Corunna, or Vigo, after having shown a bold front for a few days to enable Moore to concentrate his divisions. On 1 December Baird's infantry started their withdrawal, covered by the Hussar Brigade. Paget, meanwhile, had persuaded Baird that it would be better to take the cavalry back to Portugal overland, by way of Ponferrada and Orense, but on 3 December, just as orders had been issued for 400 men from each regiment to prepare for the journey, a request came from

Moore for one of the regiments to be transferred to his force. This was just the opportunity that Paget had been waiting for and he promptly suggested to Baird that he take all three regiments. Baird agreed, and preparations for this 'Zieten-like march' were put in hand at once.[15] Orders were given out on the 4th for the brigade to march 'as strong as possible' the next morning. Now, instead of going by Orense, they were to go direct to Salamanca, cutting their way through the enemy. The greatest danger lay at the bridge at Zamora, where the French were said to be in force. This was better than retreating, Hodge thought, bidding adieu to a bed for some time to come.

The next day the citizens of Astorga were treated to the fine spectacle of the Hussar Brigade, and the six guns of Downman's Troop, as they paraded on the plain outside the town. 'The whole,' according to Hodge, 'turned out well and having had a two days' rest appeared something like themselves.' At twelve noon they set off on the twenty-two league march to Zamora, making their first halt at La Bañeza, four leagues on their way. The next day they rested up, assembling at the alarm posts at eleven at night to resume their march. There was a sharp frost and they moved off into the night at a 'foot pace'. The next morning, 7 December, they reached the walled town of Benevente, gloomy but clean, with well-stocked shops and comfortable quarters, dominating an extensive plain watered by the River Esla. That day a hundred men from each regiment provided the picquets, which remained mounted, 'not knowing where the enemy lay and to guard the banks of the river'. Hodge was sent off to reconnoitre along the river's edge and returned exhausted in the evening to report to Lord Paget that there were no fords and that it would be impossible to cross the river in an emergency if they had to.[16] After a little hot wine and a nap he was up again, ready and mounted to march with the Brigade at half past eleven.

That night Paget and Slade had their first row when the brigade was delayed for over an hour owing to the 7th and 10th Hussars 'mistaking the place of rendez-vous'. Crossing the Esla by the bridge at Castrogonzalo, Paget's force, some 1,200 sabres strong, entered upon the most perilous part of their journey. They marched in open column of divisions or half-squadrons, 'whenever the ground would admit of it', to make rapid deployment easier. They knew the French were somewhere about for, not far from Castrogonzalo, two or three blue lights were observed in the sky, which they thought were signals made by enemy spies. After that they travelled with the artillery portfires lit, ready for instant action. Slade thought it not the most agreeable way of proceeding, but admitted that 'it was necessary to cover our movements from the enemy, who were supposed to be near us'. Anyway it was not his night, for, after their row, Lord Paget rode alongside the column giving orders which he 'desired the general to repeat to the squadron officers of the Tenth'. But no sooner had Slade left him than Paget called one of his aides-de-camp to 'ride after that damned stupid fellow, and take care that he committed no blunder'. All this was said in the hearing of a number of officers and men, and was, Gordon thought, 'calculated to deprive the Brigadier even of the slight respect previously entertained for him by the troops'. At eight the following morning, with the men and horses 'almost knocked up', they halted on a heath near Riego di Constantino, over half-way to their destination. To avoid surprise, and because all the baggage had been sent back to Corunna, and they were without tents, they linked horses in the open, the men cooking and warming themselves at fires built from wood provided by the locals.

At midnight they moved on again in a frost so intense that in the morning their fur caps bristled with icicles. The fatigue of three consecutive night marches was beginning to tell and they began to suffer from a drowsiness that was 'almost impossible to resist'. This made steady riding impossible, for, with no rest at night and little by day, sleep frequently overtook the men and 'swerving and rolling from side to side necessarily followed'. Moreover the troops, and even the regiments themselves, were frequently mixed up because the riders did not know where they were going.

At seven the following morning, 9 December, they marched into Zamora, where for the first time, Hodge reported, they were received with 'symptoms of joy'. The citizens assembled in the market place and in the windows of the houses with shouts of '*Viva la Gran Britania y George III*', while cannons were fired and bells rung. The *Junta* invited the officers to breakfast with them, and a very good one it was. The city itself, towering above the River Douro, with its fine bridge, was well worth inspecting, but the 'fatigues of our marches by night and the duties that followed were such as to put it out of the power of any officer to examine accurately the beauties of the place'.

While the Hussar Brigade had been cutting across country to join Moore, who was now at Toro, six leagues to the east, Baird's division had almost reached Corunna. On 9 December they were suddenly ordered to halt and retrace their steps to Astorga, as the situation had changed dramatically. Early in November Napoleon had arrived at Vitoria, and soon after had pushed southwards towards Madrid. Forcing the Somosierra Pass on the 30th, he summoned the city to surrender. The Spaniards managed to persuade Moore that the city would hold out for some time and he decided to call a halt to his retreat and throw his force across the French lines of communication, in the direction of Valladolid and Burgos.

On 10 December the Hussar Brigade paraded outside Zamora, expecting to march to Salamanca, but 'whether on account of the good news from Madrid or of communications between Lord Paget and Sir J. Moore during the night', they were ordered back to Toro instead. The 10th Hussars, for some reason 'best known to those in command', were left behind at Zamora. The route, which followed the banks of the Douro, was lined with fruit trees of every description. Captain Gordon, who commanded the advance guard that day, was met 'above a mile from the town by a great concourse of people, chiefly of the lower orders,' who saluted the Hussars with '*vivas*'. At six they entered the town, where they were greeted with 'joy and illuminations'. 'The windows,' Gordon wrote, 'were filled with ladies waving their handkerchiefs, and crying, "*Vivan Los Ingleses*".' For some reason the Quartermasters had not been sent

56

forward to secure quarters, but happily there was no need of their services, as the citizens threw open their houses to the new arrivals. 'Thus,' wrote Vivian with satisfaction, 'we have concluded our junction with the greatest facility.'

Captain Hodge was by now thoroughly fed up with the Spaniards, and not at all taken in by their welcome. The fact that the French, though few in numbers, had been allowed to stay unmolested in Toro, six days earlier, corresponded little, he thought:

> with the idea of those in England of a Nation in arms which they believe and were taught to expect the Spaniards were. That a small body of the enemies Cavalry should quietly march into a considerable town without molestation – this is not the spirit which will drive the French from the country, and whatever the hopes of Romana and Blake may be, I must beg leave to profess myself less sanguine and foresee that the end of this business will be Route and retreat . . . We came to assist, not to singly stem the torrent.

Toro, he thought, 'dirty and ill built', with narrow, filthy streets. He and his friend Champion managed to get into a nunnery, which afforded them some amusement, and were shown the chapel, through a grating ten feet square, and beyond it the garden, which was the nuns 'only walk'. Hodge's 'Romantick' nature got the better of him yet again, and he could not help fancying himself as the hero of one of the tales of 'Monk' Lewis or Mrs Radcliffe of *The Mysteries of Udolpho* fame.[17]

From Toro, perched high above the river, and encircled by its Moorish Walls, the countryside and the people took on a different character.[18] They now entered the wide plain of Leon which reminded the visitors of *Don Quixote*; the people almost savage, and the immense plain miserably barren. Dr Neale, travelling with Sir John Moore's army, found their mode of living, to say the least, uncomfortable:

> their clothes and linnen threadbare; their persons shockingly filthy; houses nearly unfurnished; windows without glass; fuel dear and scarce; and their food consisting almost entirely of an execrable mess called *gaspacho*, which they eat thrice a day . . .

Some, however, were better off, for the *Alcade* of Villavendemio, one Bartoleo, with whom Gordon was quartered on the night of 12 December, kept a clean and comfortable house, although it was only one of the mud-walled thatched variety. The sight of the kitchen made Gordon almost imagine himself back in England, with its blazing log fire, whitewashed walls, polished utensils and the 'carcasses of above fifty sheep, goats, and hogs – chined dried or salted – with a plentiful stock of black puddings and sausages; and a large supply of bread, baked for winter provision, of rye and indian corn'. This abundance was shared by another guest, the parish priest, who was so taken with Gordon's uniform that he insisted on strutting round the room wearing his pelisse and fur cap, flourishing a drawn sabre 'to the great dismay of the women and imminent danger to the links of black puddings and sausages'.

* * *

The Hussar Brigade was drawing closer both to Moore's cavalry, the 18th Hussars and the 3rd Hussars of the King's German Legion, commanded by Sir Charles Stewart, and to the enemy.[19] First blood, however, fell to the 18th Hussars. On 11 December it was learned that French cavalry were at Medina de Rioseco, on the Valladolid – Leon road, and at Rueda, between Nava and Tordesillas, and the Hussars were ordered to keep on the alert. The next day Stewart sent his aide-de-camp, disguised as a peasant, into Rueda. He returned with information about the number and position of the enemy, and on the night of the 13th a detachment of the 18th Hussars, under Major Otway, entered the town unobserved. The enemy were thrown into confusion, many were sabred on the spot, and others were captured, together with a convoy of wagons, loaded with cotton destined for France and said to be worth £80,000. Hodge, writing some days later, put the value at £30,000, which would be shared out by the 18th Hussars. 'Such prize money'. he added enviously, 'rarely falls to the lot of the Army'. The men of the 18th returned from Rueda bringing with them a colonel and twenty-seven men, who were the objects of much curiosity, as all wanted to see the first prisoners taken in the campaign. Dr Neale examined them on the 14th, at Alaejos, and found them to be 'stout, good-looking men, Poles, Prussians, Swiss, and French', some of whom had only just arrived in Spain after a long march from Berlin and Danzig. They had bivouacked constantly, and their feet were 'in a dreadful state of mortification, from being frost bitten'.[20]

Paget and his Hussars were now probing eastwards from Toro, with the dual tasks of locating the enemy and of screening Moore's movements. Since the affair at Rueda it was safe to assume that his dispositions were now known to the enemy. On 11 December the 15th Hussars patrolled the country ten miles in front of Morales de Toro and two days later pursued the French outposts fourteen miles along the road to Tordesillas, where Francheschi lay with 1,200 cavalry. On the 12th Hodge recorded that the 'dastardly Spaniards' had surrendered Madrid and that the British army ought now to retreat, but Moore clearly did not agree, for the army continued advancing. On the 14th they marched to Tordesillas, which had been abandoned by the French, and where they found the 15th already in quarters, with the 10th a little way in rear, the 18th being on their right flank. The latter, some of whose privates were wearing the broad buff leather belts and gauntlets they had taken from the French Dragoons at Rueda, were the envy of the other regiments.

That same day Moore learned from a captured despatch that Napoleon, apparently ignorant of Moore's true position, was marching towards Valladolid in an attempts to cut off his supposed retreat to Portugal, leaving

Soult with a mere 18,000 infantry and 1,200 cavalry out on a limb in the area of Saldana and Carrion. Moore decided to take the chance of giving him a 'wipe' before Napoleon could come to his aid. The axis of the British advance was swung northwards towards Sahagun, and Baird, whose advance guard had now reached Benevente, was ordered to join Moore at Valderas.

On the 16th the Hussars set off from the area of Pedrosa del Rey northwards towards Medina de Rio Seco, through open country 'adapted to cavalry'. The weather continued clear but frosty – during the day it was warm enough, but the nights were now intensely cold. On the 17th they marched from La Mota to Villabragima, a distance, Gordon claimed, of only three leagues. The Quartermasters of the 15th Hussars, well out in front, surprised a French foraging party, which abandoned its gleanings in its hasty retreat. General Slade, Colonel Grant and some other officers pushed on to Medina, a league away, where they were welcomed by the inhabitants with the news that 600 French cavalry had left only an hour before. But for Slade leading them by the longest route, Gordon thought, the 15th would probably have caught them. The next day, 18 December, much to their disgust, they were ordered to march away from the enemy, towards Villalpando, a movement which, Gordon recalled, caused considerable discontent. On their arrival there Lord Paget altered the brigade structure of the cavalry, keeping the 10th and 15th together under Slade, but taking the 7th away and giving it to Stewart.

On the 19th Lord Paget and Slade's Brigade, accompanied by four of Downman's guns, set off again after the French in worsening weather. During the day they passed flocks of merino sheep, whose shepherds, clad in goat or sheepskin hooded cloaks, and armed with huge iron crooks, reminded one observer of so many Robinson Crusoes. At Mayorgà, which they entered during a snowstorm, they were close behind Debelle's Brigade. After a short halt they resumed their march towards Sahagun, and at Melgar de Arriba, two leagues further on, they found a fine convent 'in which', Gordon wrote, 'we had the good fortune to deposit General Slade, who seemed happy to take shelter from a heavy fall of snow in a place which promised such comfortable quarters', while the rest moved on to Melgar de Abajo, where they halted.[21]

Lord Paget now decided to take a leaf out of General Stewart's book and the next evening, the 20th, he summoned the commanding officers and adjutants to his quarters 'for instructions for a night attack upon Debelle at Sahagun'. The plan, in the best traditions of Hussar operations, was simple and daring. The 10th and the guns, under Slade, were to follow the right bank of the Cea, surprise the French in Sahagun at first light and drive them through the town to the opposite end, where Paget and the 15th, having marched by the left bank, would be waiting for them. The Squadron and Troop officers of the 15th were given their orders at ten o'clock that night, and at one in the morning the regiments fell in. Tale recorded how the 15th:

assembled in order, and without confusion; for so well had our clever Adjutant marshalled and trained his couriers, that all points [heads of

59

troops] were communicated with simultaneously, and thence to all the more subordinate; and herein was displayed the inimitable squad regulations of Colonel L[on]g . . . Whether in barracks, quarters, or on the line of march, the sergeant held his own Squad, and was more or less held accountable for their conduct.

The 10th, however, were late in starting because, according to Gordon, the Brigadier insisted on delivering a fiery speech which ended with the stirring cry, 'Blood and Slaughter, March!' This they did accordingly and, as Slade recalled in his diary, 'a more dreadful night troops could not be exposed to'; it was particularly dark, with a severe frost, sleet falling and snow drifting in many places to the depth of four feet. One man broke his leg and an inconceivable number of horses fell during the march. These hazards were added to by the numerous small streams that flowed into the Cea, all of which could only be crossed where the ice was thick enough to bear the weight of the guns and limbers of the artillery.

The 15th, on their side of the river, picked up Captain Thornhill of the 7th Hussars and the twelve men of Lord Paget's escort, and Tale recalled how they proceeded on their way in almost total silence, broken only by 'the continuous pattering of the horses' hoofs upon the snow, the muffled clink (we were cloaked) of spur and scabbard, scabbard and spur, or an inner growl accompanied by a naughty word at the stumbling of man or animal on our uneven track.'

Towards five in the morning the leading division of the 15th fell in with a French outpost, which they charged, capturing five men. Unfortunately the remainder got away and managed to raise the alarm in Sahagun. As day broke Paget, leading the 15th round the outskirts of the town, arrived at the rear to find the enemy formed in close column of squadrons, facing the road to Carrion. The French, eight squadrons strong, started moving off to their left as soon as they saw the British, and Paget, ordering the 15th to form 'open column of divisions', followed them on a parallel course, with some eighty yards between them. As soon as he came abreast of them he wheeled the 15th left into line, and charged, 'just as you have seen us do at Ipswich,' he told his brother Arthur. Tale was so benumbed with cold that

for fear of losing the grip of my sword, I twisted the buff knot to an extent that became painful; but this proved a bootless precaution, for on wheeling into line for the charge, the temperature of the blood mounted at once from below zero to the boiling point.

With bugles blowing, and with cries of 'Emsdorff and Victory!'[22] the 15th crashed into the now halted enemy, who were formed in two lines, the 1st Provisional *Chasseurs à Cheval* in front, with the 8th Dragoons in the rear. Gordon described the moment of impact: 'The shock was terrible, horses and men were overthrown, and a shriek of terror, intermixed with oaths, groans, and prayers for mercy, issued from the whole extent of their front.' The first line was thrown back upon the second and both broke and fled, hotly pursued by the 15th. The melée, which lasted about ten minutes, was, however, fiercely contested, many individual combats continuing on the ground after the participants had been unhorsed. 'Hard knocks indeed were given and received.' Tale recalled, and as dawn broke 'frightful gashes and streams of gore were made visible . . . Horses galloping about *sans rider*, riders *à pied* running after their horses; the moans and tortures of the wounded writhing in anguish from a cold and freezing atmosphere – the dying and the dead!' The French later accounted for their tenacity by saying that they thought they were being bowled over by Spaniards, and that the disgrace was too much for them. Eventually over 200 of the enemy escaped down the Saldana and Carrion roads, which the British had failed to block. Some of the Hussars tried to follow them, but, much to Gordon's disgust, were recalled by Lord Paget, wild with bloodlust and with blown horses.

Meanwhile Slade and the 10th, in spite of what Gordon called their 'dilatory proceedings', had reached the bridge at Sahagun on time, only to find the town deserted. They pushed on through the empty streets emerging at the far end in time to discover that the 15th 'had not ten minutes [before] charged and put them to rout'. Their arrival caused some confusion, as they were at first taken for French reinforcements, and the pursuit was called off in order to face this new hazard. When the affair was over Paget assembled the 15th and thanked them for their gallant conduct, at the same time scolding them for being too eager to dash on the enemy during the pursuit. The French lost 220 killed, wounded and taken prisoner, including Colonel Dud'huit and twelve officers of the Dragoons, and Colonel Dugens and three officers of the Chasseurs. The 15th lost two men killed and twenty-six wounded, among whom were Colonel Grant and Lieutenant Jones, the former wounded slightly on the forehead and the latter severely in the face. 'It is probable,' commented Gordon, 'neither of them would have been hurt if our fur caps had been hooped with iron like those of the French Chasseurs, instead of being stiffened with pasteboard.' According to Tale the British wounded seem to have fared worst:

> One poor fellow (Hawkins) I think, received over half a score of sabre-cuts, indeed may be said to have been almost made mincemeat of; he lived to reach Haslar hospital. Another trooper (Vokins) had a frightful cut across the face . . . and at first sight the cut he had received seemed of such magnitude as to give an appearance of his face having been divided into two parts, from a sabre-cut across his nose and into his cheeks. . . . He was ultimately restored to health.

On the 22nd Dr Neale visited the prisoners in the Convent at Sahagun. Like those taken at Rueda, they were fine specimens 'from all the different nations subject to France', dressed in dark green with large white cloaks. Their horses were poor animals, smaller and slighter than those of the British, much out of condition, and nearly a third of them with sore backs. He particularly admired the brass helmets of the Dragoons:

> Of the old Roman shape, with a high crest, from which hangs a quantity of black horse-hair. . . . I have now in my possession one bearing the marks of four sabre cuts, not one of which had penetrated to the scalp beneath. Indeed I have examined all the wounded with attention, and find that while our men are most desparately wounded about the face and head, there is not a single Frenchman cut deeper than the hairy scalp. You perceive what an immense advantage this gives the wearer of a helmet, over the wearer of a fur cap; and I do hope that this new fashion may be laid aside immediately.

Many of the prisoners were in a deplorable condition from the effects of exposure, and Neale had to have the boots ripped off many of them, whose feet were 'in a state of complete mortification'. They were cheerful enough though, fiddling and dancing away in the Convent refectory' as if they were enjoying themselves in the hey-day of the vintage in the midst of France'. What a contrast they were to the Spaniards, 'gliding along . . . muffled in old chocolate-coloured cloaks and montero caps, or standing for hours beneath a dismal piazza, brooding over their national calamities'. Several of the French officers wore the '*Croix d'Honneur*' of the 'celebrated Legion of Bonaparte' on their breasts, while several of the privates had 'honorary badges'.

After the battle the loot taken from the French was auctioned in the convent courtyard. According to Lieutenant Jones, considerable sums of money and all the French baggage had been taken, including 'a great quantity of plate but the 10th Drns. choused the Regt. out of it'. One onlooker was amazed at the sort of things carried by the French officers; along with a silver ewer and basin beaten together into a lump, and the handles of a few silver knives and forks 'were a thousand glittering trinkets which the plunder of . . . many a Virgin Mary had afforded'.[23]

By the evening of 21 December the infantry had reached Sahagun and, for the next two days, the army rested while Moore considered his next move. He knew that Soult was still at Saldana, but he also knew that there was not much time left to him before the French on the Ebro, and Napoleon, to the south, turned their attentions to him. Before he was caught in a trap, however, he decided to attempt one last stroke at the French. On the 23rd orders were issued for an advance towards the bridge at Carrion, prior to an attack on Soult at first light on the 24th. For these operations, which were to be supported by 10,000 Spaniards of Romana's army, Moore's force was divided into three. Baird was on the left at Sahagun, with the 10th and 15th Hussars covering his front; Fraser was at Grajal in the centre, covered by the 7th Hussars, and Hope was on the right, at Villada, with the 18th and 3rd German Hussars. 'The French,' Hodge wrote on the 22nd, 'have taken up a strong position having their right at Saldana and their left at Carrion, each place five leagues distant from this, but their advanced posts are pushed much further forward'.

According to Hodge 23 December was 'one of the coldest evenings and the ground so slippery that the horses could scarcely stand'. Nevertheless, as the army moved forward, spirits were high. At last, after weeks of marching to and fro under the most trying conditions they were going to be allowed a go at the enemy. At the very moment of the advance, however, Moore learned that the whole of the French army was on the move from Madrid, with the Emperor himself at its head. He had done what he had set out to do and now it was time to cut away. The army was halted, the attack was cancelled and, much to the fury of officers and men, orders were issued for a general retreat across the Esla to Astorga, where Moore hoped to make a stand with the help of Romana's troops. Hope's and Fraser's divisions were to march by way of Mayorga and Valderas, the bridge at Castrogonzalo and Benevente, where they were to be joined by Baird's division, which was to march by way of Valencia de Don Juan, where there was a ferry across the Esla.

On Christmas Day, 1808, Moore and the reserve followed the route taken by Hope and Fraser, leaving the cavalry to cover their withdrawal. On 26 December Baird's division forded the Esla at Valencia. As they waded through the icy water the angry and frustrated soldiers plucked the 'royal favours', handed to them when they entered Spain, out of their headdress. Within twenty-four hours there was not a single one of the scarlet cloth cockades 'about the size of a hal'penny' to be seen. 'Perhaps,' Private James Gunn of the 42nd Highlanders speculated, 'they found their way back by the stream to where they came from.'[24]

CHAPTER FOUR
The Unfavourable Retreat

The successful extrication of the British army from Napoleon's trap was largely due to the way in which Paget handled his five regiments of Hussars. In appalling conditions, ('cold beyond measure,' Berkeley Paget thought, 'one would imagine oneself in Kamschatka') on lame and exhausted horses, they kept the French cavalry screen under constant pressure, concealing Moore's movements and giving him two clear days to get away.

On Christmas Eve the 7th Hussars remained halted all day surrounded by villages full of the enemy. That night was the third Hodge had not had his boots off, 'even to be cleaned'. Berkeley Paget spent the most unpleasant Christmas Day he could remember, shivering at the head of three squadrons on the Carrion road, while Kerrison went off in search of the enemy with the fourth. He found them in a nearby village, charged them and took twelve prisoners, 'the greater part of them Germans', but his right arm was broken in the scrimmage. In the afternoon they retired in a snowstorm to Grajal, which they reached at about six, wet and tired, 'not having passed a very merry Xmas'. On the right flank, near Villada, the 18th Hussars attacked a hundred French cavalry, killing fourteen and taking six prisoners, while the 3rd German Hussars, in a similar skirmish, took thirty more. Each time the Hussars went into action, whatever the odds, they were victorious.

On Christmas Eve the sick and wounded had been moved back to Benevente, and by the time Slade and the 10th Hussars rode back through Sahagun on the following day the town was deserted. There was no more ringing of bells, all the shops were shut, 'and not anything to be got for love or money'. On the road they had passed the bodies of twelve Frenchmen; they had been stripped naked by the locals, who were unlikely to have a pleasant Christmas either when the French cavalry caught up with them.

On Boxing Day the entire brigade, together with its horse artillery, assembled 'in a plain, a league from Grajal', on the first stage of their retreat to Valderas, nine leagues to the south-west. It was now raining hard and the road was two feet deep in liquid clay. The march itself, following the banks of the Cea, was uneventful until, as they were about to pass the town of Mayorga, some villagers came up to them saying that the French were 'in possession of the place'. Soon after, Hodge saw their cavalry forming up on the hills beyond the town. Lord Paget immediately pushed on with the 10th Hussars,

64

while the left squadron of the 15th was, Gordon recalled, 'ordered to support the troop of horse artillery . . . and the rattling of the guns as we galloped through the streets completed the panic of the inhabitants'. The two leading squadrons of the 10th, headed by Adjutant Duperier and eight skirmishers, 'fell in with the enemy's advance [guard] in the streets, and after a little skirmishing drove them out of the town into the plain beyond', where they discovered two squadrons of *Chasseurs à Cheval*, formed on a rising ground about a mile away. As the 10th moved off at a trot, the Brigadier kept stopping to adjust his stirrup-leathers and Lord Paget sent an aid-de-camp forward to hurry him along. This not having the desired result, Paget finally lost his patience completely and ordered Leigh to take over command of the attack.

Leading one squadron briskly up the hill through the slush, with the second in support, Leigh and Quentin halted at the summit, under a smart fire, to allow the horses to get their wind back. The Charge was sounded and in a few minutes the French were overthrown, with the loss of three killed, many wounded and forty or fifty prisoners, 'who presented most dreadful spectacles of bloody heads &c.' 'Howard of the 10th got a cut in the arm,' Hodge recorded, and a 'few privates were wounded, but slightly. The French were the 15th Regt good-looking young men, but not very well mounted.'

In their hurry to get into action many of the heavily-laden Hussars had abandoned their corn-sacks in the town, 'meaning to pick them up on their return', but there was no opportunity to go back, and 'loud and long were the complaints; but there was no time to insist upon a restitution of the rations'. As a result of the delay caused by this action it was dark before they reached Valderas. The town was packed with troops and the Hussars had to put themselves up as best they could. 'We were on horseback thirteen hours,' Slade wrote in his diary 'and a most severe day it was.'[1] All five regiments were now assembled and the Hussars began shooting any horses or mules that were lame, or 'in other respects unfit for work', and the next morning, as they prepared to move off, Gordon counted forty carcasses lying in the streets. That day, 27 December, was almost as bad as the one before, the roads, already extremely 'heavy' from the thaw on the 24th, not being improved by the rain that now fell constantly. As the long column of men, horses, mules and guns made its slow progress across a bleak landscape it started to overtake stragglers from the infantry, who were getting their own back on the inhabitants, whose cry was now '*Vivan los Franceses*,' by setting fire to the villages they passed through.

The head of the column reached the bridge at Castrogonzalo at five in the evening and Hodge halted on the heights to watch the last of the infantry crossing over it. They were in the highest order, he wrote, and it was heartbreaking to see so fine an army retreating. The 3rd German Hussars were left to guard the approaches to the bridge, while the 15th Hussars were sent off to St Cristobal, on the right bank of the Esla above the bridge, where they found good quarters and plenty of forage. The remainder pushed on across the plain to Benevente, three miles away, where everything was in chaos. The whole army, including the commissary department from Zamora, was milling about in the narrow streets in search of quarters. Two regiments of infantry and three batteries of artillery were installed in the castle and, according to Commissary Schaumann, were busily cooking over large fires 'fed with broken antiques'. The 10th were unable to find quarters in the town and were put up in a large convent 'on an elevation' outside it.

That night, 600 *Chasseurs à Cheval* of the Imperial Guard, under the command of Lefebvre-Desnoëttes, arrived at Castrogonzalo and at dawn started attacking the German picquets. All day, in torrents of rain which later turned to snow, the latter managed to hold off the French, even taking an officer prisoner, but in the evening they withdrew across the river, blowing the bridge behind them. Leaving twenty or so men on duty with the outlying picquet, the remainder of the regiment was ordered to unsaddle and be ready to continue the retreat the next day. Major von Linsingen, however, worried in case the river was forded and the picquets surprised, ignored these orders and kept the regiment saddled all night.

At daybreak on the 29th the outlying picquet, consisting of some sixty men drawn from the various Hussar regiments under Major Otway of the 18th, detected the enemy cavalry advancing towards the bridge. Finding it blown, the enemy immediately set about searching for a ford. The vedettes of the outlying picquet having been called in, Major Otway ordered them forward to hold off the French, while a warning was sent back to the town. By this time, however, the enemy had succeeded in swimming their horses across, just above the bridge, and now had three squadrons of *Chasseurs à Cheval*, and a small mixed squadron of Mamelukes and *Chevaux-légers* on the British bank. Otway, outnumbered, fell back until he reached the suburbs of Benevente, where he halted and formed line across the road with his flanks protected by some garden walls. At this moment a further sixty men of the 7th and 10th Hussars, part of the inlying picquet under Major Quentin, and a sergeant and twenty-five men of the 18th Hussars came galloping up and Otway decided to take the offensive. Charging forward, the British Hussars rode over the leading French squadron, taking its officers prisoner, but, coming rapidly up against the enemy's supports, were forced to retire. Lord Paget, 'twirling his moustachios',[2] now appeared on the scene, accompanied by General Stewart and three troops of the 3rd Germans, who, having remained saddled all night, turned out very quickly. As Hodge, riding with this body, entered the plain he saw the French 'formed nearly half-way between the river and us and our Picquet sharply engaged with them'. They were 'keeping up a great fire with their carbines and, as we advanced, we met many of our own men returning terribly wounded and others bringing in prisoners and wounded of the Enemy.'

Lord Paget, ordering a second charge to be made, galloped back to Benevente for reinforcements. This second attack, which Hodge says was led by Quentin, got stuck in some deep clay and was less effective than its predecessor. After some fierce hand-to-hand fighting the British were pushed back, with the French hard on their heels, right up to the walls of Benevente, which were packed with hundreds of cheering spectators. Carried away by their wild pursuit, the French failed, however, to notice the rest of the 10th and 18th Hussars, formed by Lord Paget at the edge of the town, until it was too late. The latter suddenly charged the left flank of the French, who broke instantly. There followed a wild race, over the three miles of level plain, back to the river, which the French only just won. They plunged across, under the carbine fire of their pursuers, and formed up on the far bank, only to be scattered by two or three rounds from the guns of Downman's troop, firing 'Colonel Shrapnell's shells'. 'For so short a business,' Hodge wrote in his diary that day, 'it was a very sharp one.'[3]

Lefebvre-Desnoëttes had apparently seen the British infantry leaving Benevente and thought that only one regiment had been left behind as a rear-guard. As Napoleon's orders were to find out whether the British were taking the road to Zamora or Astorga, he had decided to push on as quickly as possible. The French, who, according to General Stewart, were all 'tried soldiers', who fought in a manner 'not unworthy of the reputation which they had earned in the North of Europe', lost fifty-five men killed, seventy wounded, and seventy taken prisoner. The only person to belittle the achieve-ment was Slade. 'Had the picquet shown less gallantry and a little more address,' he complained, 'we could have got between them and the river and have taken them all; for by the time I came up with the 10th Hussars they began to retreat, and Lord Paget did not approve of them being followed across the river.'

From his bedroom window, high up in Benevente, Verner saw 'the smoke from the shots on the plain below'. He dressed quickly and leapt on to his horse. As he galloped across the plain towards the firing he passed a group of Hussars escorting a French officer, who gave him a friendly smile. This was none other than Lefebvre-Desnoëttes, who had been taken in the headlong dash for the river. Within an hour the French commander, with a 'proper cut in his face', was relating his experiences to Berkeley Paget and friends, who were 'cramming him with Tea and Toast which he preferred to anything else', while outside the Spaniards howled for his blood. He told Hodge that Bonaparte would never forgive him, 'as those Regts had never been beaten before'.

There was considerable argument about who was actually responsible for his capture. The 10th afterwards claimed that he had been taken by a private of the regiment, one Levi Grisdale, who was promoted to Corporal by the Prince of Wales as a reward. Another claimant was a young Hanoverian of the 3rd German Hussars, Johann Bergmann, who took part in all three charges that day and cut down a French officer during the second. He declared, in a sworn statement, that Lefebvre surrendered to him, but that an English Hussar came up at the same moment and led him away. Verner had a story that a man of the 7th was involved in the capture. Apparently he possessed himself of Lefebvre's watch, which he handed over to his captain, who passed it on to Vivian. The latter returned it to its rightful owner, who 'refused to take it, saying the soldier who took him was entitled to it'. In the end Vivian kept it for himself, but gave the soldier who had looted it, 'what he considered to be the value'. 'The man in the 10th,' presumably Private Grisdale, apparently got Lefebvre's pistols.[4] There was a great deal of looting going on at the time and Tale came across Colonel Elley, the Adjutant General, in the middle of the plain, giving a German Hussar 'a most unmerciful thrashing with the flat of his sword'. The culprit had dismounted and was in the act of 'easing' a Frenchman's valise of its contents 'instead of being with his regiment'.

The prisoners, 'chiefly Poles, Italians, and Swiss, also a few Germans', were collected together and put in one house. They were powerful-looking men in the huge black fur caps and 'handsome red pelisses, with gold lace and black fur' of the *Chasseurs à Cheval* of the Imperial Guard. The wounds inflicted by both sides were frightful. According to several accounts French heads and arms were lopped off wholesale, while many of the British were badly cut about the head, because their tall fur caps had no chin-straps and fell off at the first blow. Captain Meyer of the German Hussars recalled that some of his men had been saved from injury by making their own chin-straps out of lengths of silk and ribbon.

After the action the 7th Hussars 'remained on the plain till evening, during which time,' Hodge recalled, the enemy 'amused us by throwing howi[t]zer shells at us without doing any mischief.' About midday Vivian saw a large group of officers appear on a hill across the river, and from 'the number of attendants, and more especially from there being some Mamelukes of the party,' they had every reason to suppose it was Bonaparte himself. Later some French officers crossed the river under a flag of truce to arrange about Lefebvre's baggage. Vivian spoke to them and was quite impressed: 'Their dress was superb, and their appearance and manners altogether most perfectly that of gentlemen, and their opinions most liberal.' Best of all they 'freely abused the Spaniards.'

That day the army retired to La Bañeza, four leagues back along the road to Corunna but before leaving Benevente the remaining supplies were burned on hugh fires in the garden of the monastery, which had served as a stores depôt. To Schaumann's despair salted meat, biscuits, boots, shirts, collars, stockings and the most magnificent English woollen blankets were consigned to the flames. Hundreds of casks of rum were broached in the streets, to be scooped up by the inhabitants. As the 15th Hussars entered La Bañeza they met a fresh detachment of the regiment entering from the other end of the village. According to Tale the newcomers were 'redolent with polish, pipeclay, and Day and Martin', while the rest of them were 'so grimy, so bedimmed, as to give the appearance of having a chimney-sweeper's soot-bag shook over them'. That evening Lefebvre, in a dry set of Sir John Moore's underclothes, dined at Headquarters, in the full glory of his *Chasseur* uniform, with Sir John's own sabre at his side, in place of the one lost on the plain of Benevente. The Hussars assembled at their alarm post soon after midnight and, leaving Lord Charles Manners and Hodge, with a squadron each of the 10th and 7th

Hussars, 'to remain there till morning' as a rearguard, set off an hour later for Astorga, four leagues away. The road was one mass of empty canisters, cartridge paper, wadding and other artillery stores, which had been hurriedly abandoned. Further on the road was blocked by the carcasses of horses and mules and by burning artillery carriages.

On the morning of 31 December the rearguard entered Astorga, to find it filled not only with British troops, but also with 10,000 ragamuffins from Romana's Spanish army, who Hodge described as 'a miserable, half-starved, ragged, indisciplined, motley crew'. Far from co-operating with Moore, the Spanish General was now clogging up his only line of retreat. Almost every house in the town contained Spanish soldiers, either dead, or dying, of malignant typhus, and the Hussars, the last to arrive, were 'very badly put up'. Adjutant Jones, searching out the quarters he had occupied on the way out, found his poor landlady lying dead at her door. 'If our Christmas was gloomy,' wrote Gordon, 'the New Year did not afford us brighter prospects.' At eight o'clock in the evening of 31 December, 1808, having already turned out once for a false alarm, the Hussars assembled at the alarm post, with orders to wait until the last of the infantry had marched out. At midnight they too turned their backs on Astorga and set off on the next stage of the retreat, to Bembibre, eight leagues away 'over the mountain Manzanal'.[5]

'At dawn of day,' Hodge wrote, 'we entered the mountains of Galicia when, as we could be of no further use, the infantry took the rear guard.' The road, which was extremely steep, was at first knee-deep in snow, but by the time the Hussars came up it had been so packed down by the infantry, and the frozen surface was so treacherous, they were forced to dismount and lead their stumbling horses. During the night they overtook the rear of Romana's army, which, apart from the artillery train, fortunately turned off on to the road to Orense. That same night they were forced to abandon a number of sick and wounded, together with the cartloads of cotton, captured by the 18th at Rueda, which were soon snapped up by the enemy. On the afternoon of 1 January, 1809, they passed through a large village of the 'Mauregatos', a strange people, said to be of Moorish descent, who possessed a 'distinct costume, and different manners from the surrounding inhabitants'. The village had been set alight by the retreating British infantry, a common occurrence now as stragglers wandered off in search of firewood or plunder. Occasionally they unearthed *caches* of wine and, drinking themselves into a stupor, 'perished in the flames they had kindled'. Gordon accounted for the increasing breakdown in discipline by the Spaniards now treating them like enemies, hiding their provisions and pretending to be unable to supply the necessities of life 'even when ample payment was tendered'. This, together with the haphazard way in which provisions were distributed on the march, was beginning to cause discontent in the marching columns, with the officers morose and the men openly remonstrating.

When the 7th Hussars rode into Bembibre at midday on 1 January Hodge found the small town 'so thronged that we could scarcely get a place to sit down and many men and horses remained all night in the streets'. Berkeley Paget had 'the mortification to learn' that the mule which carried his 'Canteens and a small Portmanteau with some snuff, Books, Sponges &c.' had escaped from his servant and was 'irrecoverably gone'. The 15th came in about four in the afternoon, but the town was full and they were sent on to the village of Mansanassa [Matachana] half a league further on, where they enjoyed a few hours rest after 'three successive night marches'. During the night the picquets of the 7th and 10th, posted on the main road, were pushed back to Bembibre by the enemy who luckily failed to press home their attack.

At four in the morning the Hussars turned out at the alarm post in Bembibre where they waited for two hours before moving off. During this wait a party was put to work 'burning a quantity of officers' baggage and regimental stores'. The army was now about to enter the mountains again and there was a feeling at Headquarters that the French would abandon the pursuit. Suggestions to the contrary were not well received, and there was an unpleasant scene when Captain Cochrane of the 15th, who had been sent to reconnoitre the main road back to Astorga, returned with the story that his patrol had been driven back by a regiment of *Chasseurs à Cheval*. He was greeted with scepticism and abuse by the Adjutant-General, Colonel Elley, who accused him of giving false intelligence and of retreating before part of what was obviously Romana's cavalry *en route* to Ponferrada. According to Adjutant Jones, however, Cochrane's patrol, after he left it, continued to skirmish with the enemy 'in a most gallant manner' in spite of the fact that their horses were in an 'exceeding bad condition and really unfit for duty'. At six in the morning, Hodge wrote, 'we marched and had not been gone an hour when accounts were brought of the French having entered the town, where they took some of our baggage, sick men and stragglers.' His dog Turk, who had followed him faithfully 'during the whole march' turned back into the town and, to his sadness, he 'never saw him after'.

In the late afternoon the 15th, once again taking the rearguard, halted in the small village of Cubillos, which was already occupied by a company of the 95th Rifles. Later, as the regiment waited in the semi-darkness for the quartermasters to allocate billets, the village was attacked and firing broke out between the French and British riflemen. When the enemy had been repulsed the 15th moved out and bivouacked in the open in front of the village. Several large fires were lit and 'working parties were sent under the orderly officer and the quartermasters to break open the houses, and abundant supplies of bread, meat, wine, corn, and hay, were found, which proved highly acceptable to both men and horses'. During the night stragglers were attracted to the fires, like moths to a candle, and it was with sickening horror that Gordon discovered that the rustling in the bushes near his bivouac was caused by the mutilated remains of a British soldier trying to drag himself to safety.

By now the horses were 'knocking up' badly. In the 15th they had been unable to trot since leaving Bembibre, and in the 7th, according to Verner, the situation was not much better:

The horses not only became jaded and unable to carry their riders, but for want of shoeing we lost numbers. One morning there were no fewer than sixty left behind for this cause, the greater number of which were shot. One of my horses lost a shoe; by the greatest good fortune it was picked up. I always carried spare nails in the top of my cap; the difficulty was to get the shoe put on as none of our farriers were to be found.

Lack of shoes was not confined to the horses: 'several of the men were marching barefoot, and the moment a man was killed or fell off his horse . . . his boots were upon another person's legs'. When their horses could no longer carry them the men dismounted and beat them along with the flats of their sabres, and when unable to stagger further, 'they took off their kit and cloak and shot them'. What was 'most provoking', Verner recalled, was that when they arrived where the stores were collected there were kegs full of spare shoes and nails, which would have saved hundreds had they had them with them. In his opinion the artillery and infantry had by far the best of it, especially the latter. All that the infantryman had to do at the end of the day was to

go to his quarters, take off his belts, rub over his firelock, and set about making himself comfortable. We have, after putting up our horses, to look after our Billets, then go for forage, to another place for rations, and by the time all this is done, and before almost the men can get anything to eat, it is time to march.

Gordon complained bitterly that the 15th had done all the outpost duty since the start of the retreat. It seemed, he wrote, to be a 'settled system of our leaders to save the Tenth and Seventh as much as possible, out of compliment to the Prince of Wales and Lord Paget.' But these two regiments, who had now reached Villafranca, were in an equally bad way. Verner's remarks on the state of the horses of the 7th Hussars have already been quoted, and in the 10th, according to Slade, things were not much better. During the retreat so far Captain Darby and seventeen men had died of fatigue and sixty horses had been destroyed.

The 15th spent the morning of 3 January skirmishing with the 3rd Hussars and 15th Chasseurs of General Colbert's brigade, in the country between Cubillos and Caçabelos, 'celebrated in *Gil Blas*, fenced with hedges, and intersected with corn and turnip fields'. Slade came out to see what was going on, but soon left, saying that he had to make a report to Sir John Moore who, according to Gordon, told him that the proper post for a general officer 'was at the head of his brigade or division when in the presence of the enemy'. Gordon thought that the General must have 'considered the Tenth as the head of his brigade', for they saw no more of him.

In the early afternoon the 15th were ordered to rejoin the main body of Hussars at Villafranca and retired slowly, while the enemy 'followed at the same pace along the high road, with a band of music playing at the head of their column'. At Caçabelos they suddenly seemed to realize how weak the 15th were and promptly charged them. There was some fierce hand-to-hand fighting at the entrance to the town, during which a marksman of the 95th Rifles, Tom Plunkett, shot dead General Colbert, and one of the 15th decapitated a French Chasseur 'at a single blow'. Several accounts of this day's skirmishing mention that the French cavalry had a rifleman mounted behind each man, who would dismount when any good position 'or bushes by the side of the road, gave them any advantage to give our men a few shots'. At the same time the French Chasseurs would dismount, rest their carbines on their saddles, 'with their horses standing in front of them for a sort of defence, and give us a few shots as well'. During the day some of the 15th Hussars, 'who had got drunk and were unable to march' were butchered by the French cavalry. One of those missing, presumed killed, was Private Smith of Gordon's troop, a veteran of Villers-en-Cauchie. He had fought well at Benevente, acquiring in the process thirty or forty dubloons; thereafter he was scarcely ever sober, and on this occasion had been left with the baggage and 'dismounted men'.[6]

Villafranca was the usual scene of complete confusion. Not only was the town packed with troops, but there was also a large stores depot, and Verner thought it 'most provoking to see the indiscriminate way in which vital supplies were destroyed'. He remembered the river running black with powder, and cannon balls 'nearly as plentiful as stones'. The abandoned artillery pieces were made unserviceable by cutting the spokes of the wheels, 'but for want of time these attempts in many instances failed'. 'The confusion in Villa Franca,' Hodge wrote in his diary, 'was dreadful. All the stores, ammunition, and heavy baggage was ordered to be destroyed and the river and streets were full of the wreck.' During the night the stables where Lord Paget's horses were put up caught fire and Elphi Bey, 'subject of so many noble portraits', Harlequin, and a French horse, taken by the 15th at Sahagun, were suffocated by smoke. According to Hodge, Lord Paget's groom 'was so much scorched it is not known whether he will recover.'

Some of the Hussars now started to plunder the houses of the inhabitants, and that afternoon a private of the 7th Hussars was executed, as an example to the others. According to various accounts three men were detected 'in the act of stealing some wearing apparel of the inhabitants, and in the attempt to break open a box'. As Schaumann pointed out, thousands had done the same, and much worse, but this time Sir John Moore happened to be passing. George Napier, one of his aides-de-camp, claimed that he and Captain Pasley had caught one of them plundering a house in broad daylight, and that he had struck Pasley while being seized. In the event the three culprits were marched to an open space where all the troops then in Villafranca were formed up and forced to draw lots for their lives. The loser, Private Day, of Captain Treveake's troop, 'previously a very steady, good soldier', was led out and shot. The brigade then filed past the body 'and proceeded on their route'. 'The sight was distressing,' Berkeley Paget thought, 'and notwithstanding the absolute necessity of making an example, one could not but feel extreme compassion for the unfortunate creature.'

The whole army was ordered to retire to Lugo, a distance of sixteen leagues. From now on the road followed a succession of defiles and strong passes, most unsuitable for cavalry, and one squadron only of the 15th was left behind, together with the 3rd Germans and the light brigade of infantry, to form the rearguard. Leaving Villafranca the *Caminho Réal* followed the side of a deep valley, with tremendous precipices on either side, clad with tall chestnuts and oaks. It was a nightmare march, Vivian recalled, 'over a most immense mountain, on which several hale men were soon dead from the intense cold and fatigue'. The cavalry marched at a rate 'almost incredible', the 7th Hussars taking only twenty-six hours to complete the journey to Lugo, including a four-hour halt, 'but this rate of marching had the effect of destroying the horses, which never recovered from it'. General Slade, who, now that both Lord Paget and Sir Charles Stewart had been struck down with ophthalmia, was in command of the cavalry, wrote in his diary that they left Villafranca at four in the afternoon, on 3 January, halted for a couple of hours at Las Herrerias and reached Lugo between ten and eleven at night on 4 January.[7]

Berkeley Paget, who 'could not have conceived so bad a march as the army made', arrived about midnight at the little village of Los Nogales, after climbing the mountain, fifteen miles up and eight down. The horses were dropping with fatigue and some of them had to be shot for want of shoes. He himself, after the loss of his canteens, had for several days now been suffering 'much from want of food'. He had eaten nothing except what he could pick up from his friends, whom he was 'scrupulous of calling upon', as they were not much better off than himself. 'About midnight,' Hodge wrote:

we reached the highest mountain in Galicia, which we found covered with snow, the road covered with baggage of all sorts, Artillery, men, women and children laying frozen and freezing to death without a possibility of rendering them assistance, and our horses, with those of the Artillery, so fatigued they were dropping every hundred yards, where we were obliged to cut their throats and leave them. It snowed the whole way over the mountain and so piercing a wind I never remember. A Sergeant of ours fell dead from his horse, overcome by cold and fatigue. When we reached Los Nogales the horses were obliged to be lined in the fields and the men [to] lie down with them, and the only astonishment is that one half survived.

The 15th Hussars, following behind the 7th, reached Los Nogales at nine in the morning of 4 January. They, too, had made a dreadful march and had been forced to destroy fourteen horses. The scenes they had witnessed were much as described by Paget and Hodge. Amid the horrors they passed the bodies of two soldier's wives, one of whom 'had been delivered of twins only three days before', and another 'with an infant at her breast'. Fortunately the children in both cases were alive and were picked up by some of the infantry. Dr Neale, being of an enquiring turn of mind, had the curiosity to 'count the dead horses and mules for the space of two leagues, and at a moderate calculation their value amounted to more than twenty thousand pounds'. This great loss he attributed, quite correctly, to want of shoes. 'Horse-shoes, as they are made in England, are so extremely heavy,' he continued, 'that no Dragoon can well carry more than four.' He advocated using 'Light Turkish ones', and making every Dragoon 'occasionally shoe his own horse, which is not a very difficult operation'. The 15th halted at Los Nogales for two hours, and then carried on to Constantino, where they arrived between three and four in the afternoon. During their march they had passed 'all the fine Spanish brass artillery, the carriages of which had been burned'. At one stage, Gordon recalled, they had been overtaken by the two ophthalmic cavalry leaders; Lord Paget 'looked very interesting', with a white handkerchief bound over his eyes, his horse led by the fearsome Colonel Elley. After a day of torrential rain Gordon was glad to obtain some wet straw in the loft of a miserable hovel, in the company of a dozen officers, soldiers and servants, 'all distinction of rank being levelled by the distress and danger to which all were equally exposed'.[8]

That night the 7th and 10th were at Lugo, where Berkeley Paget managed at last to assuage his appetite with some bacon and eggs, kindly provided by some officers he found in the quarters allotted to him, and he 'never made a more hearty meal or enjoyed one more'. He calculated that they had now marched nearly 700 miles in thirty-three days, with only eight halting days.

On 5 January the army remained quiet. During the afternoon the 15th Hussars came in from Constantino, but had great difficulty finding quarters, and had to be content with the shelter provided by the 'piazzas in the plaza'. Adjutant Jones sent Cornet Laroche back to Corunna, sick. 'Sick, indeed,' he exploded in his journal, 'why the whole army is sick and sorry too! and in addition extremely mutinous.' That night Dr Neale hurriedly finished off a letter home, as a friend was just about to leave for Corunna in charge of three officers of the Imperial Guard taken at Benevente. They were, he wrote, 'good-looking men with enormous moustaches,' in scarlet jackets adorned with gold lace, but their 'manners and address' completely betrayed 'the rank which they held in society before the revolution'. Perhaps he was referring to an incident, later reported in *The Times*, concerning a French colonel, taken at Benevente and sent under escort to Corunna. On arriving at a town near Lugo:

the party were unable to procure a breakfast either by entreaty or money: the Frenchman laughed at the embarrassment of our Officer and observing that we had yet much to learn in the science of campaigning, begged to be allowed to cater for the party; he called the man of the house, and on his appearing, knocked him down with the hilt of his sword: he then commanded him to provide breakfast, adding, that if he delayed, he would help himself. The inhospitable host profited by the hint, and in a few minutes provided a profusion of everything.[9]

The next morning the rearguard, still consisting of part of the 15th Hussars and a few companies of the 95th Rifles, came in from Los Nogales. In the afternoon the enemy appeared. The whole army was turned out and marched out about a league on the road back to Villafranca. Nothing, however, 'passed beyond a little skirmishing,' and the cavalry returned to their quarters in the evening. Otherwise the day was spent replacing equipment and reorganizing the regiments, while biscuit, rum and salt beef, from the 'sea-stores' sent up from Corunna, were issued out. It was in Lugo, wrote Tale, who had been horseless ever since leaving La Bañeza, that 'the gloom and sulkiness . . . was in a manner dissipated by an order to brush up and look out for a fight'. Those 'of the dismounted' were ordered to put the 'flint and steel' of their carbines in 'ignitable order, be prepared to shoulder them, and march to glory'.

During the next two days, the 7th and 8th, a strong French corps arrived and took possession of the hills in front of Lugo. On both days the army marched out, as Sir John Moore tried to tempt the enemy to do battle, with the Hussars taking their place in the British line. Captain Gordon, moving up to his position, was amazed at the change that had come over the British infantry, who 'with the prospect of being led against the foe . . . had at once recovered all those qualities for which British soldiers are peculiarly estimable'. Every order 'was obeyed with alacrity' and there was no trace 'of the discontent and insubordination which had been so general for the last few days'.[10] At length Moore realized that the enemy had no intention of swallowing his bait and, as his supplies were running low, he decided to continue the retreat to Corunna. During the afternoon of 8 January Slade and the 10th were sent back to secure the vital bridge over the Minho, at Rabade, halfway back to Bahamonde. As darkness fell the artillery was pulled out and, later in the evening, the infantry began their march. The 15th Hussars assembled by the town gates and, as they waited for the infantry to leave, the left squadron of the regiment was ordered to take charge of 35,000 dollars which had been left behind. 'Sealed bags,' Gordon wrote, 'each containing 500 dollars, were distributed to the troopers, and in this manner about £8,000 was saved to the nation.' The additional weight of nearly two stone added to the weight already carried by the worn-out horses only added to their distress.

In spite of the fact that they had already, as Hodge put it, 'borne the brunt of the business the whole way,' the Hussars were again ordered to form the rearguard, and this time the task fell to the 7th, 'which then consisted of about 150 effectives'. Berkeley Paget, who was in charge, kept huge fires burning all night and did not abandon the advance posts until nearly five in the morning of the 9th, when the French discovered that the British had left undetected. Two hours later they crossed the Minho at Rabade in pouring rain, driving some 2,000 stragglers before them. The bridge was then blown, 'but not,' Slade reported, 'so effectively but that the advanced guard of the French contrived to harass our rear most exceedingly.' From here on the *Caminho Réal* to Corunna was one long trail of stragglers, bare-footed, exhausted and starving, the appearance of order and discipline, so noticeable at Lugo, having been rapidly dispelled. Every wayside hovel was packed with men who preferred to stop where they were and risk being shot, or worse, rather than continue their seemingly hopeless march. To the 7th fell the disagreable job of flushing them out and pushing them on. 'Wherever they found straw,' Vivian recalled, 'they rolled themselves up in it,' and tried to hide from his men, who found 'the only means was to prick with our swords in order to discover them.' According to Slade it was 'a most fatiguing march, as we did not go above two miles an hour, being obliged to regulate our pace by the infantry, and it rained incessantly for thirty-six hours.'

That afternoon the 7th and 10th rode into Bahamonde, after a march that was 'the most uncomfortable thing that could be imagined'. Leaving their men to fend for themselves, huddling together in a nearby field, the officers of both regiments packed themselves into a nearby hovel. The 15th pushed on to the inn at Guitirez, where Lord Paget and the Hollands had put up on the way out. It was crowded with officers and men sheltering from a violent hailstorm, but they managed to get 200 horses into a large stable. Adjutant Jones decided to relieve the men of their money-bags and, seizing some mules 'by dint of force', sent off 30,000 dollars in the charge of Sergeant Roberts. At eleven o'clock that night the bugles sounded and the 15th formed up on the road, while the tail end of the army filed slowly past.

The 7th and 10th at Bahamonde were roused at seven, and at nine set off on another 'dreadful night march'. The high road, once so smooth, was now so broken up by the weather and traffic that the infantry had to plough their way through mud over a foot deep. With daylight on the 10th 400 French Chasseurs appeared, driving before them a solid phalanx of stragglers, who had somehow managed to achieve a semblance of military order. Perhaps this was the body of stragglers which, according to *The Times*, a sergeant of the 43rd had formed up 'regularly into sub-divisions and commenced firing and retiring in a slow and orderly manner'. Some of the infantry regiments appeared almost deserted and both Gordon and Verner recalled seeing one march into Betanzos which consisted of two sergeants carrying the colours 'and not more than thirty men with them'.[11]

During the afternoon the 15th entered Betanzos and at four o'clock the 7th and 10th retired through the infantry reserve, leaving behind a squadron of the 18th Hussars, under Lieutenant-Colonel Jones, and eighty men of the 10th, under Lord Charles Manners. As the 7th gave up their duties with the rear-guard, Vivian summed up the hardships his regiment had suffered:

Scarcely, since the retreat from Grajal commenced [had the regiment] had the saddles off their horses' backs for above five or six hours at any time, and seldom so long; having been almost constantly wet, without the means of changing; having lost our camp-kettles, from the mules which carried them dying or knocking up in the mountains, and consequently having no meat to eat but was toasted on the point of the swords . . .

That night Adjutant Jones recorded in his diary that General Slade had gone off to Corunna pleading sickness, only to return unexpectedly during the evening. Gordon, an assiduous collector of gossip where his Brigadier was concerned, claimed that Slade, having left the army with Sir John Moore's permission, established himself in comfortable quarters, 'took a dose of Camomil, and retired to bed'. Unfortunately for him Lord Paget, also recuperating in the town, got wind of his presence and forced him to return to his brigade 'in a soaking rain, regardless of his pathetic remonstrances and internal commotions'.

The next morning, 11 January, the army resumed its march to Corunna. All the way from Betanzos the French cavalry hung about the edges of the rearguard and there was skirmishing at the bridge at Burgo, some two leagues short of Corunna. Losses were light on both sides, although the enemy succeeded in carrying off General Baird's travelling coach and baggage. At long last the sea came into view and everyone's spirits rose, only to be sadly dashed a few moments later when it was obvious that there were very few ships in the harbour, the main fleet, which had been ordered round from Vigo, having been delayed by adverse winds.

Moore, now confronted with the task of holding the French at bay until the transports arrived from Vigo, formed his army up on a chain of low hills outside the town. The cavalry rode on into Corunna, taking up their old quarters in the barracks at St Lucia and in the town itself. Tale thought what a 'melancholy display . . . the King's Hussars' now made, compared with 'their efficient and soldier-like appearance a few weeks before'. They were now 'almost horseless, bootless, shoeless, ragged, dirty, and something worse'.

The town of Corunna presented a picture of uninterrupted bustle, with the streets full of troops, 'and the inhabitants, both male and female, transporting cannon and ammunition to the walls'. Even some of the shopkeepers, shutting up their premises, hurried to the town gates to share the guard duties with the British sentries posted there. Hodge, who could hardly move with 'colic' and pain in his bones, was not too hopeful about their chances of survival once the British left. The next morning, as the officers of the Hussar Brigade were enjoying their first decent breakfast for weeks, two tremendous explosions shook Corunna to its foundations, 'broke the panes of the windows, and made the plaster and tiles fall from the roofs and ceilings'. Apparently 12,000 barrels of powder, sent from England for the use of the 'patriots', but never issued by the *Junta*, and stored in two buildings near St Lucia, had been blown up on Sir John Moore's orders to prevent them falling into the hands of the enemy. According to one observer the explosion and the immense column of dense black smoke which hung over the town all day was a 'magnificent sight, but it did great damage to the city, which rocked as with an earthquake and several men were killed'.

After this noisy start the rest of the day passed off quietly. The Hussars, apart from those on picquet duty with the outposts, remained in their quarters. For one thing 'the bad state of the shoeing and the excessive fatigue they had undergone completely rendered them unfit for service', nor 'did any of the ground about Corunna admit of the Cavalry acting with any good effect'. There was plenty to be done, however, in the way of 'interior economy'. In the quarters of the 15th Hussars a Regimental Court-Martial was assembled to try those who had committed offences during the retreat and had, so far, escaped justice.[12] Those who were barefooted were issued with boots or shoes from the central stores, and later the regiment paraded 'in Watering Order' for an inspection of the horses, after which about fifty were destroyed. Finally, much to everyone's relief, the transports from Vigo started coming into harbour. The following day was much the same; more transports came in, while outside the town the army still faced its pursuers.

The next day, 14 January, the 7th Hussars started to embark, and Berkeley Paget, at his brother's suggestion, went aboard the *Anne*, Hired Armed Brig, carrying Brigadier-General Stewart with despatches. By nightfall most of the sick and part of the horses and guns of the artillery had been loaded. On the 15th more transports arrived and the sick and dismounted men of the 15th Hussars were embarked, together with the rest of the Royal Horse Artillery and the Wagon Train, who managed to ship all the horses that were worth taking home. Those of the Hussars were not so lucky, for, following General Moore's orders that only thirty troop-horses from each regiment were to be embarked, harrowing scenes were taking place on shore. Many hundreds were shot on the beach at low tide, Adjutant Jones wrote in his journal, in the hope 'that the tide on its way might wash them out to sea'. Others were simply driven over a cliff. The town, Gordon recalled, 'exhibited the appearance of a vast slaughter house'. Wounded horses, mad with pain, were to be seen running through the streets and the ground was covered with the mangled carcasses of 'these noble animals, for in consequence of their uncertain aim, the men were latterly directed to cut the throats of the horses, instead of attempting to shoot them'.

When the 10th and the 3rd Germans started embarking the next day they could only load very few of their horses. The 'arrangement that was made for the transports,' was so bad, 'the horses were rowed about the harbour till a transport could be found to receive them.' Gordon reckoned that the 7th and 10th Hussars embarked ninety horses between them, the 15th Hussars thirty, and the 18th Hussars and the 3rd Germans none at all, having, it is said, been forced to destroy 290, sound as well as lame. Of Hodge's troop, originally eighty-five strong, thirty-five horses were shot, only nine being considered fit for service.[13]

At about half-past three on the afternoon of 16 January, as Colonel Long, who had come in with the fleet and at once reported for duty at headquarters, noted in his memorandum book, 'the French began an attack which lasted until dark at night,' and 'Sir John Moore [was] desperately wounded and Sir D. Baird the same.' When the action was over he returned to Corunna and attended Sir John Moore in his last moments. Moore died at eight o'clock, just as the evening gun was fired on board the Admiral's ship. The army drew off during the night and, together with the wounded, was taken off in the ships' boats.

Before dawn on the 17th the rearguard stepped into the waiting boats, 'without having experienced the slightest molestation from the enemy.' However, before they could all be got off, a squall suddenly blew up and drove two of the transports on to the rocks in the middle of the harbour. In the midst of this confusion the French managed to establish a battery on the heights of St Lucia, which commanded the harbour and, at about eleven o'clock, they opened fire on the shipping. 'Cut and run was the order of the day,' wrote Tale, as the captain of his vessel 'in common with many others, separated from his anchor' and set sail 'the breeze being propitious'. Many of the ships fouled each other in their haste to get to sea, carrying away yards, bowsprits and rigging, and Vivian saw several run aground on the rocks between the Island of St Antonio and the citadel. After the troops had been taken out and put aboard other vessels they were burnt. 'Perhaps,' he wrote, 'no fleet of transports ever got under way so quickly,' and in less than half an hour the bay was clear. A 74-gun ship stood in towards the French battery and, opening fire, eventually silenced it, while her boats took off the remainder of the rearguard.

The fleet lay off Cape Prior during the night. In the morning it was joined by the 74 with the rearguard on board, and the whole fleet set sail for England. Safely on board a British ship, with young FitzClarence still in attendance, General Slade was full of gratitude to the Royal Navy. 'It is not in the power of language,' he wrote, 'to do justice to the exertions of the navy in getting us off.' It was evident to him that without their aid they would have been 'obliged to have left many thousands behind'.

The misfortunes which the army suffered during the retreat did not end with the embarkation for England. The troops were no sooner on board, thoroughly mixed up and dispersed throughout the fleet, than a gale blew up and any attempt to sort them into their proper units proved impossible. As a result, some transports came home empty, while others, as Gordon recalled, 'carried more than double the number of men for which they were intended,' and the sick and wounded, in particular, suffered badly. Corporal Tale found himself on a hospital ship packed with the sick and convalescent, for many of whom it was 'their last living home'. Once on board, 'as several weeks had gone by without an opportunity of peeling or indulging in a wash, those refreshing and invigorating operations were now put into practice'.

Commissary Schaumann returned on the *Nimrod*, which carried twenty-two officers and 220 men, apart from the crew. On the first night out there was confusion in the cabin. Officers of the rank of Colonel Alten and Major Hay of the 18th Hussars, for instance, had taken possession of the bunks, while the rest of them had to lie packed together like sardines on the floor. They formed three rows; 'the first row spread out their legs and allowed the second to lay their heads between them, and the third lay with their heads between the legs of the second.' They were given the same sailor's fare as the men; in the morning a 'pailful of porridge or gruel, with a large lump of butter floating on the top of it'; at midday they had 'peas and salt meat with a portion of rum which looked quite black'; and at night a little hard cheese and some ship's biscuit. Major Griffith, of the 15th Hussars, returned nursing his sick nephew. 'The dirt, stink, & wretchedness of a transport,' he was to write later to his sister, 'added to the tumbling' they got in the Bay of Biscay, seemed to be making his patient worse, but fortunately the regimental surgeon was also on board 'so that he had every assistance necessary', and was soon on the mend.

The homeward passage was 'rough, gusty, and disagreeable', and the fleet was soon scattered. Many vessels were wrecked and the remainder, driving up Channel, were, in Vivian's words, 'glad to put into any port; and the soldiers, thus thrown ashore, were scattered from Land's End to Dover'. Gordon had the terrifying experience of nearly being wrecked off the Isle of Wight, when the Master of his vessel mistook the 'light of the Needles' for a star and was only put right in his reckoning by the Paymaster of the 15th. 'The ignorance of the shipmasters in general,' he wrote, 'was so gross that it is surprising so few of the vessels were lost.' When his ship finally anchored in Stokes Bay on 24 January there were only two or three hospital ships there. More transports came in the next day, but there was a violent storm which lasted for several days, during which 'several of the fleet were wrecked and others incurred imminent danger'.

The worst disaster of all befell the *Despatch* Transport, George Fenwick Master, with part of Captains Treveake's and Dukenfield's troops of the 7th Hussars on board. About half past three on the morning of 21 January she was 'driven upon the rocks near Coverack, and all on board perished except seven private Dragoons'. According to the *Gentleman's Magazine*, the dead, apart from Major Cavendish, Captain Duckenfield [sic], and Lieutenant Waldegrave, consisted of 'Eight non-commissioned officers and about 60 privates of the Regiment . . . with 5 women and 32 horses'. With them went down the whole of the linen, three-quarters of the plate and a complete set of tea kettles, dishes, and plates 'adapted for service', belonging to the officers' mess.[14]

'Thus,' wrote Adjutant Jones, 'ended this destructive and disastrous campaign', in which, he believed, they had lost everything including their honour, the final insult being Napoleon's boast that he had driven the English easily into the sea. From the moment the Hussar Brigade had disembarked at Corunna 'big with expectation and high in hopes', they had, in slightly over eight weeks, marched some 873 miles through extremely mountainous country, in bad weather, with bad food and worse accommodation. They had fought several successful skirmishes with their opponent's battle-tried cavalry, including the classic night action at Sahagun, and at Benevente they had put Napoleon's much-vaunted Imperial Guard to flight. They had, on the whole, justified the faith of Lord Paget and the Duke of Cumberland in the efficacy of well-trained light cavalry, even if they had at times, as at Rueda, sought glory when discretion would have been of more advantage to Sir John Moore. While the campaign had ended unfavourably for the British Government, the

Hussar Brigade could take some pride in the fact that they had done their duty with discipline and endurance. Their newfangled dress and equipment had suffered considerably, and had proved, in some respects, to be far from practical, although the Hungarian saddles had worked well and few horses seem to have been disabled through sore backs. The real disaster was the loss of so many fine horses, which was directly caused by a dire shortage of shoeing facilities. When an infantry officer asked why so many apparently fit horses were being destroyed, he was invariably told that 'from the roughness of the road, hardened by continued frost, they cast their shoes, and that they had not a nail to fasten those picked up, nor a shoe to replace those lost; and they added that there was not a spare nail or shoe in any of the forge carts, which retired with the cavalry'.

The casualties among the men were, if the returns are to be relied on, extremely light. Subtracting the figures given by Oman for January, 1809, from those given for October, 1808, the 7th Hussars had the heaviest losses of ninety-seven, which included the fifty-six men drowned in the *Despatch*. The 10th and the 15th lost twenty-four men each, the 18th lost seventy-seven, and the 3rd Germans, who probably saw more action than the others, and who suffered forty-six casualties at Benevente alone, lost fifty-six.[15] As for the Brigade Commander, he had been a great disappointment to Lord Paget and far from the ideal of a *Beau Sabreur* in the true Hussar style. Fortunately for him he was never again to serve with Lord Paget and for years after the treatment he had received at his hands still rankled. Shortly after Lord Paget's death, in April 1854, Slade wrote of him that he 'was a most gallant soldier; but of so unfortunate a temper he rendered it almost impossible to serve under him'.[16] As for Lord Paget himself, Corporal Tale spoke for the ordinary soldier, whose voice, in the Hussars at any rate, has been seldom heard:

To say that he was liked by the soldier, would convey but a faint idea of his popularity; he was almost idolized – ay, worshipped by them. All had an opportunity of witnessing his abilities as a cavalry officer; and his noble beauty, winning and captivating manner when addressing the men, secured him in the enviable enjoyment of every conceivable wish which a great and good commander should look for – the heart and affections of all under him. It was a common expression amongst the troopers that they would follow him to [Hell].

* * *

Throughout January, 1809, England waited anxiously for news of the army in Spain. There were plenty of rumours but very little reliable information. A bright spot in the general gloom was the arrival of the captive Lefebvre-Desnoëttes. On the 12th *The Times* reported his departure from Plymouth for Reading, where he was to 'remain prisoner on parole'. He was 'about 35 years old, and was most splendidly drest' with the star of the Legion of Honour on his breast.[17] The next day, in a letter to Mrs Fitzherbert, the Prince of Wales wrote of his 'state of anxiety about the news from Spain', which he thought would be of the 'utmost importance' as it would almost certainly bring accounts of the embarkation of the army and 'probably of a most desparate engagement previous to its being accomplished'. He had received the 'best accounts' of the conduct of his regiment, which were 'extremely gratifying'.

By the 22nd there was more definite news and Colonel Bloomfield had the melancholy task of writing to Sir John Lade, on behalf of the Prince, to announce the death of 'poor Darby', who had succumbed to the fever in spite of 'every possible attention . . . that skill and care cou'd effect'. His body, hastily buried at Corunna, was disinterred, shipped home, and reburied in Falmouth on the 25th.[19] About the same time Harriet Cavendish read in the papers that both Frederick Howard and Agenor de Grammont had behaved most gallantly, which made her 'quite adore them'. 'A young man unused to such scenes, distinguishing himself in them, does make me enthusiastic,' she wrote, unaware that her cousin George had perished in the loss of the *Despatch* on the 21st. On the 24th the Duke of Clarence told George that his mother had been 'very unhappy and even ill' on his account, but the letter he had received from, and the 'accounts of General Slade', would set her up again.

By the 28th, when the storms had abated, and as arrangements were being made at Portsmouth to collect the army 'on board their proper Regimental transports', it was learned that many of the vessels had put into Falmouth and Plymouth. The next day, as the weather was still bad, and the men increasingly sickly, it was decided to disembark them. As the boats unloaded their cargoes of sick and wounded in Portsmouth harbour the full extent of the disaster was revealed to the waiting public. When the ragged, filthy and exhausted soldiers, riddled with typhus, came ashore the country was horrified. Of the 34,000 who had set out to liberate Spain some 28,000 returned. The losses of the campaign amounted to 5,998, of whom 3,809 had perished on the road or in hospital, and 2,189 had been left prisoners in French hands. Although forewarned, an earlier and inept decision of the Medical Board in London to close the hospitals at Gosport, Plymouth and Deal on the grounds of economy meant that there was not a single bed ready to receive the 6,000 sick who eventually turned up. 'When our brave troops were embarking here to aid the Spaniards,' declared the *Hampshire Telegraph*, on 30 January, 'we never anticipated such a result to their campaign as we have been the painful witness of these few days.' Fortunately the Portsmouth area had had a very efficient Inspector in the person of Dr James McGrigor, later to become Wellington's chief Medical Officer in the Peninsula. Immediate steps were taken to set up temporary hospitals in barracks, and in hulks, transports and prison ships anchored in Spithead. The Navy offered the use of Haslar Hospital and some 1,400 cases were found accommodation there. The surgeons of the Guards were ordered down from London and every civil practitioner around Portsmouth was employed.[20] In addition, private citizens played their part, conveying the troops to the Town Hall in coaches, 'where they were provided with a good dinner consisting of soup and roast beef'. It was impossible, General Dyott wrote in his journal, on 2 February

> to imagine anything at all like the streets of Portsmouth from the crowds of officers, soldiers, dragoons, and dragoon horses; as the greater part of the troops from Corunna were disembarking; such miserable tattered beings I never saw, so wan and worn out, both with respect to drapery and general appearance, was never before exhibited.

Similar scenes took place wherever the troops landed, particularly at Plymouth where Corporal Tale disembarked on 30 January. The sick and incapable were deposited in the town, while a 'motley and queer-looking group of several score of the King's Hussars were prepared to march *à pied* and join the home squadron', having succeeded in mustering only one troop-horse. According to Vivian,

> The haggard appearance of the men, their ragged clothing, and dirty accoutrements – things common enough in war – struck a people only used to the daintyness of parade with surprise. A deadly fever filled the hospitals at every port with officers and men, and the miserable state of Sir John Moore's army became the topic of every letter and the theme of every country newspaper along the coast.

The 3rd German Hussars, Major Heise recalled, did not cut 'a very brilliant figure', landing without horses and baggage, but were not, on that account, any less well-received:

> 'D-n all the horses,' said a thorough John Bull in reply to the dispiriting observations of a bystander on the state of the regiment, 'Yorkshire has horses enough to mount them again – Thank God the lives of the brave men are saved'.

At Plymouth the local charities made strenuous attempts to cope with the flood of sick, wounded and distressed soldiers' women and children, 900 in number, who had been landed 'all ignorant whether their husbands were dead or living'. A Committee of Gentlemen sat day and night

> to afford supplies of food, cloathing, and assistance to those who required immediate aid, and every woman, of every description, who has a second garment has given it to the sufferers. Every house has become a hospital; for every family receives a sick or wounded person, giving food, and necessaries of all kinds. Notwithstanding these exertions, great numbers are dying every day; all business gives way to the calls of suffering humanity. Ladies in person attend the sick and wounded, dressing the wounds of the soldiers themselves; thus supplying the want

of a sufficient number of medical men, at the same time that many of the wounds, from not having been examined, were in a putrid and most offensive state . . .

'Now indeed' *The Times* reported on 30 January, 'we have the miseries of war brought home to our own doors; for the scenes here are beyond any pen to describe.' In all the 'Charitable Fund' in Plymouth had relieved '753 women with clothes and money, 525 children with clothes, and 124 pregnant women, who received additional relief on account of their situation'; so that the number of women and children 'relieved by the liberality of the town and its neighbourhood amounted to over 1,400.'

CHAPTER FIVE
Old England Once More

During the first weeks of February, 1809, scattered parties started arriving at their regimental headquarters. Adjutant Jones, having seen his men of the 15th Hussars off from Portsmouth, was in Romford on 7 February, in time to see the first division of the regiment arrive 'in as good order as could be expected'. Corporal Tale describes the 'joyful reunion' at Romford, where all were immediately set to work:

> No come-day, go-day, God-send-Sunday goings on; energy and emulation pervaded all. His Royal Highness was often with us and shared barrack accomodation. With such able and willing materials to work with, it ceases to create surprise that an incredibly short space of time elapsed before we were again in the saddle.

First the men were inspected by the Surgeon and found to be 'in a tollerable state of health & Cleanliness'. Then forms were issued to be filled up with details of the losses of arms, accoutrements, clothing, necessaries and appointments sustained during the campaign. Stragglers had to be gathered up and fresh remounts obtained. No more than eight to ten horses per troop had returned and the arms and appointments were 'deficient in proportion'.

On 18 February Major Leitch came in with the party from Falmouth and Plymouth, with nineteen more horses, having left a number of sick behind on the way. A week later the first of the remounts arrived at Romford, and on the 28th regular drills commenced. There was an unfortunate reminder of the hardships and frustrations of the retreat when Captains Griffith and Gordon, still harbouring ill-feelings on the subject of Lord Paget's 'nursing' of the 7th and 10th during the retreat, refused to assent to the presentation of plate to Lord Paget.

During March new boots and clothing were given out and the sick began to come in, with various tales of their treatment. The 'Countess Dowager Stanhope', of Chivering Heath, had been particularly public-spirited, paying for the sick soldiers out of her own pocket; but others, like the doctor in Sherborne, less generous, sent in their accounts, while the 'overseers at Petworth' so importuned the Adjutant with demands for payment that he told them to send their 'exorbitant Bills for attendance on sick men to the War

Office as the Regt would not pay it'. The news of the retreat took a long time to penetrate to the depths of the country and it was not until 14 March that the Adjutant started receiving letters 'from the relations of numbers of the men enquiring after their safety'.

On 18 April, the 15th paraded in full dress for the first time and four days later turned out for the half-yearly inspection, the District commander expressing 'his entire satisfaction at the high state of discipline in which the Regt appeared notwithstanding its recent losses'. Their experiences on campaign had prompted some sensible changes in dress and equipment. For a start, the new remounts were bought regardless of sex or colour, whereas previously mares had been excluded and the colours regularized by troops. Certain colours were more popular than others – brown muzzles and dark bays were supposed to have more endurance and stamina, and chestnuts and light bays greater speed – so they were now ballotted for by troop captains. The black leather bridlery, which seldom looked good 'except when fresh from the influences of "Warren" or "Day & Martin"'[1] was replaced by brown, which was easier to clean, while the use of saddle soap 'nourished its properties and preserved its pliability'. The topheavy cardboard-lined fur caps were relegated to full dress and peakless shakos, which afforded better protection, adopted in their place.

Similar scenes took place in the 7th Hussars at Guildford. On 20 February courts of enquiry were set up to assess the losses of the regiment, the extent of which can be gauged from the total sum claimed, which was, in round figures, £6,630, while a further claim was made in July for £602 for 'Extraordinary wear and tear' on the surviving articles.[2] In the end the regiment received some £5,500 in settlement, although some items were still being discussed in 1812. The officers also put in claims for the loss of camp equipment and other articles, such as a 'tent complete'; 'extra necessaries for the men'; 'dollars'; '2 English horses destroyed by order of the Commanding Officer'; 'a pair of canteens'; ' One Mule which cost 80 Dollars'; 'my Irish charger'. They were allowed compensation of £2,147, of which Berkeley Paget, who, it will be recalled, lost his mule and canteens on the retreat, received £152. When the regiment turned out for the half-yearly inspection, the District commander reported that the clothing, accoutrements, and appointments of the regiment had suffered 'much injury from their recent service in Spain', but the 'artificers and tradesmen' were busily engaged in forwarding the necessary repairs.

The *Hampshire Telegraph* reported the progress of the 10th Hussars from its port of disembarkation to Brighton Barracks. The regiment had been under the necessity of shooting about 540 horses in the course of their retreat and previous to its embarkation, but when they passed through Southampton on 2 February, 'they had no less than 19 baggage waggons in their train'. During the week ending 18 February stragglers continued to pass through Brighton, 'on their march to rejoin their respective regiments,' and there was growing concern at the 'considerable sickness' prevailing among them. On the 25th the paper announced that Grisdale, 'the brave fellow of the 10th Light Dragoons, who so gallantly took the French General Lefebvre prisoner' was at Brighton with his regiment. He was, we are told,

> a tall, well-made, and well-looking man: his countenance is ruddy and expressive, and strongly indicative of his possessing that resolute spirit, which should at all times characterize the Briton and the soldier. We have not yet heard that he has been rewarded for the above service, but we trust that his merits may, and, we are convinced they will, be taken into consideration by his Royal Commander.

The hint appears to have been taken and on 6 March it was reported that 'by command of his Colonel' Grisdale had been 'raised to the rank of Corporal, as the first step to his future promotion'.[3] At the end of March the 10th Hussars were in sufficiently good order to be reviewed by Lord Charles Somerset, who commanded the District, and in May they underwent the usual half-yearly inspection. Attached to the Inspecting Officer's report was a return of 'Articles wanting to complete the 10th L.D. for active service', which listed fur caps, dress jackets, sashes, overalls, sabretaches and saddlery. By the Prince's birthday, when the regiment paraded dismounted with the Militia, these deficiencies seem to have been made up, apart from the lack of horses. In a few months the Duke of Clarence wrote to George, 'your friends the Tenth Hussars will be compleat and fit for everything'.[4] The next day he and the Prince spent five hours looking at the young horses and the day after that three hours with the men.

The list of missing articles submitted to the Inspecting Officer had been signed by Quentin who, as second Lieutenant-Colonel, was now acting as Commanding Officer of the 10th, Colonel Leigh having been caught out cheating the Prince over the sale of a horse. The Prince wanted Leigh not only out of the 10th but also 'Newmarket and the Turf', and his friends warned Leigh that he had 'not a day, not an hour, to lose' in obeying his patron's commands. He had also, according to the diarist Farington, been swindling the men by supplying them with articles 'at a very advanced price, by which He put money in His pocket'. In June an adverse report was made to the Prince, which was forwarded on to the King, and Leigh would almost certainly have been court-martialled had not the former exerted his influence in favour of his friend.[5] In the end the matter was settled by Leigh resigning his lieutenant-colonelcy, to which Major Palmer was promoted, 'being the next officer in succession on paying abt. 1000 guineas'. Thus on 3 May, 1810, the date of Palmer's promotion, were sown the seeds of the rivalry which was to have such a drastic effect on the future careers of the officers of the Prince's Regiment.

In the meantime their fortunes were to be indirectly affected by two celebrated scandals which took place in 1809. The first concerned the Commander-in-Chief, the Duke of York. On 27 January, at the very moment that the army was limping home, the Member for Okehampton, Colonel Wardle, rose in the House of Commons and made certain accusations against the Duke, the gist of which was that his mistress, Mrs Mary Anne Clarke, was in the habit of slipping names into the promotion lists after the Duke of York had approved them and that the proceeds of these secret sales of commissions went straight into her pocket. There was an enquiry in the House and at first it looked as though the Duke would escape with being accused of mere carelessness. Mrs Clarke, however, with nothing to lose, was soon telling everything she knew, a great deal that she did not know and much more than the Duke could 'repel', in particular that the Duke, on parting with her in 1806, had given her an annuity of £400 'contingent upon correctness of conduct', which sounded very much like hush-money. In the event the House acquitted the Duke of corrupt practices by a majority of eighty-two, but public opinion was against him. As a result he resigned as Commander-in-Chief and was succeeded by the veteran and pedagogic Scotsman, Sir David Dundas, the author of the celebrated drill manual. According to Lord Moira, the King 'promptly censured and altered several of the Duke of York's regulations', forbidding, somewhat late in the day, 'the dressing our Light Dragoons like mountebanks and calling them Hussars'. Another of the King's ideas, which he found rather more incredible, was 'a disposition . . . to make all the Light Dragoons heavy again'.

The second incident concerned Lord Paget, who had for some time been conducting an affair with Lady Charlotte Wellesley, the wife of Sir Henry Wellesley, and sister-in-law of Sir Arthur. On 6 March, 1809, much to the excitement of London society, they eloped. Henry Wellesley laid an action against Lord Paget, which was undefended, and received £20,000 damages, and Captain Cadogan, Lady Charlotte's brother, challenged Paget to a duel. This unfortunate business, combined with the fact that Paget was in any case senior in rank, made it difficult for him to serve with Sir Arthur in Portugal and for the rest of the Peninsular campaign the British cavalry was deprived of its most outstanding leader.

In October 1809, the 15th moved to Godalming and Guildford, and the 10th took over their quarters at Romford. On the 25th the country celebrated the fiftieth year of George III's reign. At Guildford, after the ringing of bells and a church service, the general order 'proclaiming a General Amnesty & remission for all military offences' was read out, and the sole prisoner, Farrier Girling, was set free. At ten o'clock 'A great number of the inhabitants came to the Barracks . . . & sang God Save the King in full chorus after which they saluted the Regt with three times three'. When the officers returned at six o'clock the following morning from a ball given by Lieutenant Whiteford's father at Vale Lodge they were relieved to find that 'so very exemplary was the conduct of the men that not one of them was out of quarters a minute after the sounding of the retreat, neither did any man of the Regt misconduct himself in any shape or was guilty of the least impropriety.'

On 21 December, the first anniversary of Sahagun, 'the Trumpets played God Save the King at daybreak gave 3 cheers & a party of men assembled in the Barrack Yard & sang a song composed by themselves on the action of

88

Sahagun'.[6] The Duke of Cumberland came down on the 27th and the officers presented Colonel Grant with a sword which had been voted to him for his bravery on that occasion. They then sat down to 'an elegant entertainment attended by the band of the Horse Guards blue from Windsor & the day passed with the greatest hilarity,' the Duke and Colonel Grant leaving Guildford at one o'clock in the morning. The men received ten guineas per troop, subscribed by the field officers and captains, which 'was expended in an entertainment which they conducted with the utmost propriety'.

* * *

Early in April, 1810, serious rioting broke out in London and the 15th, then stationed at Hounslow, were hurried to the capital to act in the unfamiliar role of 'aid to the civil power'. The cause of the unrest, the wealthy baronet and radical Member of Parliament, Sir Francis Burdett, had for many years been a thorn in the flesh of the Tory government. A champion of parliamentary reform and catholic emancipation, he spoke out loudly against the harshness of the prison system and the burden of war taxation. In June, 1809, he embarked on a crusade against military flogging, which was to put him in direct conflict with the Hussars. After the return of the army from Corunna government was split between those who advocated continuing efforts to liberate Spain and those who wished to create a diversion, in Austria's favour, by an attempt to seize Antwerp. In the end both sides had their way and the country's military resources were divided. In April,1809, Sir Arthur Wellesley returned to Portugal with a considerable force and in June the largest army that had ever sailed from England, 40,000 men and a naval force to match, commanded respectively by Lord Chatham and Sir Richard Strachan, was despatched to Walcheren. After much delay, incompetence and misunderstanding between these two, Britain's finest army was allowed to rot in the fever-ridden marshes of that notoriously unhealthy island. Public opinion was angered by these events, and when Parliament assembled in January, 1810, Burdett and others set about attacking the government. On 26 January they succeeded in a motion for a full enquiry, which, in spite of much opposition, was held in secret and, on 30 March, cleared the ministers involved.

Meanwhile, on 19 February, one John Gale Jones, an apothecary and secretary of a Westminster debating society, the *British Forum*, 'placarded' Westminster, attacking the government's attitude to the press. Two days later Jones was hauled before the House and committed to Newgate Prison. Burdett sprang to his defence and on 12 March declared that Jones's imprisonment was illegal, and that if 'the privileges of the House contravened the law of the land, privileges must go'. His motion for Jones's release was defeated by 139 votes, but he had yet not finished fighting. On 24 March he published an open letter in Cobbett's *Weekly Political Register* entitled 'Sir Francis Burdett to his Constituents denying the Power of the House of Commons to imprison the People of England'. This was like a red rag to a bull and on 6 April Burdett

89

was himself found guilty of a breach of privilege and committed, by a majority of thirty-seven, not to Newgate but to the Tower of London.

The attempts of the Sergeant-at-Arms, Mr Colman, to deliver the warrant to Sir Francis, and the latter's attempts to avoid arrest, lasted for three days and could be classed as high comedy, were it not for the serious rioting which took place outside his house, No 78 Piccadilly, and in the surrounding streets and squares. The riots led to the memorable charge of the Life Guards down Piccadilly on the morning of 7 April, which earned them the title of the 'Piccadilly Butchers'. Later that day, as ugly crowds assembled along the Thames as far as the City, the Tower guns were loaded, the ditch was filled with water and an order was sent out to all the troops within a hundred miles of London summoning them to the capital. The 15th Hussars received it at three o'clock and an hour and a half later reached London, where picquets were mounted and 'strong patroles' sent out into Piccadilly and the surrounding area to keep the mob quiet 'who were assembled in very considerable numbers in those parts'.

Sir Francis reacted to this show of force by demanding from the Sheriffs of Middlesex the protection of the law, 'either by calling out the *Posse Comitatus*, or such other as the case & circumstance may require', as his house was 'beset by a military force'. The next morning, 8 April, the Sergeant was again refused admission to No 78, rioting continued all day and Piccadilly had to be cleared several times; many people were hurt and every street lamp smashed. A local resident, Miss Berry, was told by a neighbour that the crowd had pelted the Life Guards from behind the railings of Green Park, whereupon a troop was dismounted and, fixing bayonets, drove them 'without mischief to the walk on the other side of the pond, and keeping that [side] next to the street clear'. Picquets and patrols were again found by the 15th Hussars and Tale once again found himself in Piccadilly trying to keep order in the crowd, who hailed them, good-naturedly, as 'the little hairy-mouthed fellows', and compared them favourably with the 'Household Brigade', whose harassing and unpleasant duties in the maintenance of order and the repression of outrages had drawn upon them hatred and abuse'.

It rained hard that night, which helped to disperse the mob and keep the streets quiet, and it was still raining when three squadrons of the 15th paraded in St James's Street the next morning, before marching to No 78. At ten o'clock, while the Burdetts were still at breakfast, the Sergeant, armed with a government indemnity, arrived and ordered an attack on the house. Lord William Lennox, a pupil at Westminster, described how a 'body of troops was drawn up in front of the house, and a posse of constables, descending the area, burst open the windows and doors. One, bolder than the rest, had mounted a ladder, and having thrown open the sash was about to enter the drawing-room, when he was intercepted. The calm dignity with which the "friend of the people" shut the window, calling out not to hurt the intruder was deeply affecting.' Sir Francis refused to leave and was hustled out, protesting loudly 'in the King's name' against the violation of his person and house. 'It is superior force only,' he cried out, 'that hurries me out of it, and you do it at your peril.'

Safely secured in a 'glass coach' he was driven off, preceded by two squadrons of the 15th and two troops of the Life Guards, with Mr Read, the Magistrate, at their head. The coach itself was surrounded by two more troops of the Life Guards and one of the 15th. Next came two battalions of the Foot Guards, marching in open order, and finally another party of the 15th. Westminster had to be avoided at all costs, so, while the Foot Guards continued down the Strand to the Tower, the cavalcade turned north and proceeded to Aldgate High Street, followed by an immense crowd, shouting, hallooing and hurling abuse at the troops.

The Foot Guards arrived at the Tower just before twelve noon and formed a line covering the gateway. The main cavalcade arrived fifteen minutes later, providing a 'grand military spectacle', as it wound its way on to Tower Hill. The 15th, whose arrival was now greeted with boos, intermingled with cheers for Sir Francis, opened out and formed a two-deep circle around the entrance, through which the prisoner's carriage passed. As Sir Francis alighted, crossed the bridge and was received by the Lieutenant of the Tower, a gun was fired to announce his safe arrival. The mob now began to stone the 15th, who retaliated by cutting at them with their swords, forcing many of them into the moat, 'without mischief, as there was but little water'. The cheerful abuse of Sunday now gave way to anger. Sergeant Tale recalled 'a knot of scoundrels', who 'ensconced themselves behind some railings, and brickbatted us to more than our heart's content'. Another eye-witness described how, because of their 'foreign trappings and whiskers', the 15th had been mistaken for a 'German Corps', notwithstanding the 'soldierlike conduct and manly forbearance of this gallant corps'. Luckily the error was dispelled by the language of the 15th, 'but no such error could have existed had the soldiers been dressed according to their old regulations'.[7]

With Burdett safely in the Tower, the troops returned to their quarters, pelted with mud and stones by the crowd. Opposite Trinity House their patience finally cracked. According to Miss Berry, the Life Guards, 'after long bearing the insults of the people in the most exemplary manner', fired some of their pistols and carbines, killing two persons and wounding several others. Fortunately the heavy rain 'helped to drive home the idlers and lookers on, of which every great mob in a great town is half composed'. Eventually the troops were led across London Bridge and returned to their quarters by way of the south bank. Little sympathy was felt for the soldiers engaged in this 'hateful duty' and in the City there was surprise that they had been permitted to open fire without the permission of the Lord Mayor. By 9 April, according to Lady Sarah Lyttleton, the 'mobbing is quite over . . . and neither soldiers nor black-guards are to be seen about the streets', and for the rest of the month London remained quiet, although people now cheered the Foot Guards, and jeered, or worse, at the Life Guards.[8] At the end of the month, after a series of reviews, the troops dispersed and returned to their quarters.

Meanwhile Sir Francis was comfortably housed in the Tower, where, in return for his parole not to pass the gate he was given the run of the precincts, a privilege that was taken away, for a time at least, after he witnessed the flogging of some of the garrison. With the prorogation of Parliament at half past three on the afternoon of 21 June, Sir Francis's imprisonment came automatically to an end and precautions were taken against a renewal of the rioting. At eleven o'clock in the morning the 15th Hussars arrived back in London, taking up their former quarters, with orders to 'wait in readiness the requirements of the Civil Power'. But they were not needed, for when Sir Francis emerged from the Tower he went straight to Putney by water, and thence to his country seat in Wimbledon, much to the mob's disappointment. Deprived of their hero 'the enormous troops of "unwashed artificers" who accompanied on foot a long train of shabby carriages, and squadrons of people on horseback' trooped home via Newgate, where they collected the newly-released John Gale Jones and bore him off in triumph through the streets of London. Lord William Lennox remembered 'the fineness of the day, every window filled with well-dressed persons wearing garter blue ribbons; processions with bands of music; banners inscribed "Trial by Jury", "The Constitution", "Freedom of Election", added to the brilliancy of the scene'. Decked out in 'garter blue watch ribbon and favour', he shouted, as he 'ever did afterwards, "Burdett for Ever!"'

Meanwhile Cobbett, the proprietor of the *Political Register*, had also fallen foul of the government. In the summer of 1809 the mutiny in a Militia regiment stationed at Ely had been put down by four squadrons of King's German Legion Dragoons, stationed at Ipswich. The ringleaders were court-martialled and received five hundred lashes each at the hands of the German Dragoons. The public outcry over their treatment lingered on and was the reason for the mob's fury at the prospect of 'German' troops being employed, during the Burdett riots. Cobbett had erupted in an emotional leader:

Five hundred each! Aye, that is right! Flog them! Flog! They deserve a flogging at every mealtime. Lash them daily! What! Shall the rascals dare to *mutiny?* And that too when the German Legion is so near at hand? Lash them! Lash them! They deserve it. Oh, yes! They merit a double-tailed cat! Base dogs! What! Mutiny for the price of a knapsack? Lash them! Flog them! Base rascals!

The Attorney-General promptly filed an information against Cobbett for sedition, but it was not until 15 June, 1810, that he appeared before the King's Bench and was found guilty 'of a most infamous and seditious libel'. He was sentenced to two years in Newgate, a fine of £1,000 and was bound over to give 'security for His good behaviour after His imprisonment shall have terminated, Himself in £3,000 & 2 other persons in £1,000 each'. Apart from the expense of the sureties, which was crippling, and the separation from his family, which was distressing, Cobbett's imprisonment was not uncomfortable, as he was lodged in a small suite in the house of Sheriff Wood, for which he was charged the not inconsiderable sum of twelve guineas a week. The severity of the sentence was a direct reflection of the attitude of society to Cobbett's 'offence'. On 5 August Mrs Jordan wrote to George, who was back in Spain, 'I dare say you were not sorry to hear that *your friend Mr Cobbett* has found his way into Newgate where he is to amuse himself for *3 years*. He still writes, & I sincerely hope that he will compose something that will add 4 years more to his present agreable situation.'

* * *

That autumn the King's favourite daughter Amelia fell ill and her death in November severely upset the balance of his wandering mind. On 31 December, as he showed no sign of improvement, the Prime Minister, Mr. Perceval, moved for the appointment of the Prince of Wales as Regent, under certain restrictions and limitations, which were to last for a year, and on 5 February, 1811, the Regency Bill became law. The establishment of the Regency heralded a re-awakening of the Prince's military interests, which had lain dormant for some time. Freed at last from the shackles of his father's antiquated ideas, he could now carry into effect the projects closest to his heart. As, albeit temporary, sovereign, the Prince had three immediate objectives as far as the Army was concerned. In the first place, he wanted the Duke of York back at his old job, secondly he wanted Lord Paget back in command of the cavalry in the Peninsula, and thirdly he wanted to modernize the dress of the Army which, in his view, was now impractical, old-fashioned and dreary. After being subjected to considerable pressure, Perceval agreed to the first of these wishes and on 11 May the Duke of York returned to Horse Guards.[9] In his second aim the Prince was less successful, for quite apart from the coldness between the Wellesleys and the Pagets as a result of the elopement, there remained the problem of Lord Paget's seniority. On 20 June Lord Edward Somerset, commanding the 4th Dragoons in the Peninsula, echoed the current rumours that Lord Paget was to waive his seniority of rank and was to go out to command the Cavalry, for which purpose Lord Wellington was to have the local rank of general; he owned he should not be sorry if it were true. Another correspondent from the Peninsula wrote: 'Send His Lordship to Us and brisk and favourable be the breeze . . . Lord P. is the only Cavalry Officer we have, the rest are mere Pretenders who require his example to become *any thing* themselves!' In the event the obstacles proved insurmountable and Paget was not to serve overseas again until the Waterloo campaign.

The prospects looked better for the Prince's scheme for changing the dress of the Army. His brother was back at Horse Guards and there was no more talk of turning back the clock and converting his beloved Hussars back into mere Light Dragoons. The Duke of Cumberland was determined to get in on the act and, according to Lord Paget, was stirring heaven and earth to become Inspector-General of Cavalry. Paget was certain that the four Hussar regiments would soon be assembled and that Cumberland would 'exercise' them. There was nothing, he wrote, that he should 'enjoy so much as to see them together and not to have the trouble of working them'. In the event he was right about one thing, but not the other, for on 17 June a grand review of the Hussar Brigade did take place on Hounslow Heath before the Prince Regent and the Dukes of York, Cambridge and Kent, but, contrary to expectation, Paget was once again in command. The Brigade consisted of the 10th, 15th and 18th Hussars and two troops of horse artillery, with the Duke of Cumberland at the head of his own regiment.[10] After the inspection of the line by the Royal party, various complicated manoeuvres were carried out 'on the gallop in perfect order,' as usual on Hounslow Heath, partly obscured by the clouds of peaty dust. After several charges, supported by the Horse Artillery, the line was formed and a Royal Salute brought the proceedings to a close. 'It was truly fine,' Charles Paget told Sir Arthur, 'and Paget was quite in his element.'

Afterwards the royal party, the staff and officers of the brigade repaired to The Castle in Richmond, where about 200 persons sat down to a most sumptuous *déjeuner*. According to Charles Paget it was of the most luxurious style, 'as Turtle, Fish, Venison of the best quality was provided; as Champagne, Hock, Burgundy, Claret, Vin de France, and Hermitage was drunk in copious libations; as Peaches, Nectarines, Grapes, Pines, Melons, and everything most rare in the dessert way was provided in abundance, it was a feast worthy of the magnificent piece of Plate, which had been (unknown till the moment) in *readiness* to present to Paget by the Prince, the Dukes, and the Officers of the Hussar Brigade.' It was a far cry from the rigours of the retreat to Corunna, and the next day Paget's father, Lord Uxbridge, sent round to The Castle to pick up the bill.

At the height of these scenes of military splendour, the voice of Sir Francis Burdett was once more raised in the House of Commons, against the 'odious, disgraceful, and abominable practice' of military flogging. Speaking the day after the review, he claimed that many serving officers supported his views, in particular the Duke of Gloucester, who had for the last three years kept his regiment, the 3rd Foot Guards, 'in a high state of discipline without having recourse to flogging'. In the 15th Hussars, on the other hand, 'a regiment long distinguished for its efficiency in the field, and for its peaceable, modest, and proper demeanour in every respect . . . more cruel punishments had taken place within a very few months after the Duke of Cumberland was appointed to the command, than had taken place in that regiment ever since the period of the Seven Years' War'. He went on to cite some of the cruel punishments he had seen with his own eyes in the Tower of London. Yet, he continued, it was remarkable that British Officers managed to discipline foreigners without recourse to the cat-o'-nine-tails. The Portuguese, who 'were allowed to have arrived at greater proficiency in discipline' were never flogged and even the

Great Frederick had eventually given up the Corporal's stick in favour of 'a very mild system'. In this country, 'the system of cruelty and torture had been introduced principally with a view to Germanizing our soldiers; but the German soldiers in our pay were quite astonished at this mode of discipline, as nothing like it had been practised in Germany during their recollection. If British officers could make good soldiers of Germans, Portuguese and every other nation without flogging, what a scandal it was to this country to say that it was necessary with the English alone!' The motion was defeated by ninety-four votes to ten.[11]

* * *

In June, 1811, immediately after the Prince Regent's review, the 10th Hussars returned to Brighton where they settled once again into their routine of drills, parades and inspections, interspersed with the pleasures of a popular seaside resort. A new generation of officers was now coming into the regiment, more exquisite than the earlier hard-drinking set and less amenable to discipline. Colonel Leigh, as we know, had departed under a cloud and Quentin had the command, with Palmer as his second-in-command. Many of the officers who had taken part in the Corunna campaign were serving abroad, either on the staff or with other regiments. George FitzClarence, in the Adjutant General's department in the Peninsula, had a narrow escape during the battle of Fuentes d'Onoro, which took place on 3–5, May, 1811. According to the *Gentleman's Magazine*, having observed the fall of several French Hussars in his immediate neighbourhood, 'he followed their example, without the same cause, and in the subsequent confusion succeeded in regaining the British lines'. He was slightly wounded and by 10 August, now a captain, he was back in England.[12]

Lord Edward Somerset was in Spain commanding the 4th Dragoons and Frederick Ponsonby, having fought with the 23rd Light Dragoons at Talavera, was now commanding the 12th Light Dragoons. In May, 1808, the eccentric Captain Mellish had been appointed aide-de-camp to General Ferguson and fought at the battle of Vimiero. On 14 January, 1809, he set sail for the Peninsula a second time, in the company of General Dyott. As they stood down the Channel the latter reflected in his diary on the change in Mellish's condition, 'from having lived in a style of high life, considered a first rate Buck of the age, racing for more money than any other individual of his day, the companion and friend of HRH the Prince of Wales; now become the companion of a *cabin* and humble attendant on a Major-General'. On his arrival Mellish was employed as Assistant-Adjutant-General to Craufurd's celebrated Light Division and was always up to pranks of one sort or another. He was eventually sent home by Wellington because of his excessive gambling, and certainly Lord Edward Somerset did not think much of his military abilities. He told his brother that he thought Fitzroy Somerset '*equally* as well entitled to a Majority *without* purchase as such a man as Mellish who had one given to him . . . & who never sticks to his duty for many months together.'

In August, 1811, the 10th acquired a new cornet in the person of the Marquess of Worcester, the eldest son of the Duke of Beaufort. His uncle, Lord Edward Somerset, wrote to the Duke on 4 July congratulating him on his choice of regiment, as his Royal Highness would not have been pleased if he had 'preferred' the 7th Hussars. Immensely tall and thin, with a pale face and a large highbred nose, the nineteen year-old Marquess had, while up at Oxford, fallen under the spell of one of the most celebrated courtesans of the age, Harriette Wilson. The daughter of a Mayfair clockmaker, Harriette was, in the words of Sir Walter Scott, 'far from beautiful, but a smart, saucy girl, with good eyes and dark hair, and the manners of a wild schoolboy', characteristics which endeared her to the 'Dandy Set' in particular. At the age of fifteen she was established as the mistress of the Earl of Craven and after that she never looked back, numbering among her 'patrons' many of the great names of the period. The story of her affair with Worcester comes mainly from her own memoirs, but references to her in the letters of Lord Edward Somerset, Worcester and the Duke of Beaufort confirm much of her story and reveal how troublesome her attentions were to one of the highest families in the country.

After their first meeting Worcester pestered Harriette until she agreed to accompany him to Brighton. Thus, early in August, 1811, Worcester and his 'Harry' set up house in Rock Gardens, Brighton. Their household consisted of Worcester's footman, Will Haught, or 'Hort', 'a stiff, grave, steady person of about forty', dressed in the Beaufort livery, 'as stiff as himself', a coachman, a groom in livery, an under-groom and a soldier servant. The late summer days passed in a whirl of riding parties, dinners and plays. On one occasion Harriette, who already knew several officers of the 10th, including another new subaltern the seventeen-year-old Edward Fox Fitzgerald,[13] Augustus Berkeley and the Count de Grammont, was invited to dine in the mess by Colonel Palmer, being the only woman present among thirty diners.

Worcester took his military duties very lightly and, when he persisted in neglecting the eight o'clock drill parade, was put under arrest by Colonel Quentin. 'By G–, if he vas the King's son,' Harriette makes the Colonel exclaim, 'I vould put him honder arrest,' a speech which Worcester thought was the most vulgar and disgusting he had ever heard, as, after all, 'what has a King's son, or a duke's son, to do with the usual discipline observed to lieutenants in the army?' Eventually Harriette took to 'regularly attending parade, like a young recruit', in a fetching version of the regiment's uniform, with a little grey fur stable cap with a gold band. Watching the proceedings from Worcester's barrack-room, she noted every detail, especially Sergeant Whitaker's instruction of the sword exercise, which went like this:

'Tik nutiss!! the wurd dror is oney a carshun. At t'wurd suards, ye drors um hout, tekin a farm un possitif grip o' th'hilt! sem time, throwing th'shish smartly backords thus! Dror!!! Here the men forgetful of the caution which had just been given them, began to draw. 'Steady there!! Never a finger or a high to move i'th'hed'.

On 31 October the officers dined with the Prince, and Creevey, who was also present, thought they looked 'very ornamental monkeys in their red breeches with gold fringe and yellow boots'. Occasions like this drove Worcester to despair, for when the Prince Regent was at the Pavilion he was duty-bound to attend on his Royal Colonel and every minute he was away from Harriette was torture to him.

Harriette took an interest in regimental matters and when a deserter was 'taken up' she interceded on his behalf, but Worcester was unsympathetic. The deserter was court-martialled by Grammont, Worcester and another officer and was sentenced to receive 500 lashes. When Harriette asked what Quentin thought about the sentence, Worcester told her that, much to his astonishment, Quentin had said that he would not inflict one quarter of the sentence, as, in the first place, the man was young and, in the second, 'he hated the system of flogging altogether, believing it to be a punishment most of all cultivated to harden the men'.

It is possible that Harriette's account is a garbled version of a case which came to the attention of Sir Francis Burdett. On 28 October he wrote to the Prince Regent saying that, on 12 August, the Prince's birthday, a private of the regiment, one Nathan Wilson, was found out of barracks at nine o'clock in the morning, 'for which he was tried by court-martial the following day and sentenced to receive two hundred lashes; which sentence was carried into execution the next day'. This was not, however, the first that had been heard of the matter. On 11 September Rear Admiral Henry Warre had written a letter to the Prince's secretary, Colonel McMahon, which had been forwarded to the regiment.[14] Nathan Wilson happened to be the brother of the Admiral's 'Taylor at Finchley', who had told him that by 'some great inattention' the unfortunate private had received 220 lashes. The Admiral's only motive in writing was to prevent 'unpleasant circumstances being brought before the public', especially after what had recently passed in the House of Commons on the subject. However, he hinted that Wilson's friends would be prepared to drop the matter, 'by the Man's discharge, and some compensation from the party whose duty it was to see the Prisoner received no more punishment than the Court Martial awarded'.

This thinly veiled threat, coming from a Rear Admiral, required immediate attention and Quentin passed it straight on to Palmer, who had supervised the punishment, and who replied on the 18th, assuring the Admiral that the facts stated in his letter were untrue:

The man Wilson, whom he alludes to, was certainly sentenced to, & did receive 200 lashes, but *only* 200, of which the Adjutant of the Regiment, who (as usual) took down the number on paper, and whose authority . . . is most to be relied on, and could have no motive but his duty to actuate him, will make oath. Fortunately the surgeon of the Regiment, Mr Morrison from the attention he paid at the time is enabled to make oath of the same, nor am I aware of anyone who can contradict him, altho' I know that a report to that effect was circulated at the time, & which originated with the Farriers of the Regt. who flog by turns but who on this occasion, by accident or design, and I strongly suspect the latter, shifted their places in the ranks & thereby occasioned the doubts of those who calculated the punishment by the number of Farriers & the turns which came to each.

As regarded the threat of repercussions in the House, Palmer, himself an MP, was sure 'nothing could be easier to prove than the absurdity and danger of the system of a total abolition of corporal punishment'. No one in the regiment had been punished since the debate in the Commons except Wilson and the result was that, if it had not been resorted to, 'a general mutiny must have been the consequence'. The conduct of the men was now as 'orderly & creditable as ever & fully justifies the propriety of the step taken'.[15]

In his next letter Sir Francis was in full possession of the facts. First of all he drew the Prince's attention to the age of the court-martial, which consisted of 'Captain de Grammont, President, twenty-three years of age, Smith, twenty-one years of age, Cotton, twenty years of age, Hill, twenty-one years of age, Fitzgerald, seventeen years of age'. He then named the Farriers who had given twenty lashes each in turn. As there were only nine of them, the first, George Ellis had two turns to make up the two hundred, but so, apparently, did the next man, John Adams. 'So it appears,' Sir Francis continued, 'Wilson received twenty lashes more than his sentence although he twice during the punishment begged for forgiveness of Lieutenant-Colonel Palmer.' This was a man who had served in Sir John Moore's army, had his horse shot under him at Benevente 'at the taking of General Lefevre', suffered all the privations of the retreat, and during six years' service was 'never in the guard house nor as a prisoner in any sense of the word'. His only crime was being absent at nine o'clock 'on his Colonel's birthday'. Sir Francis thought Wilson deserved remuneration for exemplary good conduct, rather than for redress for such sufferings for so slight an offence. On Monday 23 October, he claimed, Colonel Palmer had called Nathan Wilson from the ranks and asked him whether he wanted his discharge or money, to which Nathan Wilson replied (and Sir Francis repeated his Christian name because 'his Royal Highness might find hereafter that his Christian name was of great consequence') that he could not answer. Four days later Colonel Palmer had threatened to court-martial him again for 'refusing to answer some questions in his parlour'. He concluded by saying that he relied on the Prince's 'benevolent heart' to judge what should be done on this occasion. The final outcome, whether Wilson accepted discharge or money, is not known.

* * *

Meanwhile, the Prince had been working on his improvements for the dress of the Army and throughout the months of August and September a Board of General Officers, headed by the Duke of Cumberland, assembled to discuss the new uniforms for the cavalry and approve samples provided for their inspection. The results of these deliberations were unveiled in October, and received immediate notice in the Press. On the 23rd a Light Dragoon private paraded in the new uniform 'fully equipped, in the Riding-House, Carlton House', for the approval of the Prince and the Dukes of York and Cumberland. Princess Charlotte, the Prince's daughter, rode by at the time and noted that Cumberland – 'Prince Whiskerandos' as she called him – was the only one who could drag himself away from the proceedings to say 'Good morning'.[16]

Having settled sartorial matters to his satisfaction, the Regent repaired to Brighton, where, on the 31st, he saw the 10th in their new uniforms.[17] This was the first time that the Prince had 'minutely inspected' his regiment since its return from Spain and he had each horse brought before him in turn, rejecting about fifty. According to *The Times* he 'inspected them in a very particular manner', which did not escape the notice of Berkeley Paget:

You see how he has been amusing himself at Brighton. I fancy his whole soul is wrapped up in Hussar saddles, caps, cuirasses, and sword-belts. . . . Didn't you see that he dismissed each Horse with a 'tap of his cane'? He has heard that is a German, or Prussian custom, or some nonsense of that kind. What a pity it is that you are not a Hussar now, You would be in high favour again, now that the rage is upon him.

In December Berkeley Paget wrote to his brother Arthur that the cavalry, the Hussars excepted, were 'amazingly disgusted' with their new uniforms, which he had heard were 'abominable'. In January, 1812, he wrote again on the same theme. An officer of the 23rd Light Dragoons had told him that the new uniform would cost about three hundred pounds, and none of the existing ones, which were 'new and altered on their return from Spain last year', would be 'convertible to any purpose whatsoever'.

One of the Men was the other day dress'd out in a Pattern Jacket &c. just sent down to the Regiment, and upon being turned loose in the Barrack was hooted and quizzed by the Men with 'Who's that damned Frenchman?' Pleasant! You may depend upon there'll be a Row. The officers grumble, and when that is the case, the men are very apt to follow their example.

The row was not long in coming. On the opening of Parliament, on 7 January, 1812, Sir Francis Burdett delivered a long speech in which, after reviewing the evils of the time, he set about the Army once again, with his accustomed hyperbole. The land was in a state of terror; 'Military possession was taken of the country; depots, and barracks, and fortifications were formed'; 'Mercenary Germans' and foreigners were scattered over the kingdom, 'as if England could not defend itself and must have recourse to Germans, who had not been able to defend their own country'. Not only, he went on, was the country over-spread with foreigners, but even our own soldiers were compelled to wear the 'German Dress and whiskers; as if the whiskered face of a German was more formidable to the enemy than the smooth open countenance of an Englishman'. He continued with a further attack on flogging, repeating many of his earlier remarks about 'a flogged nation', and the destruction of the liberty of the press. 'You must have seen in the Report of the debate on the first day', Berkeley Paget wrote to Arthur, on 10 January, 'what a *grievance* Burdett made of the new uniforms and alterations. . . . I own I thought him right, though it was misplaced on such an occasion.'

However inappropriate and trivial Burdett's attack on German whiskers, there was no doubt that he was right about the state of the country. A poor harvest in 1811 had led to a corresponding increase in the price of bread, and the retaliatory measures taken by France and America in return for having their ships searched for contraband resulted in manufacturers being unable to sell their goods and to high unemployment. During the last weeks of 1811 serious unrest broke out in Nottinghamshire, Derbyshire and Leicestershire, culminating in the destruction of the newly-invented machinery, which was supposed to be the cause of the unemployment. Mobs of so-called 'Luddites' roamed the countryside breaking up the lace-making machinery and the streets of Nottingham were placarded with notices offering rewards for the delivery of the Mayor, dead or alive. Eventually the military were called out and several regiments were moved into the area, including the 15th Hussars. Sergeant Tale had all the soldier's inborn distaste of such duties:

> Of all the services which a soldier is called upon to perform there is none so unpalatable to him as that of waging war against a domestic enemy. Credit the military seldom get, be the results what they may; but rather odium on almost all occasions . . . If lenient, and excesses follow, the soldier is blamed for apathy, and denounced as one paid by his country undeservedly; if energetic and vigorous, he makes a severe example or two, and thereby prevents the perpetration of mischief, he is charac-terised as blood-thirsty; although his promptitude in the emergency might not only have prevented the destruction of much property, but also the loss of many lives.

On 12 May the news of the assassination of the Prime Minister, Perceval, reached Nottingham, 'upon which the lower orders expressed a savage joy by assembling in a tumultuous manner & parading the Town with Drums & Flags, lighting bonfires.' The 15th Hussars were confronted by crowds of women 'with arms akimbo and clenched fists stuck upon their hips', who faced and dared them to ride 'over women'. The troubles spread to Cheshire,

Lancashire and Yorkshire, and on 11 June a camp was formed near Sutton Coldfield 'in consequence of the disturbed state of the country and the system of organisation that was discovered among the manufacturers'.

* * *

Throughout 1812 the Beauforts worked hard to break up the romance between Worcester and Harriette, the Duchess being most virulent in condemning her son's 'absurd attachment . . . for this vile profligate woman'. But when Worcester returned to Brighton from leave Harriette was still with him, and when his troop was ordered to a small village near Portsmouth, to guard prisoners-of-war, she marched with them, riding alongside the officers, Captain de Grammont, Worcester and Lord Arthur Hill, dressed in her regimental 'cap and habit'. On arrival they 'all lodged together in the same deplorable pothouse'. It was here that they experienced the results of Burdett's eloquence in the Commons. Attending the theatre in Portsmouth, they had no sooner seated themselves in a large stage-box when some sailors in the gallery began hissing and pelting them with oranges and made such a racket that they were 'obliged' to leave the theatre before the first act was over. Worse still, on their way back to the inn they were followed by a whole gang of tars, yelling 'Mounseers – German moustache rascals, and bl-dy Frenchmen'. Harriette did not know whether the sailors had objected to their 'dragoon uniforms' in general, 'as being a German costume', or whether it was the Frenchman de Grammont 'who had caused all the mischief'; clearly she had not read Burdett's speech, which perhaps the sailors had. After being 'hissed out of Portsmouth with much *éclat*', they returned to their humble village, 'looking rather wise at each other'. Looking back on the episode, she decided she had enjoyed the company of Arthur Hill, who 'had something comical about his manner', but had found de Grammont as stiff and unnatural as his shirt collars. The latter was not particularly popular with either officers or men, although he was undoubtedly 'a very handsome, gentlemanlike Frenchman', and as Harriette had always heard, 'a very brave one'; but he was severe with his men, ill-tempered and 'a decided fop'.

The Duke now sent his man of affairs, one Robinson, 'a notorious swindler of his acquaintance', to Harriette with a proposal. If she would take an oath that she had delivered to him or to the Duke every letter, or copy of a letter, from Worcester in her possession she might make her own terms. Harriette's lawyers advised her that the letters were worth £20,000, but, she claimed, she offered to return them if the Duke and Duchess would behave towards her with 'somewhat less of ill-will'. She was still waiting for an answer when she learned that Lord Wellington, at the request of the Duke, had asked for Worcester as one of his aides-de-camp. For a time Harriette considered going with him, but gave the idea up in favour of a year's separation, after which they intended to marry. In Worcester's presence, Mr Robinson agreed to pay Harriette a quarterly allowance while he was away and promising to write 'at least a foolscap' to her every day and, calling on God's blessing upon his 'adored wife', Worcester was dragged out of the house by Lord William Somerset, just in time to catch the Falmouth Mail. Had it not been for his uncle, Harriette thought, he 'would have preferred love to glory, and given old Wellington the slip'.

Worcester left London for Plymouth on 30th April, attended by Will Hort, and on 6 May Lord Edward wrote to the Duke:

> I am happy to hear Worcester is coming out to this country on Lord Wellington's Staff, & it is very gratifying that the latter should have proposed it in so obliging a manner – I hope it will be the means of breaking off that abominable connection, which I am not surprised to hear has made you so uneasy, I should think the sooner Worcester leaves England the better.

He was supposed to leave Lisbon on the 30th, so he was probably with Wellington by 22 July when the battle of Salamanca was fought, and he was certainly with him when he entered Madrid. 'Lord Wellington collected the ladies of the place for a ball,' Lord Edward wrote on 13 August, 'which Worcester amongst others seemed to enjoy very much . . . he performed a waltz with great *éclat* – but the beauty of the females was not very brilliant.' It is from Madrid, on 28 September, that the first of Worcester's surviving letters to his father is dated. He had been sent by Wellington to Sir Rowland Hill, in Estremadura, but on the way back he had lost his way and ended up in Madrid, where he was put up by an officer of the 95th Rifles. If they had 'more Cavalry & Ld.Uxbridge we might do great things,'[18] he wrote. He had heard rumours that the 10th Hussars were 'certainly coming out' and asked whether his father knew anything about it. He was obviously enjoying Madrid, where there was 'a great deal of good society':

> The women I think (that is the Higher Class Grandees d'Espagne) are in general tolerably well educated very pleasant & *highbred* & for the most part Handsome & I am become a *great Spaniard* and have got very much attached to the people who are individually very good people. The men are the most obligeing Civil Creatures & all seem fond of the English both men and women. The language (in which I have made tolerable proficiency) is such a delightful change from the Portugese that it is quite a pleasure to hear it talked. We have had two or three Balls & festivities & today there is to be another Bullfight. . . . In short if the people were richer this place would rival London for amusements of all kinds.

On 1 November he arrived back at Headquarters at Rueda and two days later told his father that he had been introduced to Sir Edward Paget by Lord Wellington. He wished they had some more of the same family, 'or at least Ld.Uxbridge & some Hussars, for the Cavalry want something or other to infuse a proper spirit into them.'

By 28 December Worcester was back in Lisbon. It was now certain that the Hussar Brigade was to be sent to Spain and he intended to 'make the next campaign with them'. He had heard that his cousin Henry Somerset was coming out as Acting Adjutant of the 10th – 'a very good thing for him, but a bad one for the Regiment'. Lord Edward, too, thought it was an excellent thing that Henry Somerset was to see some active service, which was a 'fine school for a young man', and his father Lord Charles Somerset seemed 'to rejoice at it extremely'. He thought it 'unfortunate' that Captain Henry Wyndham, the eldest of Lord Egremont's three natural sons, was to be 'one of the party'. He had recently married Henry Somerset's sister Elizabeth, but as this particular branch of the Somersets was notoriously poor, Lord Egremont had strongly disapproved of the match, and was still continuing 'inexorable' and refusing neither to 'see nor forgive his son'. The Hussars would 'form a noble re-inforcement & by sending them out immediately', he thought, they would arrive in good time for the opening of the campaign.

When Harriette learned that 'the brave and dandy warriors of the Tenth' were about to be sent abroad and there was no chance of Worcester coming home after a year, as had been planned, she set out for Falmouth with every intention of joining him. Here she learned from a newly-arrived officer that Worcester was supposed to have left Lisbon and 'gone up to the army with someone', believed to be a Mrs Archdeacon. Harriette knew all about this person, who was the sister-in-law of the Paymaster of the 10th Hussars and who had already made an 'attack on Worcester's virtue at Brighton'. She had been living with her husband in Lisbon before being 'run away with by the Marquess of Worcester'. When, however, Harriette heard that it was 'whis-pered about Lisbon' that, should she attempt to join Worcester, the English Ambassador had the power to 'get her put on board an American ship and send her to America', and it was confirmed that Mrs Archdeacon had indeed gone 'up to the army to join Lord Worcester', she returned to London 'disgusted with the whole set of Beauforts'.

Harriette now decided to place herself 'under the protection' of a young and wealthy Hampshire gentleman and even agreed with the Duke to settle for an allowance of £300 a year for so doing. However, when she least expected it, she received a letter from Worcester claiming that Mrs Archdeacon had followed him up to the army, 'whether he would or not, and he had sent her back immediately, and wished her dead for her disgusting assurance'. Harriette wrote immediately cancelling her agreement with the Duke, but he, having by now also heard of Mrs Archdeacon, replied that she might starve if she did not like to live with another man. Finally, after much wrangling over Worcester's letters, which were still in her possession, the Duke agreed to pay her £200 a year, provided she never wrote to Worcester again, or held any communication with him. Worcester, however, continued writing to her sister Fanny, and finally wrote such a pathetic letter to Harriette herself that she felt she had to answer it. Almost immediately her annuity was stopped and the affair came to an abrupt end. Lord Edward Somerset's letter, written to the Duke on 26 January, reveals the part he had taken in persuading Worcester to abandon Harriette, once and for all:

> I am very happy to find that my conversation with Worcester on a certain subject had given you some satisfaction. I shall most willingly renew the communication whensoever I meet with a fit opportunity. . . . Absence, as you observe, is the best thing for both parties; for . . . if he stays abroad some time longer, there is a chance of the Lady's patience being exhausted, & of her forming another connection. If any thing of that sort could be proved, I will answer for his giving her up directly. When I spoke to him on the subject, I ventured to assure him, that I had no doubt you would willingly settle a reasonable annuity upon her, provided he would promise distinctly to have no more communication with her, & I am happy to find that in doing so I entered into your wishes.

All were anxious to hear of the arrival of the brigade, which he expected to be 'most brilliant', as it was to be hoped that the arrival of the 10th would help to keep Worcester in Spain.

*   *   *

On 18th August, 1812, the Prince Regent attended a splendid review of his regiment on Hounslow Heath, which gave the 'numerous body of spectators' a first glimpse of the Prince's new uniforms. The 23rd Light Dragoons kept the ground and the saluting base was guarded by a party of the Life Guards, some of whose officers were wearing the Prince's new helmets. Towards the end of October four troops of the 10th moved into Knightsbridge Barracks to carry out public duties, in place of the Life Guards who were about to depart for the Peninsula. On 1 December they were on duty for the opening of Parliament when, according to one onlooker, there were some muffled catcalls. But if the Hussars were still being jeered at for their moustaches and 'German' dress, it was nothing to the reception given to the Prince's new uniforms, not only by the press and public, but also by informed military opinion. One correspondent lambasted them at length in the January, 1813, number of the *Royal Military Chronicle*. Seeing 'several nondescripts' while crossing Horse Guards Parade, he discovered that they were men of the 13th Light Dragoons in their new dress. It was fortunate, he felt, that they were in a country where the prejudice against French uniforms was not so prevalent as in Spain or Portugal, otherwise they would have required 'an efficient guard to protect them from the natives'. As for the heavy cavalry, they were now 'a sort of modern antique' which reminded him of the 'older wardrobes of some of the theatres'. He hoped sincerely that he would never live to see the day when it would be necessary to model the British Army on that of the French before we could beat them.

This *cri de coeur* was echoed in the House of Commons when, on 8 March, the Army estimates were debated. One speaker after another railed against the 'military milliners' who had so transformed the appearance of the Army. The new uniforms were 'foolish' and in 'ridiculous taste'. The Life Guards had gone abroad 'worthy of Grimaldi' the clown, adorned in pantomimic pomp and feathers, and looking like 'the Rinaldos of an epic poem'. Lord Palmerston, the Secretary-at-War, made a gallant attempt to defend the changes. They had been made 'not to make them appear fine gentlemen in the streets, but because it was thought they would be conducive to their comfort and be beneficial to the service', and in any case he thought the House was 'peculiarly unfit to judge' the dress and equipment of the Army. To which Mr Whitbread retorted that he could not see why, 'when their opinion was the same as that of every man they met in the streets, as well as the persons who were condemned to wear these trappings, only fit for a mountebank'.[19]

A letter in the March number of the *Royal Military Chronicle* rounded off the debate with an ironical defence of whiskers:

even the French seldom place a man in the flank companies of their regi-ment unless he has a formidable pair of whiskers or moustachios; and we all know the importance attached to them by Cossacks, the Croatians, and all the Northern tribes. A good weather-beaten frontispiece is as becoming to a soldier as the assumption of whiskers and a martial appearance is absurd and ridiculous in a parcel of shoemakers, attorney's clerks, and cock-milliners, the refuse of the Inns of Court, and the heroes of Cranbourne-alley.

'Where in the world,' he asked, 'shall we see such a family as that of our revered and beloved monarch, every one of whose illustrious sons wears whiskers?' Some of the Spanish Guerrillas, 'who, by the bye, have likewise mustachioes and beards, often frighten their own horses as much as the French; and others of them would frighten the devil.' They were certainly 'more soldierlike and martial', and he, for one, would continue to wear them 'until interdicted by order'.

* * *

During the whole of this lengthy and ineffectual discussion, for the introduc-tion of the new uniforms proceeded regardless of it, the Hussars had been preparing, once again, for war. On 15th December the 15th Hussars started their march from Manchester and on 1 January, 1813, the 18th Hussars left Brighton, embarking at Portsmouth on the 12th. The 15th were inspected at Chichester on the 13th and embarked on the 15th and 16th. The 10th arrived ten days later, embarking on the 26th and sailing three days later.

On 17 January the transports carrying the 15th and 18th Hussars assembled at Spithead and the following day the fleet weighed anchor, Colquhoun Grant, in command of the 18th Hussars, just managing to catch it, and actually coming aboard his ship while it was under sail. They entered the Bay of Biscay on the 22nd and, running before a northerly gale reached Cape Finisterre two days later. There they were becalmed for two days, giving Adjutant Jones time to arrange for the horses to be removed and the stabling cleaned. For the next six days they beat southwards down the coast of Spain and Portugal until, on 1 February, the wind moderated and came fair off the mouth of the Tagus, where they took on a pilot and lay to for the night. The next morning they slipped past the rock of Lisbon and on into the broad calm waters of the Tagus.

CHAPTER SIX
Black Giant and Red Dwarf

'He's who has not seen Lisbon,' say the Portuguese, according to Mr Commissary Schaumann, 'has not seen a good thing.' As the transports carrying the 15th and 18th Hussars dropped anchor on 2 February, 1813, the prospect opening before them was certainly impressive, with the St Julian fort, the distant view of Belem and the city itself, built like Rome on a series of hills, forming 'to the eye one of the most grand and pleasing sights that can be conceived'. As soon as he could, Lieutenant Woodberry of the 18th hurried ashore, landing at the steps leading up to the wide expanse of the Praça do Comércio, known to the Portuguese as the *Terreiro Do Paco*, the palace terrace, in memory of the palace destroyed in the earthquake of 1767. It was also known, particularly by the British, as 'Black Horse Square', on account of its noble bronze equestrian statue of King José I. Woodberry thought it the finest piece of workmanship he had ever seen, but a more critical officer, a celebrated sportsman and keeper of hounds, noticing that the king had one of his stirrups twisted, declared a 'nation ignorant in such matters, even in their public monuments, not worth saving, never admired aught, nor was seen again in good humour, during his stay in the country'. After a good dinner at Mrs Benson's, Woodberry went to the opera where, considering that the actors repeated verbally what the prompter read out, 'and that often louder than the action', they managed to get through their parts 'with much spirit'. The music was pleasing and they danced a 'sort of pas-de-deux with castanets, called a bolero, and fandango, but with very little grace'. On closer inspection, however, Lisbon turned out to be something of a disappointment. Adjutant Jones thought it 'a fine city, but buried in filth, the nation at least five centuries behind the enlightened state of the English,' although it was some consolation that the air, soil and climate were, at that time of year, equal to any in the world.[1]

The next day the troops continued disembarking, 'much admired by the Portuguese'. Some of the missing transports came in and part of the 15th and 18th marched into Belem Barracks 'without provisions, forage, or anything except stones to lay on'. On 5 February the 2nd Life Guards left Belem on their way up country and the 18th Hussars moved to the nearby village of Luz, leaving the 15th as the sole occupants of the Barracks. Luz turned out to be a 'most enchanting and romantic' place, surrounded by plantations of oranges,

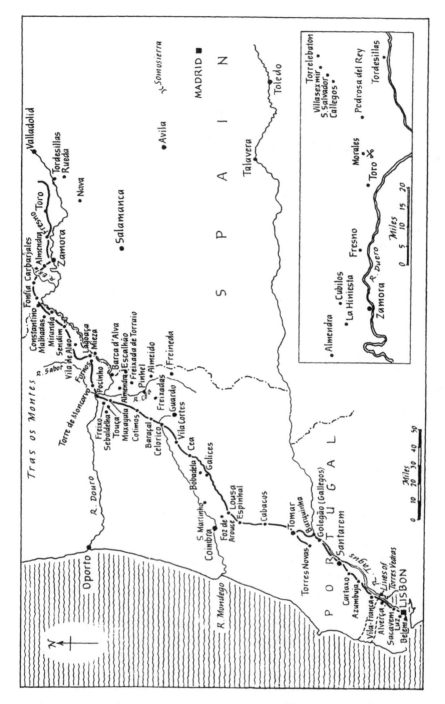

From Lisbon to the Duoro, 1813

olives and vines, watered by numerous fresh water streams. Woodberry thought that, judging from its appearance, the barracks had probably been a monastery.

Settled into Belem Barracks, 'empty & badly managed, also extremely filthy', the 15th Hussars set about tidying the place up. The missing transport turned up on the 7th and the regiment went out foraging 'for three days' straw and barley'. The ration meat and bread were generally good, but no wine was allowed to the troops stationed in Belem and Lisbon. The Adjutant was having a difficult time trying to get hold of various supplies for the regiment, as the organization of General Peacocke, the town commandant, and his staff was 'so excessive bad' that nothing was 'to be procured without considerable delay & much difficulty'; in general things appeared 'excessively mismanaged'.[2] The Hussars still had no brigade commander, but on the 8th Colonel Grant was appointed to the post and Adjutant Jones became effectively the Brigade Major, the start of a partnership which was to be the source of much annoyance and ribaldry. In the meantime the latter pressed on with getting the 15th ready for the march up to the army. The non-commissioned officers were paraded in full marching order and then the whole regiment 'turned out very servicelike and certainly much to the astonishment of the Portuguese'. The Marquess of Worcester was still in town and sent glowing reports of the 15th and 18th to Lord Edward, who relayed them on to his father, giving 'the decided preference to the horses of the 15th'.

On 13 February the first part of the 10th Hussars arrived, after a passage of sixteen days, bringing with them George FitzClarence's younger brother Henry, newly commissioned in the 15th. Between the 14th and the 17th they disembarked and, when fully ashore, were inspected on the sands near Belem Castle by Colonel Grant, who pronounced them to be in 'very fine order'. The men were physically 'good subjects', healthy and well-appointed, and the horses well selected and in very fine condition. However, by the time Colonel Palmer arrived two days later the men were already 'very much subject to drunkenness', having quickly discovered that unlimited supplies of wine could be bought for almost nothing.

Released from their cramped quarters aboard ship, the officers of the 10th were quick to sample the delights of Lisbon. 'The town was almost in ruins,' Edward Fitzgerald wrote in a letter home, 'and, moreover, dirty and dangerous to walk about in after ten o'clock at night,' as one was likely to be anointed from an upper window. 'They first throw the *perfume* and then they cry out *agua va!*' On the 15th the British Envoy, Charles Stuart, gave a ball at his house in Benefica, attended by a great company, mostly Portuguese, although there were several Hussar officers among the guests, including Woodberry, Hesse and Smith, all of the 18th, and the ubiquitous Worcester, who was the life and soul of the party, 'dancing country dances all the evening, until the last hour when waltzing commenced'. The band of the 18th made a great hit with the locals, with a new waltz, written especially for the occasion, and named after Woodberry.[3]

Meanwhile preparations continued for the brigade's march 'up-country' to join the rest of the army. Before they could be given their 'routes' they had to be issued with camp equipment and arrangements had to be made for the transport of the regimental baggage. The 15th had already made a start, with the Adjutant buying eight 'public mules' for £160, but more would be required, as each regiment was allowed fourteen, to carry the bulkier objects like the cooking kettles, the surgeon's panniers, and the paymaster's books. Rations for men and horses, supplied by the commissariat, required a further one hundred to a hundred and fifty per regiment. The regimental train was further swelled by the animals carrying the personal baggage of the officers, and their stocks of food, wine and tobacco. Apart from his private animals, each officer was allowed one public mule for his own use, but, even so, many personal belongings had to be left behind. Apart from the innumerable bits of uniform and civilian clothing, carefully listed in his diary, Woodberry managed to take with him a bearskin bed, a Hussar pipe 'complete', writing and dressing cases, breakfast and dinner services, and his racing jacket. They were carried by a horse, a pony and a mule, which, together with his two chargers and two French greyhounds, were in the charge of a valet, a groom and a soldier servant, and Woodberry was by no means exceptional.[4]

By 15 February the 15th Hussars were 'ready for immediate service', while the 18th were nearly so, with 'only a few of the horses to shoe up'. Those who remembered the disastrous shortage of shoes and nails during the Corunna campaign were taking great care to see that such a thing did not happen again. On the 16th Jones received the 'Forge Waggons & the Waggon Train establishment with them', and two days later the 'Portable Forges & their appointments from England', one of which was allocated to each squadron. The next day the farriers practised with them and found them 'good of their sort but the implements not sufficiently large to make shoes with'. In addition each man carried a spare set of horseshoes and 'more than a proportionate number of nails'. According to Sergeant Tale, 'So sacred was this reserve store considered, that . . . scarcely a set was called into requisition from their first deposit at Lisbon to the landing of the regiment at Dover from Boulogne' in 1814.

On Sunday the 21st the 10th, 15th and the garrison of Belem paraded for divine service in the magnificent riding school of the Prince Regent's palace, and afterwards marched past in the Plaça de Jeronym 'in good order'. This was followed, four days later, by a parade of the whole Brigade for General Peacocke, who arrived on the parade ground, which was no larger than St James's Square, accompanied by a large staff, 'some on horses, others on mules and asses'. After a 'General Salute' and a march past in 'open column of Divisions', the 10th and 18th returned to their quarters and the 15th went through the 'whole manoeuvres of a field day and were much admired and praised by the General'.[5] Behind the brilliant *façade*, however, the high state of discipline in which the Brigade had arrived was beginning, in the 10th and 18th at any rate, to crumble, owing to the ease with which cheap drink could be obtained. After their initial bout of drunkenness Colonel Palmer had assembled the 10th and warned them that, while he would do everything he could for their good, every man who was reported to him would be punished. He then gave them a second warning, before inflicting corporal punishment, by trying and 'breaking' four Sergeants, 'which was a very strong measure, and particularly inconvenient at such a moment, as these were perhaps the best Sergeants in the regiment'. In the event nine men were punished for drunkenness and neglect during the regiment's stay at Belem, but there were other offences that incurred the usual ferocious reprisals, so denounced by Sir Francis Burdett; 'selling corn sacks' (460 lashes); 'stealing a shirt' (300 lashes); and 'absent from stables' (100 lashes). By these means, Colonel Palmer later boasted, by the time the regiment left Belem 'it was in as good order as any regiment in the service'.[6]

The 18th had similar problems, although Colonel Murray was less inclined to order a flogging. In a letter to his second-in-command, Major Hughes, dated 8 February, he recommended that a man who had refused an order to carry corn was to 'be marched for *three hours* with *two carbines clubbed*', but he was to 'take this exercise in the shade as it is not one that is easy to practise in this climate'. He was convinced that no severity would stop the men selling the horses' corn, and the only way to check the practice was 'for the officers to be vigilant in visiting their stables'. 'Example,' he continued, was 'the only legitimate end of punishment, and . . . if each offence met with severity, it would be to take from punishment the only benefit that can be derived from it.' He was fully convinced 'of the impolicy of frequently resorting to the utmost extent of power in our hands, and therefore do not intend to flog these men'. This moderate regime was not, however, very effective, and Woodberry, sitting on his first court-martial, had to admit that, while no one could detest corporal punishment more than he, 'subordination must be kept up or we shall all soon go to the dogs'.

March went by without the Brigade receiving its 'routs'. There had been a flurry of activity in the Somerset camp when the Duke, in a letter dated 15 February, announced the 'departure of H. Wilson for Lisbon'. Lord Fitzroy Somerset was requested to send Worcester 'a preremptory order to join without delay at Freinada', and friends in Lisbon were drummed up to report 'if the lady is actually arrived there'. Lord Edward, in his reply, said that he did not believe that Worcester had the 'most distant idea of marriage,' or that it was 'his desire that she set out for Lisbon,' but her influence over him still seemed such that it was 'extremely desirable to separate them as soon as possible'. Before he could finish his letter another arrived from the Duke, dated 2 March, announcing that Harriette was not now coming to Lisbon and informing him of the agreement made with her. Lord Edward was delighted and hoped they might flatter themselves that the connection was entirely at an end. 'Of course,' he wrote, 'you will stipulate in the deed that the annuity is to be given only on the condition that all communication with Worcester shall entirely cease.' On the 22nd Edward Fitzgerald reported that Worcester had run away with 'a Mrs Archdeacon, a very pretty young woman', and had 'got her hid somewhere' in the town; he thought 'Mrs Wilson's castle-building' would soon fall to the ground.

Throughout the month preparations for the march continued apace and Adjutant Jones, now carrying out the duties of Brigade-Major, was even busier with two other regiments, besides his own, to look after. On the 9th the 15th Hussars paraded 'in complete marching order as they are to march for the army with Forge Waggons etc.', and three days later he inspected the 18th Hussars but 'found them indifferent'.[7] There were plenty of rumours as to their eventual destination going the rounds, Edward Fitzgerald writing home, somewhat inaccurately as it turned out, that they were

> to go to Gallegos [Golegão] about three leagues in advance of the whole British army, and on the borders of Spain, to take the outpost duty immediately, . . . Our horses are in capital condition and if we could keep it all the way up to the army I think we should make an example of some of them.

On the 25th Woodberry reported that Colonel Palmer had been ordered to Tomar to take up quarters for the Brigade, but there was a change of plan and Major Robarts, also of the 10th, was sent in his place. Woodberry thought that they would now march in a few days; Tomar was six days' march from Luz and 'about 7 from the army', and it was probably Wellington's intention to keep the Brigade as near to their source of supplies as long as possible.

* * *

By the beginning of April the crops were sufficiently advanced to provide the cavalry with much-needed green forage, the re-clothing and equipping of the army was complete, the vast requirement of transport assembled and Lord Wellington ready to commence his campaign. On 2 April the march up-country began with the first division of the 18th Hussars leaving Luz for Cartaxo. The next day the 15th 'paraded in complete marching order with 3 days forage & provisions . . . & every article apportioned as it is to be carried up the country'. On the 5th the right wing of the regiment marched for Sacavem 'in the most beautiful order imaginable with 2 days forage & provisions cooked'. Sergeant Tale recalled that they began their march, 'laden like bees'. Three days' supplies of bread, meat, corn, hay, and wine, giving an 'aggregate of between sixty and seventy pounds', and although this burden was not borne every day, whenever possible, 'never less than two day's consumption had to be carried'. Lieutenant Jones reckoned that the average weight carried by the horses was twenty-one stone.

The 10th were the last to leave the now half-empty barracks at Belem, on the 7th, and moving by wings, or half-regiments, so as not to put too much strain on the villages where they were to be quartered each night, the Brigade moved north, along the right bank of the Tagus, through Sacavem, Azambuja, Cartaxo and Barquinha, where they left the wide flat banks of the river. By the end of the month the three regiments were assembled in the area of Tomar. The villages they had passed through were, as Woodberry put it, 'Frenchified, that is ruined and almost deserted', a legacy of the days when the French had been holed up there in front of the Lines of Torres Vedras. The countryside around Cartaxo was 'all laid waste' and three-quarters of the houses in Santarem were 'completely gutted'. On the top of one of the church towers Woodberry spotted seven skulls hanging up and was told they were 'of traitors, who plundered the churches & assisted the French'. But although ruined, the towns provided adequate shelter for the troops each night as the cavalry generally cantoned in villages, the horses doing better under cover than in bivouac. As a result the cavalry had no tents, like the infantry, but Woodberry thought 'a bad house is better than a good tent', so they were 'not the losers by the arrangement'. When they did bivouac they generally took advantage of a neighbouring wood, but, while most officers had tents, the men had to make themselves wigwams with the boughs of trees.

At this juncture Colonel Palmer handed over command of the 10th Hussars to Major Robarts and departed for Lisbon, there to embark for England. Although he subsequently claimed that he returned home because he understood that Colonel Quentin was on his way out, and because his 'proper post', as second-in-command was with the depot in England, Lord Edward Somerset voiced a fairly general opinion that he had gone home 'for the purpose . . . of prosecuting his old claims on the mail coach business', and that he had chosen 'an extraordinary time to relinquish the command of the regt just at the opening of the campaign'.[8] Before leaving Lisbon Palmer sent a note to Adjutant Jones informing him that Henry FitzClarence had been 'appointed to the 10th & that it was done by his, Colonel Palmer's, request to the Prince'. The following day Jones 'gave up' the said Lieutenant FitzClarence to the 10th, probably with a sigh of relief, because the young man appeared to be even less amiable than his elder brother and was not settling down well with the 15th, where his fellows thought him 'overbearing and obstinate'. He was also very tactless and in an argument 'as to the relative merits of the German troops and our own, . . . was extremely violent & gave great offence' by his abuse of the English light cavalry. Palmer, knowing the Prince's interest in the boy, clearly felt he would be better off in the 10th, where he could keep an eye on him, but he was a born troublemaker and it was not a wise move.

On 22 April the 15th Hussars reached Tomar, after marching from Golegão, 'thro' a beautiful wild country in a fine day & were well put up'. They were joined the next day by the 18th, while the 10th halted farther back at Golegão and Torres Novas. During this first part of the march the inexperience of the brigade, particularly the 18th Hussars, had begun to show, and in particular the officers were beginning to regret the vast amounts of baggage they had brought with them. Woodberry thought that 'no regiment ever moved up the country with a greater train of baggage than the Hussar Brigade and the Life Guards,' and, as a result, almost everyone was 'anxious to dispose of part of those *comforts* which was thought indispensible'. One officer who had a 'Tandem' built, at the cost of at least a hundred guineas, 'purposely for this country's service sold it with harness & c., complete . . . for 4 dollars'. Some officers had given away their 'Portable Beds' and tents, or sold them 'for very inconsiderable sums', although those very articles were now found to be 'indispensibly necessary'. He thanked God that he had all his baggage safe and that, although it weighed nearly 400 pounds, his mule and pony carried it well.

The men had now 'commenced rompa-ing' every place they stayed in, Woodberry wrote. Their daily ration of a pint of wine was apparently not enough and hardly a day went by without one or other regiment halting to carry out sentences awarded for drunkenness, neglect of duty, absence from quarters and other misdemeanours. Between 5 and 29 April eleven men of the 10th Hussars were flogged, receiving between them nearly 3000 lashes. Three Sergeants were reduced to the ranks. A typical incident occurred near Barquinha, on 26 April, when a guard of the 18th Hussars, Sergeant, Corporal and all, broke into a village wine house and managed to get through nearly a pipe of wine before they were discovered in a 'beastly state of intoxication'. Four days later, a mile out of town, the Sergeant received 200 lashes, the Corporal 300 and one of the Dragoons 200, the two remaining Dragoons being pardoned. The 15th seem to have been the best behaved, for, on the same day, the Adjutant released the only two prisoners without punishment, 'from the genl. good conduct of the men'.[9]

On 24 April Augustus Schaumann, who had been in the Peninsula ever since the Corunna campaign, took up his duties as commissary to the 18th Hussars. He did so with many misgivings as the report of his predecessor of the 'ludicrous pretensions' of the officers 'was not an edifying one'. Two days later he dined with Woodberry and Burke, entertaining the 'Johnny Newcomes' with many of the old solder's tales familiar to readers of his memoirs. 'This man was at the Siege of Badajoz,' Woodberry wrote in tones of awe. 'The account he gave of the Town during the first two days after it was took, is beyond anything I before heard.'

*　*　*

At the beginning of May the Brigade left Tomar and, moving now by regiments, marched northwards towards the valley of the Mondego, and the rest of the British army, some five days march away. On the 1st the 15th arrived at Cabacos, after a march of five hours on the very worst road & in the midst of a torrent of rain', only to be put into miserable quarters, as the town and the adjacent villages had been 'dreadfully rompéd'. The 10th Hussars expected to leave on the 5th, by which time the weather had turned 'quite fine again'. They had been turning out at two in the morning for the previous two days, in order to march in the cool part of the day, and from now on they were expecting to bivouac each night, as Tomar was, Fitzgerald wrote, 'the last town in our Rout capable of holding more than two troops'. It was, moreover, a 'good place for grub', and he had managed to get 'a nice buttock of beef for dinner'. Worcester was apparently still with the regiment and Lord Edward had great hopes that his 'last business at Lisbon' would not turn out as serious as they had feared. Mrs Archdeacon's 'character & conduct previous to her connection with Worcester was so notorious' that the husband was unlikely 'to have recourse to a legal process' and he trusted the affair would end without any further notoriety. 'It is to be hoped,' he concluded, 'the operations of the campaign will direct his mind from this new object, and that as he grows older, he will grow wiser.'

By the 6th the 15th Hussars had swung to the north-east and were at Galices, in 'wild but romantic country under the sierra'. Much of the luxuriant valley of the Mondego had been destroyed, Jones noted, the Portuguese, 'a good sort of dirty people' having been 'shamefully used by the British as well as the French & all their property destroy'd.' The next day they reached Cea [Seia] where they halted for one day as the weather had turned bad again. The 18th Hussars, meanwhile, were having problems; 'nothing but mistakes,' Woodberry wrote in disgust on the 9th; 'My God! what an unfit person Colonel Murray is to command the regiment.' They had just settled down for a day's rest when they were ordered to turn out again and march for Cea. The Brigadier was at Maceira, waiting to see them pass, but unfortunately the 'unsoldierlike state' of their march, 'owing to the short notice, caused him to make some very severe remarks on Colonel Murray's conduct,' which the latter made worse by mistaking his orders and halting the regiment there, instead of marching them on to Cea. Colonel Grant had waited there to inspect them on their arrival, but they did not get in until midnight, having ridden sixty miles all through the 'apathy of Col. Murray'.

Schaumann's description of Colonel Grant portrays an arrogance only to be equalled, in later years, by Lord Cardigan:

We had only been two days at Cea when the trumpets sounded and summoned us to move further afield. Our destination was Almendra. And now the dear old troubles with the forage started afresh. Every day we Commissaries were called before Sir Colquhoun Grant to be reprimanded, and to listen to peremptory orders and threats. Our protests and proposals, based upon the experience of many years, were as good as useless. He imagined everything would be the same here as in England, and thought it exceedingly strange that we should dare to contradict so great a man as he thought himself to be. Was he not six feet tall, and had he not a huge black moustache and black whiskers? And was he not in addition, aide-de-camp, equerry and favourite of the Prince Regent? His whole manner bore the stamp of unbounded pride and the crassest ignorance, and he tried to conceal the latter beneath positive assertions which he did not suffer to be contradicted.

Schauman failed to get the 'smallest help' from the officers of his regiment, who were no better than their commander. The whole crowd were 'like fledglings; they only knew how to open their mouths to be fed'; if anything was lacking 'the officers knew no other remedy than to exclaim to one's face in a cold and stately fashion: "I shall report it".' How different things were in the 1st German Hussars.

On 11 May the 15th reached Freixadas, only seven leagues from Wellington's Headquarters at Freineda. By the 13th the whole Brigade was assembled in the area. Jones visited the 10th at Alverça to enquire 'into the state of the corps' and found it in 'tollerable order but requiring a rest'. The state of the shoeing was 'so so & they had lost a horse or two and a mule'. Colonel Murray and the officers of the 18th were sent for by Colonel Grant and reprimanded 'for the bad order' of the regiment, which Jones declared was 'for the present unserviceable'. These were pretty strong words, but he had found 'no shoes, no nails & worse than all no system with no energy in the Regt'.[10]

The army was gradually moving up into its final positions for the advance and during the rest of May the Commander of the Forces rode from division to division making sure that all was in order for the final push. It had been a difficult task getting the army, riddled with sickness, into good shape, and the endless complaints from home infuriated him. One evening, needled by criticisms in the House of Commons over the slowness with which the cavalry had been brought to the front, he unburdened himself in the hearing of Judge Advocate General Larpent. 'The men who did come,' he said,

> could not have been here sooner, and perhaps had better have come still later; that more cavalry he could not have employed had he had them at Lisbon for want of transport for food; . . . that even now he could not have brought up the Hussar brigade into the field, unless by draughting home the three regiments whose men he lately sent back, and thus setting at liberty their transport; . . . that every two dragoons employed a mule to feed the men and horses, and that all this difficulty was quite unknown at home.[11]

He still found time to relax, however, and Woodberry, seeing him out hunting, was able to leave posterity a subaltern's eye view of the great man. 'Marquess Wellington,' he wrote on 14 May,

> hunts every other morning; his dress yesterday was blue coat, white waistcoat, white neck hand[kerchie]f & grey overalls & round hat. He is an extraordinary man. For the morning after the famous retreat from the neighbourhood of Burgos, to his present cantonments, he order'd the hounds out & was actually hunting himself. His dress is always very plain & he swears like a Trooper at anything that does not please him.

1. Frederick the Great returning to Sans-Souci, after the Potsdam Manoeuvres, September, 1784. The Duke of York is on the King's left, with Lafayette on the extreme right of the picture. Engraving by A. Clemens after Edward Francis Cunningham. *(Anne S.K. Brown Military Collection, Brown University, Providence, R.I.)*

2. George III, the Prince of Wales and the Duke of York reviewing the 3rd Dragoon Guards and the 10th Light Dragoons, 1800. Mezzotint by J. Ward after Sir William Beechey. *(The Author)*

3. The Encampment at Brighton, 1796. Mezzotint by J. Murphy after Francis Wheatley.
(The Parker Gallery)

4. Light Dragoons embarking for the continent, 1793. Oil painting by William Anderson.
(National Maritime Museum)

5. The Prince of Wales in the uniform of the 10th Light Dragoons, 1801. He wears the old pattern Light Dragoon uniform with the 'Tarleton' helmet, so much beloved by George III. In fact vestiges of Hussar clothing can already be seen, notably the sabretache hanging from the sword-belt. Coloured etching by one of the Dighton family.
(Army Museums Ogilby Trust)

6. The first meeting between the Prince of Wales and Princess Caroline of Brunswick. The Prince is in the dress uniform of the 10th Light Dragoons. Oil-painting by H.Singleton.
(Baltimore Museum of Art, where it is described as the Prince of Wales and Mrs Fitzherbert*)*

7. The 10th Light Dragoons arriving at Brighton Camp, 1803. Oil painting by an unknown artist. *(National Army Museum)*

8. Light Dragoons in camp, c.1803. Privates saddling up. Pen and wash sketch by Captain Thomas Ellis, 17th Light Dragoons. *(The Author)*

9. Light Dragoons in camp, c.1803. Privates in stable dress grooming horses. Pen and wash sketch by Captain Thomas Ellis, 17th Light Dragoons. *(The Author)*

10. Ernest Augustus, Duke of Cumberland, in the uniform of the 15th Light Dragoons, c.1808. Oil painting by Sir William Beechey. *(Army Museums Ogilby Trust)*

11. Lord Paget in the uniform of a General Officer of Hussars, c. 1809. The officer of the 7th Hussars in the background is wearing the peakless shako introduced after the Corunna campaign. Engraving by Meyer after Peter Edward Stroehling. *(The Author)*

12. 'Well known Swells at Ipswich'. Hussar officers driving 'Four-in-hand'. Watercolour by Robert Dighton Junior, 1807. *(The Author)*

13. Officers and men of the Hussar Brigade, 1807. From left to right, Private 7th Hussars, Officer 7th Hussars (possibly Kerrison), Officer 7th Hussars, Officer 10th Hussars (possibly Quentin), Private 10th Hussars, Sergeant 15th Hussars, Officer 15th Hussars (possibly Forrester), Private 15th Hussars. Watercolour by the Author after Robert Dighton Junior. *(Anne S. K. Brown Military Collection, Brown University, Providence, R.I.)*

14. Review of the Worcester Militia on Southsea Common, 14 October, 1800. Painting by Richard Livesay. *(Southsea Castle Museum/Portsmouth City Council)*

15. View of Corunna harbour from the elevated ground which commanded the town. The Tower of Hercules can be seen in the left middle distance, and the fort in the middle distance. *(The Parker Gallery)*

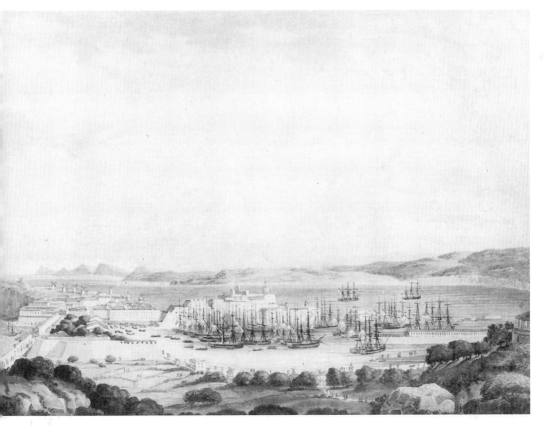

16. The attack near Sahagun, 20 December, 1808. A Private of the 15th Hussars attacking a French Dragoon. Watercolour by Henry Collins, 15th Hussars, 1811. According to Captain Gordon both British and French went into action cloaked.
(The 15th/19th The King's Royal Hussars)

17. Encounter between an 18th Hussar and a French Chasseur à Cheval at Benevente, 29 December, 1808. Watercolour by J. Garside, a musician in the regiment.
(The Royal Collection)

18. The Plain of Benevente, 1808. From the Corunna sketchbook of Sir R. K. Porter. *(British Museum)*

19. "The Pass of Manzanal". This view of "one of the noblest public works in Europe...", was "taken at a time when the natural Horrors were much heightened by many spectacles of suffering humanity". From *Sketches of the Country, Characters, and Costumes... in Portugal and Spain* by the Rev. William Bradford, 1823. *(British Museum)*

20. Henry, Marquess of Worcester, in
    the uniform of the 10th Hussars,
    with the regimental pattern sabre
    presented to every officer of the 10th
    by the Prince of Wales. Watercolour
    by J. Cosway, c.1814.
    (The Duke of Beaufort)

21. Harriette Wilson. Anonymous
    lithograph published by R. Jones.
    1823. *(British Museum)*

22. The view of the Pavilion and Steyne at Brighton with the promenade. The central circular
    part of the pavilion, and the buildings on either side, are clearly seen in the background.
    (The Author)

23. Colonel Quentin, 1807. Coloured
engraving after Robert Dighton
Junior. *(The Author)*

24. Lieutenant Edward Fox Fitzgerald,
10th Hussars, c.1811. The only son
of the ill-fated Irish patriot Lord
Edward Fitzgerald, he was brought
up by his grandmother, the Duchess
of Leinster, to whom he wrote
numerous letters from the Peninsula.
(The Author)

25. "A View of the Castle of Belem at the entrance of the Port of Lisbon," 1793. Engraving
by Wells after Noel. *(British Museum)*

26. "A view of the Praça do Commercio at Lisbon taken from the Tagus," 1793. Known to the British Army as "Black Horse Square", from the bronze statue of King José I, visible in the left of the picture. Engraving by Wells after Noel. *(British Museum)*

27. The 10th Hussars in camp in the Peninsula. Watercolour by Denis Dighton, 1813. *(The Royal Collection)*

28. The 10th Hussars charging French Infantry, c.1813. This is an imaginary scene; the Hussars should be wearing shakos not fur caps, but it gives a good idea of the use of the curved light dragoon sabre. Watercolour by Denis Dighton. *(The Anne S. K. Brown Military Collection, Brown University, Providence, R.I.)*

29. Hussars bivouacking by a church in the Peninsula, c.1813. Judging from the peakless shakos, the regiment represented is intended for the 10th. They seem to be mainly officers. Watercolour by William Heath. *(National Army Museum)*

30. The charge of the 7th Hussars at Orthes, February, 1814. Oil painting by Denis Dighton. This shows the 7th in the old white-faced uniform worn with the new shako in an oilskin cover. *(The Marquess of Anglesey)*

31. Robert Dawson Bolton, who died of wounds received at Mendionde in 1814, in the uniform of the 18th Light Dragoons, with his brother-in-law, James Hewitt Massey-Dawson of Ballinacourt, M.P. Watercolour by Robert Dighton Junior, 1802. *(The Author)*

32. Captain Thomas Wildman, 7th Hussars, in the new uniform introduced in 1814 and worn at Waterloo. The Waterloo and Peninsular medals were added later. Miniature by Samuel J. Stump. *(The Author)*

33. Captain J. Dolbel, 18th Hussars, painted at Bordeaux, May 1814. The unusual beard gives the subject an almost mid-nineteenth century appearance. Miniature by J. Dagoty. *(The Author)*

34. The three Wyndham brothers, natural sons of the Earl of Egremont. From left to right, Harry in the uniform of an Aide-de-Camp to the Commander-in-Chief, George in the new uniform of the 20th Light Dragoons, and Charles in the new uniform of the 10th introduced in 1814, just before the Quentin Trial. Oil painting by Sir William Beechey, 1814. *(Lord Egremont)*

35. The last word in the Quentin affair, the satirical cartoon, "The Siege of St Quentin", published 1 December, 1814, by W. N. Jones, No. 5 Newgate Street. *(British Museum)*

On 18 May, having already inspected the Household and Spanish cavalry, Wellington, accompanied by a numerous suite of general and staff officers, rode out from Freineda to some ground six miles beyond Freixedas to review the Hussar Brigade. After inspecting the line, with the 10th on the right flank, the 15th on the left, and the 18th, as junior regiment, in the centre, he took the salute as the three regiments marched past by half-squadrons. The ranks of men, in their blue jackets, profusely braided with white cords, and grey overalls looked magnificent, the red facings of the 10th and 15th and the red shakos of the latter making high points of colour. The horses of the 10th, Schaumann noted, were all half-blood animals, worth from thirty to forty guineas apiece, while the officers were mounted on thoroughbreds worth anything from a hundred to a hundred and fifty guineas. The day was remarkably fine and Woodberry thought the appearance of the 18th 'much superior to what it was expected; the men turned out in very high stile & upon the whole astonished the two Royal regiments in all our manoeuvres'.

According to Schaumann, Colonel Grant, a tall black-whiskered figure in an enormous cocked hat and feather, galloped hither and thither *ventre à terre* supervising the intricate movements of his brigade, and everywhere he went he was closely pusued by Adjutant Jones, 'a small man with fox-red hair, a red moustache and red whiskers', who 'also wore a red shako'. The sight of this pair was so ludicrous that henceforth they were 'never spoken of in the Brigade except as the Black Giant and his Red Dwarf'. Wellington 'expressed himself highly pleased at our appearance,' Woodberry wrote, and was not flattering them, he had the vanity to think, when he said that the Brigade was the finest he had ever seen in his life. 'The review was managed in masterly stile,' Jones wrote in his journal, '& drew from the Commander of the Forces excessive praise. The 15th certainly never looked so well as at this period.' The next day, the 19th, with immaculate timing, a letter arrived from Lord Wellington, 'containing the appointment of Lt. & Adj. Jones to the Staff of the Army in the Peninsula & with it his appointment as Major to the Hussar Brigade'.[12]

* * *

The day after the review the campaign of 1813 began in earnest. Wellington's plan, formulated with his characteristic attention to detail, simple in conception and precise in execution, was to be dramatic in its results. The French, depleted by the removal of many of their best troops to replace the losses of the Russian campaign, were strung out over a front of two hundred miles, their right flank resting on the River Douro, in the north, and their left on the Tagus to the south. They were some 55,000 strong, with a further 40,000 in the north of Spain, whereas Wellington hoped to take the field with 'near forty thousand British, and, on the whole, a hundred and fifty thousand of one sort or another'. His plan was to bluff the French into expecting a direct frontal assault in the area of Salamanca, while he, in fact, passed a large force northwards, and then east, through the 'impassable' *Tras os Montes* region, in an attempt to turn their position on the Douro. 'When the French . . . hear that we have thus crossed the Douro,' Larpent wrote on 15 May:

> and turned their position, they must either assemble and give battle which I think they will not do, or they must at once go beyond the Ebro, and then I suppose we shall attack Burgos and cross after them. Anyhow I expect a good long march at the outset.

He was right. While Wellington and Hill with 30,000 men feinted towards Salamanca, the rest of the army, under Sir Thomas Graham, with the Hussar Brigade at their head, set off on their secret march through the mountains.

They left their comfortable quarters just in time, as the supply of forage for the horses was beginning to run out. By 15 May the 18th Hussars had been 'obliged to send near 2 Leagues for green forage', the entire produce of the fields near to them, including the new crops, having been consumed by the neighbouring 15th Hussars. The regiment was 'daily assailed by the women & children with tears & moans begging us leave them a little to subsist upon'. Overtaking the bridging train, '10 waggons each drawn by 14 horses or mules', in the charge of men of the Royal Artillery, the Hussars reached their first obstacle, the River Douro, on the evening of the 20th. The next morning the two left squadrons of the 15th 'passed the river and encamped on the left [sic] bank in a beautiful olive-grove'. 'The River Douro,' Captain Thackwell of the 15th wrote, 'is beautiful beyond description, and about 130 yards across at the ferry, the current in many places very rapid,' and indeed, when the rest of the Brigade crossed on the 22nd, three horses of the 10th fell out of the boat and had to be swum ashore by one of the troop sergeant majors. It was three miles down into the gorge, 'not unlike Cheddar', and another three miles up to the town of Torre de Moncorvo, which was 'surrounded by hills like Bath'.[13]

For the next few days Graham's force followed the right bank of the Douro, travelling north-east through a countryside reminiscent of Devonshire. The little thatched villages were poor but clean, and, as the French had not penetrated the region, there were few signs of war. On the march to Fornos, on the 24th, the enemy were seen quite clearly on the other bank and it was 'Pickets out!' for the first time. That night Woodberry wrote in his journal, 'Thank God we are now drawing near those reptiles the French. They are now in sight at Merza [Mieza] in Spain, but the Douro is between us or they would not sit in their quarters so quietly.' The 'Red Dwarf', also writing up his journal, was briefer, noting that 'the enemy was this day on the opposite bank of the Douro – mounted picquets for the cover of the Brigade'. That night he issued orders to the Brigade discontinuing the sounding of reveille or retreat, 'nor any other sound of the bugles except for field duties, or to turn-out'. The trumpets could sound 'for stables as usual', but no bugle was to sound when the Brigade was together, except by order of the 'Officer commanding the Brigade . . . when it will of course be taken up by the bugles of regiments'.

The next morning they marched 'as usual right in front', that is, led by the 10th Hussars. The weather was now getting hot and it was very pleasant to camp in the river meadows at the end of the day, perhaps even to have a quick plunge in the river. On one of these balmy evenings, when the Brigade lay in adjacent fields near Vila de Alao, Woodberry launched into one of his purple patches:

How delightful is the enjoyment after a long and fatiguing march thro' a burning sun, to recline on a portable bed in your tent, under a fine grown shady oak tree. How beautiful the prospect of the Troop bivouacked, the horses all picketted to the neighbouring trees. Spain is seen distinctly, a French camp at a distance of a league; the country round in a flourishing state of cultivation; a distant view of the Forageing Parties belonging to the Brigade; the Camp all alive, the men cleaning their horses, cooking, &c., &c . . . .

On the 29th the Brigade reached its next obstacle, the Esla, 'a formidable river in a military view', very fast and as wide as the Thames at Kew Bridge, and camped between Carbajales and the ford at Almendra, which the Brigade-Major went off at once to investigate, riding across it to ascertain its depth. It was defended by 'a strong detachment of cavalry & some guns', occupying a position 'extremely strong by nature'. The next day, a Sunday, the Brigade rested and preparations were made for the crossing, which was to take place on the Monday. After breakfast Major Hughes made his own reconnaissance of the ford. Like Jones, he rode across it, but was forced to retire when the French picquets on the hills moved down to the bank on his approach. He found the stream rapid and requiring either daylight or 'a perfect knowledge' to find. It was, moreover, 'irregular & too deep for infantry' and commanded by heights.

Before dawn on the 31 May the Hussar Brigade, a troop of horse artillery, the 51st and Brunswick-Oels regiments, supported by a 'Brigade of guns 9 pounders' on the heights, were ready to make the crossing. As day broke the Hussars, accompanied by the infantry, plunged into the swirling waters, but unfortunately their guide, Captain Clements, 18th Hussars, 'not having exactly recollected the direction, . . . confusion and distress . . . equally awful and afflicting' ensued. Major Hughes described how, as many of them wandered off course, 'horses got into the chasms of the rocks, plunged and threw their riders, the Infantry were carried off their legs, others were dragged by the stirrups of the Dragoons to the opposite banks.' 'Some,' he continued, 'fell near the banks on their backs (the weight of their packs keeping them down) and were dragged out; the simple expedient of a rope would have saved most.' Sergeant Tale, in common with others, had several infantrymen clinging at once to his legs and stirrup leathers, while he carried 'as many of their fire-locks' as he could manage. One of the Brunswickers seized hold of his horse's bit 'with a death-grasp' and he was forced to push him away. 'What his subsequent fate was' he knew not, but he still sickened and shuddered 'at the thought of that horrible scene'. According to the Brigade-Major seventeen infantrymen were drowned and the 15th lost one horse. Had the French defended the position, he thought 'they would have destroy'd the troops which attempted to pass, but by some unaccountable neglect' they failed to discover what was going on until part of the advance guard had gained the opposite bank. The chaos of the crossing provided a perfect excuse for lost kit and, according to Sergeant Tale, whenever the commanding officer subsequently inspected the regiment, prior to the day's march, the invariable reply to any query about missing equipment was 'lost in crossing the Esla'. 'Bless me!' he would exclaim, 'that Esla must be choked with camp equipage.'[14]

The right squadron of the 15th now joined the advance guard and together they dashed up the hill to Almendra, where they surprised a French picquet, consisting of an officer, who was caught shaving, and fifty men of the 16th Dragoons. Another three miles of a 'Bagshot Heath road, sand and pines', before the Moorish church of Zamora came into sight, and the Hussar Brigade was back on the old route they had followed in 1808. As the 18th trotted along 'Captain Grammont of the 10th Hussars came galloping past & informed us that two squadrons of the enemy's Dragoons were advancing towards us.' When they appeared, the Hussars 'dashed at them and knocked them over in fine style', pursuing them up to the walls of Zamora. The Brigade-Major felt that Captain Thackwell 'led the squadron too far & was much too precipitate & eager in the pursuit of the enemy,' but to Sergeant Tale the whole episode was 'the maiden fleshing of our swords' in the campaign, and 'gave a spur and incentive to further brushes'.

After the initial crossing, a bridge, consisting of nine pontoons, was thrown across the Esla and the rest of Graham's force crossed over dry-shod. That night the Hussar Brigade camped at La Hiniesta and Cubilos, on the outskirts of Zamora, 'without corn & all without cover'. The prisoners, who were led into Zamora that night, as Wellington was being fêted by the populace, confirmed that, as in 1808, the French cavalry were no match for the British in open combat. The next day, 1 June, the pursuit continued, the Brigade halting for the night at Fresno, where, according to Woodberry, the 10th Hussars made themselves comfortable in all the best quarters. That same night Major Gardiner's Troop of the Royal Horse Artillery was formally attached to the Brigade.

At dawn on the 2nd they set off again, following the flat sandy road, with the river curving gently on the right. At Toro they learned that the French rearguard, consisting of cavalry, infantry and artillery, was not far ahead, and the column, led by the 10th Hussars, followed by the guns and the 18th, with the 15th bringing up the rear, broke into a sharp trot, which soon increased into a canter. They kept this pace up for six miles or so until, as they were approaching Morales, they came face to face with a 'squadron of observation' of the 16th Dragoons drawn up across the road. The leading squadron of the 10th immediately formed from divisions into line and, while they were doing so, two of Gardiner's guns were unlimbered, firing nine rounds at the enemy with little effect. The squadron then charged, with Colonel Grant and Major Robarts at their head, overthrowing the enemy's front rank, which fell back in confusion on its supports. Private Porter of the 10th Hussars described how:

the right half squadron, and that is A troop, fought and beat a whole regt of French cavalry. When they first fell in with them, the French gave them three cheers, and our troop cheered them in return and the troop charged them three times before they retreated and when they did the rest of the Regt came up and pursued them.[15]

As the enemy went about, the centre squadron of the 10th came up on the left of their leading squadron and formed line with it. The third squadron took up a position 'slightly refused' on the left of the other two and, according to Worcester, it now became 'a chase across country over the prickly-pear hedges, the pace being so good that the rest of the Hussar Brigade in support could not get up'. The enemy were driven helter-skelter some two miles to Morales, where they reformed and charged the 10th, 'in high stile'.

When the rest of the Brigade finally came up, they found the enemy, 'amounting to 12 to 1500 Dragoons', partly in line and partly in column, on the right of the town of Morales. Colonel Grant now halted the rest of the Brigade, which was in column of threes, sent the guns to the rear and advanced again without deploying. Major Hughes thought this 'injudicious' and, off his own bat, persuaded the short-sighted Colonel Murray to form the 18th in open column of squadrons. At length Grant ordered the Brigade to deploy into line and, with the 10th on the left, the 18th on the right, the 15th in support and skirmishers out in front, it 'advanced very briskly upon the enemy,' with Colonel Grant at its head. Woodberry, out with the skirmishers, had a good view of the ensuing 'bustle and confusion', as the French tried to make 'their best way off, while the 10th was hacking and cutting them about in all directions'. Major Hughes soon found himself in the midst of the enemy, his horse blown and he himself so exhausted that, on hitting out at one of them, he nearly fell off his horse. One fired a pistol at him, and just as another was 'giving point' with his sword, Worcester, followed by the 10th, came to his rescue. According to Henry Wyndham

a general pursuit ensued for about two miles in which many of the enemy were killed wounded and taken, until we arrived at a defile, being a bridge over a morass in rear of which on a height the enemy had a large column of about thirteen squadrons of cavalry, light guns, and behind the hill two Regiments of infantry.[16]

The 10th halted, but the 18th carried on and some 'stragglers too eager for the pursuit', crossed the bridge and were roughly handled by the French. Captain Lloyd, a quartermaster, a sergeant and a private, all of the 18th, actually reached the crest of the hill, 'cutting down all who opposed them, before they knew the regiment had stopped, and they were took in their attempts to rejoin'. The enemy now brought up his guns and in Wyndham's account:

got the range of the squadron with shot and shell and did a little execution killing two or three horses, and wounding two men. We immediately retired in good order and formed out of their range behind a small height; by this time the 15th and 18th were up and formed. Shortly after the enemy withdrew their force from the height and retired.

The results of this 'very handsome affair', which Wellington felt 'reflected great credit upon Major Robarts and the 10th Hussars and upon Colonel Grant, under whose direction they acted', were two officers, 202 men and 160 horses taken, besides those killed and wounded, the latter of which probably amounted to seventy, not to mention 'a lady in disguise, the wife . . . of a French officer who was found dead among the others on the field of action'. The 10th Hussars lost Lieutenant Cotton, who, according to Henry Wyndham, was 'shot through the heart and lungs and cut with a sabre over the head while we were rallying our men by the bridge,' and one man killed. Colonel Grant received a slight wound on the thigh and nine men of the 10th and 18th were wounded, 'part of them severely', one of them, Job Upton, of the 18th, having a leg shot off while riding alongside Hughes. Henry Wyndham was much impressed by the behaviour of all the young officers which was 'not only highly creditable, but particularly bold and gallant', and there was 'scarcely one of them who had not his sword into or through the body of two or three Frenchmen'. All in all, the Brigade-Major concluded that night, the 'business was very handsomely done' and, recalling, perhaps, their performance in the Corunna campaign, 'the first the 10th had ever been concerned in of any consequence'.

Woodberry had never seen men 'so mad for action as the Hussars were', noting that 'out of the number of prisoners we took, hardly one was to be discerned without some dreadful cuts on the heads and bodies'. Larpent saw them the next day, at Toro, 'much cut and wounded, covered with blood, wounds neither washed nor dressed,' and this in spite of Major Jones's application for 'medical aid for the wounded enemy' the previous evening. Larpent tried to buy some of the captured horses, which Woodberry had brought into Toro to sell for the benefit of the Brigade, but 'they were all half-starved and the service having seized the best hundred and fifty for government, the remainder, which were sold by auction, were most miserable'. Nevertheless forty-seven of them fetched over 219 guineas, which was more than the Government allowance for chargers and was eventually divided among the Brigade as prize money.

'This French Brigade,' wrote Henry Wyndham, 'of which we have made so severe an example, and particularly the 16th Regiment, is one which has been five times before now engaged with British cavalry, and has been generally

122

successful, especially against the heavy brigade of General Slade.' Apparently they had not intended to stand and fight, but had, according to Woodberry, mistaken the Hussar Brigade for Don Julian's Spanish lancers, who were dressed 'something like', and 'were determined to take the shine out of them, but they found out their mistake immediately the charge was made, when all were anxious to escape'. A prisoner at Pedrosa del Rey told Henry Wyndham that 'out of the 16th Regiment, 500 strong, only five remained that were not either killed or wounded'. They found Captain Lloyd here, where he had been 'suffered to remain', slightly wounded, having given his parole, 'that a French Captain should be sent to them in exchange'. He had apparently sold his liberty 'so dearly that the French were greatly enraged and after cutting him down from his horse they beat him with their swords so that he could hardly move'. After they had calmed down a bit they were intrigued to know 'who that great black fellow in a cocked hat was,' who had distinguished himself so much during the fighting.

The victory at Morales, one of only a handful of successful cavalry actions of the Peninsular War, may be attributed as much to the quality of British horseflesh as to the dashing hunting-field style of the officers. After months of green forage and little action, the horses of the Hussar Brigade were fat and liable to get blown easily. Yet, and much to the surprise of some of the officers, they managed to keep up a fast canter and gallop for nearly six miles. Being mainly blood, or three-parts bred horses, particularly in the 10th, their speed was phenomenal and the smaller and badly-fed French horses were bowled over like ninepins.[17]

*   *   *

The next day the Hussar Brigade marched out of Morales with the 15th 'most devilishly mortified they had no hand in the late skirmish'. At Torrelebaton, on the 4th, the army closed up and marched in 'order of battle' and the Hussars fell in with Don Julian Sanchez's cavalry, 'a despicable body of banditti mounted on small Spanish & French horses in something like hussar uniform, with lances, flags, and English helmets'. The next day, at Penaflor, where they bivouacked in pouring rain, they were joined by the 14th Light Dragoons and the 1st King's German Legion Hussars, the most experienced cavalry regiment in Wellington's army. On the 6th, Woodberry wrote, the whole army was 'so well concentrated that it could form in battle order in less than two hours'. According to Major Jones the march that day had been 'long, tedious & unpleasant' and the Brigade 'badly put up as to water & forage & convenience'. The next day they crossed the Carrion River, unopposed, and marched *en parade* through Palencia, 'among the thundering cheers of the inhabitants', but that night, at Villalabon, 'the men of the Brigade behaved extremely ill . . . & plundered the inhabitants excessively'.

The next morning the Black Giant and his Red Dwarf were on the warpath. Woodberry recalled that the bugles had sounded at ten o'clock, and when the

Brigade formed up to march, 'the *Officer's Call* directed us round Colonel Grant and the Brigade-Major expecting some compliment on turning out so quick'. On the contrary, they received a severe lecture on the conduct of the men, who had 'broke open & robbed the church and every house in the village'. The officers were ordered to inspect the kit of every man at once, and two of the 18th and one of the 10th were brought out of the ranks, having bacon in their possession. 'They were,' he continued, 'immediately tried by a Brigade Court-martial . . . and received, instead of the bacon, six hundred lashes each.'[18] After which the Brigade proceeded on its way to Tamera, where it was 'exceedingly ill put up'. It rained hard all night, with 'very few of the horses & men under any sort of cover & the 18th Hussars without corn'. In Woodberry's opinion the events of that day and night 'did considerable injury to the Brigade'. Lord Edward Somerset was now very near the Hussars, in Santoyo, and on the 9th he wrote to the Duke telling him about the 'brilliant affair' at Morales, in which both Worcester and Henry Somerset had been, 'conspicuously active & forward'. Unquestionably there was never a finer Brigade than the Hussars, but he had not 'seen a sufficiency of them yet' to decide whether he liked the 10th or the 15th best, although he considered the horses of the 18th inferior to the other two. (See map p. 130)

On the 10th they crossed the River Pisuerga, only one hour behind the French, and that evening, at Villastandino, they were welcomed by the inhabitants dancing fandangos to the accompaniment of three tambourines. The next day they were in sight of Burgos and, on the day after that, the army moved on the town, by way of the heights of Isar. Wellington pushed the Hussar Brigade and Ponsonby's heavy dragoons forward on the left flank, where they were opposed by large numbers of enemy cavalry. At about two in the afternoon the Hussar Brigade prepared to charge twelve squadrons, who had thrown out their skirmishers, 'but they retired before it reached them under cover of a fortified village'. Leaving the 15th Hussars to watch the left flank, the rest of the Brigade, together with 'the German Cavalry', Ponsonby's and Long's Brigades were detached to the right, where the French army had, by some strange blunder, failed to retire on Burgos in sufficient time, so that 'our cavalry & guns crowned the heights under which the whole of the French army was obliged to pass'. As they ran the gauntlet of British artillery, the cavalry made repeated charges on them, but so steady were the enemy's columns, and so fierce the volley and artillery fire which their squares poured upon them, that they were forced to take shelter on the high ground. As night fell the cavalry withdrew and the French retired safely into Burgos. The next morning, at two o'clock, Cornet Eversfield, who was on picquet duty, 'discovered the enemy springing mines at Burgos' and, at about five o'clock, there was a tremendous explosion as the Castle went up. The French the '*retired* in much *hurry*', by the road to Vitoria. According to the Brigade-Major, 'Lord Wellington was much gratified by the destruction of Burgos & proceeded with the army to turn their right flank.'

As the French retired north-east Wellington plunged due north into the mountainous country around the headwaters of the Ebro. After two long marches of seven and six leagues, the Hussar Brigade, with Ponsonby's, D'Urban's and Alten's cavalry brigades, the artillery, the 4th and Light Divisions, crossed the Ebro by the bridge at Puente Arenas and camped around Villarcayo. The weather had been very hot and the Brigade was 'excessively fatigued', the horses having been for several days without corn. But the British were now nearer to the sea and Wellington gave orders for a new supply base to be set up at the port of Santander.

Setting off early each morning, the army now turned eastwards, towards Vitoria and, skirting Medina, emerged from the mountains on the 18th to find General Graham's force engaged with 8,000 French in front of Villalba. That night the Hussar Brigade camped near Berberana, on the Burgos-Bilbao road, cold and wet, for the weather had suddenly changed, and 'very much in want of bread'. They rested up the next day, in very wet weather, with little or no shelter. Major Jones, resuming his Adjutant's hat, took the opportunity to deal with some regimental business, ordering much-needed boots from Mr Garner in Worcester and writing to Mr Greenwood, the regimental agent, about the men's overalls.

Cornet John Dolbel of the 18th now had a chance to write to his father, recounting his experiences at Morales. He had shot a dragoon with his pistol, with his left stirrup cut, and without his hat, pelisse or valise. His horse had been shot under him, but he had taken one belonging to a French officer as a replacement. He was now sixteen miles beyond Burgos, pursuing the enemy and skirmishing with him daily. He was without shirts or socks, travelling forty miles a day, but was in good spirits, unlike Woodberry's friend Smith, who was depressed about something; 'being absent from Mrs S[mith] must be the cause of it, if so it is a very frivolous one for an Hussar'.[19] On the 20th they reached Subijana, having just failed to cut off the French, who were now concentrating in the Zadorra valley, in front of Vitoria, where they would have to make a stand, if their immense baggage train was to reach France in safety. 'After tomorrow,' Woodberry wrote, 'we must either advance or die of hunger,' and Sergeant Tale recalled that, having, 'in the rapidity of our late marches, outstripped the commissariat, the bivouac at Subijana was more remarkable than any other I recollect for empty insides and pinching hunger'.

*   *   *

At daybreak on the morning of 21 June the army marched towards the enemy positions in the Zadorra valley and at a quarter to eight the action began with General Hill's corps, together with Morillo's Spaniards, ascending the heights to the left of the French position. At nine 'the affair became general', but the Hussar Brigade, who had made their way by 'unfrequented paths and woods', guided by a local peasant, halted in close column and dismounted on the banks of the Zadorra, near the village of Nanclarres. They were kept here, in reserve, behind the 3rd Division, for nearly three hours, during which time they could see Soult and his staff, quite clearly, on the summit of the Arinez knoll, in the centre of the French position. As the French gradually withdrew down the valley towards Vitoria, General Kempt called the 15th Hussars over the river and they advanced at a gallop, 'crossing the narrow bridge one by one, horseman after horseman'. As the Brigade moved forward the cannonade, Major Jones wrote, 'became tremendous & the action hot along the whole line'. They continued moving slowly until they reached the outskirts of the town, 'where several brigades of cavalry had been collected', and here they waited 'for a tedious and wearisome length of time', passive spectators of the battle, which was raging all around them and victims of the occasional stray round.

At about three o'clock the French centre was driven in on Vitoria, leaving their left wing exposed and the Hussar Brigade was hurled into the gap in an attempt to cut off the left flank. According to Major Hughes of the 18th the Brigade advanced rapidly, 'but the arrangements of Brigadier Grant being highly imperfect (or rather, he having made none) the rear of the regiment was halted while he advanced with the left (Captain Turing's) squadron. They halted and Hughes ordered some skirmishers out under Captain Turing, to annoy a French column to their front, but Turing 'waved his sword, cheered, and charged'. It was a most unfortunate business; Hughes tried to stop them, but it was too late and on they swept into the column, with the loss of Captain Turing killed, Cornet Forster severely wounded and several men killed and wounded. Until then, Captain Thackwell recalled, the Brigade had not been engaged, 'but suffered some loss from the enemy's artillery'.

At four o'clock the enemy was driven from Vitoria with the loss of 160 pieces of cannon & in the utmost confusion'. Lord Wellington, according to Thackwell, ordered the 15th to 'pass the flats, leaving Vitoria to the right, and endeavour to cut off the enemy's retreat', and the Brigade at length advanced. Before they could catch up with their quarry, however, they had to pass what Captain Kennedy described as 'the many obstructions in the shape of trunks of trees, high-standing corn, vineyards and hamlets', which prevented them from charging. It was at this point in the action that Sergeant Tale captured two French officers, the first of whom 'was plainly caparisoned, his headgear or brass-mounted helmet ornamented with horsehair', but the second prisoner was 'a magnificently dressed officer of our own kidney, young and handsome, whiskers and moustachios in an embryo state, but be-furred and be-silvered from head to heel'.

As the Brigade passed Vitoria Major Hughes was ordered to go through the town and, leaving the left squadron under Captain Carew, he swung off with the other two, the 10th following hard on his heels. 'The confusion and alarm of the enemy,' he wrote, was the only thing that saved them. The town gates were blocked with artillery drivers, tumbrils and cavalrymen, but somehow they managed to squeeze through and became engaged 'in desperate and individual street-fighting'. In a letter to his brother, written after the battle, he gave more details:

We succeeded in driving the enemy through the town, while women were screaming and jumping on balconies, Frenchmen firing from others, and Spaniards stabbing them in the streets, and we were followed by the 10th. As the men followed the French through the different streets, we got there in a very broken state. On the other side [of the town] stood a crowd of carriages, horses and baggage.

At this very moment King Joseph, accompanied by his bodyguard of a hundred Hussars, was fleeing through the town and would almost certainly have been taken, Woodberry thought, if Captain Kennedy's troop of the 18th had not 'ran after a set of fellows and plunder'd and did not support their captain who was very near to being taken'. According to Kennedy himself, some of his men stopped in the town for some minutes, 'in the midst of plunder, wine, and spirits of all sorts', and in such a situation it was not to be wondered that the men, 'after a long and fatiguing day in warm weather, should instantly drink, and consequently get drunk, and in this state Lord Wellington happened to come up and see some of them'.

Meanwhile the remaing squadron of the 18th, and the 15th Hussars, passed round the left of the town, where they ran into the whole of the French cavalry 'formed to protect the retreat of the King and their infantry'; 'it was here,' Woodberry recalled, 'that the Hussar Brigade was damn'd for ever.' Colonel Grant, apparently not realizing that over half of the brigade had peeled off into the town, ordered a charge, and the four squadrons, greatly outnumbered, advanced and rode over a column of infantry. But the attack failed and Woodberry, slightly wounded, was chased back to the starting place 'by a whole squadron of the enemy'. When he halted to re-form his men, he saw Carew in the hands of the enemy, and a squadron of the 15th retreating. He heard Carew shout out, 'Come along, Woodberry,' but his men refused to follow him, and that was the last he saw of him.

The 18th and 10th emerging from the eastern gate of Vitoria were immediately counter-attacked and driven back into the town, but they rallied and returned to the charge. A squadron of the 10th, under Henry Wyndham and Worcester, managed to disperse the guards surrounding the mass of the enemy's baggage. Although blown and disorganized by their wild ride, the 10th held off repeated enemy attacks to recover the baggage, while Wyndham and his squadron continued the pursuit. Worcester, coming up with Joseph Bonaparte's carriage:

found himself separated from him [King Joseph] by a mill stream, & while he was making a detour to pass it, His Majesty made his escape on foot, but his carriage was found full of various effects, gold watches, snuff boxes, & money, embroidered coats &c. &c.

One officer afterwards described the French baggage train, which was enormous and weighed down with the accumulated plunder of years of occupation:

On that occasion there fell into our hands upwards of 400 carriages, of all sorts and sizes, with two, four, and six horses and mules, containing all Joseph's court, the wives and families of the French civil *employés*, and of those Spaniards who were in his service. The main road was so choked with carriages, with their doors open and steps down, the mules and horses standing in them, that we were obliged to go into the fields along the sides. I can only compare it to the inmates of the carriages (allowing for the foreign shape and fashion) in Hyde Park, when it is at its height on a Sunday, being taken with a sudden panic, which must spread to their servants, and for them all to jump *out* and off, and tucking up their petticoats, and doffing the box coats, to run for their lives, under bare poles, across to Kensington Gardens, leaving the carriages and horses to take care of themselves.

Six of Joseph's carriages were captured and much valuable property found in them. Several hundred of the typical French long narrow ammunition waggons were also taken, some of which contained, under a tier of musket ammunition, 'a range of treasure in boxes and barrels'.

The 18th Hussars were by now totally out of control and the 'example of the Spaniards', Major Hughes claimed in their defence, 'the confusion, and the riches scattered about, tempted the men to help themselves'. This would have been 'fair and right', he thought, 'if there had not been at the time a great deal to do'. As it was the regiment was 'utterly broken, and fit for nothing', and it was with great difficulty that he managed to collect a handful of men, with which he took some guns about half a league beyond the town.

That night, with the French in full retreat, the army bivouacked in pouring rain on the great road beyond Vitoria, and the Brigade-Major summed the day's events up in his journal. It had been 'a great day', he wrote,

the enemy was completely & greatly defeated with a loss of 10,000. The loss of the British army is about 3000, or from that, including Spaniards, to 5000. The Hussar Brigade lost Captains Turing & Carew of the 18th killed, Captain Hancox, Lieut Finch & Cornet Forster of the 15th and 18th wounded, also 127 men & 91 horses killed, wounded & missing. The 18th Regt behaved ill, did not charge home & remained to plunder.

* * *

The French armies were now split. Reille, after halting for some time at Salvatierra, pushed northwards towards France. Joseph reached Pamplona, to the east, in disorder, his rearguard harassed by the Light Division, and, passing men and supplies into the strongly fortified town, he, too, fled into France. Foy fell back across the Bidassoa River and joined Reille in France. Only Clausel remained at large, somewhere near Tudela, south of Pamplona,

128

planning to enter France by way of Saragossa, and Jaça, in the east. Wellington sent Graham to cover St Sebastian while he followed the French into the Pyrenees and set siege to Pamplona. In six weeks his army, in a series of left hooks, had marched 600 miles, crossed six great rivers, invested two fortresses and driven 120,000 French veterans back within the confines of their own borders.

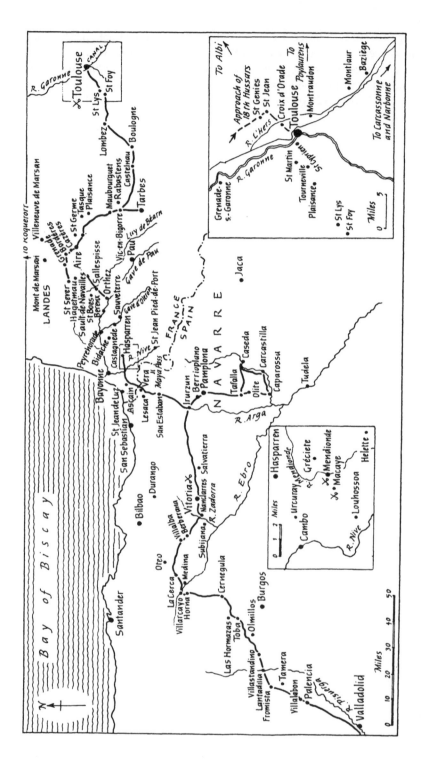

From Valladolid to Tolouse 1813–14

CHAPTER SEVEN
The Assassin's Nest

Exhausted by long marches and short rations, the Hussar Brigade followed the Light Division along the 'great Pamplona road', the incessant rain adding to their already considerable sufferings. 'The weather dreadful & the roads much cut up by the enemy,' Major Jones wrote on the 22nd at Salvatierra; 'the rain continued the whole night & the army were in want of provisions in the open field, buried in mud.' The next day was no better. 'The miseries of this day's march,' he wrote, 'almost inconceivable. Baggage, guns, horses, women, children, stuck fast in bog & the army exhausted with fatigue & want of provisions.' Everyone was talking about the 'affair' of the 18th Hussars. In Worcester's opinion they had disgraced themselves 'by their cowardice in the field & their infamous conduct out of it plundering Friend & Foe'. The next day, 24 June, the Brigade halted at Bacaicoa and the 18th Hussars were made to deliver up their plunder to be divided. One man had no less than 740 quarter-dublons in his kit, and Major Hughes collected about £2,600, not counting the jewels and clothes which he gave to the paymaster 'for the general benefit of the regiment'. Schaumann remembered seeing 'huge and beautifully kept ledgers belonging to the Royal Treasury, wonderful maps, and expensively bound books from the Royal Field Library, trodden underfoot, and sodden with the rain'. Regretfully he noted that the 'unmarried ladies belonging to the French army, most of whom are young and good-looking Spanish women, dressed in fancy hussar uniforms, and mounted on pretty ponies, or else conveyed in carriages, were first robbed of their mounts, their carriages, and their jewels, and then, most ungallantly, allowed to go.'[1]

Among the booty Corporal Fox of the 18th 'found' Marshal Jourdain's bâton, but a drummer of the 87th stole most of it, leaving him with just the golden cap pieces. These Major Hughes sent to Wellington, who graciously thanked him and the officers of the 18th, enclosing a ten-dollar tip for the Corporal. Eventually the bâton was re-assembled and sent to the Prince Regent, who was highly flattered. 'You have sent me,' he wrote to Wellington, 'the staff of a French Marshal, and I send you, in return, that of England.'[2] The rest of the army was jealous of the riches the 18th Hussars had acquired, Major Hughes wrote, but the truth of the matter was that several of the officers were implicated in the transactions. Hughes claimed that he himself 'cautiously avoided ever to accept the diamonds, Orders, crosses, and jewellry', which were offered to him, and which he might 'without inconvenience' have put in his sabretache, but Woodberry reckoned that Burke had acquired 'near two thousand pounds' and Dolbel as much again. All this time the brigade had been literally starving and, while the 'fledglings' squabbled over their jewels, experienced campaigners like Schaumann concentrated on more practical plunder, rifled from the 'royal kitchen wagon', like the hermetically sealed tins, some of which, when opened, disclosed 'a wonderful roast joint or fowl in aspic, perfectly fresh and delicious to the taste!' Others contained preserved fruit or jam. Every evening some of these tins were opened and Schaumann and his friends enjoyed them immensely. All Tale got was a 'haversack of biscuits', which he shared with his 'pet steed', but his reward came soon after when he was made 'acting Sergeant-Major to the regiment' and 'mounted an additional *chevron*'.[3]

The next day, near Pamplona, Colonel Grant was sent for by Wellington, who 'expressed himself in strong terms' against the 18th, and 'desired' him to 'state his opinion of their conduct to the officers in the plainest manner', adding that had they done their duty they could have taken King Joseph 'at the time the 15th charged so gallantly on the left of the town'. On the 26th, still in pouring rain, the brigade marched round the south side of Pamplona and, that evening, at Noain, Colonel Grant assembled the officers of the 18th, and informed them of Wellington's displeasure at the insubordination of the regiment, particularly the conduct of the men in Vitoria itself, numbers of whom the Duke had seen plundering the streets. 'He was likewise,' Woodberry noted, 'very much displeased with several of our officers, who was there likewise instead of being in the field; and to finish he had to inform us that his Lordship was determined if he heard any complaints against the regiment, he would immediately dismount us, and march the Regiment to the nearest Sea-port and embark us for England, and at the same time send the Commander-in-Chief his remarks upon the subject.' That the officers of the 18th were not the only ones guilty of plundering is clear from an entry in the Brigade-Major's journal that night, in which he states that Captain Booth and Lieutenants Mansfield, Finch and Barrett, all of the 15th Hussars, were told that they 'had disgraced themselves by participating in the plunder which had been taken on the day of Vitoria & were ordered to give it up forthwith'.

The next day the Brigade marched south to Tafalla, where they were received with acclamations. The inhabitants had never seen British troops before and they dragged the men into their houses and plied them with drink, with disastrous results. An hour later Wellington and his staff arrived and the Hussar Brigade was 'obliged to change their quarters'. When the 10th turned out, the 'most disgraceful scene' occurred, with 'three fourths' of the men 'rolling on their horses, quite drunk'. Major Robarts ordered the captains to 'select one or two of the worst men in their Troops' and these, twelve or so in number, were made 'an example of for the benefit of the whole'.

* * *

News was now received of Clausel's attempt to return to France and the 4th Division, accompanied by Grant's and Ponsonby's Brigades, was sent off to intercept him. On the 28th they marched due south from Olite to Caparosso, by the River Arga, which they followed back, in a north-easterly direction, through wild and uncultivated country to Caseda. Captain Wodehouse of the 15th, sent out to reconnoitre from Caparosso, found the enemy leaving Tudela, on the Saragossa road, and chased their rearguard for two miles or so. The next day they remained on the north bank of the Aragon, but there was no further sign of the enemy.

That day there was another sale of Vitoria plunder. Sifting through the sporting guns inlaid with gold and the silk underclothes embroidered with the red 'J' of King Joseph, Schaumann came across a sackful of 'candlesticks, teapots, silver ingots, bearing the treasury mark, plates, knives, and forks', which he bought for half their proper value. What astonished him most, however, was 'the vast number of military and court uniforms, belonging either to the King, his marshals, or to other dignitaries and officials of his entourage, made either of fine cloth, or brown, blue, and scarlet velvet, and covered with gold lace'. They were rapidly turned into jackets and forage caps, and nearly every officer in the brigade had one, while their 'vindictive Spanish muleteers' bought the crosses of the *Légion d'Honneur* 'at any price' to hang on their mules' tails.

The next day they turned due west and made their way back across country to Olite, where they settled into quarters. Relaxing comfortably, with his favourite grog and 'segars', Schaumann ran over in his mind the discomforts they had recently endured:

> Every morning at three o'clock the trumpets called us to water and feed, at four o'clock to saddle and bridle, and at 4.30 to march. As a rule it was still dark when we left our night quarters. . . . We hardly ever halted until late in the afternoon, and frequently had to ride a distance of two or three miles to water. Then we had to draw our rations, divide them up with our fellows, and cook them, so that by the time we had seen to our saddles and cleaned them, it was frequently ten or eleven o'clock before we got any rest.

It had been difficult waking up in the mornings, and one or other of the regiments was usually late on parade, when 'Grant would curse and swear and rave like a madman'. Waited on by a team of servants, in some comfortable house, it was easy enough for him to get a good night's rest and reach the parade ground 'first and in comfort'.

The Hussar Brigade had reached heights of glory, but not for long. In the three weeks since the 'handsome' affair at Morales, the flaws and weaknesses in their 'fine' façade, known previously only within the Brigade, had become common gossip. The 18th, in Woodberry's words, had been 'damn'd for ever'. An Irish regiment, full of Irish hotheads, they had never been properly part of the Hussar Brigade, having missed the training ground of Ipswich and the guiding hand of Lord Paget. Although they had fought with the other three regiments in the Corunna campaign, they had never really made up for this slow start and always seemed slightly inferior to the two 'Royal' regiments.[4] Their Commanding Officer, Colonel Murray, was not respected, in or out of the regiment, nor did the Red Dwarf, for one, think much of Major Hughes, his successor. They had no Adjutant, although Colonel Palmer kept trying to get the 10th's old Adjutant Duperier sent out to give them a hand, and without a strong commander, like Lord Paget, they were headed for disaster. The 10th and 15th more experienced regiments, both left in the charge of their junior majors, had only just managed to scrape through. In the former, with Quentin away sick, in recently liberated Hanover, and Palmer at home, pursuing his father's claims in Parliament, the seeds of discontent were beginning to germinate. And as for the raging, swearing Black Giant, his days were numbered.

* * *

The small town of Olite, once the residence of the Kings of Navarre, lay in the centre of a hot dusty plain, covered with vineyards and olive gardens. The grapes were just ripening when the Hussars took up their quarters and Sergeant Major Tale recalled how 'the face of the country presented a rich aspect, teeming with this beautiful fruit'. There were plenty of cheap and good vegetables, cherries at a penny a pound, 'pears and plumbs, onions, beans, peas, lettuce, pork, sheep; in short a most plentiful Spanish market'. In spite of this abundance, however, signs of war could be seen everywhere, for it was here that Mina, the *Guerillero*, jokingly called the 'King of Navarre', had chiefly harried the French. The invaders had been forced to barricade themselves in convents and similar buildings, with the result that many of the most beautiful were in ruins. Outside the gates of Olite, the royal residence, an old Moorish castle, had been totally destroyed only the year before and a few broken columns were all that remained of its former magnificence.[5]

The inhabitants of this pleasant spot were, according to Schaumann, 'gloomy and ill-natured', particularly the peasants, 'who used to walk through the streets at night in gangs and carried carbines under their cloaks', and were soon to tire of their British guests. The Hussar Brigade was to stay there for the next four weeks, resting up and keeping an eye on Pamplona, now being besieged by a Spanish army under Don Carlos. When the Hussars arrived they were almost starving and 'truly ridiculous prices' were given for the 'eatables' at the sale of the deceased Captain Carew's baggage on 1 July. The 10th Hussars seem to have been either the richest, or the hungriest, for the highest bids were placed by Worcester, Arthur Hill, Henry FitzClarence and Horace Seymour.[6] While the men gorged themselves on fresh bread, grapes and wine, the officers settled into a leisurely peacetime existence, punctuated by inspections, courts-martial, 'watering order' and punishment parades. On 4 July, Edward Fitzgerald wrote to his grandmother, describing the change in his situation. In the first place he had dismissed his servant, who had been all right in 'snug quarters', but had become careless and disagreable on the march. In his place he now had 'a capital French servant', taken, with some baggage, in the skirmish near Burgos. This paragon combined the talents of valet, shoemaker, tailor, cook and interpreter, as he spoke German and Spanish. 'The Prince,' he thought, would be highly delighted that his 'Dolls' were the only ones 'kept engaged' at Vitoria, and that they had 'come on' so brilliantly. All in all there was nothing to do in Olite but learn Spanish, flirt and talk of England. There was much strolling about in the public gardens, which were ablaze with oranges, roses and narcissi, and the nuns, in the convent opposite the town gates, were kind enough to declare 'that they preferred Hussars' to the redcoats they had seen from their windows.

On 1 July Worcester gave a ball 'in his quarters' and after that there was one nearly every night. Lieutenant Connolly of the 18th Hussars gave one on the 4th, which was attended by 'all the respectable & the rag, tag and bobtail of the town', and at which 'waltzing was the go nearly all night'. Three nights later it was Worcester's turn again. He had engaged the Band of the 18th, but they failed to turn up, so an NCO was sent off in search for them. He eventually found 'the whole in a room dancing completely naked, except having their pelices across their shoulders'. Woodberry understood there had been some women present, but had not heard whether 'they were strip'd or not'. The ball itself, he wrote, would 'beggar all attempts at description'. The mixture of all the respectable women, and all of 'another description, . . . was beyond anything'. The former, finding themselves in such company, left in disgust, much to the amusement of 'the bucks who brought the latter company'. 'Fandangoes was the rage; the women danced them, and many behaved in a very immodest manner.' Woodberry, who was not usually given to prudery, 'left rather early, not at all pleased with the evening's diversion.'

The behaviour of the 18th at Vitoria and Wellington's subsequent remarks on the subject were still the main topics of conversation in Olite. According to Woodberry, during the battle Major Hughes had ordered Dolbel to take charge of twenty men, 'who were placed sentry over the carriages, baggage, &c.', but 'he immediately commenced plundering many of the prisoners & persons of rank'. At a dinner not long after Wellington had been told by a Mme Guize, that, 'if it had not been for a Private Hussar, an officer of Hussars would have plundered her of everything', and that 'after she had delivered up her husband's sword to him and likewise a beautiful double-barrelled gun', he took a ring off her finger. Understandably furious at this disclosure Wellington demanded a written explanation from Dolbel, who admitted taking the gun and the sword, but utterly denied the 'ring business', and so matters rested for the time being.

The author of *A Hussar's Life on Service* provides some interesting details of life in quarters. The 'guests' were entitled only to 'house-room, beds, linen, and lights'. They were allowed army rations of wood for cooking, but seldom took them, as this was 'in general furnished abundantly' by their 'hosts'. On arrival, they were generally presented with a small cup of chocolate, a biscuit and a glass of water, handsomely served (at least where the French had not been) on 'large massive silver waiters'. Improvements to the billets, like the construction of chimneys or the filling in of empty window frames with oiled paper, were carried out by the men. 'Useful articles of furniture were often required . . . and the handicraft men in the regiments, who consisted not only of carpenters, masons, smiths &c. but individuals of callings little to be expected in military life, were in great requisition.' The astonishment of the *patrons* was considerable and they 'hardly knew their improved tenements from these little additions to the comforts of their guests of another climate'. In general, civility and good humour, and a desire not to inconvenience their hosts or their families, were the 'surest passport' to a comfortable existence.

No sooner had the Brigade settled in Olite than orders were received transferring the 18th Hussars to Alten's Brigade in place of the 14th Light Dragoons. The other regiment in the Brigade was the 1st Hussars of the King's German Legion and, on hearing the news Colonel Murray, who was still recuperating in the Bishop's Palace in Palencia, thought that the 18th might now learn something, as the 1st Hussars were 'first-rate & always kept their horses in the highest condition when others are starving'. They were also 'perfect masters of outpost duty' and much might be learned from them 'if the 18th would believe they did not know everything better than anybody else when in fact they are more deficient than anybody'.[7] At the same time Colonel Grant was removed from the command of the Brigade, to be succeeded by Lord Edward Somerset. Giving the news to his brother on 2 July, Somerset wrote that the 10th and 15th were 'infinitely superior in every respect to the 18th' and he considered himself 'very fortunate in getting them'. The general opinion in Olite seems to have been that, while Colonel Grant was allowed 'to be the possessor of Courage and Resolution', he wanted 'judgement', and that one of the reasons for his removal had been that Wellington was 'not at all pleased' with the way he had handled the brigade during the battle. The officers of the brigade were delighted. 'Grant went to Lord Wellington,' Woodberry reported, with a certain amount of satisfaction, 'to remonstrate with him and Lord Wellington gave him leave to go back to England immediately, which Grant accepted.' All his horses and 'finery' were to be disposed of that day, and he was to set off for Santander the next day. 'God be thanked we have got rid of the Black Giant,' Woodberry concluded, but the Red Dwarf remained. On the 5th, as Grant left Olite, Sir Stapleton Cotton, commanding the cavalry, accompanied by Lord Edward, arrived to inspect the three regiments in watering order. Cotton was dressed in his superb scarlet and gold uniform of a General Officer of Hussars, and all his staff were also in Hussar dress.

The first week in Olite ended grimly. The junketings with the ladies of the town had aroused the jealousy of the male inhabitants and, on the morning of 8 July, a private of the 15th Hussars was found murdered. This was only the beginning, for on the evening of the 9th the body of Private Wilks, also of the 15th, was found by the south gate of the town, and two days later the bodies

136

of an artilleryman and a musician of the 18th Hussars, by the name of McNorton, were found, the latter buried in a wood between Olite and Tafalla. 'This poor fellow,' Woodberry wrote, 'was an excellent player on the Clarinett,' and was the first man of the band they had lost. According to Schaumann, the Spaniards were so jealous that no Hussar seen merely 'joking with a girl' was safe. They killed two men of the 10th Hussars close to the gate of the town and tore their eyes out, which were found afterwards about twenty feet away from the bodies. Schaumann himself was one of their prime targets, and they started shooting at the windows of his chief muleteer while the latter was 'quietly lying in his room at night, and the bullets almost grazed his ears'. Finally, things reached such a pass that orders were issued that no one was to go about unarmed.

By now many were getting weary of their 'enforced idle life' and were longing to get out of 'this town of assassins'. Each day was the same as the one before, Fitzgerald wrote, except when there was a ball, where there were always plenty of partners to be found. As for the dancing, the 'Fandangoes and Bolero' were the most ungraceful bearlike performance he ever witnessed and he flattered himself that some of the officers of the 10th danced them a great deal better than most Spaniards. The monks having offered a general absolution to the the ladies of Olite 'in favour of the English officers . . . they now foot it famously . . . and they generally get absolution the next morning for having danced with us the night before.'

Fitzgerald usually dined at five, went to bed at nine and got up at six to play tennis in the town's court, after which he breakfasted on the chocolate, which his servant made so admirably that it put him in mind of Holland House. There was much visiting and dining out between regiments, but sometimes their culinary efforts ended in disaster. When Smith and Blackett of the 18th invited Stuart and Seymour of the 10th to share a 'pidgin pie and quarter of mutton', they managed to burn everything. Seymour 'did not like the joke & after attempting to eat a little of the Pie, and pick the mutton bone without success', went home, giving his hosts 'great umbrage'. Woodberry's dinner the next day was more successful and he and his three guests worked their way through 'soup, 2 roast fowls, 2 rabbits, (boil'd with onions), Beef Stakes [sic] & onions, Peas, Potatoes, & a Rice Pudding'. While at Olite Woodberry penned the definitive description of the eating habits of the Spaniards, whose mode of living was 'certainly not congenial to that in England':

The first orders [of society] take in the morning, either in bed, or soon after they rise, chocolate with cakes or toasted bread, having first drunk some cold water, which is always brought with the chocolate. They dine from 12 to 2 o'C[loc]k, seldom later. The tables are about 8 feet long and 6 wide, covered with one large table cloth, and a plateau is generally placed in the centre, with figures in wax and bottles of wine corked, placed round the brim of it; bread covered with a napkin denotes the place of each of the party. The dinner consists of soups and a variety of dishes which encircle the plateau. Each person sitting opposite to a dish, whether of meat, fish, or vegetables, fills his own plate, carves the contents and hands it round, so that during the whole time of dinner, if a large party, they are continually passing and repassing plates. With something of every sort that passes the Spaniards always fill their plates, they are moreover very great eaters. Some of the dishes are palatable to Englishmen but their meats are covered with oil and garlick; their soups are good; the meat is generally boil'd in large unshapen junks, or in pieces and mixed with potatoes mashed in oil. The Spaniards rarely eat salt and pepper. They seldom use a knife, except in cutting up the contents of the dish next to them (and occasionally stabbing each other), a piece of bread & a fork answer their purposes. . . . The Fish is a side dish. Generally after the soup are two dishes, one of meat boil'd & boil'd fowls together, and the other a sort of stew with sausages, of which garlic is the material ingredient. Strangers eat and drink as they please, no healths [are] drunk &c. There is not that reserve or respect observed by the servants who attend the table as in England. They laugh at a joke, set you right where they think you wrong . . . ; both men and Maid Servants are dirty, slovenly & awkward.[8]

A rest of nearly a month enabled the Hussars to make good some of the 'wear and tear inseparable from a long and continued march' and, apart from the farriers, all the regimental tradesmen, saddlers, shoemakers and tailors, 'were pressed into stitching operations'. Major Griffith wrote to Hodge that the 15th Hussars were still wearing the 'large red *chacos*' with which they had left Lisbon; they were 'heavy, hideous, unbecoming, unserviceable, villainous affairs altogether'. The 10th had not received theirs yet, but looked 'very well in their old black ones'. Generally they were still mustering 'between 50 and 60 file a squad[ron]', which was rather stronger than most of the other brigades. But in spite of the 'fine and salubrious' climate and the 'open and dry' situation, there was a lot of sickness about.[9] Sergeant Major Tale put it down to the effects of 'the grapes, or the juice therefrom', which was 'as common as *aqua pura*, and as easily procured'.

The end of this idyllic life was heralded on 25 July by two new arrivals. The first was Captain Duperier, at long last appointed Adjutant to the 18th Hussars. 'Mr Dupree our new Adjutant arrived this morning,' Woodberry recorded in his diary, adding that he was 'originally Adjutant to the Tenth Hussars', that he had risen from the rank of private 'through merit', and that reports spoke highly of him. If this was the same person as the 'coxcomb' du Pré, who had so annoyed Landsheit way back in 1803 he must have been one of the longest serving soldiers in the regiment. Colonel Murray, whom he had visited on his way to Olite, thought he would be a 'great acquisition' to the 18th, who had not had such an Adjutant for many years. The second arrival, Colonel Quentin, had also called on Colonel Murray, who found him 'on the whole very well - considering that he never can expect to be quite well'. De

Grammont who had also been at Palencia, sick, 'being nearly recovered', returned to Olite with his Commanding Officer.

* * *

The very next afternoon, as Quentin was dining with Major Robarts, Major Griffith and Lord Arthur Hill, orders came for the Hussar Brigade to leave Olite. Without any idea of the reason for this sudden summons, they marched at daybreak and right through the heat of the day without halting. At five in the evening they reached Huarte, at the head of the defile which leads down from the Pyrenees to Pamplona. Here they found Picton's and Cole's Divisions engaged with the enemy, and confusion everywhere. While Wellington had been busy on the left flank, supervising the siege of San Sebastian, Soult had struck at the British troops holding the Maya and Roncesvalles passes over the Pyrenees. After fierce fighting, the British had fallen back and were now holding off superior forces only a league and a half north of Pamplona. The Hussars had been summoned to help plug the gap. In a tremendous thunderstorm they retired to the neighbouring villages in search of food, and settled down to a wet and uncomfortable night.

The next morning, 28 July, Soult attacked the British left flank at Sorauren. The right flank, considerably 'refused', between Pamplona and Zabaldica, was not attacked, although some infantry and about three thousand cavalry demonstrated against it. The 10th and the 18th, together with Gardiner's guns, were posted here and spent most of the day skirmishing with parties of French cavalry, who were trying to turn their flank. On turning out at daybreak, Hughes found the 10th Hussars engaging the enemy with pistols, which they 'laughed at'. During this skirmishing Captain Harding was wounded and one man taken prisoner. They had used up their ammunition and were falling back when Hughes was ordered to take their place with the right squadron. Using their carbines, the 18th 'almost immediately drove them back to their bounds with the loss of two or three killed or wounded'. Both sides then stood looking at each other for more than an hour, while the French exchanged insults with their opponents. According to Woodberry, their officer, whom they thought was either English or Irish, taunted them with cries of 'Why don't those dashing officers of the Tenth come on,' and, when Kennedy and some men of the 18th drove them back 'across the rivulet', called out, 'Come on you flashy officer of the 18th, why dont you come over the pudle[sic]?' In the course of the day Captain Gordon of the 10th was wounded in the arm and Worcester had 'a narrow escape, being knocked off his horse by a musket ball, which struck his pouch belt', giving him a nasty bruise. Horace Seymour had his horse shot, George FitzClarence told Mrs Fitzherbert, while his had been 'grazed on the nose with a ball'. They had taken 'a great part of the enemy's baggage, and 4,000 prisoners'. He had been into France and sent her some oakleaves he took from a tree to crown himself conqueror. He also enclosed some box he wore in his hat 'during the

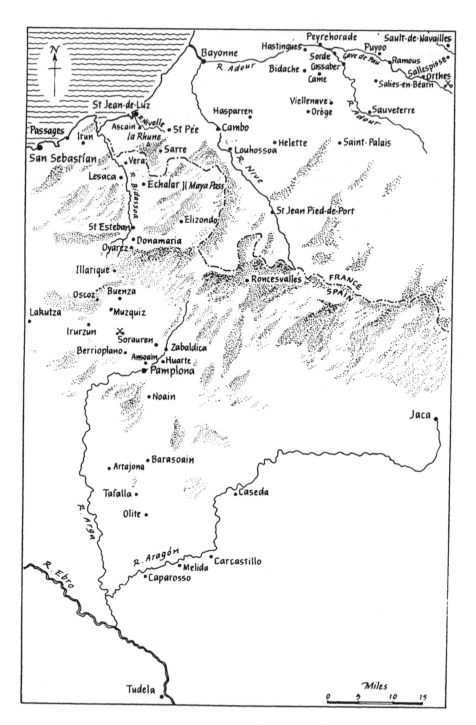

The Approach to the Pyrenees, 1813–14

whole of the action, as it was fought on the anniversary of Talavera'.

The French retired the next day and the Hussars followed the advancing infantry across to the Roncesvalles road. On the 31st they moved into cantonments in the villages at the foot of the Pyrenees and spent the next few days refitting and occasionally patrolling through the passes. By 5 August the army was 'put up' in French villages, except for the cavalry, which was still on the Spanish side of the Pyrenees. The French losses since 20 July were put at 20,000, 'besides the whole of the cattle and provisions they had brought for the garrison of Pamplona, who were consequently now 'feasting on horse-flesh'. There had been occasional brushes with the enemy, as when, on the 7th, a Sergeant's party of the 10th, patrolling towards St Jean Pied-de-Port, was cut off on a mountain track by French infantry and had to 'dash' their way out, with the loss of one man wounded and one taken prisoner. On the 10th the Hussar Brigade was relieved by the 14th Light Dragoons and the next day marched to the rear. On the 12th they returned to their cantonments south of Pamplona, but this time the 10th and Brigade Headquarters were at Tafalla, the 15th at Artajona, 'a small, pretty, clean, regular town', and the 18th at Olite.

* * *

The men of the 10th had been extremely drunk at Olite, prior to Colonel Quentin's arrival, and were even worse at Tafalla. There was plenty of looted money about, wine was plentiful and those who were hard-up were treated by the comrades. Faced with this situation, one of the first things Quentin did in Tafalla was to call for the regiment's courts-martial book and was amazed at the 'wonderful punishments' that had been inflicted, many of them exceeding the permitted limit. Like Colonel Murray with the 18th, he initiated a 'different system', putting culprits in irons, or making them walk up and down 'with kits on their backs'. But, before the new system could prove successful, Colonel Palmer returned from England, having failed to get a staff appointment at home, and so avoid serving abroad under Quentin, with whom he was now on very bad terms. By way of getting his own back, and venting his animosity, he proceeded to undermine the Commanding Officer's efforts. As a result the 'system' failed, the 'excesses of the men became intolerable' and flogging was once more resorted to, although there was a notable reluctance on the part of the Farriers and trumpeters, one of them a 'Negro', to carry out their duties. All this was carefully observed by the Red Dwarf, who later testified that at this time the regiment 'certainly became very slovenly, and the conduct of the men very bad; drinking and behaving extremely irregularly, and apparently very inattentive to their duty'. Typical of Palmer's lack of co-operation was his failure to pass on to Quentin, who was away at the time, a report made by the regimental surgeon to the inspector-general, stating that the sickness in the regiment was the result of drunkenness, 'want of necessaries' and a 'disinclination to personal cleanliness'. Palmer not only failed to mention it to

Quentin, but also to Lord Edward Somerset, so that no action was taken. He also, according to Quentin, failed to support his efforts to get the officers to attend to the welfare of their men, pouring scorn on the stream of regimental orders issued to this end. For the moment, however, the bad state of affairs in the regiment was not apparent outside Tafalla, where life was returning to normal.

They had hardly been there a week before the cut-throats were out in force. On the night of the 17 July one of them attacked Henry FitzClarence with a knife. 'The villain meant to stick him in the groin,' Fitzgerald wrote two days later, 'but luckily missed him by inches' giving him, instead, a nasty cut in the thigh, 'five inches in length and three in depth'. The Spanish were very jealous of the English in Tafalla and Fitzgerald was taking care 'not to insult them, being resolved not to get stuck by a Don!' 'A country town in England offers but few resources,' wrote one officer, 'but a town in Spain still less; and though Tafalla could boast a Juego de Billar, and even a small fives court, we found some difficulty in passing our time.' As things gradually quietened down, they could turn their minds to domestic matters like dress and promotion. At brigade headquarters Lord Edward was busy growing proper Hussar whiskers and moustachios. On 24 August he wrote to his brother that the moustache was considered indispensable for an Hussar and, although he was 'never an advocate for imitating foreign troops', he had adopted it and wished he could with a little difficulty equip himself 'with all the other costume of an Hussar General, the dress of which is very handsome & splendid'. Worcester, now back at Headquarters, wrote that his uncle made 'a good Hussar', and 'must be perfect now his mutton-chops are grown'. His constituents in Gloucestershire 'would stare nearly as much to see him' as did the men of his own regiment, the 4th Dragoons.

Fitzgerald was worrying about 'getting his troop'. Henry Wyndham had gained his majority and was about to go home, with despatches, and the Adjutant, Samuel Bromley, had just received his captaincy 'without purchase', which meant that Fitzgerald was now top of the list of subalterns. 'In case Mr Ogilvie is in London,' he wrote to his grandmother on the 26th, he would purchase for him, 'if he is able', otherwise he would have to make up his mind to having somebody put over his head from another regiment, as nobody in the regiment had served 'the time allotted by the King's regulations' except himself. During the first week in September Henry Wyndham left for England, carrying the despatches announcing the fall of San Sebastian, which had been taken on 31 August, after a bloody assault in which the Allies had lost 2,500 men. His troop was to be taken over by George FitzClarence, who was still at Headquarters, and Lord Edward thought his going home a very 'fortunate circumstance' for his wife, Elizabeth, the daughter of the fortune-hunting Lord Charles, whose marriage to his natural son was so much disapproved of by Lord Egremont.[10]

George FitzClarence returned to Tafalla on 10 August, the same day that his brother Henry rode over to Olite to visit his friend Woodberry. Things were still going badly for the 18th Hussars and promotion was a sore subject with them as well, for, to their disgust, the vacancies caused by the deaths of Captains Turing and Carew had been filled by officers from other regiments. In addition, one of these new officers, Captain Croker, reported that London was full of how the regiment had run away at Vitoria. On top of this Lieutenant Rowle, who had been sent to Bilbao 'for the sea-bathing', had coolly embarked for England without leave. This was almost certainly the 'W.R.', a 'young, rich, and a fine-looking fellow' who, according to Gronow, had a stud of horses 'remarkable for their blood', three English grooms, a 'light cart to carry forage, and a fourgon for his baggage'. All went well until he came to go on outpost duty, 'but not finding there any of the comforts to which he had been accustomed' he departed for England, telling his 'astonished sergeant that campaigning was not intended for a gentleman'.[11]

As if this were not enough, Major Hughes learned that Dolbel's version of Mme Guize's ring story had never been forwarded to Headquarters. He hurried off to Lesaca, where he had a stormy interview with the Commander of the Forces, who, notwithstanding, afterwards invited him to dinner. Wellington told him that he thought 'the men of the 18th at Vitoria behaved more like Rebels and Banditts than a Regiment of Hussars,' but when Hughes asked if he had anything to say about their courage, he replied that he thought them 'very brave but too impetuous'. The Black Giant seemed to have done the dirty on them, behaving towards the 18th 'like a villain', and it was to him they were indebted for not forwarding Connolly's or Dolbel's statements, drawn up 'in vindication of their characters'.

Otherwise life at Olite was much as it had been before, with a succession of balls, usually given by Woodberry, and described in detail in his diary. The female company usually consisted 'of the immodest', Major Hughes bringing 'one of the most notorious of the country round', a dancer from Pamplona, who waltzed delightfully. Woodberry opened one ball with a 'Donna Senora Zacarras Nabasques', with whom he performed a Spanish 'Bolera, and received some praise from the females for the execution'. He was beginning to find that he was quite a favourite in Olite and would have been very proud, 'was it not for their cursed cutthroat husbands'. He gave another ball on 8 September when 'Eight Senoras' honoured him with their company and they danced 'nine sets'. Once again the music was provided by the Regimental Band, who 'played some of the most favourite tunes, which much delighted the Spaniards, particularly Paddy Casey'.

Not surprisingly, relations with the local men went from bad to worse, and on several occasions groups of officers returning from a party had to use their swords to hack their way through gangs of citizenry. Either because of his foraging activities or, as he claimed, his numerous love-affairs, Schaumann was a particular target. There was even a plot to kill him, which only failed 'because the brutes fired too soon and in too great a hurry', although they did manage to hit his servant. Afterwards 'a troop of them passed by with guitars and castanets playing a sort of serenade through the streets' to ascertain the effect of their shot. If his account of his various conquests has any truth, it is not surprising they were out to get him:

> In the first place there were the donnas Francisca and Stephania from Seville, the daughters of a wealthy landowner, who were very responsive. Then in Lieutenant Backer's there was a handsome beauty who was the wife of a Spanish colonel, and who took no pains to conceal her attachment to me. I also had a pretty girl who paid me many visits; and finally the legitimate spouse of an organist, who always availed herself of her husband's duties in the church, in order to come to me.

*　*　*

The decision to remove the 18th Hussars from the Hussar Brigade was finally implemented on 14 September when they received orders to move out of Olite, now earmarked for the newly-arrived 7th Hussars;[12] and the following day, 'with much rejoicing', they left the 'inhospitable and gloomy assassin's nest know as Olite'. Schaumann was particularly relieved at the change of quarters as, what with the heat and his 'lovemaking with the ladies of the place', he was feeling 'very low', and his 'ague showed signs of returning'. They passed round the southern side of Pamplona, which was still holding out, and on to the great road to Vitoria. On reaching Irurzun on the 17th they turned north into the mountains and three days later went into quarters around Oscoz, 'a fairly large and flourishing village, with houses built in a style which was reminiscent of Switzerland'. The girls here were pretty and wore their hair in two long plaits, but, because they were shy and their Basque unintelligible, Schaumann and his friends had to console themselves 'with the beauties among the soldiers' wives', whom they courted 'in the fragrant woods' and with whom they 'dallied on the grass and among the flowers'.

The 10th and 15th remained in the area, although, partly because of shortage of forage and partly out of a need to keep a close eye on Pamplona, the latter left Artajona, and moved west and south to Larraga on the banks of the Arga River. Writing from there on the 28th Major Griffith gave a description of the 'easy life' they were leading; never, except for three days when they were 'without bread before the battle of Vitoria', had they been 'distressed for food'. He was in an excellent house, this family consisting of a young husband and wife, and her sister, who was 'an uncommon fine girl, and so fond of battledore and shuttlecock' that he was worked to death by her, but his Spanish was improving daily. They usually breakfasted on the staircase, little cups of chocolate being ranged along the banisters, and dinner was 'a scrambling sort of business'. 'Never in this world,' he thought, 'did people understand comfort so little as the Spaniards.' He had heard that his 'friend Colonel Grant' had got a Brigade of Light Dragoons, so that, although he was still in the country, they would seldom come in contact again, 'and never on duty'.[13]

On the 20th Worcester wrote home saying that Quentin, Charles Manners and 'young Fitzgerald' had been staying at Lesaca, for the past ten days, but had now returned to the regiment. 'All the talk' was of a move being likely to take place soon, which he hoped with all his heart would happen, as he was 'quite tired' at their state of inactivity, but he imagined that 'nothing of consequence could be attempted' until Pamplona had surrendered, which would probably not be that fortnight. However, in spite of these protestations, four days later Lord Edward was writing 'respecting Worcester's going to England this winter', which he did not really see any impropriety in, provided there was no probability of a '*Winter's campaign*'. That same day, the 24th, George FitzClarence, passing through Muzquiz, broke his journey long enough to take a little 'cold pidgeon' off Woodberry, by way of lunch. 'I don't like this buck,' Woodberry wrote afterwards, as much as 'his brother the Lieutenant'; 'This fellow,' he thought, 'uncommonly high and proud.'

The 18th Hussars were now, at long last, brigaded with the highly experienced and efficient 1st Hussars of the King's German Legion, under the command of General Alten, whose handsome letter of welcome, Woodberry copied into his diary on the 23rd:

He felt himself highly flattered and honoured by the Commander of the Forces in having so gallant a regiment as the 18th added to his Brigade, and strongly recommended to the officers not to relax the Discipline of the regiment, but to bring to punishment any man who committed the most trivial crime; that the fate of the whole army is often entrusted to an Hussar Regiment, and strongly reprobated drunkenness in an Hussar. . . . The duties of Hussars in the field are so various & require so much practice & experience that too many opportunities cannot be taken to instruct the men in them, and the Major-General will find great pleasure in giving that assistance which his experience may enable him to do.

This high-minded exhortation did little, however, to dampen the high spirits of the officers of the regiment, who soon settled back into their old routine. 'The favourite amusement at parties in this part of the country,' Woodberry wrote on the 21st, 'is dancing and singing.' The ladies sang 'very agreeably' at the slightest invitation, but they suffered from the common fault of all Spanish women, namely 'bad teeth'.

At the beginning of October part of the 10th Hussars moved to the village of Barasoain, north of Tafalla. Writing from here on 7 October, Fitzgerald reported that the garrison of Pamplona was 'reduced to the last extremities', with only forty horses left and 'but a quarter of a pound of mouldy bread a day', and it was expected 'to surrender immediately'. He was sorry to say that the regiment was 'rather sickly', which, it was said, was 'owing to the bad water at Tafalla'.

On the 9th Wellington, in a series of surprise attacks, drove Soult back from the line of the Bidassoa River into France and, following close on his heels, took up a position on the northern slopes of the Pyrenees, covering the Nivelle River. Headquarters moved from Lesaca to the small town of Vera, on the Bidassoa, which Worcester thought was an improvement, although they were far from being in hunting country. France, from what he had seen of it, must be a most beautiful country; he and the Prince of Orange, now serving on Wellington's staff, had, while on 'Patrole into a French village', surprised a French Picquet, but managed to get away without difficulty.[14]

As the fall of Pamplona grew imminent, it was feared that the garrison might try and escape, and on 16 October the Hussar Brigade was ordered to supply parties to observe the southern side of the town. Two days later three troops of the 10th were moved nearer to town and on the 20th they were reinforced by the right squadron of the 15th. The following day Fitzgerald wrote from the village of Salinas de Pamplona that the garrison was 'now reduced to the last extremities' and was expected 'some night before the 28th to blow up the works and make a bolt'. He had heard from no less an authority than Sir Stapleton Cotton that, when the town fell, the cavalry would advance. The weather was much colder than he had ever felt it in England, and, when not on duty, he sat in his quarters, which had neither window glass nor shutters, wrapped in his cloak, scarcely able to hold a pen. Grammont, the day before, had gone into Pamplona with a flag of truce, bearing a summons to surrender from 'Don Carlos d'España', which they refused to do, unless they were allowed to return to France unmolested.

The 7th Hussars arrived at Olite on or about 12 October and Lord Edward thought them a 'great acquisition' to his brigade, which was now the strongest in the army. He liked what he had seen of them 'extremely' and the officers seemed 'a very gentleman-like & smart set'. They were now commanded by Colonel Vivian, who had arrived at Bilbao with part of the regiment on 29 August, but by the time the rest had been collected a month had gone by. On 30 September Vivian heard that the missing fourth squadron had arrived at Passages, and two days later set off for Olite with the troops that he had with him. The first day's march to Durango went well and he wrote home that the conduct of the men deserved praise 'much beyond' any he could bestow on them. They were 'in all points' as complete, the horses looking just as well and the men 'as healthy or more so' than they were 'at the best of times in England'. On the 6th Captain Wildman, with his troop at Linzarza, wrote to Major Hodge at the depôt in England that the regiment was then to march, in two divisions, to Olite. On the 10th they passed through Buenza, where a party of the 18th Hussars turned out for them. Two days later they passed within two miles of Pamplona and so on to Olite. There, on the 20th, Vivian wrote that he was quartered in the house of a woman, married to an Irishman, named Murphy, who had deserted her and gone to America. 'Grant, who was here before me,' he continued, 'would never speak to any of them; indeed he could not, and they disliked him very much.' The men were all well, but they got 'sadly drunk' now and then, for which he had 'tickled a few of them', but with strong wine at sixpence a quart it was really no wonder.

A long letter, which he wrote to Hodge at the Regimental Depot on the 27th shows how the Commanding Officer had to plan ahead and make his own decisions about his regiment's domestic needs, even when on campaign. On the subject of clothing he wrote:

If Lord Uxbridge has no objection I propose that he should give the men Overalls instead of Pantaloons for the Clothing of 1813 and in this case Prater may at once commence making overalls the same as we now have, only tell him to make them very stout and strong. Those he last made were not. . . . Prater may begin making up the Stable jackets for 1813. The same pattern exact as we have now. If we return we can easily put on blue collars & yellow lace, but here whilst wearing white collar'd jackets & white lace it would not do to have yellow laced stable jackets.

On the subject of fresh drafts of men and horses, he warned Hodge that they would need about a hundred men and a hundred and fifty horses, and he was to use his 'best exertions' to recruit them, each to 'be good of their sort, the larger the horses the better'.[15]

Hodge was kept well-informed of what was going on by others besides the Commanding Officer. Wildman reported that the regiment 'in general both on foot & mounted' looked as well as he had ever seen them in England, with the men healthy & well and turning out 'as much the Lilly Whites as ever'. They had had some 'few punishments for disposing of the second blankets', but there had been very little 'drinking or irregularity'. They were living 'uncommonly well', but it was 'but stupid work' and he hoped they would advance soon. Major Thornhill described how the Governor of Pamplona had proposed 'by way of capitulation' marching his troops into France, with the promise 'not to serve during the war', but his terms were rejected. The garrison were now down to half-rations of bread & horseflesh'. 'The tops of the Pyrenees,' he wrote:

are already covered with snow; for my part I think I have more of the swallow in me than the woodcock; I envy a summer snipe & dont much like bivouacking in a snowdrift, but still that is better than being devoured by Flees [sic] & hushed with buzzing night flies to one's slumber.

* * *

On Sunday 31 October, just as everyone was reconciling themselves to wintering in Olite, 'where Pipeclay was in high request' and eating and drinking their only employment, they received news of the fall of Pamplona and their marching orders at one and the same time. The next day, in pouring rain, the 7th moved to within a league of the city. Vivian and Major Kerrison arrived just in time to see the garrison, '3,500 Men, excellently cloth'd &

147

appointed, and looking in general very well, considering their late circumstances' march out 'with Drums Beating, Colours Flying, and cries of "Vive l'Empereur!"' Having laid down their arms to the Spaniards, they 'were march'd off under escort', but some were 'beastly drunk, and these, the moment they dropt behind the Escort, were seized, stript to the skin, and murder'd by the Guerillas & peasantry'.[16] While this was going on three troops of the 10th moved up and Sergeant Major Wells, who was acting Adjutant, was sent into the Arsenal to select seventy carbines for the use of the regiment.[17] The same day the 15th moved up the Arga River and plunged northwards into the mountains towards Oscoz. As they passed round Pamplona, the 'poor inhabitants, now nearly famished, ran out to meet the loads of bread and other provisions coming in which they bolted like pointers'.

The next day, 2 November, the 7th Hussars were ordered to Berrioplano, a village on the Great Road west of Pamplona, which meant passing round the town. Vivian requested Don Carlos for permission for the regiment to march through it, which proved impossible as only one gate had been unblocked. Instead they marched 'close round the glacis and halted before the main entrance, when all the officers had leave to go into the town'. Wildman thought it the finest city he had ever seen in Spain. The Cathedral was magnificent, 'the buildings good, the squares and streets broad, well-pav'd & *clean*, the pradas . . . very handsome and well planted with avenues of trees, and the whole far surpassing even Astorga'. They saw thirty-six British prisoners, whose captors had treated them very well, providing them with the French rations of four ounces of bread and five of horseflesh a day. Lord Edward acquired the French commander's cook, 'a smart young Frenchman', and hoped his talent in the *cuisine* would turn out as good as he expected.

The order to march reached the 18th Hussars at Oscoz at midday on 1 November and was so urgent that the men had to throw away their dinners half-cooked. They marched at three 'in wretched weather' for Illarique, their route leading from behind the village across some lofty wooded heights. Schaumann, for one, never forgot 'the roar of the mountain streams, mingled with the cry of the eagles, the sound of their horses's hooves and the singing of the Hussars', which made 'a curious melody'. Occasionally the long trail of horsemen passed a sturdy Biscay peasant, 'with his blue baretta on the side of his head, and his cloak carried on his mountaineer's stick'. Higher up, as they followed the track, which twisted northwards towards St Esteban, in the upper Bidassoa valley, they came across gangs of peasants hard at work improving the perilous road under the supervision of British officers. At one point a sharp twist in the road revealed a magnificent panorama stretching as far as the Bay of Biscay and for a moment the Hussars gazed down on France herself. Major Hughes description of the journey was less idyllic. He had a cold and spent the night of 1 November quartered with the padre of Illarique. They marched again on the 6th, 'a very fine day tho' it had snowed in the night', halting at Oyarez and Donamaria, 'a straggling sort of village lying in a valley high up in the mountains', a few miles short of St Esteban, where Hughes dined with General Alten.[18]

The next day was foggy and Hughes' cold was much worse. They marched to Echalar, following the winding course of the Bidassoa, down to a point near Lesaca, where they turned north into the mountains. At Echalar they halted for another two days, during which time Hughes gave orders for the 'new overalls to be worn' and everything was made 'preparatory for an attack'. They marched again at four o'clock in the morning on the 10th, in 'a beautiful moonlight & very warm', turning off north into the mountains towards the Pass of Echalar. At length they found a guide in the person of a Provost-Marshal, who conducted them 'down the side of one of the steepest Pyrenees, where there was neither pass nor road', to the point where they were supposed to meet up with the 1st German Hussars.

The leading regiment of Somerset's brigade, the 7th Hussars, was not far behind. On 3 November they arrived at Buenza after two forced marches, which were especially trying. 'The worst goat path in all Wales,' Vivian wrote, was 'a garden walk compared to it', and they still had eight more leagues 'of still worse roads' before they reached France. Two days later, 'at Barasoain', Wildman found 'capital' stabling, and plenty of provisions, including mutton, bread and wine. They had not had much barley 'of late' for the horses, relying on wheat, Indian corn, straw and some bran, but they were looking very well 'and in good working condition'. The men were healthy and well behaved, and the officers 'living like Princes giving Dinners &c. in great style'. They reached St Esteban on the 7th, one day behind the 18th, after a six-hour scramble over mountains and roads, if possible, ten thousand times worse than the roads Vivian had described before. In one troop alone nearly twenty horses had lost their shoes and, all the way down the line, the farriers had worked hard 'putting things to rights'. St Esteban, Vivian thought, must once have been an exceedingly good town; it was about 'half as large as Truro', with several very good houses, 'but completely destitute of furniture'.

The 15th Hussars did not reach St Esteban until 12 November. Griffith had been billetted with a priest, probably the same one Hughes had stayed with at Illarique, 'an enlightened man', who comforted him with the assurance that they would all perish in the snow unless they got out of the Pyrenees that month. The sublimity of the scenery compensated to some degree for their miseries, but the forests and valleys were inhabited by the most wretched and ignorant people, little better than savages, who had a language of their own called 'Basquenz'. He might as well have attempted to explain himself in Spanish to the natives of Llanrwst. The 15th remained at St Esteban until 19 November, when they received orders to return to Spain and go into cantonments along the River Arga.

The object of moving the cavalry forward had been to support Wellington's planned offensive, which was delayed by bad weather until 10 November. On that day the British and their allies drove the French from a line of prepared positions along the Nivelle River, watched from the summit by 'the Great

Lord' and 'many amateurs', including Lord Edward Somerset, Colonel Vivian and Mr Commissary Schaumann. 'It was,' Thornhill told Hodge, 'a sort of parade fight like a Lord Mayor's Day.' Vivian wrote that it was 'quite beautiful to see our fellows facing the batteries & breastworks & the coolness with which the French retired more like a preconcerted arrangement of a field day on Wimbledon Common than a regular set to.' The 18th Hussars had arrived in time to take part in the battle, in close support of the infantry, but with their usual bad luck one of the men had been caught by the Commander of the Forces chasing sheep. On the 11th the 18th Hussars reached the banks of the River Nive and the next day were at St Pée, on the main road running east from St Jean-de-Luz to Cambo. The 7th Hussars had been halted at Sumbilla, 'above three leagues to the rear, during the action, and two days later moved down to Sarre, where they remained 'near a week, expecting that a fresh advance would open the country' for them in front.

* * *

The army, held up by continuous rain, was now jammed between the Rivers Nivelle and Nive, unable to move. Everyone tried to make themselves comfortable in country through which the enemy had passed. It 'was hardly possible to imagine more complete destruction than it exhibited. In the houses which they occupied 'there was not a particle of furniture of any kind remaining.' The beds, chairs, and tables had all been cut up and burned, and 'there was not a hole nor a corner that had not been ransacked and plundered'. According to the author of *A Hussar's Life on Service* the disadvantage of being with the cavalry was that, during the winter, 'with a view to saving forage in front, or if the country will not permit our use, or to ensure our horses plenty, and consequent efficiency', they were 'occasionally sent back . . . or left behind at a considerable distance'. For precisely these reasons the bulk of the cavalry was, to their 'inexpressible mortification', now sent back into Spain. Back across the mountains they went, 'in the most wretched weather, over such roads as never before were seen', to the villages around Pamplona. The wear and tear of these marches was dreadful; in a week or ten days a man and his horse were almost barefoot. By 25 November the 7th were back along the River Arga, generally very well put up, although Wildman, for one, would never be in 'good humour' while they remained in the rear.

The charms of Pamplona, where everything could be bought, even Windsor soap, and Smyth's Lavender water, were lost on those, like the 10th Hussars, who had been stuck on the banks of the Arga all this time. At length, however, the brigade received orders to advance once more into France. The general feeling was pleasure at the thought of taking the outpost duty in front of the whole army and spending the winter in France instead of the miserable villages about Pamplona. Any change from Spain must be one for the better, and anyway the climate in France was supposed to be milder and the forage more plentiful.

Meanwhile the 18th Hussars were gaining much-needed experience of outpost duty, having been working alongside the 1st German Hussars on the banks of the Nive ever since the beginning of November. They were quartered in St Pée, but the weather was so atrocious that it was only with the greatest difficulty that the officers could get about to visit the outposts, which faced the enemy across the river, which was easily fordable. On the 16th, near Ascain, Sir Stapleton Cotton, the *Lion d'or*, whose dress and horse appointments were said to be worth £500, was completely submerged with his horse in an immensely deep puddle and was only rescued after 'some hard knocks' by Hughes and the General's orderly. Marshal Beresford 'also had a swim' that same day, and on the 30th, when General Alten inspected the 18th Hussars, Hughes deigned to venture out with an umbrella which was almost immediately blown inside out by the wind.[19]

Early in December Wellington decided to force the Nive and swing the right of his army northwards towards the banks of the River Adour to prevent the French using it to supply the besieged city of Bayonne. The resulting battle, which lasted from 7 to 14 December, involved the 18th Hussars in sporadic skirmishing in the worst of weathers. 'Our boots,' Schaumann wrote, 'even if we had several pairs in use, were never dry. We always had cold and wet feet. The very sight of the stone floors in the house . . . made one shiver; while the smoking chimneys drove one to desperation.' After the battle the 18th Hussars went into quarters at Urcuray, and from then on were engaged in daily skirmishes with the French outposts. On the 17th Hughes received orders to take two squadrons to assist the Spanish General Morillo in an operation near Mendionde, a village in enclosed country east of Cambo and south of Hasparren. The following morning he joined Morillo with a squadron of the 18th and one of Germans, and advanced, with his flanks protected by Spanish riflemen, or *Caçadores*. Crossing the bridge at Mendionde, they moved up the high road driving the French picquets before them. Almost immediately they came under heavy infantry fire and, as they were withdrawing, were shot at from a wood which the Spaniards had precipitately abandoned. At this moment Hughes was hit, but managed to stay on his horse and rode off. Captain Bolton continued to withdraw the squadron of the 18th, but was forced to charge the enemy cavalry in order to gain time for the *caçadores* to retreat. The Germans, who had retreated by another road, got off with the loss of only one horse, but Bolton, who took his squadron too near a wood occupied by enemy infantry, was wounded and taken prisoner. Woodberry and Croker were also slightly wounded, and three men and ten horses were captured by the French.

Hughes, meanwhile, had ridden back to Mendionde, with a bullet lodged in his breast, in great pain. There his friend the *curé* gave him a glass of wine and he struggled on to Urcuray, where Pulsford, the assistant surgeon, was called out and 'began to extract the ball but his knife was bad & it was tightly lodged'.

Eventually Chambers, the surgeon, arrived and 'completed the operation which was rather tedious', but not perhaps so painful to Hughes 'as to the spectators'. 'Poor Bolton' was not so lucky. The following morning Hughes received a 'very handsome letter' from the French Colonel of *Chasseurs à Cheval* reporting that his prisoner was '*griévement blessé*' and asking him to send a surgeon and a servant to attend him. This was done the next day, 20 December, but they returned the same evening with the news that Bolton was dead. They brought his watch and personal effects with them, together with a message that he would be buried with full military honours as 'becoming a brave soldier'.[20] The affair at Mendionde did little to improve Wellington's opinion of the 18th. It seemed, Wildman wrote, 'the general opinion that they were too precipitate'; and when General Alten called on Hughes before leaving for England he promised to see the Duke of York and the Prince Regent about the regiment's affairs.[21]

CHAPTER EIGHT
Into France

The 7th Hussars were the first of Somerset's brigade to leave Spain, on 14 December. After five days' marching, during which they crossed into France by the bridge of boats at Irun, they reached the town of Cambo on the right flank of the army. Wildman's troop had no sooner settled into quarters in Urcuray on the 20th than they were sent out to reconnoitre. He found the country to the front covered by Alten's two Hussar regiments, but to the right it was totally unprotected. Between three and four thousand French were in and about St Jean Pied-de-Port, from which there were two roads. One, the main road to Bayonne, ran through Urcuray, but the other, which followed the banks of the Nive through Macaye to Bas Cambo, was totally unprotected.

The author of *A Hussar's Life On Service* describes the procedure when the Hussars took up new quarters. On arrival, written orders, or *billets*, on the houses of individuals, were issued by '*Monsieur Le Maire*, or *Le Prefet*', and distributed according to rank. Next the quartermaster scribbled with a piece of chalk on the 'doors of our hosts sundry illegible characters, intended to imply that the Casa of Don Fulano, or la Maison de Mons.Tel, is intended to be, without the permission of either one or the other, the domicile of a certain officer in the British Army'. The French had a similar system and the Hussars were accustomed to read on the doors, as they followed the retreating enemy, 'Logement du General Clausel, Logement du General Villete, &c.', long after these great folks had 'withdrawn their precious persons' and as good men, if not better, had taken possession. In the house allocated to him in Urcuray Kerrison found Major Hughes propped up in bed nursing his wound, but 'doing very well, the ball having glanced round his ribs'. The 18th had left just as the 7th marched in and Hughes had 'managed' it that Kerrison should come into his quarters.

By the 22nd the whole brigade and its troop of horse artillery was posted on the right bank of the Nive, where the three regiments took it in turns, a week at a time, to post a captain's picquet on the high road and a subaltern's 'to the right of that towards the river'. Verner, at Hasparren, was tolerably well supplied with forage and provisions. He was quartered in a comfortable farm-house two or three miles from the town, where Sir Stapleton Cotton's headquarters were also situated. Wildman, writing to Hodge on Christmas Day, thought the country and climate delightful, and the more so the further they advanced. They had suffered some heavy rains for a day or two, but at other times the weather was more like May in England and the sun very hot. Their Christmas dinner had been 'by no means despicable, a fillet of excellent veal, some ham, soup, & plumb pudding, and three bottles of claret', quite a difference from Spain. The people were good looking and civilized, and civil 'beyond measure, but very much astonished' at the invaders paying them for what they took. They were 'a different race of beings, and their habitations fit for an Englishman, with fire places, & glass windows'. Butter and milk were plentiful and they were carrying on the war 'in a very jolly manner'. Lord Edward wrote the following day that outpost duty was 'much pleasanter than quiet quarters in Navarre' as it afforded him a daily occupation, particularly as many of his 'people' were as yet 'rather inexperienced'.

The 15th Hussars arrived at Cambo on 22 December and on New Year's Day, 1814, the 10th moved up to take their turn of outpost duty at Urcuray, and the convalescent Hughes exchanged the company of Kerrison for Quentin. He was living a regular life and mending well. Each day, after having his wound dressed, he shaved, washed, put on 'clean things', had his bed made, to which he returned, took his breakfast, read his book and received his visitors. Colonel Quentin, Major Howard and George FitzClarence had all paid calls on the 27th. He had usually dined with Kerrison and the doctor, and 'sometimes one or two others, conversed with the people of the house & then retired to bed'.

On the 4th the whole army turned out, expecting a fight, and remained in position for three days, when the French gave up whatever they had intended and 'the *Lord*' had the army 'again in cantonments'. After this burst of activity things remained quiet for some days until the enemy started 'annoying' the foraging parties again. The British were forced to forage right under the noses of the French, and 'by some blundering', as Hughes put it, were losing a man or two each day. On one occasion the enemy captured thirty mules belonging to the Artillery.

At this particular juncture Captain de Grammont was sent by Wellington to England, on French royalist business. The employment of a relatively junior officer in such a diplomatic mission came about because the army was now very close to the de Grammont family estates at Bidache, and a royalist agent, a M.de Mailhos, appeared at Headquarters bearing 'congratulations' to the Count 'from the persons now on his cidevant estates', together with their 'wishes for old times and old landlords'. According to M.de Mailhos they also wanted a prince of the house of Bourbon to join the army, Louis XVIII to be proclaimed and the standard of the Bourbons raised. Wellington was sceptical of these claims and sent for de Grammont to ask his opinion. De Grammont saw no reason for 'discrediting' them, so Wellington sent him at once to London with a letter to the King from M.de Mailhos. De Grammont returned on 16 January, in company with Colonel Abercrombie with despatches, in 'a little cockleshell of a sloop' in the middle of a terrible storm.[1]

On 9 January the 15th Hussars took over from the 10th and Major Griffith replaced Quentin in Hughes' residence. The approaches to Urcuray were, by now, virtually impassable, with the 'animals plunging every now and then in mudpools and holes up to their girths'. It was a country of 'mountain, hill, and vale', and at this season it was 'villainous'. Both men and horses 'fared scantily', relying on the Commissariat supplies which had to come from the depôts at Passages and St Jean-de-Luz. But with the appalling road conditions issues were uncertain, and could seldom be depended on. For a fortnight or so the fertile valleys of Macaye and Mendionde supplied them with excellent hay and the dreariness of their existence was occasionally 'relieved by an enlivener, in the shape of a turn-out in marching order on a foraging excursion', when the enemy generally 'scented' them out, 'and, being infantry, had all the local advantages for a fight on their side'. The object of these 'affairs' was 'solely to procure hay and grain from the vicinity of the enemy, and retreat . . . the moment that any liklihood appeared of committing the troops in a serious skir-mish'. Vedettes were posted to prevent surprise while the men were off their horses collecting the hay and corn in the farmhouses and granaries. When interrupted, 'the subsequent retreat on our quarters, after an exchange of a few shots, have not only been mighty entertaining, but given opportunities of instruction to our young officers'. On the 8th Somerset wrote that they were foraging 'rather close to each other' and the following day issued a Brigade Order on the subject. After specifying the areas which the regiments were to forage the next day, he ordered that in future, when a regiment was foraging in the Macaye valley, the officer commanding was to send a report to General Morillo, at Louhossoa, who would 'push forward some parties of infantry to cover the foragers on his being required to do so'. General Morillo had his own depôts of forage in the area, and the Hussars were ordered to respect them.[2]

The 10th were allocated the Macaye valley for the next day, the events of which were subsequently to become the subject of the minutest examination, with the result that every detail of the operation has been recorded. Their orders did not reach them until after dark, when it was too late to send a message to Morillo, but at eight o'clock that evening the acting adjutant, Sergeant Major Wells, detailed a subaltern to go to Louhossoa at daybreak, with a request for a covering party of one hundred men.

At dawn on 10 January, according to orders, Quartermaster Benjamin Eyres set off in search of forage and, finding a supply in some houses two or three leagues from Cambo, he set off back to the regiment. After the sentences of two or three courts-martial had been 'put into execution', the main body had set off for the Macaye valley, halting *en route* at Louhossoa, where they found forty or fifty Spanish infantry waiting for them. When Colonel Quentin complained that these were not enough, he was told that there were picquets out in front who would assist him. Sending Captain Lloyd back to Louhossoa to try and get some more, he continued on to the isolated church of Macaye, where the 15th had one of their outlying picquets. The country here is very enclosed, with high banks and hedges, and deep lanes, reminiscent of Devon. The Hussars passed to the right of the church and filed down a narrow lane leading into the valley, where they dismounted, while the troop sergeants went off in search of forage. When they returned FitzClarence's and Stuart's troops were ordered into the valley with instructions to forage close to the Spanish picquets, taking care to place a chain of vedettes and to keep a sharp look out. Almost immediately the French were seen advancing from the opposite hill, but when FitzClarence asked the Spanish picquet officer to cover his troop while they continued to forage, he replied that his orders were to retire.

Captain Harding was about to send his troop down into the valley when the sound of firing was heard. Colonel Quentin immediately called him back and led the rest of the regiment away from Macaye church, leaving the two troops in the valley to their own devices. FitzClarence and Stuart now formed their troops in 'column of divisions', about three hundred yards behind the Spaniards, throwing out skirmishers, in an attempt to rally them. As the French advanced the Spaniards fled, the two troops were 'put about' and sent to the rear, while the two FitzClarences and Fitzgerald remained behind, vainly beating the Spaniards back to their posts with their swords. Eventually Captain Lloyd turned up with a 'covering party' of *caçadores*, three companies strong, who succeeded in driving the French back, just as the picquets were about to give way. FitzClarence and Stuart managed to extricate their troops and rejoined the regiment about two leagues to the rear. An hour or so later, when Major Jones taxed Quentin with the loss of part of two troops, he admitted that he *had* lost a few men and horses, but not to any great extent. In fact the losses were five men and four horses. The object of the expedition had been to collect enough forage to last the regiment for three days, but when it returned to its quarters at six o'clock in the evening, having been out for nearly ten hours, it brought back barely sufficient for thirty horses for one day.[3]

The next day Wildman summed up the difficulties of operating in such close country. A cavalry regiment 'in single files, marching thro' deep lanes, in a hilly enclosed country' was all but defenceless against 'ever so small a force of infantry'. A strong infantry picquet was now occupying Gréciete, between Mendionde and Hasparren, and the Hussars *sometimes* had covering parties when they foraged. The French had 'done a great deal by the judicious mixture of their force', as when, at Mendionde, their cavalry had drawn the squadron of the 18th Hussars into 'a cross fire of their sharpshooters'. As if to confirm his remarks, the 7th Hussars had an incident on the 16th, very reminiscent, if less serious, than the Mendionde affair. Captain Heyliger, in command of twenty men of each troop of the regiment, set off to forage in the country to his front, but the enemy had concealed a party of *Tirailleurs* 'in some ditches on his left, who fired upon him just as he was entering the village, and wounded himself and one troop horse'. The ball went through his right arm and 'lodged in the muscles near his back bone', having 'enter'd his side and ran round the ribs'. Wildman hurried to the scene and found Heyliger in great pain, being helped by two officers and the assistant surgeon of the 15th Hussars, who refused to do anything until the surgeons of the 7th arrived. 'Irwin & Moffat came at last and extracted the ball, after which he suffer'd greatly in being convey'd home to his Quarters abt. five miles distant.' Like

Hughes, however, whose wound was remarkably similar, he made a rapid recovery. By 26 January he was doing 'as well as to be able to sit up at dinner', and on 12 February Thornhill could report that he was 'nearly quite well'.

In spite of the strictures of the Brigade-Major and the flow of orders repeating his earlier instructions, 'affairs with the enemy' continued, the 10th losing a further six men and four horses, and the 15th several more, during the last week of January. Wildman was highly critical of Jones, complaining that he took all 'the little arrangements' out of the regimental officers' hands. A foraging party, he thought, 'should arrive . . . before daybreak and with as much secrecy as possible, and on no account march in open light along the side of a hill in front of the enemy's out-posts; and from there descend into a village in a valley'. On 13 January Robbins reported to Hodge that he did not think that they had 'two days forage of any description' within their lines. Corn they got very irregularly and seldom as much as five pounds per horse. 'Having to go two or three leagues a day,' he continued, 'and then to forage just under the enemy's videttes, out at daybreak & not in till 3 or 4 in the afternoon has made the outline of the horses appear strong indeed'. By 20 January the forage was exhausted around Mendionde and Macaye, and alternative measures had to be taken to save the horses from starvation. A substitute was sought for, and found, in the 'green and round tops of gorse, gathered in abundance in the neighbourhood', chopped and 'bruised', and mixed with the corn ration, when available. Schaumann claimed that he was the first to bring this local custom to the attention of the authorities, after it was pointed out to him by a 'rustic of the district'. The 'matter was immediately reported to the general, and having tried it, it was approved', but owing to the prickles, the gorse had 'first of all to be crushed otherwise the horses would not touch them'. It was a not entirely successful expedient, however, and as February came in with bad weather and the whole country was turned into a quagmire, the condition of the horses grew steadily worse. On the 12th Thornhill informed Hodge that the 7th Hussars had lost several horses that had 'dropped down dead on the way from the outposts', and the rest were 'like the nags of "Warwick & Talbot Salisbury and Gloster" dropping down their heads before the Battle of Agincourt'. In short they were looking 'sad & forlorn, the fatal effect of eating gorse without corn'.

With the forage running out there was an end to the vicious scrapping and the opposing outposts settled down on the best possible terms. According to Wildman, writing on 3 February, the French had brought all their picquets close to theirs, so that, on most posts, there was a 'French sentry at one end of a little bridge, and an English or Portuguese on the other'. The French were 'extremely civil and always anxious to converse', but 'all except official communications' had been expressly forbidden. The 10th Hussars struck up a particularly close relationship with the French 21st Chasseurs, 'from having been all this winter opposite each other', which was on occasions carried to extremes. On visiting a distant picquet and enquiring for the subaltern, who spoke fluent French and German, Captain Gordon was told that he was 'over at the enemy's picket' as Captain Le Clerc, of the 21st Chasseurs, 'a relation of Josephine, was one of his friends'.

Behind the lines life was now pretty comfortable, at least for the officers, who, Wildman wrote on 11 January, were 'growing as fat as pigs on French living'. Campaigning in France was definitely *a gentlemanlike service*'. There was an excellent market at Hasparren, where 'every kind of meat, poultry, salt fish, and even tea & coffee' could be bought, although the prices, Thornhill thought, 'were infernally dear, with meat at three shillings a pound, geese at twenty shillings a piece, and sixpence for a bantam's egg.' Every farmhouse had enough plates for a large Mess, 'ranged in racks, like England', and the houses beautifully clean, and Wildman thought there was no reason why an officer 'should not sit down, in *quiet times*, to as Gentlemanlike a Dinner, as he would in England, and be more fit for his duty than if he lived like a pig'. The locals, Major Griffith thought, were, if anything 'too civil', and quite over-whelmed them with kindness. There was a 'remarkably fine handsome fellow' in Wildman's house who had served with the *Chasseurs* of the Imperial Guard, and who well remembered 'seeing us before at Benevente.' The lower orders, in general, spoke 'the Pyrenean lingo', and he seldom met with any who spoke good French, except for the priests. Everyone was waiting impatiently for the advance to begin, but the roads were still impassable. On 4 February the 10th Hussars left their quarters to go to Passages to collect their new clothing. They marched via St Pée and Irun, and the journey there and back probably took them ten days. They returned just in time, however, because a sudden sharp frost hardened the ground sufficiently to make movement possible, and the army was at last set in motion.[4]

* * *

Soult was now holding a lining running north from St Jean Pied-de-Port, at the foot of the Pyrenees, to the Adour River. Wellington's plan was to turn the French left with Hill's Corps, while Beresford acted against their centre and right, all the time drawing Soult further away from Bayonne, which had been invested by Hope's Corps. Vivian's Hussars were to act with Beresford, and Somerset's with Hill. The advance began on 14 February, with Hill pushing the French back past Helette, south and east of Cambo. By the evening of the 16th he was in possession of a line running north-west from St Palais to Orège, while, to the north, Beresford was pushing towards the Adour. Wildman and his 'Brother of the 4th', who was staying with him, saw the first day's advance 'to perfection', and spent the day running occasional errands for Sir Stapleton Cotton. 'It was,' he told Hodge, 'a very pretty sight.' When the Hussars marched on the 16th it was high time, as the horses were dying of weakness after being turned out to grass, and the men were 'worn out with chopping and bruizing gorse'.

On the 17th Hill made a demonstration towards the Gave d'Oleron, while the 4th Division and Vivian's Hussars occupied Bidache, pushing their outposts the following day north towards Peyrehorade and Hastingues, where the Gave d'Oleron and the Gave de Pau joined and flowed into the Adour. On the 18th the 10th Hussars moved to Came, only two miles from Bidache, where the gaunt grey ruins of de Grammont's family seat stand to this day. According to Schaumann it had been occupied during the Revolution by soldiers who had 'through some piece of carelessness' set fire to it. When de Grammont 'made himself known, and discovered a few old people who remembered having seen him as a child', there were great rejoicings in the neighbourhood. Everybody tried to get at him and, 'while some clasped his knees and others implored him to take possession of his heritage, others stood weeping with joy'. At last a former servant of the family turned up 'who had carried Captain Grammont in his arms as a child'.

The small straggling villages through which the Hussars were now marching were full of excellent forage, the weather was fine and clear and the horses picked up surprisingly and 'began to fill out in their carcasses'. By the 22nd picquets of the 15th Hussars, at Escos, on the left bank of the Gave d'Oleron, were in touch with the right of Vivian's Brigade, and all the likely crossing places were under observation. The next day Beresford, with the 4th and 7th Divisions, drove the enemy from Hastingues and Oeynegave, into the entrenchments covering the bridge across the Gave de Pau at Peyrehorade. Soult, with his right and centre held in check, was now menaced along a front of twenty-five miles.

On the 24th, Wellington struck. While diversionary attacks were mounted at the obvious crossing places, Hill's Corps crossed the Gave d'Oleron higher up at Viellenave. Further east, at Sauveterre, the French had established a strong bridgehead and the 3rd Division, together with Somerset's Hussars, were ordered to threaten a passage, but not to actually cross. The river, swollen with rain, was flowing fast and the enemy kept up a heavy fire from behind a hill, half a mile away on the far bank. On the British side there was a mill weir built across the river 'in the shape of two sides of an angle, over which the stream was running with great rapidity'. Sir Stapleton Cotton suddenly called for a subaltern and six men of the 7th Hussars to lead the infantry across, but there was delay sending for an officer from the rear, during which Cotton fumed at the slowness of the Hussars, saying that he wished he had one of his old brigades. Eventually Captain Verner started crossing with his squadron, but when only half of them were across the French sent down some skirmishers and the order 'Files about' was given. Verner got all his men back safely, but he estimated that the infantry had lost 'not less than 300 men of whom many were drowned or shot in the river', although Vivian put the figure at five officers and forty men killed and wounded. Cotton seems to have completely forgotten that the crossing was intended to be a feint, and, as Verner put it, 'a more absurd or injudicious order could not have been given'. When Picton, who was known to have 'a thorough and rooted dislike of cavalry, more especially Hussars', arrived on the scene, there were 'very high words' between them, leading to some very strong language.

The next day the Hussars crossed the Gave d'Oleron and led the rest of the army north and north-east towards the Gave de Pau. While Vivian's Brigade crossed at Castagnede, marching through Cassaber to Sorde, Somerset's crossed by a ford below Sauveterre and headed for Salies-en-Béarn. The weather remained fine, the roads were excellent and the horses in fine condition; 'in short,' Captain Kennedy of the 18th wrote, 'the Wellington pack were in high spirits and in full cry', the scent was lying well, as the French had had 'but a short start', and he hoped they would 'be in at the death' in Paris before long. Spirits were certainly high that night at Salies-en-Béarn and the 10th Hussars got out of hand once again. Colonel Palmer and the sergeant major went to one of the houses 'where there were some men at dinner, making free with the person's wine, and eating his bacon'. As Palmer entered, the ring-leader, one Gilbert, sat fast in his chair, 'eating his bacon and looking at Palmer the while,' until the Colonel knocked him out of his chair and threw them all out. 'I never,' Palmer later stated, 'struck a man before belonging to the Regiment, but in a state of mutiny like that, it was impossible to do other-wise.' Before marching the next morning a punishment parade was held, at which Colonel Quentin told the men that if any of them got drunk again he would make sure that the regiment was made to bivouac every night. After some delay, the Brigade set off, fording the Gave de Pau, a mile below the bridge at Berenx, and driving in the enemy picquets. 'The whole army got over,' Wildman wrote, 'with a little skirmishing and one or two shots from the 6 pounders.' Turning on to the great road from Peyrehorade to Orthes, they pursued the French outposts, through Ramous and Puyoo. That night Vivian's Brigade halted at Ramous, and Somerset's near St Boes, just off the great road, a few miles from Orthes. On the same night Sir Stapleton Cotton issued a strong order, doubtless inspired by the 'irregularity' of the 10th the previous night. 'Lenity to those guilty of small offences,' he declared, tended 'too frequently to encourage the commission of offences of greater magnitude,' and when captains of troops had 'occasion to represent the misconduct of indi-viduals to the commanding officer,' the latter was bound to support them, 'otherwise the troop will of necessity become disorderly, the captain will lose his authority, and his zeal for the good of the service' was likely to be dimin-ished 'in the same proportion'.

* * *

On the 27th 'a remarkably fine morning announced a glorious day.' The army moved off at about nine o'clock, although, before the 18th Hussars could join the rest of the Brigade, seven men were flogged near Ramous. Soult's army, some 40,000 strong, lay in a good position, on a series of heights, parallel to the great road from Peyrehorade to Orthes, in front of the village of Sallespisse. 'His artillery,' Captain Thackwell recalled, 'about 20 pieces, was advanta-geously posted on the salient points of his position, and his right was covered by broken ground, a woody ridge, and the village of St Boes'. The British assault began at about ten o'clock, with, from left to right, the 4th, Light and 3rd Divisions, supported by the 6th and 7th Divisions, wheeling left off the high road and climbing steadily up to the French positions. The ground was too broken for the cavalry to act, but as they waited for the outcome of the infantry battle, Verner, at the head of his squadron, had a grandstand view of the action:

> The day was lovely, perfectly calm with a bright sun, more like summer than the month of February. The appearance was more that of a review than the moment of battle. Our infantry advanced in line – the colours flying in the centre, and the bands playing, [but] it was not long before we received a salute from the enemy, which soon let us know that we had music of different kind to attend to.

At length, after a bitter struggle, the enemy's right around St Boes gave way and the British gradually gained ground along the whole ridge. 'This,' wrote Thackwell, 'obliged his left to retire, and he took up a new position on a small eminence this side Salles[pisse]'. At the same time Stewart's Brigade of the 2nd Division, with the 13th and 14th Light Dragoons, who had crossed the Gave de Pau above Orthes, were seen racing northwards in an attempt to cut Soult off at Sault-de-Navailles on the great road northwards to Mont-de-Marsan.

As the British centre began to close on the enemy's new position, the French began a precipitate retreat upon Sault-de-Navailles and a squadron of the 7th Hussars, ordered to charge along the road to Sallespisse, took some prisoners. It was now that Wildman witnessed,

> the most beautiful sight I ever beheld; the French no sooner gave way than they ran like mad, our infantry running out of breath after them, all open to avoid the shells, and the squadrons of cavalry moving on in the midst of them. The French however rallied and three times made a stand upon very strong positions, but our artillery soon got at them, and when the infantry advanced they ran. The 21st *Chasseurs*, who near Hasparre[n] talked of taking the pipeclay out of our jackets, attempted a daring thing, to take two of our guns, but they got amongst the infantry in a narrow lane, and were almost annihilated.

It appears that Soult thought that some of the British guns were capable of being captured and gave orders for two squadrons of the 21st to gallop through a deep lane, in order to '*déboucher* on the open ground and charge them'. The officer in command pointed out the risk his men would run, 'but on receiving in reply some cutting remark, nettling to his high feelings, he gave the word, galloped forward, and he and his *Chasseurs* soon became entangled in the lanes', which were in places from ten to twenty feet deep. While in this predicament, a Portuguese regiment came up on the brink and, with a volley, laid nineteen out of every twenty on the ground. The 10th Hussars, in support, came up just after this slaughter:

These poor fellows and their horses lay so thick, with their swords and bridles still in their hands, that the road was impassable, and we were obliged to break into the fields in order to proceed in pursuit of the enemy. I think there was but one feeling, that of regret, at seeing our old friends, with their green jackets, broad belts, and chaccos [sic] with white or ticken covers, laying thus, and it was even then evident, unnecessarily sacrificed.

Among the dead the 10th found their old friend Captain Le Clerc.

Pressing on, the Hussars found the enemy fleeing in disorder towards the mud-flats which bordered the Luy de Béarn River. The 7th trotted forward along the great road to Mont-de-Marsan, and about two miles short of Sault-de-Navailles caught up with the rear of the enemy's infantry. Wheeling left off the road they charged up into them. Thornhill and the right squadron went in first, and Verner, coming up behind, passed him standing, with a long pole with a spike on the top in one hand, and holding his horse by the bridle with the other. As he galloped past he cried out, 'I congratulate you upon having taken that'. Thornhill's reply was, 'Yes, but the d— fellow has run it into my g–ts!' Thornhill's prize was one of the halberds carried by the escorts to the regimental 'Eagles', so it would seem that the 7th were very near to taking one of those coveted trophies. In any case Thornhill was not seriously hurt and managed to secure the pike and the officer who was carrying it, while the rest of the regiment took nearly seven hundred prisoners. Lord Edward Somerset, putting the figure at more like five hundred, wrote that the 'country being enclosed, they had nothing to do but to dash down the lanes, & charge their infantry as it was retiring in confusion'. They were 'so panic struck & beat that the greatest part of them were ready to lay down their arms without firing', so that they 'suffered but little'.

The 15th Hussars were now ordered to take up the pursuit, but, much to Thackwell's annoyance, the 13th and 14th Light Dragoons got in front of them. When they were within three-quarters of a mile of the river they caught up with the enemy's rearguard crossing over the flats, in total confusion, but were prevented from charging them, which, had they done so, Thackwell thought, would have resulted in 'at least 3,000 *hors de combat*'. Instead, some guns were brought up to cannonade the enemy, who replied in kind from the opposite bank. 'Had daylight lasted one hour longer' Griffith thought, they would 'have made mincemeat of some thousands', but it was getting so 'dusk' that Sir Stapleton would not let them continue the pursuit, although he had 'never felt so great an inclination to be savage'. The 15th now dismounted in column of squadrons. Thackwell remembered one of the enemy's shots removing part of a private's saddle and killing two geese in the rear; but this was the only hit they scored, which was just as well as there was by now some confusion. The 7th Hussars, coming back from the river, met the British infantry coming down the road, which became 'so jammed that for a length of time neither were able to move'. Shot and shell fell on the ground either side, but mercifully none on the road.

As night fell the enemy fled in the direction of St Sever, while the exhausted Hussars bivouacked, Vivian's at Bonnegarde, near Sault-de-Navailles, and Somerset's in houses along the great road. The out-lying picquet, which remained standing all night, was found by Colonel Palmer's squadron of the 10th Hussars. The ground was literally strewed with the dead and dying, and fifty men were sent out to 'scour the ground where the 7th had charged that day'. 'I never saw any man so cool & collected,' Wildman wrote of his brigade commander, 'and very active in bringing up the guns, and us to every point where we could be useful; we were scarcely out of a trot or gallop, except when the guns were firing, from 10 in the morning 'till near 6.'

* * *

The morning after the battle the 10th Hussars formed the advance guard of the centre column of the army, with orders to prevent the enemy destroying the several small bridges on the high road. What followed was to be another subject of close examination and debate. As the right squadron, under Colonel Palmer, set off, Sir Stapleton Cotton appeared and ordered Lieutenant Eversfield and three or four men to go forward with him to reconnoitre. A league or so down the road they came across a squadron of their old friends the 21st *Chasseurs* on the far side of a small river, busily destroying the bridge. Two of Gardiner's guns were brought up and rapidly dislodged them, while Eversfield and his party crossed by a ford, and, following the enemy, caught up with them in front of the village of Hagetmau, half a mile further on. On Cotton's orders, he pressed them as much as possible for about half an hour, until Colonel Palmer arrived, followed closely by Captain Harding with orders to charge. Palmer had just lined the party, consisting of himself, Harding, Eversfield, Fitzgerald, Henry FitzClarence, Cotton's Aide-de-Camp, Beauchamp of the 16th Light Dragoons, and five or six men, across the road, when the rest of the squadron, led by Colonel Quentin, appeared trotting up the road, whereupon the enemy 'filed off'. Palmer and his party pursued them, followed two hundred yards behind by the squadron. The enemy halted and fronted, but, seeing Palmer and the squadron coming at them, quickly went about again, hotly pursued by the whole squadron. After this skirmish, in which Harding was wounded and some men and horses of the enemy taken prisoner, Palmer asked the men if they were ready for another charge and, receiving the answer 'Yes', he led them once more at the enemy, taking some more prisoners.

The right squadron was now ordered to open up to allow the Horse Artillery to unlimber and fire a few shots at the enemy, after which the centre squadron, under Captain de Grammont, advanced, the 'Gallop' was sounded and off they went, with Palmer's squadron falling in behind them. Some distance down the road, however, a volley was fired at them from some woods on either side and the centre squadron, facing about, retired out of range. The enemy also halted, 'threw up their skirmishers' and retired. Lord Edward Somerset ordered the 10th to remain where they were until the infantry came up and they halted, having taken eighteen prisoners in all, with the loss of Captain Harding and five men wounded. That night the Brigade was quartered a league short of St Sever, which remained in French hands.

At nine o'clock the following morning, 1 March, Thackwell's squadron of the 15th Hussars, wearing their cloaks in the heavy rain, took up the pursuit. The French had slipped out of St Sever and the Hussars, passing through the town, were soon across the Adour River, where they discovered that Soult had turned east on the road to Aire, abandoning his store depot at Mont-de-Marsan. While the 7th Hussars continued northwards up the road, the 10th and 15th turned off after the French. A league short of Grenade Thackwell came up with them and pushed them back into the town, where the leading division, Sergeant Major Tale with them, suddenly found themselves face to face with their quarry lined up across the market place. As the British approached, they broke, and 'it was wheel-about and turn-about, to the tune of the Devil take the hindmost, fixing the price of heels at a premium'. A fierce skirmish now took place 'under the noses of hundreds of spectators, who lined the windows of the surrounding houses', in which a further eighteen prisoners were taken. The 6th Division now came up and Thackwell formed the advance guard to within a mile of Cazères. That night he and the right half-squadron got good quarters 'at the château of Baroness de Course', who was very polite and gave them an excellent supper. In general the French were continuing 'very civil', according to Griffith, and on their entering a new place greeted them with cries of '*Vive le roi George*'. That night a Cavalry General Order thanked Colonel Quentin and 'the officers and men of the 10th Royal Hussars for their gallant and steady conduct' on the previous day.

Soult now rallied his forces in front of Aire, covering the road from Bordeaux to Pau and Toulouse, where he had a large magazine, but on 4 March he was attacked by Hill's Corps and forced to retire down both banks of the Adour as far as Maubourguet. On the 5th Somerset's Brigade set off after him, finally halting on the outskirts of Plaisance. Vivian's Brigade, meanwhile, having carried on straight up the great road to Mont-de-Marsan, remained there until 4 March, when it moved to Villeneuve-de-Marsan in support of Hill's attack on Aire. They remained there until the 8th, when they marched to Bordeaux, accompanying Beresford, and the 4th and 7th Divisions. Four days later, as they entered the town, they witnessed the first public demonstration in favour of the Bourbons. 'Who would have thought,' Vivian wrote, 'that the British soldier would get drunk on their delicious wines, for which in England we pay 10s. a bottle, and which we purchase here for ten sous?'

By 14 March Soult had managed to concentrate his army on the left bank of the Adour and was once again threatening Hill at Aire. The cavalry picquets were withdrawn from Plaisance to within a mile of St Germe, to the east of Aire, and parties were posted to watch the various bridges across the river. Beresford's force was summoned urgently from Bordeaux, but before battle could be joined Soult learned of the fall of Bordeaux and retired on Tarbes, some eighteen miles to the south. On the 15th Somerset's Hussars were once again in contact with the enemy. At St Mont, where a bridge crossed the Adour, a private of the 15th Hussars, trapped in the church tower by a French patrol, threw the bell rope over the side, 'rapidly descended by it', mounted his horse and got clear away. The following day the enemy were in full retreat. At Tasque Captain Hancox, with the leading squadron of the 15th Hussars, drove in the 13th *Chasseurs* killing ten and taking an officer and thirty men prisoner. That morning the Brigade was late starting, held up by the 10th Hussars, whose baggage had been slow in turning out. A league beyond St Germe Sir Stapleton Cotton had spoken 'very freely' on the subject to Colonel Quentin, telling him 'how very ill the regiment was commanded', how slow they were at performing their duty, and 'how very much displeased he was with his conduct'. In vain Quentin pointed out that the roads were very bad and the regiment much dispersed; the '*Lion d'Or*' was in no mood to listen to excuses.

On 19th March Soult tried to make a stand at Vic-en-Bigorre, but was driven out of his position and forced to retire on Tarbes. The following day the whole of the Allied army was concentrated at Rabastens. Even Vivian's Brigade was there, having marched 'in four days considerably upwards of a hundred miles, and a great part of it through sands up to the horse's fetlocks'. Advancing on Tarbes by the high road, the 2nd, 3rd, 6th and Light Divisions drove the French from their positions after a sharp fight. Retiring in good order and taking full advantage of the renowned marching capabilities of the French infantryman, Soult set off due east towards Toulouse, his pursuers following slowly, in incessant rain, through a countryside intersected by flooded, bridge-less rivers. Soult entered Toulouse, the main arsenal of south-west France, on the 24th, having gained several days, sufficient to strengthen the already formidable defences of the city.

Wellington's army stumbled after him 'through a variety of villages', with Somerset's Hussars at the head of the 6th Division and Vivian's at the head of Beresford's left column. If the weather was atrocious, at least the countryside was beautiful, and good food and Bordeaux wine made this part of the campaign 'bearable'. Vivian, on the other hand, was not so easily comforted. At Muigan, near Boulogne, on the 23rd, he wrote that all the fine roads were 'past and gone', and that they were once more up to their necks in mud. The next night, at Paylauzic, near Lombez, conditions were getting worse and worse. He was in a 'still more wretched village' and his brigade dispersed 'in a completely open country, something like Salisbury Plain, cultivated without being closed'; 'a fine cavalry country,' he thought, if the ground had not been 'too deep', the wet weather having 'played the devil with it'.

On the 26th the right squadron of the 15th pushed the enemy picquets back, beyond Tourneville, although they were, in turn, driven back, later in the day, with some casualties.[5] Meanwhile Vivian's Brigade drove the enemy along the Auch–Toulouse road, as far as the Touche River, three miles short of Toulouse. Soult's whole army was now in Toulouse, with the Allies closing in, having taken seven days to march the distance the French had covered in four. Soult's men were in rags and most of the infantry without shoes; their sufferings were dreadful.

On the morning of the 28th Hill's Corps was to have crossed the Garonne, but the bridge was found to be two pontoons short and had to be taken up. The army therefore moved to its right, on to the Toulouse–St Gaudens road, leaving Vivian's Brigade on the road from Auch and Somerset's on that from Tarbes. 'The French picquets,' Thackwell recalled, 'all retired within a mile of the bridge of Toulouse, forming a semicircle, the Garonne forming the arc.' As the picquets in front of Vivian fell back the 18th Hussars followed them cautiously, until they reached the bridge at St Martin de la Touche, which was barricaded and guarded by the 10th *Chasseurs*. Ordering thirty men to dismount and attack the bridge, Vivian sent two squadrons of the 1st German Hussars across the river, above and below the village, to cut off the French. Before this could be done, however, the French abandoned the bridge and retreated along the high road towards the suburb of St Cyprien, pursued by the 18th Hussars. Suddenly 'brought up by the discharge of five pieces of cannon', which the enemy had placed in a battery enfilading the road, Vivian was obliged to 'put about' and the 18th 'who were in the front, were very steady and did it very quietly'. The French 'fired very badly indeed' and the Hussars were 'fortunate enough' to lose only two or three men and four or five horses killed or wounded; indeed, Major Hughes thought that it was a miracle the 18th were not totally destroyed in this action. 'By the Lord Harry,' Vivian wrote to Wildman on the 31st, if he had had the support of a few British infantry he would have 'been into the town'. 'You never saw fellows in such a funk.' However, he continued, 'it secured us an admirable position near the town before possessed by the enemy and Lord W. was very well pleased.'

*   *   *

That same day the 7th Hussars rejoined Somerset's Brigade, having been detached, the day after the battle of Orthes, to protect the northern flank of the army. Since then they had been scattered all over the countryside, sometimes being a fortnight without contact between squadrons. At first they were quartered at Mont-de-Marsan, but then moved to Roquefort, in the Landes, which was 'throughout one immense tract of land, cover'd with forests of pine, and occasionally opening into immense barren heaths'. Before long they came up against a 'Party of Brigands', led by one 'Captain Florian'. It was composed partly of unemployed 'Douaniers and other officers of Custom', and partly of deserters, who lived on plunder, authorized to do so by Marshal Soult in order to cut off and 'annoy' the transport of provisions to the army. Their first

166

exploit was to seize Major Thornhill, in bed in his quarters at Villeneuve-de-Marsan, on the night of 9 March while he was recuperating from the blow he had received at Orthes. Wildman described the scene to Hodge with a mixture of glee and respectful sympathy:

> A Party of these Ruffians . . . contriv'd to surprise the sentinel at the major's house, whom they made prisoner, and took the major himself out of his bed. He, however, wounded as he was, knock'd down two of them with their arms and escaped. They however got away with his saddle bags and two of his Horses, and took seven Troop Horses out of a detach'd stable out of the town.

Vivian, however, was definitely not amused. Thornhill fancied, he wrote,

> they took him for me; but they would not have caught me so! It is a bad business; very disgraceful to the regiment, and not creditable to Thornhill. . . . There never was a post so easily guarded as Villeneuve. At a bridge, at the entrance of the place, which I barricaded, and where I had a picquet, he had none. The old Fool!

According to Verner, 'Captain Florian,' dressed in Thornhill's clothes, waited on the road, 'where he expected supplies to come up to the army and as he could speak English tolerably well, he obtained all the information necessary to make his arrangements'.

His next exploit was less gallant. On Sunday, 13 March, he ambushed a convoy of mules and baggage animals on the road between Roquefort and Mont-de-Marsan, 'in the most savage manner'. 'They took an officer of the 40th [Regiment] prisoner,' Wildman wrote, 'and four or five privates, cut and maim'd the Muleteers, shot a peasant who knew one of them, and afterwards two of the prisoners who could not keep up.' The 7th sent a party out after them and managed to rescue the officer and all the plunder, but the gang slipped away into the trackless forest, leaving 'fifty-eight mules hamstrung, and their bellies rip'd open', which the Hussars had to put out of their misery. The next night Wildman took out a patrol and, early on the morning of 15 March, stumbled on a small inn 'in the wildest country imaginable', the landlord of which, after 'threats of hanging &c.', revealed that this 'formidable Banditti', supposedly 200 strong, consisted of only fifteen members, 'one calling himself Captain dress'd in Thornhill's pelisse and waistcoat, one officer, and thirteen privates', some dressed as soldiers and some as 'arm'd peasants'. Their weapons came from a store which the French had left behind to be destroyed. Acting on this information, Wildman and his patrol went straight to a village about three leagues further on, 'where they [the gang] had committed much depradation upon the inhabitants' and seized one of the brigands in a small inn. He was 'immediately recognized & sworn to by the officer of the 40th and some of the Muleteers, and Privates who had been taken' and was accordingly hanged in the market place at Roquefort two days later. The executioner was a soldier of the Brunswick-Oels regiment, who requested the duty in revenge for the death of a comrade at the hands of Captain Florian.

The following day the 7th Hussars handed over 'this agreable [sic] duty', to the 4th Portuguese Cavalry, and set off to join the Brigade. By the time they reached Auch it seemed that they were being followed by the banditti. A few nights previously someone had suddenly fired at one of the vedettes, 'who unfortunately stood fast, and after firing his carbine & pistols, *charg'd them alone'*. Unfortunately, Wildman wrote, because if the vedette had retired and drawn the banditti towards the town, they 'must have had more of them, as besides the Picquet of Foot Guards', they had the whole squadron 'under arms on foot' in little more than ten minutes. This, however, was not the last that was seen of Captain Florian, as Thornhill disgustedly reported to Hodge on 30 April:

Lowther and Uniacke dined a few days ago with the officer who took me, they say he is a good sort of fellow. I think he is a damned black-guard or he would have at least sent me back my new pelisse. I have recovered my horses, one of which I found in a French General's stable. I requisitioned them both. Congratulate yourself that you were not that unhappy major who was taken prisoner at Villeneuve one night. How lucky it was for me that Frenchmen never dream of men fighting with their fists.[6]

* * *

Assistant-Surgeon Jenks, who had recently joined the 10th Hussars, wrote in his journal that, at this time, the regiment skirmished 'almost daily, and by constant practice both officers and men acquired great proficiency in outpost duties'. Many of the men were first-rate shots, and one in particular, named Farmer, 'greatly distinguished himself as a marksman'. Jenks was a great admirer of Colonel Palmer, who, in his estimation, was 'a most enterprising officer and an admirable horseman'. Unfortunately his rosy view of the regiment seems to have been at variance with the facts.[7] On 30 March the right squadron of the regiment, under the command of Colonel Palmer, spent the day skirmishing in front of Plaisance, and that night Captain Turner's troop was quartered in a neighbouring château. The next morning the owner came to Palmer complaining that he had been plundered. Palmer went back with him and found that the house had, indeed, been 'completely ransacked'. In a blazing fury, Palmer set off after the troop and, catching up with them, 'made every man take off his things' and instituted a search, which turned up a fowl and some linen. As he was 'abusing' the men Colonel Quentin came past on his way to the outposts. To Palmer's anger Quentin remained very cool, merely saying that if the facts could be proved he would court-martial the culprit and have him punished. Recalling this period Palmer could still not keep the anger out of his voice:

I have been obliged to collar men in the ranks; I have been compelled to use personal violence with the men; I have told a man he was drunk, and he has told me very coolly that he was not. . . . I have paid out of my own pocket for robberies committed by the men. . . . Upon my oath I did not conceive my life in safety, the men were in that state of drunkenness they were mutinous. It was their constant practice, when they got into a house, to lay hold of everything.

That same day Lord Edward Somerset received a letter from the Adjutant-General, enclosing a charge which had been preferred against Sergeant-Major Robinson of the 10th Hussars for allegedly allowing his men to plunder the house of an inhabitant. In his letter he stated that complaints against the regiment had become 'so general' that steps were to be taken 'to re-establish that discipline . . . which has been allowed to relax in an unpardonable degree under the command' of Colonel Quentin, who seemed 'unequal to control a regiment of the first pretensions'. Sir Stapleton Cotton instructed Lord Edward to read this letter out to the officers of the regiment, but the Brigade Commander, considering it to be a private letter, did not make it public to the Brigade, contenting himself with making known to Quentin that part referring to himself. Lord Edward himself makes no reference to the troubles of the 10th Hussars in any of his letters, which is strange as he was not one to stint with the gossip, if he had the chance.

The next morning, when tempers in the regiment were not at their best, Lord Edward assembled the officers and conveyed to them the Commander of the Forces' displeasure. Afterwards Palmer and Gordon called on him to ask whether they were being personally blamed. Somerset replied that, 'cantoned as the regiment constantly was, in dispersed villages', unless the Commanding Officer was properly supported by every officer under his command it was impossible for him to maintain discipline and that 'when troops were scattered over a great extent of country, a great deal necessarily depended upon the troop officers'.

It is not clear precisely what prompted this outburst from the Commander of the Forces, as in the case of Sergeant-Major Robinson no corroboration was found, and, with Lord Edward Somerset's approval, Colonel Quentin reported that he considered the charge unfounded. It appears, moreover, in spite of Palmer's subsequent remarks, that only three cases of plundering by the Hussars are mentioned in Wellington's correspondence, one of which was the affair of the church at Bordéres, which involved men of the 15th Hussars.[8] Of the two remaining incidents, which both involved the 10th Hussars, one was discounted by Quentin; so much for the 'general complaints' mentioned by the Adjutant-General.

* * *

'Nature and Art,' Major Griffith of the 15th Hussars wrote home on 25 April, 'were combined to place the French Army in a situation which would have been impregnable to any but British Troops.' To the west of Toulouse a loop in the Garonne was covered by the fortified suburb of St Cyprien. To the north and east the Languedoc Canal provided a formidable ditch, protected on the eastern side by the fortified suburbs of St Etienne and Guillemerie. Beyond the canal, running roughly north-south was a long ridge, crowned with redoubts, while, beyond it, the River Ers (or L'Hers), impassable except by bridge, ran through a flat marshy land. To the south lay the suburb of St Michel and the height of Pech David.

Wellington's first plan was to attack from the south with Hill's Corps, and on the 29th and 30th the Engineers laboured to make 'pontoons of casks &c., to throw the bridge over the Garonne'. When the crossing took place on 1 April Vivian reported that they were made into 'proper April fools'. Hill had indeed crossed the Garonne, and a second river, the Ariège, below the town, but he had found the roads into Toulouse impassable for artillery and had been forced to return. The next day, in Vivian's words, 'The Lord' was now planning how to 'circumvent Mr Soult', who was 'rather a serious playfellow'. On the 3rd Vivian joined Wellington and Beresford in a reconnaissance of the river to the north of Toulouse. After a long ride, it was decided that the bridge should be 'thrown over' at a small village near Grenade, some twelve miles from the city, at daybreak the next day. The 3rd, 4th, 6th and Light Divisions, with Somerset's and Vivian's Brigades, marched at eleven that same night, reaching Grenade at daybreak. The bridge, consisting of seventeen pontoons, was set up in three hours or so, and at nine the crossing commenced. It was cloudy and showery, and the troops were looking 'rather miserable' after a night march 'drenched to the skin and up to their knees in mud'. But the crossing itself, with the bands playing the 'British Grenadiers', the trumpets sounding and the banks lined with spectators, was a 'beautiful sight'. Because the horses had to be led across one by one, it was nightfall before the 3rd, 4th and 6th Divisions and the cavalry had crossed, but the latter managed to get in some skirmishing with the enemy's picquets before it became dark. During the night the weather grew steadily worse, with 'such a flood of rain' as Vivian never saw. Dawn on the 5th revealed the river swollen and, even worse, the bridge of boats 'carried away by hulks &c., sent down by the enemy'. It had to be taken up and the three divisions and three brigades of cavalry that had crossed were completely cut off from the main body. 'Had Soult now attacked us,' Hughes wrote, 'we would have had a great deal to do, and might have been played hell with.' For the next three days the army waited, but Soult never appeared. On the 7th Vivian reported that the weather was delightful, that the river had fallen three feet and that he was expecting the bridge to be re-established that evening, when the Spaniards and the Light Division were to cross. In fact the work was not completed until four in the morning of the 8th. When all were safely across, the whole force advanced up both banks of the River Ers towards Toulouse. Somerset's Brigade moved off at about one in the afternoon and drove in the enemy's picquets facing the British right.

Leading the left wing of the army, the 18th Hussars at last redeemed themselves. They skirmished with the enemy all the way past St Geniès, until they reached the Toulouse–Albi road, which they crossed at St Jean, and ascended the heights. Vivian, who was with them, rode to the top of the hill and looked down on the bridge across the Ers, which it was vital to take intact to enable the two wings of the army to join forces for the attack on Toulouse. As he turned to rejoin the 18th, a carbine ball hit him in the arm, and apparently unharmed, he rode on down the hill and ordered the regiment to advance; but as he raised his sword arm to give the signal it snapped and he was carried off in great pain. The regiment, in column of troops, swept down the high road and, jamming the French *Chasseurs* on the bridge, 'sabred their front ranks, their rear ranks going off in disorder'. The 18th pursued them at a gallop through the village of Croix d'Orade, 'nearly three miles in the very highest style', almost to the gates of Toulouse. When they rode back, having taken two hundred prisoners, for the loss of Captain Croker wounded and four men killed, the infantry had secured the bridge. 'It was reckoned,' Major Hughes wrote in jubilation, 'the best cavalry affair that has occurred, and all the praises which we have acquired have met my most sanguine expectations, and Lord Wellington has been most kind.' Wellington later wrote that what had passed on that occasion showed that he was as ready to applaud good conduct, when he observed it, as he was to find fault.

On the 9th the army lay quiet, while Wellington made his final preparations and at five o'clock in the morning of 10 April, another fine day, the army was put into motion. The bulk of the subsequent fighting, however, was done by the 4th and 6th Divisions and the Spanish. While the latter attacked the northern height, on the ridge, the 4th and 6th Divisions moved round the back, along the bank of the Ers, to attack the French right. 'Nothing,' Thackwell wrote, 'could resist the impetuosity of these attacks, and the enemy's columns were driven into the town, and the redoubts remained in our possession.' Somerset's Brigade, acting in support of the 4th Division, had to run the gauntlet of the enemy's fire as they moved through the flats bordering the river, before swinging to their right and climbing the ridge towards Toulouse. Here Major Howard, commanding the two left squadrons of the 10th, was ordered to charge the French cavalry formed in divisions across the road in front of him. When the 10th Hussars were about a hundred yards away from them the enemy went about. The Hussars followed after them, charging up to the top of the hill, where they were halted by 'a heavy fire of the enemy's infantry'. Immediately after the firing ceased Quentin rode out to the side to see what was going on, and, when it recommenced, he gave the order 'Threes about' and the Hussars withdrew at a steady walk until they were safely out of range. Just as they were turning about a musket ball hit the hilt of George FitzClarence's sword and went into his thigh. Quentin told him to fall out and, stuffing a white handkerchief into his mouth in considerable pain, he rode to the rear. The left squadron remained on the road, while the other three, on Cotton's orders, moved further to their left to support the attack of the 4th Division.

Vivian's Brigade, which had been working its way even further round to the left in pursuit of two French cavalry regiments, now swung back to its right along the road to Toulouse through Montraudon, and it was here that an unfortunate occurrence took place. The 10th Hussars, seeing Vivian's squadrons approaching from their left front, thought they were French and moved forward to attack them. This brought them within range of the guns of the enemy's forts at St Cyprien, which opened fire, causing serious losses, including Captain Gordon, who was struck on the side, just above the hip, by a cannon shot and mortally wounded.[9] Nobody 'was ever so fortunate as the 15th have been throughout this campaign,' Major Griffith wrote after the battle, as they and the 10th had been formed together 'and during a most tremendous cannonade' they had 'suffered lightly while the 10th got knocked over terribly'. By five in the evening, the French having withdrawn into the town, the whole of the position was in British hands, and only the road running south-east to Villefranche was available to Soult as a possible escape route.

* * *

The next day, 11 April, the Hussars were sent out to keep an eye open for possible French reinforcements. Vivian's Brigade, now taken over by Colonel von Arentsschild, was sent northwards along the Languedoc canal, and Somerset's north-east along the great road to Albi. At two o'clock on the morning of the 12th the French evacuated Toulouse, marching in good order the twenty-two miles to Villefranche, cutting the bridges over the canal and the Ers as they went. At eight o'clock the Allies entered the town 'amidst the cheers of the spectators, the white flag of the Bourbonnes [sic] floating over the Capital, and the white cockade worn by all'. 'The British soldiers,' Surgeon Jenks wrote in his diary, 'were received by the inhabitants with great joy, and were decorated with the Royalist colours.' Already rumours were circulating that Napoleon had abdicated and, on the following day, confirmation came from Paris. While the army awaited the armistice, in Toulouse 'all were holiday making with officers wearing the white cockade'. The 18th Hussars, according to Major Hughes, were 'specially feasted, owing to their brilliant conduct at Croix d'Orade', and at Wellington's ball on the 14th he was actually 'accosted by him in a frank and pleasant manner'.

As Somerset's Brigade pursued Soult towards Narbonne, Major Griffith was looking forward to 'a dip in the Mediterranean', but just as they reached Carcassonne, while they 'were all in full pursuit', the news of Napoleon's abdication came upon them 'like a thunderbolt & arrested all operations & almost all power of movement so astonishing it appeared'. They were now 'all impatience and anxiety' to know what was to become of them. It was quite impossible, he thought, that so vast an army could get home 'in a minute' and he feared those last to embark would be stranded in France for two or three months. In the meantime he had nothing to do and considered himself 'more as a young gentleman making a tour in the South of France than an officer on

172

service'. On the 17th, still not believing in the abdication, Soult took up a position near St Felix, but the next day, at Puylaurens, a vedette of the 10th Hussars came in with a French officer bearing a flag of truce. Henry Somerset took him on to Headquarters and before long an armistice was announced, followed soon afterwards by a convention, under the terms of which the British cavalry were to remain in cantonments around Toulouse. Ten days later, on 27 April, Griffith was among the crowd of officers who witnessed 'the entrance of the Duc D'Angoulême to the great & populous city of Toulouse'. 'All the Civil & Military Authorities of this vast district', he wrote:

> the Generals of France, England, Spain & Portugal, with hundreds of officers of each nation in full uniform formed a cavalcade a mile in extent at the head of which rode the Royal Duke and the Duke of Wellington. Thousands of Country People crowded each side of the road for a League before we reached Toulouse, and absolutely deafened us with acclamation so that we could hardly hear the thunder of Artillery and the Bells of the Churches. . . . The streets were all covered with sand or fine grass, the lower part of the houses hung with tapestry or pictures, the upper ornamented with wreaths of flowers and evergreens. Triumphal arches, the white & fleur de lys, crossed the streets every twenty paces, and windows and even the house tops were crowded full of ladies, waving handkerchiefs, clapping hands, & calling with all their might 'Vive le Roi! Vive les Bourbons!'

That night, at the theatre, when the band struck up *Henry IV*, Griffith thought 'the audience would have battered the walls, or at least the partitions of the House down'. After hearing the Te Deum at the Cathedral, he attended the Levée, and was presented, in form, by Captain de Grammont, now the Duc de Guiche. On the following day there was a grand ball, but as he knew his 'stock of finery' would not 'keep any pace with that of the French officers' he and Dalrymple 'withdrew from the City' to their country seat at Gorgas.

Major-General Fane was now in command of the cavalry, as the 'Lion d'Or' had gone home. He was, Kerrison thought, the greatest ass he had ever seen, and could well be spared. There were rumours going around that the cavalry were to march 'up the country to Boulogne to embark', but in the meantime, as Sergeant Major Tale put it, they continued to enjoy 'warrior's rests, and more than warrior's comforts', where good living, good quarters, wine, hosts and hostesses were concerned, and 'an absence from all useless and unneccesary drills and parades'. There was, however, plenty of work for idle hands to do 'repairing the ravages committed by war', in preparation for the march home.

CHAPTER NINE
Elegant Extracts

By the end of May preparations for the dispersal of Wellington's Peninsular army were well in hand. On the 21st Larpent could report that nine or ten thousand infantry, destined for service in America, where the war with the United States still dragged on, were 'all on the road for Bordeaux', or already there. The Portuguese were to remain until the British had finished with the mules, while the Spanish, 'to the joy of all parties,' were to return home. The cavalry were to set out overland as soon as the new French government approved the final arrangements. The plan was to move in two columns, one up the Paris road, through Cahors, the other more to the left, through Angoulême, Poitiers, 'and to unite at a town on the Seine'.

On the 19th Kerrison was in Toulouse making final arrangements with the Quartermaster-General, who had 'nearly promised' the 7th Hussars the lead, a great advantage on a long march. The horses were in fine condition, he had enough clothing to start every man 'with well-mended overalls & boots', and he flattered himself that the 'Queen's Own' would look as well as 'any of them'; the whole trip to Boulogne, he felt, would 'be delightful for the regiment'. Soon all was ready, the horses unfit for further service disposed of and the baggage and 'other useless encumbrances' sent on ahead to Boulogne. Lord Edward was sure the brigade would 'appear with considerable éclat' as they marched through France and 'astonish the inhabitants'. The 10th Hussars certainly ought to do so, 'for there never was, in any regiment, such a collection of fine horses'. By the 29th the two columns, consisting of eighteen regiments, divided into seven brigades and totalling some 9,000 men, were closed up, ready to move off on their 600-mile march.

On 1 June the left column, under Major General Vandeleur, crossed the Garonne east of Bordeaux and headed north. With them went the 18th Hussars and the 1st German Hussars, the latter, according to Woodberry, 'looking very fine in their new uniforms, put on specially for the occasion'. The Paymaster of the 18th had bought a new set of musical instruments in Bordeaux and, for the first time since leaving Portugal, the band played at the head of the regiment. On 6th July they reached Calais and Boulogne, where, after handing over three horses, whose total value was 'but £30', to Louis XVIII's newly-formed *Maison du Roi*, and parting, for as little as fifteen dollars each, with the mules which had carried their belongings half way across

Europe, they settled down to await the arrival of the other column.[1]

This, commanded by Major General Fane, had set off, with Somerset's Brigade in the van, a day later than the left column. On the 7th they crossed the Dordogne at Souillac and five days later reached Limoges, which Griffith thought had 'nothing to recommend it except its charming promenades under avenues of elms along the banks of the Vienne'. Thackwell, on the other hand, was struck by the fine regiments in garrison, 'particularly some of the Empress's Body Guard, well-dressed and accoutred, fine, handsome, fellows,' as well as a battalion of King Joseph's Spaniards. Unfortunately the novelty of their situation was now beginning to pall. 'I do not think our march proves quite so agreable as was expected,' Lord Edward wrote to his brother, as they moved in too large bodies to get good accommodation and were obliged to bivouac frequently. In addition, the civil magistrates who had to allocate quarters were 'in general extremely unaccomodating'.

At Limoges Griffith complained of being 'out of order for three or four days through drinking, when hot, two glasses of stuff called *bierre* which was made of everything but malt and hops', and by the time he reached Orléans on the 24th he had to abandon his horse for a carriage. 'Posting is dreadfully tedious and expensive,' he wrote, 'but the extreme ridiculousness of the carriage,' the miserable jades that drew it, the 'shreds and patches of the rope harness, together with the postillion in a huge laced cocked hat, a great greasy queue, nearly sansculotte, and a pair of boots weighing at least twenty pounds each' were 'nearly sufficient' to repay him for the delays and 'impositions' to which he was subjected.

On 1 July the first leg of the journey ended at Mantes and several officers took advantage of the next day's halt to visit Paris. Griffith and a party of the 15th Hussars dined at Versailles, slept the night at St Germain and arrived in Paris the next morning, where he 'indulged in a luxurious warm bath'. He had been deeply impressed by Versailles and now, seeing the Tuileries, wondered what the Emperor of Russia and the King of Prussia, who were now in England, would think of our paltry royal residences. When the Brigade marched on the 3rd Griffith and his companions stayed on for another six days. On the 7th he went to pay his respects to Louis XVIII, who had entered his capital on 3 May to a subdued welcome, but he could not help feeling that 'a *very great* proportion of the people would be glad to see that arch villain Boney back again'. The latter had 'certainly done wonders in Paris', and had 'contrived to weave his name, or deeds, so completely . . . throughout the whole place that it would be impossible to efface it' without destroying half its beauty. The palaces and gardens were 'beyond description superb', but, although he was highly delighted with his visit, he still thought Paris inferior to London. Nôtre Dame was 'a Parish church' compared to Westminster Abbey; the theatres and public buildings 'would still less bear any comparison' with those in London, and there were no handsome squares and very few 'good streets'. He left Paris on 9 July, travelling by *Diligence*, and reached Boulogne two days later. That same day Major General Fane inspected the Hussars and thirteen horses of the 15th and twenty-one of the 10th Hussars were handed over to the *Maison du Roi*. At one o'clock on the morning of 16 July the 15th Hussars embarked for England. They sailed at half-past nine and cast anchor off Dover at three in the afternoon, but the tide was against them and would not 'admit' of their entering the harbour. The day was 'dark with rain', but in spite of this typically British welcome on the part of the weather, Griffith was jubilant. 'Thanks to the God of Armies,' he wrote from Dover on the 17th, 'the God of Navies, the Goddesses of Wisdom, Prudence, Health & every other God or Goddess concerned in it,' he was 'once more safe & sound in this tight little Island'.

* * *

The cavalry returned home to find the country in the closing stages of weeks of celebrations, reviews, fêtes and state visits, which had given the Prince Regent several opportunities to exercise his talents as a stage manager, and the highlight of which had been the visit of the Allied sovereigns in June.[2] They were just in time, however, for the greatest junket of all, *The Grand Jubilee*, advertised to commence on Monday, 1 August, and to last until the Prince's birthday on the 12th. Schaumann landed at Portsmouth on 31 July and hurried up to London to see the 'great victory festival'. In St James's Park and Kensington Gardens he found detachments of artillerymen 'standing ready with large supplies of rockets and other fireworks'. Everywhere there were 'pagodas, Chinese towers . . . triumphal arches, stars, rosettes, globes, illuminated names, and suitable devices formed with coloured Chinese lanterns', which also hung from all the trees in the avenues. On the Serpentine two fleets of men-of-war, 'properly manned and mounted with guns', lay at anchor in readiness for the '*Naumachia*', or naval display, showing the 'celebrated manoeuvre practised by the immortal Nelson, at Trafalgar', including 'the destruction of the enemy fleet by fireships, in the evening'. The canal in St James's Park was provided with a Chinese bridge and pagoda, as well as 'handsomely decorated boats', which were to be 'at the disposal' of those who wished to 'add this amusement to the numerous pleasures of the entertainment'. In Green Park a huge 'Temple of Peace', over fifty feet high, stood behind a battery of fifty guns. There were huts and booths everywhere, 'some offering refreshments and others sheltering brass bands', and Schaumann felt quite lost among the huge crowd, estimated at 500,000, streaming in through the park gates.

The celebrations began with the *Naumachia* and the firework display. Then the fifty guns in Green Park opened up with the first of 500 rounds, making an uproar that almost deafened Schaumann. While this was going on 'the screen of grey canvas was suddenly lifted and the Temple of Peace was revealed', beautifully illuminated with hundreds of lamps. Water flowed from lions' head fountains into golden basins and on the roof of the temple a detachment of the Foot Guards with the Royal Standard, gave three loud hurrahs.

After this *pièce de resistance*, 'adorned', according to the programme, 'with allegorical transparencies, executed by the masterly pencils of artists of the first eminence', the eating and drinking began, with the crowd wandering among the tents and booths. Schaumann was pleased to note that 'there was no disorder, no fighting, no pickpockets, and no importunate fast women', to spoil the occasion, which he left at two in the morning.

By the time the Prince's birthday came round the public was thoroughly addicted to fireworks and illuminations and in the evening a large crowd gathered in Green Park in the hope of another display. When this failed to take place, the rougher element turned nasty and began to break up the fencing around the Temple of Peace, using the wood to light a huge bonfire, which threatened to engulf not just the Temple, but St James's Palace and York House as well. Much fencing was destroyed, some sentry boxes burned, together with some neighbouring trees, and eventually, at about two in the morning, the Horse and Foot Guards were called out to disperse the crowd.

Meanwhile, in Portugal another *metteur en scène*, whose talents must surely have been missed by his erstwhile employer, was celebrating his own private jubilee. A British officer serving with the 12th Portuguese Infantry was astonished, on entering the frontier town of Chaves, 'to see one of the principal houses decorated with transparencies, illuminations, and bouquettes of laurel leaves &c'. The author of this display, which contained 'a full-length portrait, as large as life, of our dear Prince, in a Field-Marshal's rich uniform, quite in his Royal Highness's accustomed elegance and figure', was none other than our old friend Baron Eben, now a Brigadier General and Governor of that particular district of Portugal.[3]

* * *

But if he was not there in person, the Baron's disruptive spirit was still abroad in Brighton, for little more than a fortnight after the return of the 10th Hussars to their old quarters the ill-feeling festering in the regiment came to a head. Ever since 1811, when Colonel Leigh had been forced to retire and Quentin had succeeded to the command, there had been fierce rivalry between him and Colonel Palmer. This animosity had been aggravated in 1811 and 1812 by Burdett's attacks on military flogging, any reduction in which Palmer, in spite of doubling as Whig Member of Parliament for Bath, strongly opposed. In this he was supported by most of the other officers. Furthermore Palmer was quick to take the part of the wealthy and influential young officers whenever Quentin tried to instil some modicum of military knowledge and discipline into them. The remark which Harriette Wilson put into Worcester's mouth – 'What has a King's son, or a Duke's son, to do with the usual discipline observed to Lieutenants in the Army?' – summed up one of the main problems which faced Quentin in the exercise of his command.

Once the regiment was on active service it was only a question of time before these squabbles led to inefficiency and reprimands from above. But the inevitable censures, when they came, were by no means so severe as those heaped on the 18th Hussars; nevertheless the officers of the 10th could not see that they were in any way to blame and attributed their 'disgrace' to Colonel Quentin. Sometimes not on speaking terms with Palmer, he seems to have been oblivious to the depth of feeling building up against him, even visiting Paris with Captain Lloyd, 'upon the most friendly footing of personal intercourse'. When the war ended Palmer came home as quickly as possible by sea, in order to deal with private matters, and appeared at Brighton in August, rather suspiciously, just at the very moment when the feeling against Quentin reached its climax. The officers were determined to be rid of their Colonel and Palmer must have been aware of what was going on, even if he was not the instigator of the whole affair.

'The first intimation I received upon the subject,' he afterwards claimed, was when Colonel Robarts handed him the notorious letter, dated 9 August, which afterwards became known as the 'Round Robin'. It was addressed to the Prince Regent and signed by every officer of the regiment except Major Howard, who refused on the grounds of his friendship with Quentin, the Adjutant, Captain Bromley, the Riding-Master Lieutenant Holborn, neither of whom was asked, Lieutenant Meynell, who was absent, and the Count de Grammont, now the Duc de Guiche in the service of Louis XVIII, who would undoubtedly have added his name had he been in the country. In the letter the officers felt called upon to try and remove any impression of the prejudice which 'the repeated animadversions of the Duke of Wellington and the Commanding Officer of the Cavalry, in regard to the regiment' might have raised in the Prince's mind. After assuring him that they had 'endeavoured by every exertion' to maintain the discipline and credit of the regiment, they turned, as one man, on Colonel Quentin. It was their 'imperious duty', they wrote, to notice reports 'most generally circulated' to the prejudice of his military character, which was 'so unhappily calculated to throw discredit on the regiment'. Finally, they deeply regretted being compelled to appeal to the Prince 'on a subject so delicate' and hoped to be acquitted of any sinister motive. They asked Palmer to submit their letter to the Prince and to add his signature if his feelings were the same as theirs, which last, however, he was not prepared to do.

When, on 15 August, Quentin was told about the letter by Palmer, he was 'astonished and surprised', and brusquely 'declined all conversation upon the matter'. He even refused to read it, merely requesting that any complaints against him should be laid before the Prince. Palmer now stalled and decided to withold the letter, waiting, instead, for one of Quentin's absences from Brighton to approach the Prince in person. Unfortunately for him, Quentin, probably forewarned, returned unexpectedly and was present throughout the interview. The upshot was that the Prince ordered the officers to bring forward specific charges against Colonel Quentin, to be submitted to the Commander-in-Chief, which was the last thing they wanted. In addition, Quentin managed to prise the letter itself out of Palmer, on the grounds, hotly disputed afterwards, that the Prince had commanded him to do so. Quentin thus emerged victorious from the first round, having forestalled his detractors with the Prince Regent. 'The complaints of the officers,' as Palmer put it, 'could not have been communicated through a more unfortunate channel than that of the person against whom they complained.' When Quentin pressed them for charges, they replied that they did not wish to bring any forward 'and had none therefore to give'.

Before long, however, they had second thoughts, and on 20 August wrote a second letter to the Prince, disclaiming any wish to bring charges against an individual who had hitherto been so distinguished by the Prince's 'favour and protection', conceiving that nothing could justify to the 'world' and themselves 'the indelicacy of such an act'. Nevertheless they immediately referred the Prince to the two censures about which they were still smarting. Furthermore, they claimed that 'reports out of the regiment, and the general opinion of officers', were so 'injurious to the personal honour of Col Quentin, as to his conduct before the enemy', they could not refrain from stating the fact to the Prince. On top of inefficiency, they were now accusing Quentin of cowardice in the field, which was a very serious matter. It is not known what answer the Prince gave to this dangerous composition, but the next day Quentin thanked him for his 'humane consideration . . . under the present unlooked-for circumstances in the regiment', and declared himself 'incapable of shrinking from the most public investigation'.

Colonel Palmer and the officers of the 10th had clearly made a thorough hash of the business and, instead of quietly forcing Quentin to resign, found themselves with a full-scale court-martial on their hands. The Duke of York, not for a moment taken in by the fact that Palmer had not signed the original letter, ordered him, as senior officer, and the 'medium of the complaints of the others' to act as prosecutor and to frame the charges, which were to specify 'dates and facts'. Palmer, in turn, asked the officers to 'state the instances', but, as he well knew, their complaints were general rather than particular. At length they came up with three charges which they could date with certainty, and one, covering Quentin's alleged failure to support his officers, the particular dates of which they could not remember. Palmer was forced to write this last charge himself.

As to how general these feelings were among the officers, it is remarkable that the only letters in which there is any hint of the dispute in the regiment are those to George FitzClarence from his parents. Neither Lord Edward Somerset, nor Worcester, nor Fitzgerald, nor Henry Wyndham nor any other officer of the Brigade seems to have referred to the shortcomings of Quentin in any way; yet the Duke of Clarence, in an undated letter, probably written after the return of the regiment to England, and before the issue of the 'Round Robin', told his son that he was sorry to see that he was always grumbling about the regiment. 'Remember,' he wrote:

you are not one and twenty, and near three years a captain and without purchase. Recollect how much the Prince is your friend and attached to

179

the Regiment. . . . Should those captains you expect leave the regiment, and you become the senior captain, with the reduction of two Field Officers you will occasionally be in command.

With Quentin out of the way his chances would be even better. On 23 August Mrs Jordan told him that the contents of his last letter had given her much uneasiness, but she hoped all might end well. The Prince himself was furious about the whole thing. According to Princess Charlotte 'he was dreadfully occupied' about the 'affair of the 10th', 'the whole *Regiment*' were '*out of favour*' and he talked of nothing else'.[4]

The troubles in the 10th Hussars soon became public knowledge. On 7 September the *Military Register*, which had 'hitherto forborne from delicacy' to mention the subject, felt that, as it was now 'bruited abroad', they were no longer 'held by any motive from its notice'. It would be undoubtedly hard, the editorial continued, 'if a number of spirited officers, after due obedience on *active* service, should be compelled to serve, in peace, under an individual who had omitted any of the duties which should peculiarly inspire the conduct of commanders'. It then quoted from a newspaper which expressed surprise that, while two 'English' officers had been dismissed the service 'for the want of preserving proper discipline in their corps', the 'German Officer' Quentin, had not sought an enquiry at the time of Wellington's censure. To which a reader replied that 'The German officer' had been 'twenty-one years in that regiment' and that the 10th Hussars, 'under the command of the German officer,' had attained 'a state of discipline equal if not superior to any cavalry regiment in His Majesty's service'. On 14 September the same journal revealed that 'the most respectable journals' had described the officers of the regiment, now stationed at Romford, as 'so completely divided that they dine in separate rooms in the same Inn!'

* * *

At ten o'clock on the morning of Monday, 17 October the court assembled in the office of the Commissary General of Musters at Horse Guards. The President, General Vyse, sat 'as usual in this comparatively small room, with his back to the West window, looking out on the Admiralty'. On his right sat the Rt Hon Charles Manners Sutton, the Judge Advocate General, 'attended by Mr Oldham and Mr Gurney, the shorthand writer'. On their right were Colonel Palmer, his solicitor, Mr Pedder, 'Secretary to the Gas Light and Coke Company' and an assistant. On the left of the President sat Colonel Quentin, 'attended as Aide-de-Camp to the Sovereign, by the Hon. Colonel Ponsonby' and assisted by Mr Harrison of the Treasury and Mr Bicknall, the Prince's solicitor, with an orderly officer. The court itself, consisting of four lieutenant generals and nine major generals, were all on the right of the President, and in the audience sat Mr Tierney, a prominent Whig politician and near relation to Lieutenant Colonel Robarts.[5]

The proceedings began with the reading of the four charges, 'trumpery in the extreme', to each of which Colonel Quentin pleaded not guilty. The first was to the effect that Quentin 'did not make the proper and timely arrangements to ensure the success of the regiment', in its foraging operations in the Macaye valley, on 10 January, 1814, 'whereby some men and horses of the regiment were taken prisoner'. The second was that, on 28 February, 1814, during the pursuit of the French rearguard after Orthes, he 'did not make such effectual attempts as he ought to have done, by his presence, and his own personal exertions and example, to cooperate with, or support the advanced divisions of the 10th Hussars under his command'. The third, similar in wording to the second, accused him of cowardice on 10 April, 1814, during the battle of Toulouse. The fourth charge, which was very vaguely worded, charged him with 'general neglect of duty by allowing a relaxed state of discipline to exist in the regiment under his command' by which 'the reputation of the regiment suffered in the opinion of the Commander of the Forces, and of the Lieutenant-General commanding the cavalry.'

Colonel Palmer then addressed the court 'in a short but energetic speech', the gist of which was that nothing could have been further from the intention of the officers 'than to injure the individual they had been called upon to prosecute' and that their sole object had been to 'do justice to themselves, and to vindicate the honour and character of the regiment'. Had Colonel Quentin 'entitled himself to their confidence and respect, it would have been as little their inclination' to avail themselves of 'any partial errors he might have committed', but, as they had been reduced 'to the alternative of either sharing in the disgrace brought on the regiment or standing forward as his accusers', they trusted 'no unworthy motives' would be attributed to their conduct. Palmer was followed by the witnesses for the prosecution for the first charge, headed by none other than the Red Dwarf. 'This intelligent officer,' we learn, 'appeared in coloured clothes of which, however, the Court took no notice.' He was followed by Henry FitzClarence, whose imperious tone clearly grated on the Judge Advocate General, who was called to task for using the 'appellation' of Mr, instead of his military rank, which one member observed was 'like addressing a *valet de chambre*'.

The next day was taken up going through the evidence of the second charge, which was completed the following morning, and the third charge started, Captain FitzClarence, Lieutenant Charles Wyndham and Lieutenant Seymour being the only witnesses called by Palmer. The rest of the day, however, was taken up by a lengthy discussion about the two letters mentioned in the fourth charge, which Mr Manners Sutton summed up as follows:

the pith of the charge seems to be this, that the regiment suffered in the view of the general commanding in the Peninsula; and that, in consequence . . . it suffered in the view of the world at large; that I take to be the real motive of the charge . . . any acts of indiscipline or relaxation of discipline which occurred subsequently to the date of this letter . . .

cannot have this intimation of the commanding officer of the forces; from which intimation of displeasure has arisen that feeling, as the officers of the regiment seem to think, of depreciation of their services.

On the fourth day of the trial, 20 October, Sir Stapleton Cotton, now Lord Combermere, stated that he had seen a great deal of the 10th in quarters and in the field and had never met with a finer corps of officers. He did not think 'there were ever officers better disposed or more zealous', or officers he would like better to command. That was his reason for thinking, as he still did, 'that it was not their fault but the fault of their commanding officer'. Lord Edward Somerset, also in 'coloured clothes', considered that the 'relaxed state' was due to the want of 'a proper system and arrangement' in the regiment. He had not observed 'any want of attention to any directions' on the part of Colonel Quentin, but had 'conceived that at times there was a want of activity on his part'. He was followed by Colonel Grant and Brigade-Major Jones, the latter of whom testified to the change in the regiment which took place after Colonel Quentin had rejoined at Tafalla. His testimony was corroborated by Major Gardiner of the Royal Horse Artillery, who said that he had known the Hussar Brigade parade sometimes an hour after the hour of march, usually because of the 10th Hussars. Several officers then told of occasions when, for one reason or another, men, whom they had charged with some offence, had escaped punishment. Captain Turner told how, during a punishment parade held on his march to join the regiment with a new squadron, the men had laughed and shouted that if Colonel Qentin had been there nothing of the kind would have happened. Palmer interrupted him to say that this was proof of their opinion of their Commanding Officer, but Mr Manners Sutton asked whether it did not, on the contrary, show 'the want of control of the officers at the moment, that they should dare to use such expressions'. The Court then adjourned for four days for Colonel Quentin to prepare his defence.

When it re-assembled on 25 October the audience was the largest yet. Mr Manners Sutton began by reading out Quentin's speech, as the latter's English was not good enough for him to do so himself. Quentin began by recounting his medical history after he had 'broken a blood-vessel' in 1812. This had prevented him going to Lisbon with the regiment, but, in spite of a second attack, he had joined it later in Spain. It must have been obvious, he said, that he had 'very frequently felt the effects of this bodily exertion, as well as the exposure and privations incident to the service' in which they were engaged. He then turned to the two letters of censure, claiming that it was never 'hinted or stated' to him that the order of 26 February was intended for the 10th Hussars alone, 'being well aware that irregularities did occur in other regi- ments'. Hence his surprise when he learned that his conduct had so excited the attention of his superiors. If he had erred, he said, 'from any mistaken princi- ples of lenity' he considered himself sufficiently punished by the censure. He had returned to England with his regiment 'without having had the most distant intimation' which would have led him to suppose that anything which

182

had occurred during his command 'had in any manner tended to cast the slightest imputation' on his character as an officer. He had, in fact, received the thanks of his superiors for his conduct during the pursuit of the French rearguard after Orthes, and was amazed when Palmer approached him, on 15 August, with the officers' letter. The court, he continued, would find among the signatures on this letter 'not only the names of officers on service with the regiment . . . but of others who were only with the regiment a very short part of the time; . . . of others who never were on the continent with the regiment at any time; of others, who, though on the continent, were detached upon the staff and never with the regiment; and of one or two who did not belong to the regiment at the time,' but had joined since the peace. 'What sort of spirit,' he asked, 'must prevail in a regiment, in which officers, so circumstanced, could be asked to sign such a letter,' and 'what sort of spirit must prevail among the superior officers who could permit their subalterns, most of them very young men. . . not conversant with the usages of the service, to sign such a letter?'

After disposing rapidly of the first three charges, he turned to the fourth. When he returned to the Peninsula in July, 1813, one of the first things he noticed was the frequency and severity of the corporal punishments, 'many of them exceeding the limit' permitted to regimental courts-martial. He had not needed the 'repeated injunctions' of the Prince Regent to induce him to try a new and better system, whereby 'an unremitting attention of the officers to their men might, in a great measure, supersede the necessity, or at all events mitigate, the extent of corporal punishments'.[6] Had he the right to demand of troop officers their unremitting attention to their men . . . or had they a better right to demand of him 'the trial and punishment, in every case in which they thought it necessary, of men who had committed offences?' Nothing, he thought, could be more injurious to the Army than permitting officers to substitute 'severity of punishment for their own personal and constant attention to visiting quarters, as the means of maintaining the discipline of a regiment'. That he thought the officers inattentive in this respect was obvious from the repeated regimental orders he had issued on 'various points of interior management of the regiment'. Nevertheless, he had no suspicion of the strength of feeling against him. How, he asked, could he have had the co-operation of officers who held such feelings? 'I was pursuing a system,' he declared:

in which their co-operation was absolutely essential, and I have now reason to know and feel that they were pursuing another system destructive of mine; and I also now too late find that I was vainly looking for co-operation, where I ought only to have been guarding future attacks upon my honour and character.

The evidence for the defence began with a string of general officers who testified to Quentin's gallantry and worth. General Cartwright declared that if the

10th had acquired any credit by its general discipline and good appearance 'it was largely the result of the extraordinary exertions of Colonel Quentin'. Lord Uxbridge, harking back to Ipswich and Corunna days, had never had a regiment under his command 'in more perfect order, or where the discipline appeared to be better carried out'. He had seen Quentin in action on several occasions and had witnessed his courage and calmness before the enemy, particularly at Benevente. Sir Colquhoun Grant, who came next, told how he had 'regretted extremely' not finding Quentin at the head of the 10th when they arrived in Lisbon. Somewhat prophetically, he said that were he to be placed immediately in command of a brigade, 'in the presence of the enemy', he would be glad to see Quentin at the head of a corps under his orders; in less than a year he would be just so situated.

The next day Vivian testified that he had not thought that the cavalry order of 26 February applied to any particular regiment, but rather that it had been a 'general cavalry order'. He had been quartered at Ipswich for a considerable time when Quentin had been in command, Colonel Leigh being 'very little with the regiment', and it was in the highest possible order. Lord Edward Somerset told the court how the conduct of the 10th, on the march through France, had been 'extremely correct and regular,' although that was possibly due to the fact that the regiment was more under the eye of Quentin, who was making additional efforts after the Adjutant General's letter.

When the Court re-assembled on Monday, 31 October, after a break of four days, Colonel Palmer began his reply by reading out a letter from Captain Lloyd, explaining why he had visited Paris with Colonel Quentin. Previous to his arrival in England, the 'circumstances' which had 'been brought forward' at the trial were only partially known to him, and 'not supposing they would ever be the subject of public investigation', he neither 'weighed, nor considered it' as he ought to have done. One wonders how much this was the feeling of the other officers who signed the letter, and how much pressure was put on them to toe the party line. Palmer then went on to deny that he had been forced to become prosecutor; he had not committed himself 'in any manner', nor had he delivered up the officers' letter to the Prince Regent. It was Quentin who had extracted it from the officers, in the name of the Regent, although the latter had afterwards denied that he had authorized Quentin to do any such thing. As for Quentin's claim to be responsible for the state in which the 10th had arrived at Lisbon, obviously, 'the appointments of the men were good, and the horses were in good condition, but the conduct of the men, while quartered in London previously had been very bad'. When Quentin gave up the command, and he succeeded to it, an alteration immediately took place, 'and the regiment being at Guildford two or three weeks before it embarked for Lisbon they became in much better order'.

Palmer now began to delve into the courts-martial return, but the President interrupted to say that he thought he was giving himself a great deal of trouble, as his own conduct had been so satisfactory to the Court, and to the 'World', he had no need to say anything 'to put his conduct in a more proper, a more

184

exemplary, and a more honourable light', which 'elegant declaration' evinced a 'murmur, and afterwards signs of approbation by the feet on the floor, among the numerous auditory round the foot of the table'. Palmer, however, was determined to have his say. While between 19 April, and 26 June, only eight men had been punished, between 26 June, and 29 June, the number suddenly rose to twelve, as a result of the regiment having been suddenly turned out of Tafalla, after a very alcoholic reception from the citizenry. Between 29 June, and 26 July, when Quentin arrived, the total had dropped to eleven. At this point Palmer was once again interrupted by the President:

> When Colonel Quentin joined the army, and found there had been so many instances of punishment amounting to seventy-two in number, it was natural for him to endeavour to recur to the principles of lenity, recommended by the Duke of York, and to see what would be the effect of that system, so highly recommended; and to hope the conduct of the men would be as much affected by the lenity and attention of their officers as by their severity. Colonel Quentin mentioned it with great modesty . . . if he failed in that design there was certainly merit in it, though he might not be successful.

Palmer continued, unabashed. The regiment, he said, had remained at Tafalla until November, and during the three months they were there only two men were punished. The men, however, became confirmed in their bad behaviour, until their excesses became so great that, at last, Colonel Quentin himself had six men flogged for drunkenness in one day. 'I think the Judge-Advocate will agree with me,' he said:

> . . . in the necessity of contraverting such statements, which, if true must completely justify the opinion of Sir Francis Burdett, and others, on this subject, and enable them to carry their point; for certainly the practice of corporal punishment is only to be defended upon the ground of its absolute necessity, and I can have no other motive but the good of the service in stating my conviction on this point.

Palmer now went on to explain that the only reason that he had left the regiment in April, 1813, was because he understood that Quentin was already on his way out to Lisbon, and, as for Quentin's ill-health, according to the medical officers, with the exception of a temporary indisposition, 'his general health was as good as that of other officers'. After recounting, at length, the tortuous events which had led up to the trial, he turned to the specific charges, refuting Quentin's defence to each. Turning to the fourth charge, he said that Quentin's defence might perhaps be popular, 'as expressing a wish to diminish corporal punishments', but he, who was as willing as any man to listen to the claims of humanity, thought that it would be 'ruin to the service, and to the best interests of the country'. In conclusion, he left the cause of the officers of the 10th

Hussars, with confidence, to the decision of the Court, satisfied that it would be governed by that 'impartiality which is to be expected from officers of their rank and station'. He then 'took his leave respectfully, and the court closed for sentence'. Palmer's confidence was not shared by all his fellow officers. 'Your last, my dear George,' Mrs Jordan wrote, the day after the Court closed:

> tho' it could not fail of giving me great pain, yet it did not surprise me as much as you might suppose – for there was a strain that ran through all your letters . . . that made me fearful of complete success. Why should Quentin [be] more severe on you than on the others? It was not you alone that brought it *forward*. What will be the *consequence* if he is recommended to retire? Will you in that case remain in it [the regiment]?

*   *   *

Just over a week later, on 8 November, the findings were announced. Colonel Quentin was found 'guilty' of part of the first charge, for which he was sentenced to be reprimanded, 'not guilty' of the second and third charges, and 'guilty' of the fourth charge. In the case of the last charge, however, the court considered that the censure of the commander of the forces in Spain had been 'adequate to the degree of blame which attached to him', and passed no further sentence. However, they added a rider to their findings, to the effect that they could not:

> conclude these proceedings without expressing their regret, that there appears to have existed such a want of co-operation among the officers of the regiment as to render the duties of the commanding officer much more arduous than they otherwise would have been.

In approving the sentence the Prince Regent added that, while 'the nature of the combination against Colonel Quentin would call for the removal from the service of those who had joined it, he was prepared to be lenient to a corps of officers who had hitherto merited his approbation'. He therefore commanded that:

> the officers who signed the letter of the 9th of August shall no longer act together as a corps, but that they shall be distributed by exchange throughout the different regiments of cavalry in the service, where it is trusted that they will learn and confine themselves to their subordinate duties.

As for Colonel Palmer, although he had not signed the letter, he was, nevertheless, 'by his declared sentiments and his general concurrence in the opinions of the officers, to be considered in the same light as if he had put his name to that paper', and he, too, was ordered to be removed to another corps.

The day after this announcement the Adjutant General, Sir Harry Calvert, went to Romford, where the 10th Hussars were drawn up to receive him. After reading out the findings, he ordered the officers who had signed the letter 'to move forward in front of their respective troops and to return their swords into their scabbards'. He then addressed them as follows:

Gentlemen – I have the Commander in Chief's commands to signify to you his Royal Highness the Prince Regent's pleasure, that you no longer belong to the 10th Regiment of Hussars; and the Commander in Chief enjoins you to hold yourselves in readiness to join the different regiments of cavalry to which the Prince Regent will immediately appoint you.

At this point Augustus Berkeley broke the sword which the Prince of Wales had given each of the officers of his regiment across his knee and threw the pieces at the feet of the Adjutant General, who, with 'good taste and feeling . . . took no notice of this rash, though manly act'. After the parade was dismissed, the officers 'retired to their mess-room, and with one voice declared their determination to retire from the service'. The two FitzClarences dissented and were consequently asked by the others not to 'further identify themselves with their comrades'. Colonel Palmer stepped in at this juncture recommending 'coolness and temper', and advised the other officers 'to wait and see if the changes were made in an obnoxious way, and without reference to their wishes, when it would still be open to them to solicit retirement on half-pay'. Some of the men hinted that the officers should leave Romford at once, but Augustus Berkeley, for one, refused to go until the following day, and, although 'mortified by hearing cheers given for the colonel, and seeing the men's rooms partly illuminated' in his honour, he was 'not subjected to any insult'. The high estimation in which Colonel Quentin was held by the men is shown by the comments of a private in the 10th Hussars, when told that his sister had heard that the regiment 'was disgraced'. He declared that this was false and that he was sorry it was 'reported so'. There had been a 'Trial with Col Quintin' and the rest of the officers were jealous because the men adored him, for he was 'that man that will see a Private righted, so they raised false charges against him'. Porter was 'overjoyed' Quentin had 'got the day', and all the officers 'that was against him' had been discharged. Proudly he listed the regiment's recent achievements. At 'Marrallis' they 'had beat a Regt that never had been beat before, and was the Terror of our heavy horse'; at 'Victoria the 10th was in front and was first that Charg'd the Toun and sucseded well'; and 'at the battle of Toulouse they fought like Britons'.[7]

Comment on the trial was swift and varied. The feeling in military circles was that the finding was much as expected, although the editor of the *Military Register* thought it bungling and preposterous. 'We had supposed,' he wrote, 'that such as had no very strong interest would have been dismissed entirely; that those who had parliamentary interest would have remained with censure, or gone on the staff; and that Col. Quentin would have been promoted

Major-general.' As it was the result was a scandal, which affected the dignity of the Sovereign, the Constitution, and the interest of 'every honourable family in the country'. Are, he asked, 'six and twenty of the spirited offspring of the truly noble Devonshire, the patriotic Leinster, the beneficient Beaufort, the virtuous Egremont,[8] and other houses . . . to be scattered through a *select* number of regiments, for pity, and for *tuition* and *correction*, . . . the *scoff* of the idle, and the boast of the unworthy!' He concluded by urging that Colonel Palmer 'or whatever member is to introduce the subject' raise the matter for investigation by Parliament.

Palmer had pre-empted him on 15 November when, at his request, a debate was fixed for the following week. This gave him an opportunity of going through the entire proceedings. Claiming parliamentary privilege, he called Quentin a blockhead, a coward, and a liar. Not surprisingly Mr Manners Sutton said that he thought the House had exercised 'an unusual degree of patience' with Colonel Palmer's 'extraordinary course'. Nothing was more natural than that the prosecutor should be dissatisfied with the sentence, but he was surprised to hear the occasions when Colonel Quentin had shown lenity, by remitting the sentences of the men, 'hailed by gentlemen on the other side of the House as facts to his prejudice'. It seemed that he had changed sides with those Hon Gentlemen. He was followed by Mr Tierney, who, although another Whig, launched into a vitriolic attack on the men of the 10th, who, he thought, 'all deserved a great deal of punishment'. There never was a regiment 'so disgraced by breaches of discipline of all kinds'. Now, 'for the good of the service', the Prince Regent's advisers had left the colonel, who was not fit to command any regiment, to command 'this mutinous set of men' and dispersed the 'able and zealous officers' to other regiments. The barracks, he understood, had been illuminated in consequence of the trial, and even now, he had heard, 'a paper was handing about the men to vote a sword to Colonel Quentin'.

Mr Wellesley Pole, for the Government, thought that the real state of the case was simply that Palmer and Tierney, not concurring in the opinion of the Court, 'had thought proper to call upon the House to constitute itself a court of appeal'. If anything was needed to show the want of co-operation, it was only necessary 'to avert to the declaration of the hon. mover himself, that he did not communicate the orders of Colonel Quentin because he considered them absurd and ridiculous'. If there had been any wish to curry favour with great people, it would have been easier to remove 'one old, almost worn out, though meritorious officer', than 'twenty-three young men of the highest rank, pretensions, and connection in the empire'. The case would, however, be of great use to the Army, for 'it would prove to the young officers of high birth, how little their rank or connections would avail them, if they were not attentive to their duty', sentiments which were received with 'loud and repeated cheers'. A Mr Brand maliciously pointed out that when the Act of Settlement was 'resumed, as it would be, he believed, on the 17th of the next June, the commission of Colonel Quentin would be annulled, as he was not naturalised; and he should be glad when that period arrived'. Then, after four more

Members had spoken, and Palmer had made a mercifully short reply, the House divided, the motion being defeated by one hundred and seven votes.

The case continued to engage the attention of society and the press for some time to come. It was said that the Prince had named Lord Manners and Lowther, in place of Palmer and Robarts, and that he had 'insulted the dismissed officers by demanding the *return* of their *regimental swords*, a thing without example in the service'. One of the Captains, probably George FitzClarence, had returned the hilt of his, 'observing that the blade was shot away in action by the same ball that gave him a very heavy wound!!!' Mrs Jordan, with singular lack of tact, wrote to Colonel MacMahon on 1 December that her only comfort was that her sons had done nothing 'to disgrace themselves as *men* and *soldiers*', and that it was '*lamentable* to think that so many brave fellows must be SACRIFICED to support a *German*'.

Some of the press, however, held an entirely different view of things. *Bell's Messenger* thought that Colonel Quentin 'was an easy, good-natured, and perhaps indolent man, and that he was not coxcombical enough' for a regiment 'certainly the most foppish in the whole Army'. The officers, most of them young men, had 'perhaps fixed their regards upon another commander, and probably Colonel Palmer', and with the purpose of harassing and vexing Colonel Quentin, and 'compelling him to quit the regiment' had 'formed a combination against him'. *The Times* condemned the 'crude and ill formed judgement of the accusers' and hoped that the 10th would now become an English regiment of horse-soldiers, 'rather than a regiment of dancing-masters or merry-andrews'. A caricature published soon after the court-martial took an impartial view of the case, in that it thought the worst of everybody. The Prince Regent and the Duke of York are shown hauling Quentin out of a patch of boggy ground. The Prince is saying to his brother:

> 'He must be saved, for on my life,
> He hath a very pretty wife.
> And, Chief Commander of our Forces,
> You know he buys me all my horses.'

The Duke, in a clear reference to his troubles with Mrs Clarke, replies, 'Saved by a woman! How many have we known that have been disgraced by one!', while Quentin wails, 'Oh, my de-ar la-dy!'. The Adjutant General stands nearby, armed with a large extinguisher, which he is about to apply to the 'Elegant Extracts',[9] while Colonel Palmer sheathes his sword with the words, 'I could not *palm* this conspiracy on the court-martial'. Further to the right of the composition Lord Worcester addresses the FitzClarences, who wear chamber-pots on their heads instead of fur caps. 'I'll henceforth,' he declares, 'to the *Worcester* potteries and manufacture Jordans for your mother.'[10]

As the year drew to an end the *Military Register* expressed concern that 'this important case' seemed to be dying 'away from the public mind'. 'Is it possible,' it asked, 'that the brave and intelligent officers of this so highly

189

distinguished corps, are to be slid one by one, into obscurity?' On 1 December the Earl of Egremont, much to the annoyance of the Prince, gave notice in the House of Lords that, after the recess, he would move for an address to the Prince Regent that the minutes of the court-martial might be laid before the House; Palmer was to make a similar request in the Commons. When Parliament reassembled in February, 1815, Lord Egremont did indeed raise the subject, but it never came to a vote, and Colonel Palmer, who had been expected to do the same, was otherwise engaged.

* * *

Ever since the announcement of the sentence the 'World' had been waiting avidly for news of a duel between Palmer and Quentin, but, in spite of frequent rumours, nothing happened until early in January, 1815, when Colonel Quentin, accompanied by his brother-in-law Mr Lawrell, crossed over to France. Aware that Palmer was in France, they had hoped to find him in Paris, but he was away on private business, so they settled down to wait for him. When he returned on 2 February, Lawrell called on him with a challenge from Colonel Quentin, which was immediately accepted. The two met the next morning, outside the Paris barriers, Colonel Palmer travelling to the ground in one of the Duc de Guiche's carriages, attended by a Mr Thomson, the Member for Midhurst, and an eminent French surgeon. Colonel Quentin was accompanied by his brother-in-law only. At twelve paces Quentin, as the aggrieved party, fired first, but missed, whereupon Palmer, showing that 'he was influenced by no personal motive', fired into the air, an act which the *Military Register* afterwards described as 'hitherto inexplicable, unless on the part of one who had committed and meant to acknowledge wrong'. Quentin and Lawrell having 'declared themselves perfectly satisfied', the affair ended and the parties returned to Paris.[11]

Early in April the subject of courts-martial, including that of Colonel Quentin, was once again raised in the House of Lords by Lord Egremont. The Editor of the *Military Register* did not think his choice of cases very happy, and, 'as for the officers of the 10th who tried Col Quentin,' they had chiefly abandoned it themselves. The Duke of York 'concisely vindicated' the trial, saying that the greatest care had been taken in selecting the members of the Court, 'so all of them should be individuals least likely to be influenced by partial motives'. From their sentence Colonel Quentin appeared to have been honourably acquitted in every sense of the word, and the removal of the officers had been a necessity. Lord Combermere praised the conduct of the officers of the 10th while on service, but 'could not support their subsequent conduct'. 'If the commanding officers,' he concluded, 'were not supported against such combinations, he conceived there would be an end of discipline'. Lord Grey had the last crack at Quentin. 'With regard to Colonel Quentin,' he said, 'he not being a natural born subject of these realms, he should be glad to be informed . . . whether he was capable of serving in a British regiment,' a question which he put twenty-one years too late; and in any case the subject of his enquiry was, as he spoke, once again at the head of his regiment on active service.

*　*　*

On the afternoon of 17 June, 1815, the very day that Mr Brand had so maliciously predicted that Colonel Quentin's commission would be annulled, the 7th Hussars, cloaked against the pouring rain, formed divisions on the muddy *pave,* six hundred yards north of the Belgian village of Genappe, and launched themselves at the enemy. It was a manoeuvre they had carried out often before with great success, but now things were different. For the first time since the retreat to Corunna they were the pursued, not the pursuers, and their opponents were lancers, a form of cavalry they had not come up against before. Furthermore, the latter were protected on either flank by the houses of the village, from which they were about to emerge, while the street behind them was packed solid with supporting troops. Lord Uxbridge, in command of the Allied cavalry, ordered the 7th to throw themselves three times on the lance points of the enemy without making any impression; and in one of these charges Major Hodge was killed. As they pulled back for the last time, the French followed them, and as they left the shelter of the village the Life Guards hurtled down on them. Seconds later they broke and fled, giving Wellington's cavalry time to get clean away. The next day the Battle of Waterloo was fought and, although the Hussars, one brigade of which was commanded by Sir Colquhoun Grant, and the other by Sir Hussey Vivian, had their fair share of the action, the laurels of the day went to the heavy cavalry, who took three thousand prisoners and two Eagles, and disabled over thirty guns.[12]

Within days of the battle rumours began to circulate to the effect that the 7th Hussars had been 'very deficient in that bravery and heroism' which had 'hitherto characterized their meritorious conduct'. Addressing himself to the officers of the regiment through the columns of *The Times,* Lord Uxbridge wrote from Brussels, where he was recuperating from the loss of a leg, that the attack of the 7th at Genappe, although most gallantly led, had failed 'because the Lancers stood firm, had their flanks secured, and were backed by a large mass of cavalry'. The plain honest truth was that, however lightly he thought of lancers, 'under ordinary circumstance, . . . , posted as they were, they had a most decided superiority over Hussars'.

This unfortunate episode was to have two results. In the first place, following on so closely after the Quentin court-martial, it added to the Prince Regent's disillusionment with Hussars. A SUBSCRIBER referred to this in a letter to the *Military Register,* dated 2 August, 1815, when he wrote that as for Genappe, it only proved that:

the Hussar paraphernalia – the whiskers – the mustachios – the route of
horses – the drills – the field days the reviews – the trouble and expence

which have been followed up during the last six years; after all this grand preparation, when called upon at a critical moment for gallant entreprize – all, all, all, ended in shameful retreat! and the P[rinc]e R[egen]t has appointed himself Colonel of the 1st and 2nd Regiments of Life Guards, as a mark of peculiar approval and censure!

He was promptly supported by AN OLD DRAGOON, who demanded:

Shave off those mustachios, let us see the honest countenances, that we may know our friends, and dress them once again in red, that their enemies may dread them. No man, be his rank or pretensions what they may, should be suffered to gratify his capricious fancy by any innovation on the national uniform. . . . If our mustachio, whiskered, sheep-skins could not beat the other mustachio, whisker, bear-skinned fellows, it is evident these whimsical freaks do not answer.

The debate went on for months, with the furious contributors fighting over again the actions at Benevente, Mayorga, Morales and Orthes, usually to the detriment of those who had borne the heat of the day. The second consequence was the speedy introduction of lancers into the British Army, thought by some to be a retrograde step, but a development in which the influence of the Prince Regent, particularly in matters of dress, was well to the fore. 'The mustachio, whiskered sheep-skins' were before long to be joined, not replaced, by the flat-hatted, mustachioed, whiskered, plastroned, aiguilletted, cossack-trousered fellows, who, sartorially speaking, were to put the Hussars very much on their mettle.[13]

*   *   *

The subsequent histories of the Prince Regent's 'unsatisfactory' reign as George IV, and of the 'devilish' Duke of Cumberland, reviled at home but loved and respected as King of Hanover, are somewhat outside the scope of this book. The same might be said about the subsequent careers of the other senior Hussar officers. They continued to rise through the ranks, though their careers were ornamental rather than warlike. An exception was Colonel Thackwell who, as a Major General Sir Joseph, served with distinction in the second Sikh War of 1848. A Hussar general officer with combat experience in India was a rare creature indeed, and it is interesting to speculate whether the charge of the Light Brigade would ever have taken place if he had been present in Lord Cardigan's place on that fateful day. Of the junior ranks, a few remained in the Army, while others retired to peaceful oblivion, their lives recorded only in the obituaries in *The Gentleman's Magazine* or in the collections of anecdotes of sport and society that abounded in the latter part of the century.

Of the two main protagonists in the 1814 *fracas*, Colonel Quentin continued in the Army, remaining an Aide-de-Camp until 1825, when he was appointed Equerry to the Crown Stables, a post in which he served three monarchs. He died on 7 December, 1851, in his ninety-second year, a knight and a lieutenant general. Looking back over the years, Lennox thought that Quentin had not 'sufficient dash about him', although the charge of cowardice against him ought never to have been made. He was never popular with the officers, particularly as he tended to deprive them of all authority 'doing himself the duty of Colonel, Captain, Adjutant, and Riding Master'. On the other hand, he was extremely popular with the men, which Lennox put down to his being over-lenient, and this tended to cause bad feeling in the regiment.[14]

Colonel Palmer's history was more eventful, if less happy. According to Gronow, after inheriting a handsome fortune, and acquiring the £50,000 settlement of his father's mail coach claims, he was keen to invest some of his wealth, and a journey on the Lyons-Paris *Diligence* in the company of a charming widow led to his buying her late husband's property in Bordeaux, which still bears the name of Château Palmer. The employment, as manager, of a man who had already been involved in several disastrous speculations, and the unquestioning acceptance of advice on the subject of wine-making from the Regent and his drinking companions, led to all sorts of disastrous experiments. The vineyard was mortgaged, the theatre he owned in Bath was sold, the Reform Bill robbed him of his seat in Parliament, and in the end he was bankrupted. Needless to say none of these lurid details appear in the fulsome obituary in the *Bath Chronicle*, which says merely that after the election of 11 March, 1829, which he lost by two votes, he sold out of the Army. Although they both came from merchant backgrounds, Quentin and Palmer were complete opposites in character and style, and it is hardly surprising that they got on so badly together. Palmer was the very picture of a typical English country gentlemen of Whiggish tendencies, with his wealth and the parlimentary 'interest' which required so much extra-regimental attention. Harriette Wilson describes him trotting around the barracks at Brighton, in the rain, 'on an ugly little pony, his laced jacket covered by an old, short, brown, greatcoat, and a shabby round hat', the very antithesis of the dashing Hussar. According to his obituary, it would have been difficult to find a more kindly-disposed man. He was, apparently, the idol of the Bath populace, an affection that was clearly not shared by the rank and file of his regiment.[15]

Of the remaining officers, Worcester, de Grammont and the two FitzClarences continued to make their mark in society, for better or worse. With the end of the war in 1814, Worcester returned home, resigned his commission and took the seat in Parliament to which he had been 'elected' by his father in 1813.[16] With his usual impetuosity, and with considerable misgivings on the part of his family, he rushed into marriage with Georgiana Fitzroy, Wellington's niece. The couple spent some time in Paris, where Worcester, one of the first of many British officers to descend on the city, made a name for himself as a considerable dandy. According to Gronow, none excelled him in the ballroom, and as an authority in matters of taste, whether of dress, the turnout of a carriage, or the selection of horses, he was second to none. To his credit, he was one of the small group who stood by Brummell at the time of his downfall, sending him money, writing to him, and visiting him without fail whenever he passed through Calais. His wife died suddenly in 1821 and he subsequently married her half-sister, eventually succeeding to the Dukedom and devoting his life to the hunting field. His old flame, Harriette, moved to Paris in 1820, where she settled down to write the history of her life, which appeared in 1825 and was an instant success, containing as it did much piquant information about the fashionable world. She eventually married a Monsieur Rochfort, returned to England in 1846 and died a pious widow.

In 1814 a few British officers, like Worcester, had made short excursions to Paris, but after Waterloo, in addition to a large army of occupation, the city was filled with hordes of British tourists. With them came the *emigrés*, 'rejoicing in Waterloo as a victory rather than a defeat'. A few, like de Grammont, now Duc de Guiche, were accepted members of the dandy set, and would, like his brother-in-law, the celebrated Count D'Orsay, play an important part in furthering the Anglomania, which now became all the rage.[17] Chief among the fashions aped by the French dandies was the cult of the horse. The pleasures of the Four-in-Hand Club were introduced in Paris in 1815 by, among others, Captains Bacon and Arnold of the 10th Hussars. Sir Charles Smith, a great supporter of the turf, was the first man to bring thoroughbreds over from England, and 'to get up very fair racing at Valenciennes', supported by the officers of the several cavalry and infantry regiments who 'contributed their efforts to make these races respectable in the eyes of foreigners'. The preposterous Lord Henry Seymour, who was born in France and appears never to have set foot in England, founded the French Jockey Club and, in conjunction with the Duc de Guiche, 'placed the turf upon a respectable footing'.[18] After years trying to make do on the Prince's allowance of £200 a year, De Guiche's life was now 'a continued scene of prosperity and promotion'. He rose to the rank of General, serving with distinction in Spain in 1823. As *Grand Ecuyer* to the Dauphin he lived rent free, had the control of all the Dauphin's stable establishments, and appointments which brought him in not less than 100,000 francs a year. However, the July Revolution of 1830 drove him once again into exile with his royal master Charles X. He eventually retired to Versailles, where he lived 'on a limited income in quiet and retirement'. De Guiche was much admired by Gronow, who described him as perhaps the most perfect gentleman he ever met with in any country, and the 'type and model of the real French gentleman and *grand seigneur* of the olden times'. He spoke English perfectly, was quiet in manner, a most chivalrous, high-minded and honourable man who was universally loved and regretted.

George and Henry FitzClarence, in disgrace with their superiors and shunned by their mess-mates, were not destined for such a happy existence. In 1811 their father parted from Mrs Jordan, driven by necessity to search for the hand of a wealthy heiress, and the last correspondence she had with them was at the end of 1814, when they were waiting for a ship to take them to India.[19] Contrary to their father's belief that they were being well treated by the Regent and the Duke of York, she stoutly maintained that they were being victimized for their part in the Quentin business. On their arrival in India they were separated, Henry being made ADC to Sir Thomas Hislop in Madras, and George ADC to Lord Moira in Calcutta. The following year Henry was invited to Bengal by the Governor-General and died there of fever in September, 1817. George, meanwhile, after taking part in the Maratha War of 1816–18, returned overland with the despatches. Back in England on half-pay, he was a constant problem to his father, who exhorted him to avoid 'the *indolent* and *profligate* life of London', and considered, at one point, bringing him over to Hanover to act as his Equerry, to keep him out of mischief. He cannot, however, have been completely idle, for in 1819 he published a lengthy account of his travels across India and through Egypt. In October of the same year he married Mary Wyndham, the sister of his old comrade-in-arms Harry and natural daughter of the 'virtuous' Earl of Egremont.

With the death in childbirth of the Princess Charlotte in November, 1817, the royal marriage race hotted up, and the Duke of Clarence, after several false starts, finally settled on Adelaide, the daughter of the widowed Duchess of Saxe-Meiningen, whom he married on 11 July, 1818. As she was as poor as he, the couple were forced to spend the next fourteen months living in Hanover 'in straitened circumstances'. Within days of his accession as William IV, in 1830, his sons started demanding honours and titles. George claimed that he had been promised a peerage, while his brothers let it be known that they would be satisfied with the rank of younger sons of Dukes, and the King's inability, financially, to grant their wishes led to a serious family rift. As it turned out George did not have long to wait for, in May 1831, his father-in-law having settled £65,000 on Lady Mary and her children, he was created Earl of Munster. At the same time his brothers were given the rank of younger sons of Marquesses.

Elevation to the peerage did not end George's 'extraordinary pretensions' and 'inordinate ambition and vanity', his request to carry the crown at the coronation and demands that he be recognized as Prince of Wales provoking his father to make such remarks on his conduct. George never made up the quarrel with his father and kept away from Court for the greater part of his reign, falling, according to Greville, 'into comparative obscurity and real poverty'. In March, 1842, having been 'in low spirits' for some time, brought about, he thought, by 'the disappointment of the expectations he once formed, together with the domestic unhappiness of a dawdling, ill-conditioned, vexatious wife', he shot himself. A man not without talent, but wrong-headed, was Greville's final judgement on the person who had perhaps done most to stir up the ill-feeling of his fellow officers against their commanding officer and to bring down the anger of their sovereign upon their heads.

* * *

195

In the reductions that inevitably followed the victory at Waterloo, the 18th Hussars were disbanded, but another regiment, the 8th Light Dragoons, took their place in 1823. In 1840 the 11th Light Dragoons, commanded by that latter-day evocation of regency vapidity Lord Cardigan, were turned into Hussars after furnishing the escort to Prince Albert on his arrival in England for his marriage to Queen Victoria. Apart from the brief European venture in 1827, when the 10th Hussars and the 12th Lancers, brigaded under the command of Harry Wyndham, were sent to Portugal as part of an expedition in support of the regency of Queen Isabella, who was being threatened by Spain,[20] the subsequent histories of the four original regiments followed the usual light cavalry pattern of alternate home and foreign service, the latter usually in India. Of the original Hussars only the 10th took part in the closing stages of the Crimean War, the dubious distinction of charging with the Light Brigade falling to the two new regiments, the 8th and 11th. After the Crimean War four regiments of Light Dragoons remained – the 3rd, 4th, 13th, and 14th – all those who were not Hussars having been converted to Lancers – and in 1860–61 they too became Hussars, and the old 18th were re-raised. The amalgamations of the 1920s and 1960s severely reduced the number of regiments, and played havoc with their titles, but it was 'Options for Change' which dealt the death blow to the time-honoured titles. In what is, to the military historian, the strangest change of all, the 15th/19th, the descendants of the Duke of Cumberland's 'Bold King's Hussars', have of their own free will chosen to revert to being plain light dragoons, thus turning the wheel full circle. The idea that the addition of 'The' to their title makes them different and 'special' is an ironic reversal of the facts; and through a combination of 'market forces' and dubious historical argument, George III has finally had his way. The shades of 'Prinny' and 'Prince Whiskerandos' must be gnashing their teeth in fury.

Notes

1. The Colonel of Dragoons (pp 1–21)

For the education, early years, and correspondence of the royal princes, I have relied heavily on Professor Aspinall's *The Later Correspondence of George III* and *The Correspondence of George Prince of Wales, 1770–1812*. Other, more general works like Wilkins, W.H.: *Mrs Fitzherbert and George IV*, Melville L.: *The First Gentleman of Europe*, Ashton, J.: *Florizel's Folly*, Bishop, J.G.: *The Brighton Pavilion and its Royal Associations*, and Wraxall: *The Historical and the Posthumous Memoirs of Sir Nathanial Wraxall*, have provided background material. Burne, Lt.- Colonel A.: *The Noble Duke of York*, is useful as the only modern biography of the Duke of York. Information on the French nobles came from Maugras: *The Duc de Lauzun*, and Carlyle, T.: *The French Revolution*; for the Prussian reviews, *The Military Register*, 1814, Hanger, Colonel G.: *Life, Adventures, and Opinions of Colonel George Hanger* and Cornwallis: *Correspondence of Charles, First Marquess Cornwallis*; for the early history of Hussars, Warnery: *Remarks on Cavalry, by the Prussian Major General of Hussars Warnery*, Depreaux: '*Les Premiers Hussards, 1692–1721*' and Brunon, Jean & Raoul: *Hussards*. Gouaches by General Baron Barbier, 1793 and 1803, with a commentary on French Hussars. For the Duke of York's army reforms see Tylden, Major G.: *Horses and Saddlery* (1965). Strachan, H.: *British Military Uniforms, 1768–96*, quotes the relevant Royal Warrant of 27 July, 1796.

1. Minto: *Life and Letters of Sir Gilbert Elliot, First Earl of Minto, From 1751 to 1806* Edited by the Countess of Minto, II, 118–119.
2. During the latter half of the eighteenth-century it was fashionable to be painted in a version of 17th century dress, inspired by portraits by Vandyke, which soon became popular as a masquerade dress.
3. From 1730, when the dress coat became extravagantly elaborate, a simpler version came in, especially for wear in the country. Called a 'frock', it was either single or double-breasted, with a turned-down collar and could be buttoned up for protection against inclement weather. By the last quarter of the century a simpler 'frock uniform' was being adopted by the military as an undress uniform. See Waugh, N.: *The Cut of Men's Clothes 1600–1900* (1964). Three portraits of the Prince in military dress, painted about then, have puzzled historians because at the time the Prince held no military rank. The most likely answer is that he was painted in uniforms he had ordered for Prince Frederick, before they were sent off to him.
4. Hans Joachim von Zieten (1699–1786). General of Hussars in the Prussian service, known as the 'Hussar King'; Ensign, Infantry Regiment No.24 (Schwerin), 1720; Lieutenant, Dragoon Regiment VI (Wuthenau), 1726; cashiered for duelling, 1730; re-instated as squadron commander in the Leib-corps Husaren (2nd or Zieten Hussars); Rittmeister, 1731; Major, 1736; Colonel, 1741; Major-general

1744; Lieutenant general, 1756; Knight of the Black Eagle, 1757; General of Cavalry, 1760; See Bleckwenn, H.: *Unter dem Preussen-Adler*, (Munich: 1978), 196; Duffy, C.: *The Army of Frederick the Great* (1974), 98–100; Mollo, J.: *Uniforms of the 7 Years War*, (1977), 94.

5. In 1794 the firm of Trotter, of Soho Square, who supplied practically all the camp equipment for the Army was requested to open a stores depot at Portsmouth. By 1807 they had established no less than 109 similar depots. Trotter's provided tentage, and were the inventors of the bell-tent. From 1793, this replaced the inferior ridge-pole tents formerly used (Ward, S.P.G., *Wellington's Headquarters*, 14–15).

6. See Wylly, Colonel H.C.: *XVth (The King's) Hussars, 1759–1913*, 96–8, for details of the action at Villers-en-Cauchie.

7. For the Prince's relationship and morganatic marriage to Mrs Fitzherbert see Wilkins, W.H.: *Mrs Fitzherbert and George IV*. The 'Prince's uniform' refers to the blue and buff, the colours of the Whig party, which were adopted by him as a form of livery, as opposed to the blue and red 'Windsor uniform'.

8. By the time he was twenty-one, the Prince's debts amounted to some £30,000. After the fitting out of Carlton House and Brighton Pavilion, they rose to nearly a quarter of a million pounds and the Prince was forced to raise loans abroad. In 1787, by the expedient of denying that he had ever married Maria Fitzherbert, he raised sufficient support in Parliament for the House to vote him the sum of £161,000 for the payment of his debts, and a further £60,000 for the completion of Carlton House (POW: I, 272–273).

9. The MSS Notes on the life and career of Sir John Slade, compiled by his son Wyndham, contain much additional information not included in the extracts from Slade's Diary quoted in Liddell, Col. R.S.: *The Memoirs of the Tenth Royal Hussars*.

10. See also Jesse: *The Life of Beau Brummell* By Captain Jesse, 2 Vols., (1927), I, 30–33, Gronow, 10, and Ponsonby, Major General Sir J.: *The Ponsonby Family*, 224, The Prince of Wales to Lord Bessborough, 11 December, 1797.

11. Oman C.W.C.: *Wellington's Army, 1809–1814*, 198–201; *General Regulations and Orders for the Army, 12 August 1811*.

12. *Journal of the Society for Army Historical Research* Vol 49, 1971, p. 183, NOTE 1562 '10th LIGHT DRAGOONS 1794', quoting an October 1950 issue of the *Sussex Weekly Advertiser*.

13. The improvements to the mail-coach service were suggested by John Palmer, Bath merchant, theatre proprietor (and father of Colonel Palmer of the 10th) who was rewarded by being made Comptroller of Post Office by William Pitt. In 1793 Palmer was dismissed with a pension of £3,000 *per annum*. He however claimed remuneration above this figure, and the matter was brought several times before the House of Commons, of which Colonel Palmer was a Member. In May, 1808, the House endorsed Palmer's claim in principle, but the matter was not finally settled until 1813 [see Farington, IV, 180].

14. Letter to the Rt. Hon. W. Windham, 1799, quoted in Fortescue: *A History of the British Army* IV, Pt. II, 907–912.

2. Ipswich Swells (pp22–41)

For the development of Hussars at Weymouth I have used: XRH Archives, POW: IV, Landsheit: *The Hussar* by G.R. Gleig; Long MS, Jones: *The MS Journals of the Adjutant of the 15th Light Dragoons*, McGuffie, T.H.: *Peninsular Cavalry General*, Lennox, Lord William Pitt: *Celebrities I have known*, 2nd Series, Liddell, Slade MS, Tale: *Jottings from my Sabretache, by a Chelsea-Pensioner (Sergeant-Major Tale, 15th Hussars)*. For the Hussar Brigade at Ipswich: Liddell, Barrett, Long MS, Seventh L.D.: *Standing Orders for the 7th Light Dragoons* (Ipswich 1808), Jones, Wylly, Paget Brothers: *The Paget Brothers, 1790–1840*. Edited by Lord Hylton, Gronow, Elers: *Memoirs of George Elers, Captain in the 12th Regiment of Foot*, 213, Ritter, R.: *La Maison de Gramont*, POW: V–VII, Brack, Colonel de: *Avant-Postes de Cavalerie Legère*, 104, Verner: 'Reminiscences of William Verner (1782–1871) 7th Hussars', by R.W. Verner, (*Journal of the Society for Army Historical Research*, Special Publication No. 8, 1965), PRO.WO.27, Dyott, XRH: 869 MS Digest of Services, Vol 1, and Mrs Jordan: *Mrs Jordan and her Family, being the unpublished correspondence of Mrs Jordan and the Duke of Clarence, later William IV*, Edited by A. Aspinall.

1. In May, 1802, the 15th Light Dragoons were reduced by 325 men, and 244 horses, and in June by a further two troops, while the remaining eight troops were cut to 64 men and 54 horses each; in October 1804, the 10th and 15th Light Dragoons were augmented by two troops, and in December by ten horses per troop (XRH; Liddell: 72).
2. In 1792 the great de Bércheny himself retired to London, and elements of his regiment and the Saxe Hussars deserted to the royalist cause.
3. The traditional Turkish punishment of beating on the soles of the feet.
4. From newspaper reports and Colonel Long's orders (Long MS, f.338) it is possible to reconstruct the entire ceremony of execution. The garrison were drawn up; the condemned men came on the ground in a mourning coach attended by two priests. After marching along the front of the line, they returned to the centre, where they spent about twenty minutes in prayer, and were then shot by a guard of twenty-four men. The troops then wheeled into sections, and marched by the bodies in slow time. The regiment returned to barracks, leaving the recruits, 'under inspection of a Quarter Master', to bury the bodies.
5. Clothing Regulations, 22 April, 1803 (Liddell, 75).
6. Lennox, Lord William Pitt: *Celebrities I have known*, 2nd Series, I, 194–7.
7. From 1802–1806 Moore was in command of the Camp of Instruction at Shornecliffe, where the 43rd, 52nd, and 95th were trained as a Light Brigade (Oman, C.:*Sir John Moore*).
8. Notable among those who left good descriptions of Paris under the First Consul are Sir Francis Burdett, Fanny Burney (Mme Darblay), Erskine, Joseph Farington, Charles James Fox, Lady Holland, and Lord Wycombe.
9. Benjamin Bloomfield was for twenty-five years the Prince's private secretary, and keeper of the privy purse, when he was dismissed 'with a certain degree of mystery'. Dyott knew him as a subaltern at Plymouth, in 1793, when he was plain 'Jolly Ben Bloomfield'; see also Biographical Notes (page 218).

10. The 'Manby affair' does not appear in Aspinall (POW IV), but the relevant correspondence may be found in the Royal Archives, 40275–40302. Baron Frederick Eben ü Brunen, a Dane and Captain in the 10th Light Dragoons, 1804–1806, was a talented artist. He was responsible for the rifled carbine manual for the 10th, which he illustrated himself, and a series of plates on the uniforms of the Swedish Army. A great favourite of the Prince of Wales, he was employed to stage direct spectacles at the pavilion. There are notes of expenditure on several costly items of 10th Hussars uniform ordered for Baron Eben in the royal wardrobe accounts for 1805–6.

11. GOLB 367 20 February, 1805: 'His Majesty permits the 10th or Prince of Wales's Own Light Dragoons to wear Hussar Appointments'. Although the King permitted the change, he baulked at letting the regiments concerned call themselves 'Hussars'. For some years they continued to appear in the Army List as '(Light) Dragoons (HUSSARS)', even the description 'Light', which had been in use since 1759, proving too innovative for him.

12. In June, 1803, a French army marched into Hanover, and on 14 July the 15,000 strong Hanoverian Army laid down its arms, in accordance with the terms of the Convention of Lauenberg, which George III refused to ratify and authorized the concentration of the scattered Hanoverian units on British soil. The immediate response, however, was disappointing, and on 10 August the King was forced to make a personal appeal for recruits. This produced better results and on 19 December, 1803, the Duke of Cambridge was given the task of raising a corps of all arms and the celebrated King's German Legion was formed. The first cavalry regiments to be raised were one each of Heavy and Light Dragoons, followed in July 1804 by a second regiment of Light Dragoons, and in June 1805 by a second regiment of Heavy Dragoons. See Beamish, N.L.: *History of the King's German Legion*, and Schwertfeger, B.: *Geschichte der Königlichen Deutschen Legion 1803–1816*, 69–72, for a detailed description of the formation of the Legion.

13. A typical cavalry barracks of the period consisted of an enclosure with a main gate, opposite which, on the far side of the parade, stood the officers' house, hardly distinguishable from any of the hundreds of gentlemen's houses that dotted the countryside. Around the parade were ranged the rectangular barrack blocks and stables, that housed the men and horses, with the kitchens, storehouses, canteen and 'necessaries', in the rear. Sometimes the barrack rooms were built directly above the stables, and sometimes, as at Radipole, the two were separate single-story buildings. The larger barracks usually had an indoor riding-school.

14. The MS Journals of the Adjutant of the 15th Light Dragoons records two instances of privates of the 15th being punished in this manner, in both cases for a period of twenty minutes only. Private Williams was sentenced to be picketted on 10 October, 1805, and Private Kierler on 28 July, 1806. In the case of Private Kierler it was remitted from 200 lashes.

15. Elers commenting on this case says that 'the girl being found guilty, she was sentenced, *according to the Spanish laws*, to stand upon a sharp peg for a certain time. It was a very common punishment for the Dragoons when I first entered the service, and it was called picketing' Elers, 213; Lennox, *op. cit.*, I, 199, gives a

description of picketing, which he says, was still used in the US Army in 1866.

16. In 1807, at the height of the Hussar craze, only three out of the forty-nine officers in the 15th had anything like German names, and one of these was a Hanoverian who had been transferred from the 2nd Hussars of the Legion.

17. Tale: *Jottings from my Sabretache, by a Chelsea-Pensioner (Sergeant-Major Tale, 15th Hussars)*, (1847), 8–26.

18. This is, of course, a reference to Samuel Whitbread (c. 1764–1815), the founder of the brewing business and prominent Whig Member of Parliament.

19. Apart from the men's meals, the cavalry required 18 lbs of hay per horse, and straw in proportion. For the former, which might cost as much as 19d., the Government allowed between 10d. and 14d. Such 'miserable candle-end and cheese-paring economy' was enough to cut the soldier out from sharing the comforts of civilized life, and caused him to be looked upon as a pest to society rather than a defender of his country's rights.

20. Tale was promoted to Corporal 'early in 1808', being told by Adjutant Jones that it would be his own fault if he did not 'get on'.

21. There is some evidence to suggest that the 10th Hussars kept their queues until as late as 1815 (See Mollo J.: *Waterloo Uniforms*).

22. Philip Hamond, an officer in the Royal Horse Guards, wrote in 1803 that a Cornet in his regiment could live on £150 a year, besides his pay, which was only £36 more than a Cornet of Dragoons, nor did he think 'an officer suffers anything in the opinion of his comrades if he adopts a frugal plan'. As regards the income to be derived from commanding a regiment, a document dated 10 February, 1808, lists the amounts of off-reckonings (the amount of money allowed a Colonel for the provision of uniforms &c. for his regiment) owing to the Prince of Wales as Colonel of the 10th Light Dragoons. For the period 25 December, 1807, to 24 December, 1809, the total was £8808. 15s. 11d. This was for 44 Sergeants, 40 Corporals, 10 Trumpeters, 10 Hautbois [Musicians], 760 privates, 40 Contingent men and 40 Warrant men. The Band of the 10th was a considerable expense to the Prince of Wales. (XRH Archives).

23. The Royal Military College was founded in 1801. The credit for its founding can be divided between Major LeMarchant, who devised the plan, and the Duke of York who secured its achievement. A junior school was founded in 1802, at Marlow, with a complement of 100 cadets, consisting of thirty sons of officers who had either died or been maimed on active service, who were to receive free education, board, and clothing; twenty sons of serving officers, who were to pay £40 per annum; and thirty sons of noblemen and gentlemen and twenty East India Company cadets, who were to pay £90 per annum. Candidates had to be over thirteen and under fifteen, mentally and physically fit, able to write a good hand, and be well grounded in grammar and arithmetic. The subjects taught included mathematics, fortification, gunnery, tactics, military geography and history, French, German, natural and moral philosophy, riding, fencing, the use of the sabre, and swimming. The cadets were formed into one company, under an officer and a sergeant major, for instruction in the practical parts of their profession. Any cadet who, after four years, failed to pass the leaving examination, was required to quit

the college. As a result of the success of the college, the number of companies was increased to four, and the cadets paid 2s 6d a day, in 1808. (Glover, M.: *Peninsular Preparation*, 198–210).

24. Raised in 1759 as the 19th Light Dragoons, and re-numbered as the 18th in 1763, the regiment always considered itself as Irish, being known as the 'Drogheda Light Horse' although it never had 'Irish' as part of its title. They were in Ireland from 1804 until 1807, and after conversion to Hussars were not included in the first Hussar Brigade, but were sent to Lisbon in July, 1808, to join Sir John Moore's force, where they were brigaded with the 3rd Hussars of the King's German Legion. The 18th Hussars were disbanded in 1821.

3.   In the Cause of Spain (pp42–63)

Compared with the other two regiments, there is very little contemporary material about the experiences of the 10th Hussars in the Corunna campaign. Slade's diary, used by both Liddell and Wylly, is still missing, in spite of searches through the Slade family papers. On the other hand, the 7th are well served by Berkeley Paget, Hodge, Verner, Vivian, and Barrett, the 15th by Jones, Gordon, Griffith and Tale, and the 18th by Kennedy and Hughes, both used by Malet, and of course the gossipy Schaumann. Neale, a medical man, and Porter, an artist, are useful for general observations on the campaign.

1. On 22 September, 1808, the 10th received orders to have in readiness eight troops to embark on foreign service. The strength of each troop to be 1 Quartermaster, 4 Sergeants, 1 Trumpeter, 84 rank and file, and 85 horses. (XRH: 869 MS Digest of Services, Vol 1). Brereton's introduction to Hodge's diary says that the 7th Hussars comprised eight troops, with 2 Majors, 8 Captains, 6 Lieutenants, 4 Cornets, 4 Staff-officers, 6 Quartermasters, 717 Other Ranks, and 677 horses.
2. Typical of the type of vessel employed on this service was the *Three Brothers*, of about 200 tons, which was used to transport the 2/52nd Regiment to Portugal in 1808, and foundered shortly afterwards taking French troops home after the Convention of Cintra. Her single cabin had four berths, anyone else having to sleep in cots slung from the beams, only a few inches apart. The rank and file were 'packed like herrings, out of sight of daylight and assailed by a horrible stench'.
3. The Slade MS suggests that this event took place on 14 October, when a tender was sent for Slade to take him ashore as the Prince of Wales 'much wished to see him'.
4. Britain and Russia were officially at war, and the latter, fearing for her Mediterranean Fleet, decided to withdraw it. On 20 October, 1807, Admiral Senyavin's squadron of eleven vessels passed through the Straits of Gibraltar bound for the Baltic. Storm damage forced them to put into Lisbon where they were blockaded by a British squadron under Sir C. Cotton. On 3 September, 1808, Senyavin agreed to hand over his ships until the conclusion of peace between Britain and Russia, while the crews were allowed to return to Russia. Only two of the eleven ships were returned to Russia, in 1813, the rest being unfit to make the

voyage [Anderson, R.C.: *Naval Wars in the Baltic* (1910), 336–7].

5. There are several good descriptions of the town and harbour of Corunna, notably in Neale, A.: Letters from Portugal and Spain, &c., &c. (1809), and Porter, Sir R.K.: *Letters from Portugal and Spain, written during the March of the British under Sir John Moore, &c.* (1809).

6. Holland, Lady Elisabeth: *The Spanish Journal of Lady Elisabeth Holland*, 202–4. Lord and Lady Holland, doyens of the Whig party, made two journeys to Spain and Portugal, the first in 1802–05, during the latter part of which time Spain was at war with Britain, and the second in 1808–9. Lord Holland travelled entirely for pleasure. He had no official position of any kind and in 1808–9, he was requested by the government to make it clear to the Spanish Junta that his communications with them were in no way authorized by the British Government. Unlike his party, he was an ardent supporter of the war and was convinced that, with outside assistance, the patriotic spirit of the Spaniards would in time prevail against their oppressors. He was very critical of Moore's handling of the campaign, and according to General Craddock would 'give the lives of ten English to save one Spaniard' [Holland: vi–vii, 250n.]

7. The reference to the *Corunna Diary* appeared in the *Morning Post*, 21 November, 1808.

8. *The Adventures of Gil Blas of Santillane*; a picaresque romance by Alain René Le Sage (1668–1747), gives a lurid picture of Spanish life, although the author's knowledge of Spain was entirely second-hand. It was translated into English by Smollett in 1749, and like the works of 'Monk' Lewis, and Mrs Radcliffe, seems to have had a considerable following among the officers of the Hussar Brigade.

9. Plas Newydd Papers (PNP): Letter from Sergeant R. Thomas, 7th Dragoons, to Lieutenant & Adjutant Shore, 7th Dragoons, Corunna, 15 November 1808.

10. Monte Salgueiro was the name given to the lonely Posada Castillana, the sole habitation of the place, 'by our staff'. 'Salt Hill', 'an insignificant hillock near Slough', was the finishing point of the 'Ad Montem' pocession from Eton, which took place on the Tuesday of Whitsun week every three years from about 1561 until it was abolished in 1847. It was also the destination of the outings of the 'Four-in-hand' Club. See Burnett, T.A.J.: *The Rise and Fall of a Regency Dandy, The Life and Times of Scrope Berdmore Davies* (1981), 24–6.

11. Tale nearly lost his Corporal's stripes during the advance, when a driver decamped with one of the bullock carts in his charge. He was hauled up before his 'fierce and fiery little friend the Adjutant' but got away with a 'severe and trimming reprimand'.

12. Several officers refer to the works of Mrs Ann Radcliffe (1764–1823), one of the founders of the 'Gothick' school of novel writing. Her best known work is *The Mysteries of Udolpho*.

13. It is not clear why this particular detachment of the 15th Hussars was actively breaking their *parole*; perhaps they considered that they had no duty to keep their word with privateers.

14. On 29 November the 7th Hussars mustered only 520 out of the 700 embarked.

15. See Notes, Chapter 1, Note 4.

16. Hodge seems to have failed to notice the ford to the east of the bridge, which the French used on 29 December (see next chapter).
17. Matthew Lewis (1775–1818), known as 'Monk' from his authorship of the 'Gothick' novel of that name published in 1796.
18. Both Zamora, its bridge, and Toro are still recognizable from the descriptions of Gordon and others. Zamora is the grander of the two towns, and Toro is now considerably cleaner and less gloomy than it must have been in 1808.
19. See Biographical notes at the end for details of Stewart's career.
20. The affair at Rueda is described by Gordon, who says the cotton 'was said to be worth £80,000 [£4,000,000]' (Hodge; Malet, 25–6, and Neale, 251). The strengths of Paget's cavalry, at time of junction, is given in a return from the Adjutant General's Office, 24 February, 1809, as follows:

7th Light Dragoons (8 Troops)	676
10th Light Dragoons (8 Troops)	677
15th Light Dragoons (8 Troops)	675
18th Light Dragoons (8 Troops)	666
3rd King's German Legion	563
Total	3,357

21. Gordon seems to have transposed these two villages. Melgar de Abajo, with its convent, is the furthest away from Sahagun, and Melgar de Arriba the nearest.
22. Emsdorff, the first battle honour of the 15th Light Dragoons was awarded for the action which took place there on 16 July, 1760, during the Seven Years War, during which the 15th captured an entire French Infantry battalion together with its colours.
23. Porter describes finding the bodies of twelve Frenchmen who had been stripped by the peasantry, and his surprise at discovering 'a female amongst the group' (Porter: 228). It is difficult to locate the exact place where the action took place, as a railway line and new roadworks now cut through the likely area; but the large convent/monastery still stands on an eminence outside the town. The road to Melgar de Arriba now runs over the high ground, and the tracks used by the Hussars, running on both sides of the river Cea are no longer accessible.
24. Scarlet cockades with *Viva Fernando settimo* stamped on them in gold were worn by the Spaniards, rich and poor alike. When Moore's army entered Spain it was, 'out of compliment to the Spanish nation', ordered to wear the red cockade in addition to their own black one. These were issued to the NCOs and men to put on when they passed the frontier, but officers were requested to provide their own (See Gunn: 'The Memoirs of Private James Gunn', by Dr. R.H. Roy: (*Journal of the Society for Army Historical Research*, Vol 49, 1971), 96–7; Schaumann: 81; Malet: 17).

4. Unfavourable Retreat (pp 64–84)

The story of the continuation of the campaign is based on the same sources as before, with the addition of Anderson, J.H.: *The Spanish Campaign of Sir John Moore*, for the campaign in general, and Beamish's and Schwertfeger's histories of the King's German Legion for Benevente. Neale and Porter contain interesting descriptions of conditions on the retreat. For the return of the army use has been made of: Stewart, Leslie: *Letters of Mrs Fitzherbert*; Cavendish, H.: *Harry-O. The Letters of Lady Harriette Cavendish, 1799–1809;* Mrs Jordan Cantlie, Lt.-General Sir, N.: *A History of the Army Medical Department, and Dyott.*

1. The modern road from Sahagun runs over the high ground to the SE of the town, where the final skirmish took place. The old road along the river Cea is no longer accessible, but the bridge where the Hussars halted survives, and the steep climb up through the town to the far gate is virtually unchanged.
2. Oman, C.: *Sir John Moore*, 565–6, Quoting Colborne, who, at the time was Sir John Moore's military secretary, and who abandoned his master and attached himself to Lord Paget for the course of the engagement.
3. The ford below Castrogonzalo is still recognizable, as is the damaged portion of the bridge, between Castrogonzalo and Castropepe. The open plain between the river and Benevente is now criss-crossed by modern roads and a railway, and has been heavily planted with poplars on the river bank.
4. Levi Grisdale's promotion to Corporal was dated 25 November, 1808. He received a pension of 1s. 0d. per day from 9 August, 1825, after 22 years service and died at Penrith on 17 November, 1855. (Information communicated to the Royal Hussars by his great, great, great-granddaughter Miss M. Grisdale). A silver regimental medal of the 10th Light Dragoons, inscribed CORPORAL GRISDALE GREATLY DISTINGUISHED ON THE 1ST DAY OF JANUARY, 1809. THIS MEDAL IS ADJUDGED TO HIM BY THE OFFICERS OF THE REGIMENT, is listed in Balmer, Major J.L.: *British and Irish Regimental and Volunteers Medals, 1745–1895*, Vol I, 49–50; Wildman, of the 7th Hussars, had hanging over his dressing-room door at Newstead Abbey the belt and scabbard of a French cavalry officer. Wildman said it was given to him immediately after the French had been driven back to the river by an officer who was being ransacked on the ground by two Hussars. This was Lefebvre-Desnouëttes; his sabretache was formerly in the RUSI Museum.
5. On leaving Astorga, Craufurd's and Alten's Brigades, totalling 3,500 men, were sent via Orense to Vigo, with orders to embark on the transports, which were waiting there as Corunna harbour was considered unsafe. Moore's objects were to save supplies, cover the flank, and, by reducing the traffic on the road, speed up the retreat. [Anderson, J.H.: *The Spanish Campaign of Sir John Moore*, 38.] They arrived at Vigo having suffered 'shocking conditions of haste, snow, and hunger', but comparatively unmolested by the French. [McGuffie, T.H.: *Peninsular Cavalry General*, 38.] Gordon put their losses at 500. [Gordon, 207–8].
6. See Jones (CCC), 23–4; *The Times*, 24 &26 January 1809; See also the account of Bugler Green of the 95th Regiment in the *Rifle Brigade Chronicle*, 1947, 154.
7. At Las Herrerias, on 4 January, Moore received the opinions of the engineers on the ports of Vigo and Corunna, and, guided by them, decided to embark at

Corunna, and ordered the transports up from Vigo [Anderson, 40–1]

8. Ophthalmia, an inflammation of the mucous membrane that covers the front of the eyeball was a prevalent affliction during the retreat.

9. *The Times*, 30 January, 1809.

10. Adjutant Jones, however, recorded that Major Forester, Captains Seelinger and Gordon, Cornet Phillips and Assistant-Surgeon Forbes, reported unfit for duty, commenting '*sick* indeed, the wonder is they find the time to be sick'.

11. The actions of Sergeant Newman, of the 43rd, are described in *The Times* of February, 1809. The colours seen by Gordon were those of the 50th Regiment.

12. Privates Allwood and Smith were charged with plundering, and Private Ellershaw with 'losing' a sack containing 500 dollars. Smith and Ellershaw were found guilty and were punished two days later.

13. 16 January, 1809: 'The dismounted men embarked at St Lucia [Barracks] – the remaining part ordered into the citadel – 30 horses to be embarked – 309 delivered to the Commissariat and the remainder ordered to the beach to be destroyed, and the men to be embarked in such ships as room could be found in' (XRH 869, Vol I).

14. See Barrett, 327, quoting from *The Gentleman's Magazine*, and the records of the church of St Keverne for 22 January, 1809.

15. See Oman, Sir Charles: *A History of the Peninsular War*, I, 646, Appendix XIII, Corunna Losses.

16. From a letter to his son Wyndham Slade dated 2nd May, 1854, communicated to the author by Colonel Mitford-Slade.

17. Lefebvre-Desnoëttes broke his parole in 1811, and was at the head of his cavalry again in time for the 1812 campaign in Russia. He served in the campaigns of 1813, 1814, and 1815, being wounded at Waterloo. He emigrated to Louisiana, was permitted to return to France, but was drowned in the wreck of the *Albion*, which went down off the coast of Ireland on 22 May, 1822.

18. See Elers, 245, for a description of Captain Darby 'a nice handsome little man', the son of a niece of Lady Lade, of whom 'it was whispered that he was the son of the Prince of Wales'.

19. Of the 1,400 cases admitted to Haslar Hospital, 205 died, a mortality rate of 14.6 per cent. Gordon was told that they died at the rate of fifteen a day.

5. Old England Once More (pp 85–106)

Jones, Mrs Jordan, Farington, The Paget Brothers, and the four regimental histories have been useful for this period of peace. For the state of the regiments after Corunna see Tale, Griffith, Gordon, 7LD, PNP. For the Duke of York's dismissal and the other various scandals see Burne, Melville, L.: *Regency Ladies* (1926), *Harry-O, One-Leg, Farington*. For the Burdett riots see Patterson, M.W.: *Sir Francis Burdett and His Times (1770–1844)*, Jones, Tale, Wylly, Albemarle, Miss Berry, *The Times*. For Worcester and Harriette Wilson see Wilson, Somerset, Melville, Fitzgerald, Creevey. For the Prince's uniform changes see the *Military Magazine* 1812/4, the *Royal Military Chronicle* V, 1813/1, Paget Brothers, Jones, Aspinall, A.: *The Letters of Princess*

Charlotte, Hansard. For the departure of the Hussar Brigade, XRH, Woodberry: *The Idle Companion of a Young Hussar during the Year 1813*, The MS Diary of Lieutenant Woodberry; Wylly, Malet and Liddell.

1. Makes of blacking.
2. The reasons given for losses included 'thrown away by order of' Lord Paget, Brigadiers Stewart and Slade, Sir John Moore', 'cut from saddle while at Lugo', 'taken with the baggage at Mayorga', 'lost in action at Benevente', 'horse destroyed unable to carry it', 'Lost through sickness'; 'Stole when embarking', 'lost in consequence of a boat's sinking at Corunna', lost on board the *Despatch* transport, and, finally, destroyed at Plymouth, Falmouth, or Haslar hospitals, to avoid infection. The total losses for clothing, arms, and accoutrements of the 7th Hussars, were as follows: 282 pairs of leather pantaloons; 244 fur caps; 214 pelisses; 360 carbines; 448 pistols; 442 swords; 444 pairs of boots; and 532 complete saddles and bridles.
3. See Chapter 3, Note 4.
4. The same day while celebrating at the Pavilion with the Prince, the Duke of Clarence received a letter from George, announcing the battle of Talavera, fought on 27 and 28, during which the latter's leg had been grazed by a shell splinter. 'The joy was universal', the Duke wrote in reply, ' . . . your brother officers are all anxious about you, and the different male and female friends you left in Brighton'.
5. Things had apparently gone as far as framing the charges, which included one of conniving over a period of two years with John Roberts the paymaster at 'exhorbitant profits' in the supply of clothing and equipment, and for conniving with him 'in failing to credit the Regiment with the full allowances from the Govt. for postage, stationery, coal, candles, and veterinary and riding school accounts, as well as having made improper charges for NCO's expenses, remount horses, coach hire, farriers' bills, etc., contrary to his duty as a commissioned Officer, and to the breach of good order and military discipline' (Langley Moore, D.: *Lord Byron Accounts Rendered*, 122–3).
6. Wylly, 536–7, gives the words and music of this song. On 25 October, Private Thomas Smith, of Captain Gordon's Troop, turned up at the Barracks. One of few Villers-en-Cauchie men left in the regiment, he had fallen out at Bembibre 'too drunk to march', but had escaped from the French at Saragossa and made his way to the port of Gijon, where he served for a short time with the Spanish guerrillas. After being wounded in a skirmish, he was 'received on board' the Frigate *Amethyst*, and brought home. On 29 January, 1810, Private Phillips rejoined. Having escaped from his captors at Madrid, he joined up with the 23rd Light Dragoons, and returned with them to England, after the casualties sustained in their desperate charge at Talavera had rendered them unfit for further service in Spain (Gordon, 155, Jones: XI, 29 January, 1810).
7. Wylly, 172, quotes in full a letter to *The Military Chronicle* for 24 November, 1810, headed 'Military Apparel 15th Light Dragoons' and signed 'Non Sic Olim', which makes a direct connection between the 'German Whiskers' of the 15th Hussars and the behaviour of the King's German Legion at Ipswich.

8. *The Times* for Wednesday 2 May, 1810, reported that on a Sunday afternoon five Life Guardsmen taking a stroll on Primrose Hill, were attacked, and had to be rescued by no less than twenty-five of their comrades.

9. While his re-appointment as Commander-in-Chief was welcomed by the military, one officer noted with sorrow that 'in the city the reverse is the case, and to an extent I could not have believed'. It was indicative of their attitude that a Court of Common Council, in April 1809, unanimously voted Colonel Wardle a gold box worth 100 Guineas, and the freedom of the City, for his part in getting the Duke of York removed from office.

10. After Corunna the 18th Hussars landed at Plymouth and Portsmouth, between 23 January, and 8 February, dismounted, and without appointments. They proceeded to Deal and various stations on the Kent coast, where they were employed on the Revenue Service. Nine troops marched to Wimbledon to take part in the review of 5 June, 1811. There was a problem with the Turkish bells of the band, and frantic efforts were made to repair them in time. [Malet, 30–32]. Present at the Review were B and C Troops, Royal Horse Artillery, the 1st and 2nd Life Guards, the RHG (650), 2nd DG (250), 5th DG (520), 15th 'Light or Duke of Cumberland's Hussars' (650), and 10th LD (650), and the 18th Hussars. (*Military Magazine*, 1811, I, 494, Wylly, 173).

11. Burdett's efforts were, however, not without some effect, as later in 1811 a clause was inserted into the Mutiny Act which hinted to courts-martial that other punishments should be substituted for flogging, if this did not involve danger to the Army. See *Journal of the Society of Army Historical Research* Vol 20, 1941, 114 and 178.

12. George FitzClarence, who was at home nursing his wound, presented the Prince with the pouch of an officer of the 24th Chasseurs, acquired during the battle. During the Burdett riots he had attached himself to the staff of the Duke of Cambridge, who, while commanding the troops in London, had set up his headquarters at the Gloucester Coffee House in Piccadilly.

13. Edward Fox Fitzgerald was the only son of Lord Edward Fitzgerald, Irish patriot, and 'La Belle Pamela' said to be the daughter of the Duc d'Orléans and the Comtesse de Genlis. On the death of her husband in 1798 Lady Edward went to live with her mother in Hamburg, leaving her children in the care of their grandmother the Duchess of Leinster. Edward joined the 10th Hussars in 1810, from the RMC Marlow, with an allowance of £200 per annum from his step-grandfather, Mr Ogilvie; see Fitzgerald: 'With the Tenth Hussars in Spain: Letters of Edward Fox Fitzgerald' Edited by Captain D.J. Haggard (*Journal of the Society for Army Historical Research*, Vol 44, 1966).

14. Sir John McMahon, 'an Irishman of low birth and obsequious manners. He was a little man, his face red, covered with pimples, always dressed in the blue and buff [Prince's] uniform, with his hat on one side, copying the air of his master, to whom he was a prodigious foil, and ready to execute any commissions' (Raikes, III, 55).

15. POW: VIII, 3228, Sir Francis Burdett to the Prince of Wales. Rear-Admiral Warre's letter to Colonel McMahon and Colonel Palmer's reply are in the Royal Archives (18564 & 18565).

16. Aspinall, A.: *The Letters of Princess Charlotte* (1949), 10–11. Don Ferdo Whiskerandos is a character in Sheridan's play 'The Critic'.

17. On 15 March, 1811, the *Brighton Herald* announced that, 'That fine regiment the 10th Light Dragoons of which the Prince Regent is Colonel, has received His Royal Highnesses permission to assume the distinguishing epithet of "Royal", consequently, their facings, which were yellow, will now be changed to red'.

18. Paget succeeded to the title when his father, the 1st Earl of Uxbridge (of the 2nd creation), died on 13 March, 1812.

19. A Mr Bennet believed that the reason for making the alterations was largely financial and claimed that the Colonel of a regiment, made a profit of about £700 per annum, on the new articles, while the men would be worse off by £380. A great expense would be incurred by the new saddlecloths, 'to please some idle, paltry, and contemptible taste'. Objecting to the enormous expense of the uniform changes he claimed that an officer's jacket cost him £23; his pelisse £21; his pantaloons £4; his cap, belt, &c. £60. He got these figures from his tailor; while his saddler informed him that the horse furniture came to eight guineas; the total expense was £108 (Hansard).

6. Black Giant and Red Dwarf (pp 107–129)

The title of this chapter comes from Schaumann, 387. When Colonel Grant was relieved of the command of the Hussar Brigade [see Chapter 7], the officers of the 10th Hussars drew a caricature of him 'on horseback' with his brigade major, Captain Jones, galloping along behind him, with the caption 'The Black Giant and his Red Dwarf', which was stuck up on the public notice board of Olite. Jones was a fiery little red-haired man, who wore the large red shako of the 15th Hussars. The main sources for this and the following chapter are, Weller and Larpent for the general story of the campaign, and Neale and Porter for descriptions of Lisbon. For the Hussar Brigade in general, the Quentin Court-Martial (QCM), and Somerset. For the 10th Hussars, XRH Archives, Liddell, Fitzgerald, Somerset, Worcester, and Wyndham. For the 15th Hussars, Wylly, Jones, Tale, and Thackwell. The 18th Hussars are particularly well covered by Malet, Woodberry, Schaumann, Hughes and Murray. The account of the action at Morales has been taken mainly from Hughes, Jones, Liddell, and Malet, and that of Vitoria from Jones, Liddell, Malet (for Hughe's and Kennedy's accounts), Schaumann, Tale, Thackwell, Woodberry, Wylly, and 'A Hussar's Life on Service', a series of anonymous letters, written from France in 1814, but probably by Captain Charles Gordon, 10th Hussars (*The United Service Journal and Naval and Military Magazine*, 1829).

1. One of the transports, the *Canada*, with 40 men and 60 horses of the 18th, was taken by 'Yankees' on 3 February, but came into port on the 10th, having been ransomed for £3,000. The equestrian statue of King José I, is by the late 18th century sculptor Machado de Castro [*Michelin Green Guide to Portugal* (1989), 89]. The story of the twisted stirrup leather comes from 'A Hussar's Life on Service'.

2. Brigadier-General Sir M. Warren Peacocke was the Commandant at Lisbon. Being 'incapable of taking command in the field' he was sent to Lisbon by Lord Wellington 'in order, by means of every kind of interference, to make the life of English officers in Lisbon as difficult and unhappy as possible' (Schaumann, 314–2).

3. See Fitzgerald and Woodberry.

4. See 'The 18th Hussars in 1813', Extracts from Woodberry's diary, edited by W.Y. Carman (*The Journal of the Society for Army Historical Research*, Vol 36, 1958, 140–2).

5. Wylly gives the strength of the Hussar Brigade at the outset of the campaign as 540 per regiment, (6 troops of 90 men each).

6. One of the four Sergeants 'broken' was Grisdale, the captor of Lefevbre Desnöettes.

7. Jones gives the state of the Hussar Brigade on 24 February, 1813, as 72 Officers, 104 N.C.O.s, 18 Trumpeters, 1530 rank and file, 1553 Troop horses, 170 Officers' horses, 81 Baggage animals, 35 'Servants not Soldiers'.

8. Colonel Palmer's claim (see Note 13, Chapter 1) was finally settled in 1813, when Lord Liverpool's government awarded him £50,000, in addition to his pension. [see Farington, IV, 180].

9. These figures are taken from the courts-martial return produced at Quentin's court-martial (see Chapter 9); they do not appear in every copy of the published report, and the RUSI Library no longer seems to have the copy consulted some twenty-five years ago. Typical offences committed during this period were drunkenness, 'Conduct unbecoming', absence from quarters, and the loss of accoutrements.

10. Sergeant Tale had some comments to make on the problems the farriers were having in finding suitable fuel for their forges: 'At the termination of every day's stage the sons of Vulcan were put upon their mettle, and puff went the bellows; clink, clank, hammer and anvil. They were sadly put to the pinch at times for fuel. . . ; . . . I believe on several occasions the troopers turned hewers of wood and burners of charcoal'.

11. The regiments ordered home on13 March, 1813, were the 4th Dragoon Guards, and the 9th and 11th Light Dragoons. On 7 April, Wellington wrote to Sir Stapleton Cotton, setting out the various problems regarding the organization of the cavalry, in particular who was to command which brigade. He proposed to take the field as soon as the appearance of the green forage would 'serve the food of our horses'; in consequence of orders from 'Home' he had drafted the horses from the 4th Dragoon Guards and the 9th & 11th Light Dragoons and he had orders and had it 'in contemplation to draft the horses from the 2nd [KGL] Hussars; Excepting the first and second Heavy Germans all the Rgts. will have as many horses as they can mount'. He preferred to draft the horses from the 11th rather than the 13th, as the men of the former were very sickly, and by keeping the 13th he would 'have more mounted Dragoons than by keeping the 11th'. Finally, he proposed that the whole cavalry of the army should be in one Division, under Cotton's command (NAM, 7203–26).

12   On 15 April, the strength of the Hussar Brigade stood as follows: 10th Hussars, 505 men and 496 horses; 15th Hussars, 521 men and 496 horses; 18th Hussars, 504 men and 456 horses.

13   Griffith says that 'two large boats lashed together, with boards laid across them, conveyed us, 18 at a time, to the other side of the river'. It should be noted that most diarists continued to refer to the River Douro, although, properly, once they had crossed into Spain, it became the Duero.

14   It was here that Murray's horse fell on him severely injuring his knee, and damaging his eyesight (see Note 17 below).

15   See the letter of Private J. Porter, 10th Hussars (XRH).

16   In a letter to the Duke of York, dated Pedrosa, 3 June, 1813, he states that the French cavalry consisted of the 16th Dragoons and parts of the 5th and 21st Dragoons (Petworth Archives). In a letter to the *Military Register,* dated 11 December, 1815, 'A WITNESS, AND A FRIEND OF TRUTH' wrote that 'the enemy consisted of four regiments of Dragoons, two regiments of Voltigeurs and eight pieces of cannon . . . two squadrons only of the 10th were actually engaged (the 18th joining afterwards in the pursuit) and that the Hussars absolutely rode over and broke the enemy with the greatest ease'. The field of Morales is extremely satisfactory to visit as it has hardly changed at all. The country to the N and NE of the town is dead flat, and traversed by sandy tracks, some of which lead towards the hills beyond the Rio Bayas and in front of Pedrosa del Rey. The summit of these is an extensive plateau, with plenty of dead ground in which to post a large body of troops. Morales itself and the surrounding villages are virtually untouched by modern developments.

17   Murray's eyesight 'was defective' as a result of his fall at the crossing of the Esla. Two days after 'inflammation set in the knee, yet he followed the Regt. in a spring waggon in rear, till upon the representation of the surgeon that if he went on with the troops he must die, he was sent back to the hospital station at Palencia, where, with abscess and acute rheumatism he nearly died'. He remained there until 6 September, when he left for England. The hospital at Palencia was a 'passing station', of which there were others at Salamanca and Toro (communication from S.G.P. Ward). A printed return in XRH gives the casualties at Morales, viz. 10th Royal Hussars – 1 Lieutenant, 1 rank and file, 4 horses killed; 1 Captain, 1 sergeant, 1 rank and file, 10 horses missing. 15th Hussars – 1 Colonel wounded. 18th Hussars – 1 Sergeant, 3 rank and file, 3 horses wounded; 1 rank and file, 1 horse missing. Total – 1 Lieutenant, 1 rank and file. 4 horses killed; 1 Colonel, 1 sergeant, 13 rank and file, 14 horses wounded and missing. Killed – 10th Royal Hussars – Lieutenant Cotton. Wounded – 15th Hussars – Colonel Grant slightly. Missing – 10th Hussars – Captain Lloyd. XRH, Regimental Digest, Vol 1,1813, gives the losses of the 10th Hussar as, Lieutenant Cottin and private Rogers killed. Captain Lloyd, Quartermaster Cowley, Sergeant Roper, and private Shackleford taken prisoner. (Quartermaster Cowley was retrieved after the capture of Burgos, where he was found in the gaol].

18   Malet, 50–1, says butter not bacon.

19   John Dolbel of Jersey to the Rev. William Gordon Rees, 20 July, 1813.

7. The Assassin's Nest (pp 131–152)

This chapter is based on the same sources as Chapter 6. With the arrival of the 7th Hussars, however, Barrett, Hodge, Vivian and Verner come into play once more.

1. According to Oman (*Peninsular War* Vol VI, 448) Wellington had hoped to secure the 5,500,000 Francs subsidy, which had just arrived at Vitoria. In the event only one twentieth was recovered.

2. Corporal Fox did not produce the caps until 22 December, when Hughes sent them off to Wellington, who acknowledged receipt on 28 December.

3. Sergeant-majors wore four chevrons of lace on the right upper arm, points downward, surmounted in the case of the 15th Hussars by an embroidered Hanoverian or 'Guelphic' crown.

4. See Chapter 2, Note 24, for the Irish-ness of the 18th Hussars.

5. Mina's corps, in August 1813 numbering about 14,000, 'interrupted' all French supplies not accompanied by a little army, to such an extent that his infantry were dressed in French uniforms. 'however they may have annoyed and even distressed the enemy, and rendered necessary the employment of large numbers of troops to keep up communication, they never could nor would have liberated their country. ... but for our forces, all the best and accessible countries of every province were permanently subdued' ['A Hussar's Life on Service'].

6. Worcester gave 34s. for a pair of brass spurs, while two bottles of 'sause' went for 35s., seven pounds of cheese for 73s 6d., and two tongues for 27s. Woodberry gave £4 for a bridle, 'a monstrous price', and £2. 14s., for a pair of overalls.

7. The 18th Hussars were moved to Alten's brigade, in place of the 14th Light Dragoons, who were moved to Long's Brigade, in place of the 9th Light Dragoons who had returned to England.

8. See 'A Hussar's Life on Service', for a further dissertation on Spanish cuisine.

9. Griffith's letter is one of the twenty-seven written to Major Edward Hodge, at the 7th Hussars' depôt in England, by officers serving in the Peninsula and Southern France in 1813–1814. It is also a very valuable piece of uniform evidence, a subject rarely mentioned in such detail in letters from the front.

10. Mr Ogilvie, who had been Lord Edward Fitzgerald's tutor, was married to the Duchess of Leinster. On his joining the 10th Hussars, Ogilvie allowed Edward £200 per annum, paid quarterly. Haggard calls this parsimonious but it was the same amount of money allowed by the Prince to his various *protégés*. The 3rd Earl of Egremont (1751–1837) patron of the arts and agriculturist, friend of the Prince and Charles James Fox, and patron of Turner, Phillips, Northcote, and numerous other artists. 'In his rôle as patron particularly, Lord Egremont found support in the taste of the lady who for long bore the courtesy title of Mrs Wyndham'. For some reason Lord Egremont did not marry her until after the birth of six children, and on his death the earldom passed to a nephew, and is now extinct. The house and estates passed, however, to his eldest son George, created Baron Leconfield in 1859. [*National Trust Guide to Petworth*, 1984, 60–1].

11. In this connection it is interesting to read Woodberry's list of his 'Horses, Mules, Servants &c, &c,' made sometime in September, viz., 'Grey Horse – Crafty; Bay Horse – Worcester (my battle horse); Black Horse – Andalusian (late King Joseph's); Bay Mare – Morales (for Baggage); Piebald mare; Poney – 2 years old – Belisarda (for the small breakfast canteen) – in foal. She is 4 foot high; A Mule – Doctor (for Baggage); Fly & Swift – Two French Greyhouds; Vitoria – my French Prisoner – a faithfull companion (a poodle); John Porter – Valet & Cook; John Ipper – Groom; Jossa – A Portuguese Servant. Hired him at Selvadilla (very faithfull); & Kingston – A mounted Dragoon'.

12. The 7th Hussars, eight troops strong, embarked at Portsmouth on 15 August, 1813, arriving at Bilbao on 30 August (Barrett, 337). On 6 August, 1813 the four Hussar regiments were increased to 12 Troops each, with four squadrons each on active service, comprising 48 Sergeants, 48 Corporals, 1 Trumpet-Major, 11 Trumpeters, and 912 Privates. [Wylly, 200].

13. From 2 July to 6 September Grant was without a brigade. On 6 September he was given Long's Brigade (13th and 14th Light Dragoons). On 24 November he went home sick, returned again to the army, but he was still 'very sick' at Toulouse in May 1814.

14. William, Hereditary Prince of Orange (1792–1849) had been serving as an extra ADC to Lord Wellington since 1811. See Biographical Notes.

15. The 7th Hussars were issued with new uniforms, with blue facings, in 1812–1813, but the service squadrons went out wearing the old white-faced uniforms, with the new shakos, as shown in Denis Dighton's painting of Orthes at Plas Newydd (PNP).

16. 'When the garrison of Pamplona marched out on their capitulation, the Spaniards watched on the flanks of the road towards Passages, and within the short space of time in which the column passed through their lines, massacred five men, whose cries might be heard by their comrades' ['A Hussar's Life on Service'].

17. On 6 November Colonel Quentin selected 47 French carbines from the arsenal at Pamplona, for the use of the regiment, and two days later Acting Adjutant Eames selected a further 30 (XRH: Digest of Service).

18. The houses of clerics were particularly popular as billets '. . . to the south of the Pyrenees, the house of the Cerigos are almost invariably the best, and not only recommended by good fare and accomodation but are desirable from their having generally, should the divine celebs or celebite . . . not have passed the prime of life, a pretty girl, yclept a Sabrina (*niece*,) as an inmate, who does the hounour admirably' ('A Hussar's Life on Service').

19. Cotton's nickname seems originally to have been the 'Leon d'Oro' after the name of a popular hotel in Lisbon ('A Hussar's Life on Service').

20. This story is inscribed on the back of a watercolour portrait of Captain Bolton and his brother-in-law James Hewitt Massey-Dawson M.P., by Robert Dighton Jnr, 1802.

21. Colonel Vivian took over command of Alten's brigade in January 1814, when the latter had to go home sick.

8. Into France (pp 153–173)

The sources for this chapter are the same as those for the previous two, except that more use has been made of the Hodge correspondence and 'A Hussar's Life on Service'. Much of the detail of the various foraging and skirmishing operations comes from the report of Quentin's court martial (QCM).

1. Wellington also sent a memorandum pointing out the risk to which 'adherents of the House of Bourbon might be exposed by one of the family appearing' in France at that particular moment. In reply he was informed that Monsieur, as the future Louis XVIII was then called, was determined to send his sons to France. If they were refused permission to land, they would let the whole world know that it was not their fault. Every argument would be used to prevent their departure, until there was a decision as to their future. In the event of their arriving in France, Wellington was instructed not to receive them at Headquarters (Despatches, XI, 390: Supplementary Despatches: VIII, 453–4; Larpent, II, 253).

2. The Cavalry Order of 9 January, 1814, is given in full in QCM, 7. On 16 January, the strength of the Hussar Brigade stood at: 7th Hussars 513; 10th Hussars 459; 15th Hussars 466 (Wylly: 207).

3. The author visited Macaye in 1974, and it was then a completely unspoilt piece of country, with the church and, alongside it, the narrow lane, descending into the valley, just as it did in 1814.

4. Note communicated to me by S.G.P. Ward.

5. Wylly, 220. The losses of the right squadron of the 15th, during the course of the day, consisted of a sergeant killed and seven men badly wounded . . . Lt Barratt severely wounded in the arm; killed and died of wounds, 1 sergeant, 1 rank and file, 8 horses; wounded 1 officer, 5 rank and file, 1 horse; Squadron commander (Cpt Wodehouse) 1 horse killed, 1 horse wounded; Sergeant Prigg and private Burden subsequently died of wounds.

6. This account of the exploits of Captain Florian is taken from Verner, Thornhill's, Vivian's and Wildman's letters to Hodge.

7. Dr Jenks seems to have come out with the new 4th squadron of the 10th, commanded by Captain Joseph Smyth, which arrived from England, at the end of March (Liddell, 123). His diary, used by Liddell, like that of Slade, is now missing.

8. See the 'Dispositions of certain men of the 15th Hussars accused of having committed sacrilege at Bodares in France, March 2nd 1814', taken by Thackwell (Wylly, 230–1). It is not clear from this precisely what the offence was, and whether the men were found guilty or not.

9. We are told, in the pre-amble to the letters, that the author of 'A Hussar's Life on Service' died in action shortly after writing the last of them. He mentions that his regiment was in support at Orthez, which would make it the 10th Hussars, further-more Gordon was the only officer of either Hussar Brigade killed in action after 22 March, 1814.

9.   Elegant Extracts (pp 174–196)

See Note 9 below, for an explanation of the title of this chapter. The sources used for the march home are: Larpent, Hodge [C], Somerset, Griffith, Liddell, QCM, and Wylly. For the peace celebrations: *The Times*, Hobhouse, *The Military Register*; GLG, Schaumann, Farington, *The United Services Journal*, 1829. For the Quentin court-martial: Hansard, XXIX, QCM, Aspinall A.A.: *Princess Charlotte*, Mrs. Jordan, *The Military Register*, Granville. For the Genappe controversy: One-Leg, *The Military Register*, 1815, Verner, 'Correspondence concerning the death of Major Hodge, 7th Hussars, at Genappe, 17th June 1815' Arranged and compiled by Major the Marquess of Anglesey and F.R. Hodge. (*Journal of the Society for Army Historical Research* Vol XLIII, 1965). For Worcester's marriage and character: Somerset, Dale, T.F.: *The Eighth Duke of Beaufort and the Badminton Hunt*, Gronow, Lennox, *Drafts on My Memory*, Greville, Moers, E.: *The Dandy, Brummell to Beerbohm*; Gronow; Wilson; For Paris during the occupation see Moers, Gronow, Lennox. For the FitzClarences Greville; Turner; Mrs Jordan.

1.   The Prince Regent presented 500 British cavalry horses to mount Louis XVIII's newly-formed 'Guard of Honour', (whose uniforms he very probably designed). Until the discovery of the MS of Woodberry's journal, it was only known in its French translation (Helié: *Journal du Lieutenant Woodberry* [1813–1815] Translated by G. Helié (Paris: 1896)) which continues until 1815, whereas the MS finishes in September 1813.

2.   Including the appearance of the Life Guards wearing cuirasses, at the review in honour of the Allied sovereigns held on 20 June.

3.   Baron Eben [see also Chapter 2, Note 10 and Biographical Notes], served in the Peninsula, 1808–14. In 1809 he was appointed to the command of the 2nd of the two battalions of the Lusitanian Legion raised by Sir R. Wilson.

4.   Aspinall: *Princess Charlotte*, 149.

5.   Charles Manners Sutton, 1st Viscount Canterbury (1780–1845), Speaker of the House of Commons 1817 to 1835. Gas was introduced in London in Golden Lane on 16 August, 1807, by Mr Winsor, who had previously exhibited in 1803 in Pall Mall, and proved the practicability of lighting the streets of cities.

6.   Burdett's Motion of 13 March, 1812, was defeated by seventy-nine votes to six, but the Horse Guards Circular Letter of 25 March limited the number of lashes that could be awarded by a regimental court-martial to 300. In this letter the Duke of York stated that he had no hesitation in 'declaring that the maintaining of strict discipline without *severity of punishment*' was one of the criteria by which he would be 'very much guided in forming his opinion of the merits of officers' (JSAHR, Vol 20, 1941, 114 and 178).

7.   Letter of Private J. Porter, 10th Hussars, to his mother (XRH Archives).

8.   See Chapter 7, Note 10, for The 'virtuous' Earl of Egremont

9.   The nickname *Elegant Extracts* was given to those officers removed from the 10th Hussars, and refers to two popular works of an improving nature, compiled by the Rev. Vicesimus Knox (1752–1821) headmaster of Tunbridge School. They were *Elegant Extracts, or Useful and Entertaining Passages in Prose,* (1783), and

Elegant Extracts, or Useful and Entertaining Pieces of Poetry, Selected for the Improvement of Youth, (1789). In 1793 a sermon on the unlawfulness of offensive war, given by Knox in Brighton Parish Church, attracted notice, and some indignant Militia officers threw him and his family out of the Brighton Theatre. The officers brought in from other regiments, were known as 'The Prince's Mixture', after the blend of snuff favoured by the Regent.

10. Another aspect of the case, taken up eagerly by the press, was the suggestion that the Prince Regent was having an affair with Quentin's wife. In 1811 Quentin married Georgina Lawrell, sister of James Lawrell of Frimley Park, in Surrey, a gambling companion of the Prince. According to the family the liaison lasted for at least six years and it is said that several of the Quentin family bore an extraordinary facial resemblance to George III's children. See Underwood, E.H.: *The Trial of Colonel Quentin: A Brighton Scandal of 1814*, A Paper presented to the Regency Society of Brighton and Hove, (1979), 14–15. The caricature (BM 12315) 'The Siege of St Quintin', published December, 1814, is described in George, M.D.: *Catalogue of Political and Personal Satires* [7 Vols., 1949–1954], Vol. IX [1811–1819], 437–8.

11. Douglas, W.: *Duelling Days in the Army*, 134 et seq; *The Military Register*, 15 February, 1815, 698. The 'Barriers' were the fifty-five custom-posts where the main routes passed through the 'wall of the Farmers-General' built around Paris in the 1780's to limit the evasion of the duties levied on goods entering or leaving the city, which were abolished during the Revolution.

12. Major Howard was killed and Colonel Quentin was severely wounded; Captain Gunning was also killed, and one Captain and four Lieutenants wounded. Twenty-one rank and file, and fifty-one horses were killed; one Troop Quartermaster, one trumpeter, thirty-eight rank and file and thirty-five horses wounded; and one trumpeter, twenty-five rank and file, and forty-one horses 'missing'. Of the officers who had gone to other regiments Henry Wyndham was wounded defending the north gate of the farmyard at Hougoumont. Lord Arthur Hill and Henry Seymour both served on the Staff, the first as Extra Aide-de-Camp to Wellington, and the second as ADC to Lord Uxbridge, in which capacity he was slightly wounded; Captain Lloyd fought with the 18th Hussars, and Charles Wyndham was wounded with the Scots Greys, during the famous charge of the 'Union' Brigade. (Dalton: *The Waterloo Roll Call*). Charles Wyndham later achieved notoriety as the officer involved in the flogging of Somerville of the Greys (Somerville, A.: *The Autobiography of a Working Man*).

13. Lancers were first encountered in the Peninsula during the battle of Albuhera, when the 1/3rd, 2/48th, and 2/66th British regiments were virtually destroyed by them. Accounts stress the ruthlessness of the 'French' [actually Polish] lancers, who speared the wounded who were trying to surrender. For accounts of the battle and the subsequent development of Lancers see *The Military Register*, 1815; Weller, J.: *Wellington in the Peninsula, 1808–1814*, 176–7 n.; Linney, C.A.: 'The First Lancer Regiments' (*Journal of the Society for Army Historical Research*, Vol 68, 1990), 98; Collins, Major R.M.: 'Lieut-Colonel Reymond Hervey De

Montmorency' (*The Journal of the Society for Army Historical Research*, Vol. 46 1968), 97–8; Somerset: Lord Edward Somerset to the Duke of Beaufort, Villa, France, Spanish Estramadura, 3 June, 1811; *The Brighton Herald*, 30 November, 1811; Jones XI: 15 October, 1811; GLG: *Granville Leveson Gower, First Earl Granville, Private Correspondence*, 1781–1821 Edited by Castalia Countess Granville, II, 421, Lady Bessborough to GLG, 8 December 1811.

14. *Gentleman's Magazine*, Vol XXXVII, January to June 1852, 190; Lennox: *Drafts on My Memory*, I, 66–70.

15. Gronow: I, 139–40, 142–3; *Bath Chronicle*, April 24, 1851, 3.

16. Worcester became a Lord of the Admiralty in 1815.

17. De Guiche married D'Orsay's sister. His sister Corisande de Grammont (*d.* 1865) married in 1806, Lord Ossulton afterwards 5th Earlof Tankerville (1776–1859). 'She had long lived with the late Duchess of Devonshire, who was her fast friend'.

18. In 1829 De Guiche published the first of the scholarly essays, *De l'amélioration des races de chevaux en France*, which were to establish the traditions of the thoroughbred in France, and which are still classics of the technical literature of the horse [Moers, 118].

19. It is interesting to note that Nicholas Brown, possibly another pensioner of the Prince, was also sent to India where he died in 1827 (see Biographical Notes).

20. After the advance of this force, 5000 strong, to Coimbra and the Mondego valley, the Spanish backed down, and the 10th Hussars returned to Lisbon to kick their heels in their old haunt, Belem Barracks. Anglesey, The Marquess of, :*A History of the British Cavalry*, 1816–1919, Vol 1, 1816–1850, covers this period in excellent detail.

Biographical Notes

BLOOMFIELD, Benjamin (1768–1846). Cadet Royal Artillery 1779; Capt 1794; Maj. And Lt-Col 1806; Gentleman Attaché to the Prince of Wales 1806; Maj-Gen. 1814; knighted 1815; Keeper of the Privy Purse 1817; Minister Plenipotentiary at Stockholm 1824; raised to the Irish peerage 1825.

BOLTON, Robert Dawson (1779–1814). Cornet 18th Lt Dr 1802; Lieut 1804; Capt 1808–14; killed at Mendionde January 1814.

BROWN, Nicholas (1793?–1827), 'Son of the [late?] Viscount Montague'. Cornet 10th Hussars, 1805; Lieut 1806; Capt in the Army 1810; 11th Foot 1810; HP 69th Foot 1816; 41st Foot, 1825; died of cholera near Madras 1827.

BRUMMELL, George Bryan (1778–1840). Educated at Eton; Cornet, 10th Lt Dr 1795; Lieut 1796; Capt 1797–8; leader of fashion in London; retired to Calais in debt 1816; died in an asylum at Caen 1840.

BURDETT, Sir Francis (1770–1844). Radical MP for Boroughbridge 1796–1802; for Middlesex 1802–4 and 1805–6; for Westminster 1807–37; for North Wiltshire 1837–44; M. 5 August, 1793, Sophia Coutts (1771–1844); succeeded to the Baronetcy on the death of his grandfather Sir Robert (1716–1797).

CAMBRIDGE, Adolphus Frederick, Duke of, (1774–1850), 7th son of George III. Colonel in the Hanoverian Army, 1793; Lt-Gen 1798; transferred to the British service, 1803; Gen 1808; F-M 1813; Dukedom 1801; the King's resident representative in Hanover 1813; Viceroy of Hanover 1816–37.

CAVENDISH, The Hon George Henry Compton d. 1809), son of Lord George Cavendish, younger brother of the 5th Duke of Devonshire. Cornet 7th Lt Dr 1801; HP 1802; Lieut 7th Lt Dr 1803; Capt 1804; Maj 1808; drowned off the Lizard in the *Despatch* Transport 27 January 1809.

CLEMENTS, John O'Marcus. Cornet 18th Lt. Dr. 1804; Lieut 1805; Capt 5th West India Regt. 1806; 18th Hussars 1807; Bt-Maj on Portuguese Staff 1813–14; Lt-Col 1819.

COTTIN (COTTON), J. (1791–1813). Lieut 10th Hussars 1811–1813; killed at Morales June 1813.

COTTON, Sir Stapleton (1773–1865), 6th Baronet, and 1st Viscount Combermere. Lt-Col 25th Lt Dr 1794; Maj-Gen 1805; commanded a cavalry brigade in the Peninsula 1808–9; commanded the cavalry in the Peninsula 1810–14; Lt-Gen and KB 1812; Baron Combermere 1814; commanded Allied cavalry in France 1815–17; Col 3rd Dragoons 1821–9; C-in-C Ireland 1822–5; C-in-C E. Indies 1825–30; Viscount 1827; F-M. 1855.

CUMBERLAND Ernest Augustus, Duke of, and King of Hanover, (1771–1851). 5th son of George III. Lieut 9th Hanoverian Lt Dr 1790; Lieut-Gen 1798; Duke of Cumberland and Governor of Chester 1799; Col. 15th Lt Dr 1801; Gen 1803; F-M 1813; present at the battle of Leipzig 1813; took over the Electorate of Hanover in his father's name 1813; Col Royal Horse Guards, 1827; KG GCB GCH KP; King of Hanover as Ernest I, 1837.

DALRYMPLE, Leighton Cathcart (*d.* 1820). Ensign 55th Foot, 1800; Cornet 3rd Dragoon Guards 1801; Lieut 2nd West India Regiment, 15th Lt Dr 1802; Capt 1804; Maj 1812; Lt-Col 1813; CB.

DARBY, Frederick Joseph *(d.* 1809). Son of a niece of Lady Lade, of whom 'it was whispered that he was the son of the Prince of Wales'. Cornet 10th Lt Dr 1804; Lieut 1805; Capt 1807.

DOWNMAN, Sir Thomas (1773–1852). Gent Cadet 1787; 2nd Lt 1793; 1st Lt 1793; served in Flanders taken prisoner at Lannoy 18 May 1794, exchanged July 1795; Capt-Lt 1797; Capt 1802; 1st Capt B Troop RHA 1808–9; Maj 1810; in command of the Horse Artillery in the Peninsula 1811; Lt-Col 1814; Col 1825; Maj-Gen 1837; Lt-Gen 1846; Col Cmdt RA 1843; ADC to the King 1825; KCB KCH.

DUKENFIELD, Samuel George *(d.* 1809). Cornet 7th Lt Dr 1801; Lieut 1804; Capt 1806; drowned off the Lizard in the *Despatch* transport 27 January, 1809.

DUNDAS, Sir David (1735–1820). Entered RMA Woolwich; worked on the great survey of Scotland 1752–1755; Lieutenant-Fireworker, Royal Artillery 1754; Practitioner-Engineer 1755; Lieut 56th Foot 1756; Ensign Royal Engineers 1757; Capt Elliott's Light Horse 1759; Maj 15th 7th Lt Dr 1770; Lt-Col 12th 7th Lt Dr 1775; Lt-Col 2nd Horse, 1781; Col 1782; Maj-Gen 1790; Lt-Gen 1797; Gen 1802; Commander-in-Chief, 1809-1811; KCB.

DUPERIER [DU PRÉ?], Henry. Rose from the ranks to Sergeant-Major 10th Lt Dr [?]; Cornet, 10th Hussars 1808; Lieut. 1809–10; Lieut & Adjutant 18th Hussars 1814; wounded at Waterloo 1815; HP November 1821; still living 1846.

EBEN u BRÜNEN, Baron Adolphus Christophr Frederick, v., *(d.* 1832). A Danish Officer. Capt in the Army 1800; 10th Lt Dr 1803–6; responsible for the rifled carbine manual for the 10th, which he illustrated himself; Maj Regt de Frohberg 1806; Regt de Dillon 1807; served on a mission to the Prussian court with Lord Hutchinson, and was present at Friedland on 15 June, 1807; Lt-Col de Roll's Regt 1811; Col serving as Brig and Acting-Governor of Tras-os-Montes, in Portugal, 1808–1814; dismissed for 'disgraceful conduct in Portugal' 1817.

FITZCLARENCE, George Augustus Frederick, 1st Earl of Munster (1794–1842). Eldest son of the Duke of Clarence, later William IV, and Mrs Jordan. Educated at Dr Moore's school at Sunbury, and at the RMC Marlow; Cornet 10th Hussars 1808; ADC to the Hon Charles Stewart 1809–11; Lieut 10th Hussars 1810; Capt 1812–14; DAAG in Peninsula 1813; Exchanged to 20th Lt Dr 1814; ADC to Lord Moira in India 1815–1818; HP 1818; M.1819, Mary Wyndham, 3rd D of George Earl of Egremont; Earl of Munster 1831; Committed suicide 1842.

FITZCLARENCE, Henry (1795–1817). Second son of the Duke of Clarence and Mrs Jordan. Midshipman RN 1808–11; Lieut 7th Foot 1811; 15th Hussars 1813; 10th Hussars, 1813–14; Capt HP 73rd Foot 1818; Capt 87th Foot 1818; ADC to Sir Thomas Hislop in India 1815–17; Died of fever in India 1817.

FITZGERALD, Edward Fox (1794–1863). Only son of Lord Edward Fitzgerald, son of the 1st Duke of Leinster. Educated Eton and RMC Marlow; Cornet 10th Hussars 1811; Lieut 1812; Capt 52nd Foot 1814; retired to Ireland and Paris; estates restored and reinstated as Lt-Col 3rd Dragoons 1819; H.P. 1821.

GARDINER, Sir Robert W. (1781–1864). Gent Cadet 1795; 2nd Lieut 1797; 1st Lieut 1799; 2nd Capt 1804 Bde-Maj RA Corunna campaign 1808–9; Capt 1811; 2nd Capt 1812; at Siege of Badajoz 1832; Bt Maj 1812; commander of E Troop RHA from May 1813; at crossing of Esla and Morales; Lt-Col 1814; at Waterloo 1815; Col 1830; Maj-Gen 1841; Lt-Gen. 1851; Gen. 1854; Col Cmdt R.A. 1853; Principal Equerry to Prince Leopold of Saxe Coburg; ADC to George IV, William IV, and Victoria; Governor of Gibraltar 1848; GCB.

GLOUCESTER, William Frederick, Duke of Gloucester (1776–1834). Son of George III's youngest brother. Succeeded his father in 1805; entered the Army 1789; served in Flanders; Maj-Gen 1795; Lt-Gen 1799; Gen1808; F-M 1816; Col of the 6th Foot 1795–1806; Col of the 3rd Foot Guards, 1806–1834; KG.

GORDON, Alexander (1781–1872). Cornet, 15th Lt Dr 1805; Lieut 1805; Capt 3rd West India Regt 1808; 15th Hussars 1808; 60th Foot 1811; retired 1811.

GORDON, Charles J. (d. 1814). Lieut 10th Lt Dr 1808; Capt 1810; Killed at Tolouse April 1814; presumed author of 'A Hussar's Life on Service'.

GRAMMONT [GRAMONT], Antoine IX-Genevieve, Heraclius, Agenor, De, 9th Duc de Guiche (1789–1854). Emigrated to Russia; Sub-Lieut Tauride Foot 1798; Emigrated to Scotland 1800; Ensign Regiment de Roll 1802; Chasseurs Brittaniques 1804; Cornet, 10th Lt Dr 1805 as Count de Grammont; Lieut 1806; Capt 1810; Returned to French service in 1814; Lt-Gen; Grand Ecuyer to the Dauphin; married the sister of Count D'Orsay; accompanied Charles X to Scotland on his abdication in 1830, and thence to Prague; retired to Versailles where he died.

GRANT, Sir Colquhoun (1764–1836). Ensign 36th Foot 1793; Lieut 1795; 25th Lt Dr 1797; Capt 9th Lt Dr 1800; Maj 28th Lt Dr 1801; Lt-Col 72nd Foot 1802; Lt-Col 15th Hussars 1808; Col 1811; commanded Hussar Brigade January–July 1813; Maj-Gen 1814; commanded 5th Cavalry Brigade at Waterloo 1815; Col 15th Hussars 1827–1835; Lt-Gen 1830; KCB KCH.

GRIFFITH, Edwin (1786–1815). Cornet, 25th Lt Dr 1800; 15th Lt Dr 1801; Lieut 1803; Capt 1805; Maj 1811; killed at Waterloo 1815.

GRISDALE, Levi (d. 1855). Corporal 10th Hussars 1808; Sergeant 1810; Sergeant-Major 1816; discharged 1825.

HESSE, Charles (d. 1832). Cornet, 18th Lt Dr 1808; Lieut. 1809; wounded at Waterloo 1815; Capt. Staff Corps 1816; HP 1819; killed in a duel in Paris 1832.

HILL, Lord Arthur Moyses William, 2nd Baron Sandys (1792–1860). 2nd son of the 2nd Marquess of Downshire. Capt 10th Hussars 1810; Capt 2nd Dr Gds 1816; Maj 1815; Lt-Col 1819; Col 1837; Lt-Gen 1854; Col 2nd Dr Gds 1858.

HODGE, Edward (1782–1815). Cornet, 2nd Dr Gds 1798; Lieut 1800; Capt 1804; 7th Lt Dr 1805; Maj 1812; killed at Genappe 17 June 1815.

HOWARD, The Hon Frederick (1785–1815). 3rd son of Frederick, 5th Earl of Carlisle. Ensign 1801; Lieut 10th Lt Dr 1802; Capt. 60th Foot 1804; 10th Lt Dr 1805; Maj 1811; Equerry in the Royal Household 1813–15; killed at Waterloo 1815.

HUGHES, James. Cornet 1802; Capt 18th Lt Dr 1804; Maj 1812; Lt-Col 1817; Col 1837; CB.

JONES, Charles (d. 1840). Appointed from troop quartermaster to Cornet, 15th Lt Dr

1807; Adjt 1807; Lieut 1808; Capt 1813; HP 1814; Bde-Maj Hussar Brigade 1813–4; Bde-Maj 5th Cavalry Brigade at Waterloo 1815; Capt 15th Hussars 1817; Capt 37th Foot 1821; HP York Chasseurs, 1821.

KENNEDY, Cornet, 18th Lt Dr 1805; Lieut 1806; Capt 1812–22.

KERRISON, Sir Edward, Bt (1776–1853). Son of a rich miller from Bungay, in Suffolk. Cornet 6th Dr 1796; Lieut 1798; Capt 47th Foot 1798; 7th Lt Dr 1798; Maj 1803; Lt-Col 1805; Col in the Army 1814; Commanded the 7th Hussars at Waterloo 1815; Maj-Gen 1819; Baronet 1821; Lt-Gen 1837; Gen 1851; MP for Eye 1824–1852; Col 14th Lt Dr 1830; GCH KCB.

LEIGH, George [d. 1850]. Cornet 10th Lt Dr 1791; Lieut 1794; Capt 1795; Maj 1797; Lt-Col 1800–10; Equerry to The Prince of Wales 1800; married 13 August 1807 his cousin the Hon Augusta Mary, daughter of Captain John Byron (d. 1791) and Baroness Conyers (Lord Byron's step-sister).

LLOYD, James Richard Lewis, Capt 10th Hussars 1810–1814.

LONG, Robert Ballard, (1771–1825). Cornet 1st Dr Gds 1791; Lieut 1793; Capt 1794; Maj York Rangers 1797; Lt-Col Hompesch's Mounted Riflemen 1798; Maj York Hussars 1800; HP 1802; Lt-Col 2nd Dr Gds 1803; 16th Lt Dr 1805; 15th Lt Dr 1805; Col 1808; Maj-Gen 1811; Lt Gen 1821.

MACMAHON, Sir John (c. 1754–1817). Lt-Col 87th Foot 1794; disappears from the Army List in 1797 but is generally known as Colonel McMahon; MP for Aldburgh 1802–12; Vice-Treasurer of the Household and Commissioner of Accounts 1800; Member of the Prince of Wales's Council for the Duchy of Cornwall c.1802; Keeper of the Prince's Privy Purse c. 1804; Storekeeper of the Ordnance, 1806–7; Keeper of the Privy Seal, Private Secretary and Secretary Extraordinary c.1806; Auditor and Secretary to the Duchy of Cornwall c.1806; Receiver and Paymaster of the Royal Bounty to Officers' Widows 1812; Keeper of the Privy Purse 1812; PC 1812; Baronet 1817.

MANNERS, Lord Charles Somerset (1780–1855). 2nd son of the 4th Duke of Rutland; Cornet 10th Lt Dr 1798; Lieut 1799; Capt 1800; Maj 1808; ADC to Lord Chatham in Walcheren 1809; ADC to Lord Wellington 1811–12; Lt-Col. 23rd Lt Dr 1811; 3rd Dr 1812; Col 1817; Maj-Gen 1825; Lt-Gen 1838; Col 11th and 3rd Lt Dr 1839; Gen 1854; KCB.

MANNERS, Lord Robert William (1781–1835). 3rd son of 4th Duke of Rutland. Cornet 10th Lt Dr 1799; Lieut 1801; Capt 1803; Maj 1811; Lt-Col 10th Hussars 1815–19; Maj-Gen 1830; CB.

MELLISH, Henry, Francis (d. 1817). Son of an army contractor. Cornet 11th Lt Dr 1800; Lieut 1801; 10th Lt Dr 1804; Capt 1806; 87th Foot 1808; Maj Late Sicilian Regiment 1811; Bt Lt-Col 1812; HP 1816; Equerry to the Prince Regent.

MURRAY, The Hon Sir Henry (1784–1860). 4th son of the 2nd Earl of Mansfield. Lieut 10th Lt Dr 1802; Maj 18th Hussars 1811; Lt-Col 1814–22; HP 1821–1838; Col 14th Lt Dr 1853; Col 7th Dr Gds; Gen 1855; KCB.

ORANGE, William Frederick Henry, Hereditary Prince of Orange (1792–1849). Educated in England; served in the Peninsula as an ADC to Lord Wellington from 1811; Lt-Col 1813; Maj-Gen 1813; Gen commanded the 1st Corps of the Allied army at Waterloo where he was wounded 1815; F-M 1845; married Grand Duchess Anne, sister of Alexander I of Russia 1816 (for a period between March 1812 and April 1814 there was a plan for him to marry the Princess Charlotte); succeeded his father as William II of Holland 1843; KG GCB.

OTWAY, Sir Loftus William (*d.* 1854). 4th son of Cooke Otway of Castle Otway Tipperary. Cornet 1796; Lt 5th Dr Gds 1796; Capt 1798; Maj 1803; 8th Lt Dr 1804; Lt-Col HP 24th Lieut Dr 1805; Maj 18th Hussars 1808; Lt-Col HP 26th Foot in command of a Bde of Portuguese Cavalry 1810–13; Col 1813; knighted, 1815; M-Gen 1819; Lt-Gen 1837; Lt-Gen; Col 84th Foot; CB

PAGET, The Hon. Berkeley (1780–1842). 6th son of the 1st Earl of Uxbridge. Cornet, 7th Lt Dr 1798; Lieut; Capt 1800; Maj 1805; retired 1809.

PAGET, Lord Henry William (1768–1854). Eldest son of the 1st Earl of Uxbridge; 2nd Earl 1812; 1st Marquess of Anglesey, 1815. Served in the Staffordshire Militia; raised and commanded the Staffordshire Volunteers (afterwards the 80th Foot) 1793; joined the army under the Duke of York in Flanders, 1794, and subsequently commanded a brigade; Lieut 7th Foot, Capt 23rd Foot, Maj 65th Foot, Lt-Col 16th Lt Dr 1795; Col in the Army, 1796; Lt-Col 7th Lt Dr 1797; Col 7th Light Dragoons (Hussars) 1801–1842; Col Royal Horse Guards 1842; Maj-Gen 1802; Lt-Gen 1808; Gen 1819; F-M 1842; KG GCB GCH.

PALMER, Charles (1777–1851). 2nd son of John Palmer, a successful brewer and tallow-chandler and member of an old Bath family. Cornet 10th Lt Dr 1796; Lieut 1798; Capt 1800; Maj 1805, Lt-Col 1810; Col unattached 1814; Maj-Gen 1825; retired 1830.

PENRICE, John (1787–1844). Cornet 15th Lt Dr 1805; Lieut 1807; left at Sahagun 25 December 1808 with typhoid fever; taken prisoner and removed to Verdun; exchanged 1809; Capt 1813; retired 1815.

PHILIPS, Frederick Charles (*d.* 1858). Cornet 15th Hussars 1808; Lieut 1809; Capt 1812; present at Waterloo 1815; Maj 1822; Lt-Col HP 1826; Lt-Col 82nd Foot 1833; retired 1833.

PONSONBY, The Hon Frederick Cavendish (1783–1837). 2nd son of the 3rd Earl of Bessborough. Cornet 10th Lt Dr 1800; Lieut 1801; Capt 1804; Maj 23rd Lt Dr 1807; AAG Fane's Brigade 1810; Lt-Col 12th Lt Dr 1811; wounded at Waterloo 1815; Maj-Gen 1825; KCB.

QUENTIN, Sir George Augustus (1760–1852). Son of Georg Ludwig Quentin, a merchant of Göttingen (*d.* 1803). Served in the Hanoverian Gardes du Corps 1789–93; Cornet 10th Lt Dr 1793; Lieut 1795; Capt-Lieut & Capt 1797; Capt 1800; Maj 1806; Lt-Col 1810; Col 1814; Maj-Gen 1825; Lt-Gen 1838; KCB KCH.

ROBARTS, George James (*d.* 1829). 'Son of the banker'. Cornet 23rd Lt Dr 1803; Hompesch's Mounted Rifles, Capt 10th Lt Dr 1804; DAAG under Sir John Moore 1808–9; Maj; 1811; Lt-Col and HP 1814; MP; CB.

ROBBINS, Thomas William. Ensign 1st Ft. Gds. 1805; Lieut 7th Lt Dr 1808; Capt 1809; Maj 1811; wounded at Waterloo 1815; Lt-Col 1821; H.P. 18th Foot 1821.

SCHAUMANN, August Ludolph Friedrich Schaumann (1778–1840). Lieut 7th Line Bn KGL 1809–12; Commissary 1st Hussars KGL 1809–12; Deputy Assistant Commissary-General 9th Lt Dr 1812; 18th Hussars 1813; retired 1814.

SEYMOUR, Henry. Cornet 10th Lt Dr 1794; Lieut 1795; Capt-Lieut & Capt 1796; Capt 1797; major 1802-5.

SLADE, Sir John (1762-1859). Cornet 10th Lt Dr 1780; Lieut. 1783; Capt 1787; Maj 1794; Lt-Col 1795; 1st Dr 1798; Col 1802; Col commanding Hussar Brigade 1808-9; Maj-Gen commanding a heavy cavalry brigade in the Peninsula 1809-13; Lt-Gen 1814; Baronet 1831; Gen 1837; GCH.

SOMERSET, Lord Charles Henry Somerset (1767-1831). 2nd son of the 5th Duke of Beaufort. Lt-Col 103rd Foot 1794; Maj-Gen 1798; Lt-Gen 1803; Gen 1814; Comptroller of the King's Household April 1797; Joint Paymaster-General 1804-6; Governor of the Cape 1813-1828.

SOMERSET, Lord Robert Edward Henry (1776-1842). 4th son of the 5th Duke of Beaufort, known as 'Lord Edward'. Cap 10th Lt Dr 1794; Lt-Col 4th Dr 1809; Maj-Gen commanding Hussar Brigade 1813-14; commanded Household Brigade at Waterloo 1815; Col 4th Dr 1836-42; Gen 1841; GCB.

SOMERSET, Lord Fitzroy James Henry, 1st Lord Raglan (1788-1855). 8th and youngest son of the 5th Duke of Beaufort. Cornet 4th Dr 1804; Lieut 1805; Capt 6th Garrison Bn 1808; 43rd Foot 1808; Maj 1811; Lt-Colonel 1812; ADC to Wellington in the Peninsula; 1st Ft Gds 1814; Col 1815; Military Secretary to Wellington at Waterloo, where he lost an arm, and from 1819-1852; Maj-Gen 1825; Lt-Gen 1828; Master-General of the Ordnance 1852; Gen and F-M 1854; Commander-in-Chief of the British Army in the Crimea 1854-5 where he died; GCB.

SOMERSET, Sir Henry (1794-1862). Son of Lord Charles Somerset. Cornet 10th Hussars 1812; Lieut 1812; Maj Cape Corps 1823; Cape Mounted Rifles 1827; Lt-Col 1835; Col 1847; Maj-Gen. 1852; Governor of Bengal; Col 27th Foot; KCB KH.

STEWART, The Hon Charles William, 1st Baron Stewart and 3rd Marquess of Londonderry, (1778-1854). Ensign, Lieut, and Capt Macnamara's Regiment of Foot, 1794; Maj 106th Foot 1795; Maj 5th Dr 1796; Lt-Col 1797; 18th Lt Dr 1799; Col and ADC to the King 1803; Under Secretary for War 1807-9; commanded a cavalry brigade in Spain 1808-9; Adjutant-General in the Peninsula 1809-12; Maj-Gen 1810; Col 25th Lt Dr 1813; Lt-Gen and Baron 1814; Col 10th Hussars 1820; Gen 1837; Col 2nd Life Guards 1843; KG GCB.

TALE. Enlisted in the 15th Lt Dr 1806; Corporal 1808; Sergeant 1809; Acting Sergeant Major 1813; Troop Sergeant Major 1814; present at Waterloo 1815; pensioner of Chelsea Hospital.

THACKWELL, Sir Joseph (1781-1858). Cornet, 15th Lt Dr 1800; Lieut 1801; Capt 1807; wounded at Waterloo 1815; Maj 1816; Bt Lt-Col 1817; Lt-Col 15th Hussars 1820; HP 1831; Col in the Army commanding 3rd Lt Dr 1837; Maj-Gen and CB 1838; Served in the 2nd Sikh War of 1848; Lt-Gen 1854; GCB, KH.

THORNHILL, William (d. 1850). Capt 7th Lt Dr 1806; Maj 1813; Lt-Col 1815; retired 1826; KH.

TURING, William (d. 1814). Capt 18th Hussars 1808-14; Killed at Vitoria, June 1814.

VERNER, William (1782-1871). Cornet, 7th Lt Dr 1805; Lieut 1806; Capt. 1808; Acting Maj at Waterloo 1815; Maj 1815; Lt-Col 12 Foot 1818; HP 1818-26.

VIVIAN, Richard Hussey, 1st Baron Vivian (1775-1842). Ensign 20th Foot 1793; 54th Foot 1793; Capt 28th Foot 1794; 7th Lt Dr 1798; Maj 1799; Lt-Col 25th Lt Dr; 1804;

7th Lt Dr 1804; Col in the Army 1810; ADC to the Prince Regent 1811; Maj-Gen KCB commanding 6th Cavalry Brigade at Waterloo, 1815; Inspector-Gen of Cavalry 1825–30; Lt-Gen and Col of the 12th Lancers 1827; Baronet 1828; Groom of the Bedchamber to William IV 1830–37; Master-General of the Ordnance 1835; Col R Dr 1837; Peerage 1841; GCB GCH.

WALDEGRAVE, The Hon Edward, (1797–1809). Cornet 7th Lt Dr 1806; Lieut 1808; drowned off the Lizard in the *Despatch* transport, 27 January 1809.

WILDMAN, Thomas (1787–1859). Cornet 5th Dr Gds 1807; Lieut 7th Lt Dr 1808; Capt 1813; wounded at Waterloo 1815; Maj 9th Lancers 1816; Lt-Col 1819; HP 1819; lived at Newstead Abbey.

WODEHOUSE, Philip (*d.* 1846). Ensign 20th Foot 1806; Lieut 1807; Capt 96th Foot 1811; Capt 15th Hussars 1811; Maj unattached 1817; Lt-Col 1821; HP 1826; Col 1837; retired, 1837.

WOODBERRY, George. Cornet, 18th Hussars 1812; Lieut 1812–18.

WORCESTER, Henry, Marquess of (1792–1853). Eldest son of the 6th Duke of Beaufort; later 7th Duke. Lieut 10th Hussars 1811; Extra ADC to Lord Wellington 1812–1814; Maj 37th Foot 1819; resigned 1832; MP for Monmouth 1813–32; for W Gloucestershire 1835; a Lord of the Admiralty 1815–19; KG.

WYNDHAM, Henry (1790–1860). Eldest natural son of the 3rd Earl of Egremont. Ensign 31st Foot 1806; Ensign Foot Guards 1806; Lieut. 1808; ADC to Sir John Moore during the Corunna campaign, brought back the despatches and escorted Gen Lefebvre Desnouettes back to England 1809; Capt 71st Foot 1809; 10th Hussars 1809; Maj 8th Portuguese Cavalry 1811–1812; with 10th Hussars at Morales 1813; 60th Foot 1814; Lt-Col Dillon's Regt 1814; Capt. & Lt-Col Coldstream Guards 1814; wounded at Waterloo 1815; Lt-Col 19th Lancers 1816; HP 1821; Lt-Col 10th Hussars 1824; Bt Col and ADC to the King 1825; commanded the cavalry in the expedition to Portugal 1827; HP. 1833; Maj-Gen 1837; Lt-Gen 1846; Col 11th Hussars 1847; Gen 1854; MP for Cumberland; KCB.

WYNDHAM, Charles (1795–1872). Natural son of the 3rd Earl of Egremont. Cornet 10th Hussars 1813; Lieut 2nd Drs 1814; Capt 1819; Maj 1827; Lt-Col 1837; retired 1841; Keeper of the Crown Jewels in the Tower of London.

YORK, Frederick Duke of, (1763–1827), 2nd son of George III. Col in the Army 1780; Col of the 2nd Horse Grenadier Guards and Maj-Gen 1782; created Duke of York and Albany and Earl of Ulster 1784; Lt-Gen and Col of the Coldstream Guards 1787; Gen and Commander-in-Chief of the expeditionary force on the Continent 1793–1794; F-M 1795; Commander-in-Chief of the Army 1795–1809 and 1811–27; KG.

Select Bibliography

A. Manuscript Sources

Hodge (A): Typescript copy of the diary of Captain (later Major) Edward Hodge, 7th Light Dragoons, during the Corunna campaign, October 1808–March 1809, edited by J.M. Brereton (1969).

Hodge (B): Correspondence of Captain Edward Hodge, 7th Light Dragoons, 1808, comprising eleven letters to William Dacres Adams, and one to Giles Welsford.

Hodge (C): Twenty-seven letters to Major Edward Hodge, 7th Light Dragoons, from officers serving with the regiment in the Peninsula and Southern France, 1813–1814.

Hodge (D): Five letters to Major Edward Hodge, 7th Light Dragoons, from Colonel Vivian, 1813–1814.

(All the above deposited with the Regimental Museum of the Queen's Own Hussars, Warwick.)

Hughes: The papers of Lt-Colonel James Hughes, CB, 18th Hussars: (Peninsular Journals. Department of Manuscripts, University of North Wales, Bangor, 1572 & 1573).

Jones: MSS Adjutant's Journals of the 15th (King's) Light Dragoons (Hussars), 1799–1815, compiled by Lieutenant and Adjutant Charles Jones. (Regimental Museum of the 15th/19th the King's Royal Hussars, Newcastle-upon-Tyne.)

Long: The Papers of Lieutenant General Robert Ballard Long. (National Army Museum, 6807–219.)

Mellish: Mellish of Hodsock Papers. (Department of Manuscripts, Nottingham University, NRA–0893.)

Murray: Letters of Colonel Henry Murray, 18th Hussars, to his wife, 1813 (National Army Museum, 7406–34. 1–20.)

PNP (Plas Newydd Papers): MSS Papers dealing with the 7th Light Dragoons (National Army Museum, Paget Papers, 6806–43.)

PNP: Letter from Sergeant R. Thomas, 7th Dragoons, to Lieutenant & Adjutant Shore, 7th Dragoons, Corunna, 15 November, 1808. (National Army Museum, Paget Papers, 6806–43–14.)

Slade: MSS Notes on the life and career of Sir John Slade compiled by his son Wyndham Slade c. 1916. (Colonel Mitford Slade (1972)

Somerset: Letters from Lord Edward Somerset to the 6th Duke of Beaufort, from Portugal, Spain, and France, 1811–1814. (Badminton Archives 509–14–2–12.)

Woodberry: *The Idle Companion of a Young Hussar during the year 1813*, The MS Diary of Lieutenant Woodberry, 18th Hussars. See also HELIÉ for the French translation which continues the diary to 1815 (National Army Museum, 6807–267.)

Worcester: Letters from Henry, Marquess of Worcester to his father the 6th Duke of Beaufort, from Portugal and Spain, 1812–1814. (Badminton Archives 509–14–13)

Wyndham: Letters from George and Charles Wyndham, to their father Lord

Egremont. (West Sussex County Record Office, Chichester.)

XRH: Papers in the possession of the Royal Hussars (PWO); Serial 821, scrapbook and album; Serial 869, MS Digest of Services, Vol 1.; Misc correspondence with E.H. Underwood and others, on the subject of the Quentin Court-martial.

B. Published Sources

Place of publication London, unless otherwise shown

Albemarle, George Thomas, Earl of: *Fifty Years of My Life* (1877)

Anderson, J.H.: *The Spanish Campaign of Sir John Moore* (1905)

Anglesey, The Marquess of, : *A History of the British Cavalry, 1816–1919*, Vol 1, 1816–1850 (1973)

Anon: 'A Hussar's Life on Service (*The United Service Journal and Naval and Military Magazine, 1829*), possibly by Captain Gordon, 10th Hussars.

Ashton, J.: *Florizel's Folly* (1899)

Aspinall, A.: *The Letters of Princess Charlotte* (1949)

Baring Pemberton, W.: *William Cobbett* (1949)

Barrett, C.R.B.: *The 7th (Queen's Own) Hussars* (2 Vols., 1914)

Bath Chronicle, The

Beamish, N.L.: *History of the King's German Legion* (2 Vols., 1832)

Berry, Mary: *Journals and Correspondence*. Edited by Lady Theresa Lewis (1865)

Bessborough, The Earl of, & Aspinall, A.: *Lady Bessborough and Her Family Circle* (1940)

Bishop, J.G.: *The Brighton Pavilion and its Royal Associations* (1876)

Brighton Herald, The

Brunon, Jean & Raoul, *Hussards*. Gouaches by General Baron Barbier, 1789 and 1803, with a commentary on French Hussars.

Burne, Lt.-Colonel A.: *The Noble Duke of York* (1949)

Cantlie, Lt.-General Sir N.: *A History of the Army Medical Department* (2 Vols., 1974)

Cavendish, H.: *Harry-O. The Letters of Lady Harriet Cavendish*, 1799–1809. Edited by Sir George Leveson-Gower and Iris Palmer.

Creevey, T.: *The Creevey Papers*. Edited by Sir Herbert Maxwell (2 Vols., 1904)

Dale, T.F.: *The Eighth Duke of Beaufort and the Badminton Hunt* (1901)

Dalton, C.: *The Waterloo Roll Call* (1904)

Depreaux, see *Hussards*

Devonshire, Duchess of: *The Two Duchesses, Georgiana Duchess of Devonshire, Elisabeth Duchess of Devonshire, Correspondence, 1777–1859*. Edited by Vere Foster (1898)

Dighton, Robert, Jnr.: '7th, 10th, & 15th Hussars, 1808–1809. Notes on some water-colours by Robert Dighton Junior', by W.Y. Carman (*Journal of the Society for Army Historical Research*, Vol. 30, 1952)

Dolbel: A Letter from John Dolbel of Jersey, to the Rev. William Gordon Plees, 20th July 1813, passing on news from Cornet Dolbel of the 18th Hussars, 19th June, 1813 (*The Connoisseur*)

Douglas, W.: *Duelling Days in the Army* (1887)

Dyott, W.: *Dyott's Diary, 1781–1845, The Journal of General William Dyott*. Edited by R.W. Jeffrey (2 Vols., 1907)

Elers: *Memoirs of George Elers, Captain in the 12th Regiment of Foot*. Edited by Lord Monson and George Leveson Gower, (1903)

Farington, J.: *The Farington Diary*. Edited by James Greig (7 Vols., 1922–1928)

Fitzgerald: 'With the Tenth Hussars in Spain: Letters of Edward Fox Fitzgerald' Edited by Captain d.J. Haggard (*Journal of the Society for Army Historical Research*, Vol 44, 1966)

Fortescue, The Hon Sir John W.: *A History of the British Army* (1911)

Fulford, R.: *George The Fourth* (1935)

George, M.D.: *Catalogue of Political and Personal Satires* [In the British Museum] (7 Vols., 1949–1954)

G III: Aspinall, A.: *Later Correspondence of George III* (5 Vols.)

GIV: Aspinall, A.: *The Letters of George IV, 1812–1830* (3 Vols., 1938)

General Regulations and Orders for the Army, 12 August, 1811

Gentleman's Magazine, The

GLG: *Granville Leveson Gower, First Earl Granville, Private Correspondence, 1781–1821*. Edited by Castalia Countess Granville (2 Vols., 1916)

Glover, R.: *Peninsular Preparation, The Reform of the British Army, 1795–1809* (1963)

Gordon: *A Cavalry Officer in the Corunna Campaign, 1808–1809, The Journal of Captain Gordon of the XVth Hussars*. Edited by Colonel H.C. Wylly (1913)

Gramont, Duc De: *Histoire et Genéalogie de la Maison de Gramont* (n.d)

Granville, Countess: *Letters of Harriet, Countess of Granville, 1810–1845*. Edited by the Hon. F. Leveson Gower (2 vols., 1894)

Greville: *The Greville Diary*. Edited by P.W. Wilson, 2 Vols. (1927)

Griffith: 'Peninsular War Letters written by Major Edwin Griffith, 15th Light Dragoons, and Cornet Frederick Charles Phillips', Edited by Norman Tucker (*The National Library of Wales Journal*, Vol XII, No. 2, Winter 1961, Aberystwyth, (1961)

Gronow, W.R.: *The Reminiscences and Recollections of Captain Gronow* (2 Vols., 1900)

Gurwood, Lt-Colonel John: *Despatches of Field-Marshal the Duke of Wellington* (12 Vols. 1839)

Hanger, Colonel George: *Life, Adventures, and Opinions of Colonel George Hanger, written by Himself* (2 vols., 1801)

Hansard, T.C.: *The Parliamentary Debates from the year 1803 to the Present Time* (Vols., XX, XXIV, XXIX)

Haswell Miller, A.E. & Dawnay, N.P.: *Military Drawings and Paintings in the Royal Collection* (2 Vols 1970)

Healey, E.: *Coutts & Co 1692–1992. The Portrait of a Private Bank* (1992)

Helié: *Journal du Lieutenant Woodberry* [1813–1815] Translated by G. Helié (Paris: 1896)

HMC: *Historical Manuscripts Commission*, 30, Fortescue, X

Hobhouse, J.C.: *Recollections of a Long Life*. Edited by Lady Dorchester (2 Vols., 1910)

Holland, Lady Elisabeth: *The Spanish Journey of Lady Elisabeth Holland*. Edited by the Earl of Ilchester (1910)

Hussards: 'Les Premiers Hussards, 1692–1721', by A. Depreaux (*Costumes &*

Uniformes, No. 10, 1914)

Jesse: *The Life of Beau Brummell* By Captain Jesse (2 Vols., 1927)

Jones (CCC): 'Cavalry in the Corunna Campaign (as told in the Diary of the Adjutant of the 15th Hussars' by Major Lord Carnock) (*Journal of the Society for Army Historical Research*, Special Publication No.4, 1936)

Landsheit: *The Hussar: The Story of Norbert Landsheit, Sergeant in the York Hussars and the 20th Light Dragoons.* Edited by the Rev. G.R. Gleig (1837)

Larpent: *The Private Journals of F.S. Larpent Esq. Judge Advocate General of the British Forces in the Peninsula.* Edited by Sir George Larpent Bt, (3 Vols., 1853)

Lennox, Lord William Pitt: *Celebrities I have known*, 2nd series

Lennox, Lord William Pitt: *Drafts on my Memory* (2 Vols., 1866)

Leslie, A.: *Mrs Fitzherbert* (1960)

Leslie, S.: *Mrs Fitzherbert, a Life chiefly from unpublished sources* (1939)

Leslie, S.: *The letters of Mrs Fitzherbert, being the second volume of the life of Mrs Fitzherbert* (1940)

Liddell, Colonel R.S.: *The Memoirs of the Tenth Royal Hussars* (1891)

Malet, Colonel H.: *The Historical Memoirs of the XVIIIth Hussars (Princess of Wales's Own)* (1907)

Maugras, G.: *The Duc de Lauzun and the Court of Marie Antoinette* (1896)

Melville, L.: *The First Gentleman of Europe* (2 Vols., 1906)

Melville, L.: *Regency Ladies* (1926)

Military Magazine, The

Minto: *Life and Letters of Sir Gilbert Elliot, First Earl of Minto, From 1751 to 1806.* Edited by the Countess of Minto (3 Vols., 1874)

Morning Post, The

McGuffie, T.H.: *Peninsular Cavalry General, The Correspondence of Lieutenant-General Robert Ballard Long* (1951)

Moers, E.: *The Dandy, Brummell to Beerbohm* (1960)

Mrs Jordan: *Mrs Jordan and her Family, being the unpublished correspondence of Mrs Jordan and the Duke of Clarence, later William IV.* Edited by A. Aspinall (1951)

Neale, A.: *Letters from Portugal and Spain, &c. &c.* (1809)

Oman, C.: *Sir John Moore* (1953)

Oman, C.W.C.: *Wellington's Army, 1809–1814* (1912)

Oman, C.W.C: *A History of the Peninsular War* (7 Vols., 1902–1930)

One-Leg: *One-Leg, The Life and Times of Henry William Paget, First Marquess of Anglesey, KG* by Henry, Marquess of Anglesey (1961)

Paget papers: *The Paget Papers (The Correspondence of Sir Arthur Paget, 1794–1807).* Edited by H.M. & E. Paget (1896)

Paget Brothers: *The Paget Brothers, 1790–1840.* Edited by Lord Hylton (1918)

Paget, H. M. & E.: *Letters & Memorials of General the Hon Edward Paget, GCB* (1898)

Patterson, M.W.: *Sir Francis Burdett and His Times (1770–1844)* (2 Vols., 1931)

Ponsonby, Major General, Sir J.: *The Ponsonby Family* (1929)

Porter, Sir R. K.: *Letters from Portugal and Spain, written during the March of the British under Sir John Moore, &c.* (1809)

POW: Aspinall, A.: *Correspondence of George, Prince of Wales, 1770–1812* (7 Vols.,

1963–1970)

QCM: *The Trial of Colonel Quentin of the Tenth, of Prince of Wales's Own Regiment of Hussars, by a General Court-Marshal, held at Whitehall, on Monday, the 17th of October, 1814; and continued by Adjournment, till the 31st of October, 1814* (1814)

Raikes, T.: *A Portion of the Journal kept by Thomas Raikes Esq.* (4 Vols., 1856)

Raymond, J.: 'George IV: A Re-appraisal' By John Raymond. (*History To-day*, Vol. 12, 1962)

Read, F.: *The Duke of Lancaster's Own Yeomanry* (1992)

Ritter, R.: *La Maison de Gramont* (Paris: n.d.)

Royal Military Chronicle (7 Vols., 1810–1813)

Royal Military Chronicle (New Series, 6 Vols., 1814–1817)

Schaumann: *On the Road with Wellington, The Diary of a War Commissary in the Peninsular Campaigns, by August Ludolf Schaumann, Deputy Assistant Commissary-General in the British Army.* Translated and Edited by A.M. Ludovici (1924)

Schwertfeger, B.: *Geschichte der Koniglichen Deutschen Legion 1803–1816* (2 Vols., Hanover, 1907)

Seventh LD: *Standing Orders for the Seventh Light Dragoons* (Ipswich 1808)

7LD: 'The Life of a Cavalry Regiment, A Report on the Anglesey papers dealing with the 7th Light Dragoons' By T.H. McGuffie (*Journal of the Society for Army Historical Research*, Vol 38, 1960)

Smith: *Military Dictionary* [1779]

Somerville: *The Autobiography of a Working Man* by Alexander Somerville with a Preface by Brendan Behan (1967: First Published 1848)

Strachan, H.: *British Military Uniforms, 1768–96* (1975)

Tale: *Jottings from My Sabretache, by a Chelsea Pensioner*, (Sergeant-Major Tale, 15th Hussars), (1847)

Thackwell: *The Military Memoirs of Lieut-General Sir Joseph Thackwell.* Edited by Colonel H.C. Wylly (1908)

Thal, H. Van: *Ernest Augustus Duke of Cumberland & King of Hanover* (1936)

Times, The

Trevelyan, G.M.: *British History in the Nineteenth Century and after* (1782–1919) (1945)

Turner, E.S.: *The Court of St. James's* (1959)

Tylden, Major G.: *Horses and Saddlery* (1965)

Underwood, E.H.: *The Trial of Colonel Quentin: A Brighton Scandal of 1814*, A paper presented to the Regency Society of Brighton and Hove, (1979)

Verner: 'Reminiscences of William Verner (1782–1871) 7th Hussars', by R.W. Verner (*Journal of the Society for Army Historical Research*, Special Publication No.8, 1965)

Vivian: *Richard Hussey Vivian, 1st Baron Vivian, a Memoir.* Edited by The Hon C. Vivian (1897)

Ward, S.G.P.: *Wellington's Headquarters* (1957)

Warnery: *Remarks on Cavalry, by the Prussian Major-General of Hussars Warnery, Translated from the Original* (1798)

Wellington, The Duke of: *Supplementary Despatches, Correspondence, and Memoirs, of Field-Marshal Arthur, Duke of Wellington, KG* (15 Vols., 1872)

Wilkins, W.H.: *Mrs Fitzherbert and George IV* (1914)

Wilson, H.: *Harriette Wilson's Memoirs of Herself and Others* (1929)

Wraxall: *The Historical and the Posthumous Memoirs of Sir Nathanial Wraxall*, by H.B. Wheatley (5 Vols., 1884)

Wylly, Colonel H.C.: *XVth (The King's) Hussars, 1759–1913* (1914)

Index

235

242

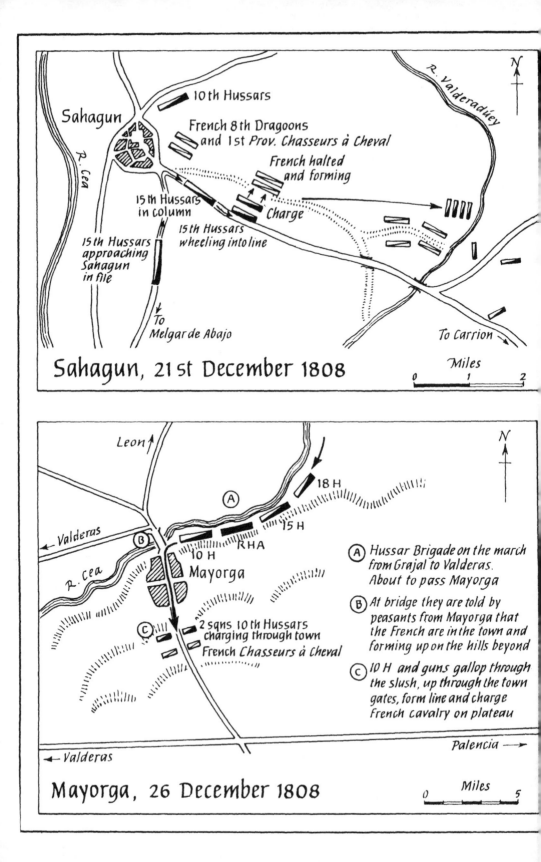

Sahagun, 21st December 1808

10th Hussars

Sahagun

French 8th Dragoons and 1st *Prov. Chasseurs à Cheval*

French halted and forming

R. Cea

15th Hussars in column

Charge

15th Hussars approaching Sahagun in file

15th Hussars wheeling into line

R. Valderaduey

N

To Melgar de Abajo

To Carrion

Miles
0   1   2

Mayorga, 26 December 1808

Leon

18 H

N

(A)

15 H

Valderas

(B)

RHA

10 H

R. Cea

Mayorga

(C)

2 sqns 10th Hussars charging through town
French *Chasseurs à Cheval*

(A) Hussar Brigade on the march from Grajal to Valderas. About to pass Mayorga

(B) At bridge they are told by peasants from Mayorga that the French are in the town and forming up on the hills beyond

(C) 10 H and guns gallop through the slush, up through the town gates, form line and charge French cavalry on plateau

Valderas

Palencia

Miles
0   5

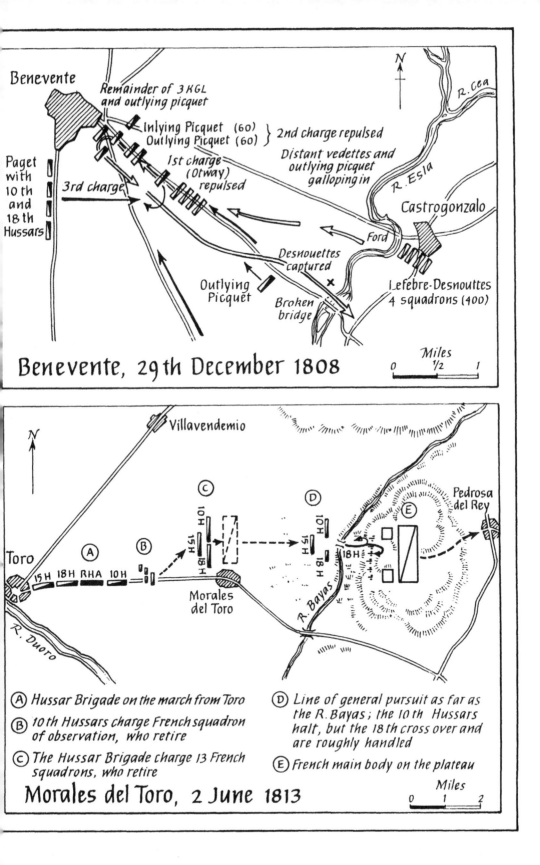

Benevente, 29th December 1808

Benevente

Remainder of 3 KGL and outlying picquet

Inlying Picquet (60)
Outlying Picquet (60) } 2nd charge repulsed

Distant vedettes and outlying picquet galloping in

1st charge (Otway) repulsed

Paget with 10th and 18th Hussars

3rd charge

R. Cea

R. Esla

Castrogonzalo

Ford

Desnouettes captured

Outlying Picquet

Broken bridge

Lefebre-Desnouttes
4 squadrons (400)

N

Miles
0   ½   1

Morales del Toro, 2 June 1813

N

Villavendemio

Toro

ⒶHussar Brigade on the march from Toro

15H 18H RHA 10H

Ⓑ

Ⓒ
10H
15H
18H

Morales del Toro

R. Bayas

Ⓓ
10H
15H
18H

Pedrosa del Rey

Ⓔ
18H

R. Duoro

Ⓐ *Hussar Brigade on the march from Toro*

Ⓑ *10th Hussars charge French squadron of observation, who retire*

Ⓒ *The Hussar Brigade charge 13 French squadrons, who retire*

Ⓓ *Line of general pursuit as far as the R. Bayas; the 10th Hussars halt, but the 18th cross over and are roughly handled*

Ⓔ *French main body on the plateau*

Miles
0   1   2